WITHDRAWN

FV.

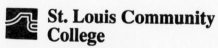

Women of the Renaissance

WOMEN IN CULTURE AND SOCIETY

A series edited by
Catharine R. Stimpson

❦

WOMEN OF THE RENAISSANCE

Margaret L. King

THE UNIVERSITY OF CHICAGO PRESS
Chicago and London

MARGARET L. KING is professor in the Department of History at Brooklyn College and the Graduate Center, City University of New York.

Originally published as *Le Donne nel Rinascimento*, © 1991 Gius. Laterza & Figli Spa, Roma-Bari.

The University of Chicago Press, Chicago 60637
The University of Chicago Press, Ltd., London

00 99 98 97 96 95 94 93 92 91   5 4 3 2 1

ISBN 0-226-43617-9 (cloth)
ISBN 0-226-43618-7 (paperback)

Library of Congress Cataloging-in-Publication Data

King, Margaret L., 1947–
    Women of the renaissance / Margaret L. King.
        p.   cm. — (Women in culture and society)
    Includes bibliographical references and index.
        1. Women—History—Renaissance, 1450–1600. 2. Women—Europe—
    History. I. Title. II. Series.
    HQ1148.K56   1991
    305.4′094—dc20   91-19960
                                                                          CIP

♾The paper used in this publication meets the minimum requirements of the American National Standard for Information Sciences—Permanence of Paper for Printed Library Materials, ANSI Z39.48-1984.

FOR MY PARENTS

CONTENTS

SERIES EDITOR'S FOREWORD

In 1678, a Venetian noblewoman, Elena Lucrezia Cornaro Piscopia, earned the degree of "doctor of philosophy" at the University of Padua, the first woman ever to take a Ph.D. Famous for her learning, she was thirty-two, unmarried, and attached to a Benedictine convent. Her degree, however, was a consolation prize. For neither the Catholic church nor the university had been prepared to grant her a degree in theology, which she had wanted. After her partial triumph, she got sick and—health never regained—died six years later.

Cornaro is one of the hundreds of vivid figures who appear in *Women of the Renaissance*, a grand panorama of an epochal period in Western history. Beginning in Italy in the fourteenth century, the Renaissance became a European and English movement that reclaimed Greek and Latin culture, revitalized Western art and architecture, established early modern political and economic practices, and drew a heroic, secular picture of man that dominates us still, particularly in the humanities.

In 1977, the Renaissance historian Joan Kelly asked a question as elementary and audacious as that of the child in the legend who wondered where the emperor's clothes had gone, "Did women have a Renaissance?" Kelly then postulated that they did not. More specifically, she described contractions in the lives of Italian urban women, ironic counterpoints to the expansion in the lives of their husbands, sons, and brothers.

Kelly's work was one element of a wide, deep, and spirited development in Renaissance studies: the exploration of the lives of women, the meaning of gender, and the structure of families. Meticulous, fascinating, and comprehensive, *Women of the Renaissance* draws on this scholarship "to visit (the) Renaissance women in their varied classes and endeavours" who lived from 1350 to 1650 in Western Europe and England. Margaret L. King asks that we listen to the voices of contemporary scholars and to a collage of voices of Renaissance men and women—the

Venetian woman who longed to be a theologian, the bishop who condemned such ambitions.

King organizes her book around three great themes. The first is that of women as family members, as daughters, wives, mothers, and workers, the roles available to the majority of women. No matter what her class, and class did matter intensely, a woman was the sinful daughter of Eve, a carrier of the viruses of lust and licentiousness. Church, state, father, and husband had to control her. During the persecution of witches, which both Catholics and Protestants carried out, the daughter of Eve was pictured as having descended even further to become the consort of demons. Carefully but pungently, King shows women exercising the one legal power they did have, that of making their wills and disposing of their dowry. More often than men, they left legacies to women.

King's second theme is that of women within the church. Family and circumstance forced some women into convents, but many women chose claustration. For a holy life permitted the vile daughter of Eve to transform herself into the immaculate daughter of Mary. The convent had other offerings for women: education, freedom from marriage and family life, and a place in which to strive for holiness and sainthood. For King, the ecstatic visionaries of the Renaissance are its heroines. Despite their exceptional accomplishments, the Catholic church maintained its rigid theories of gender and expectations of women's place and nature. Heresy, of course, thrives when orthodoxy seeks to kill the vital and the different. Women were attracted to the "deeply and marginally heretical." They were punished for their deviance. Yet, King suggests, the Catholic church may have treated women more generously than Protestantism. To be sure, Protestants believed in elementary education for girls. Catholicism, however, gave women a choice between sanctity and procreative marriage as an appropriate life course. Protestantism gave them only procreative marriage.

King's study of holy and charismatic women leads logically to her third theme—women of might, influence, and power. They were writers and scholars like Cornaro who fought for education, rulers like Caterina Sforza who fought for political and military strength. Perhaps their supreme embodiments are Joan of Arc of France, burned as a heretic, and Queen Elizabeth I of England, buried with honor. King shows how consistently the Renaissance adapted classical motifs and figures to picture women. A metaphor for the woman of might was the Amazon, at once fearsome and free.

Did women have a Renaissance? King excavates an "obdurate substratum of Renaissance thinking about women: their role is to reproduce, their home is their fortress and their prison, their destiny is endless work with needle and spindle." However, King also calls on the work of David Herlihy, a major historian of Europe. Herlihy suggests "Something changed in the Renaissance in women's sense of themselves, even if very little changed or changed for the better in their social condition." Cornaro did take a degree in philosophy. The consciousness of women's consciousness, of women as potential creators of public culture, shifted. So doing, it helped to make possible this general history of women in the Renaissance, this much-needed and welcome book.

Catharine R. Stimpson
Rutgers University

INTRODUCTION

The woman of the Renaissance is many women—mother, daughter, widow; warrior, manager, servant; nun, heretic, saint, witch; queen, martyr, seeker. This book attempts to visit Renaissance women in their varied classes and endeavors, to do many things in a small space.

Renaissance women are defined broadly and simply: all women whose lives unfolded between 1350 and 1650, and occasionally the grandmothers of the earliest and granddaughters of the latest. The setting is western Europe, city and country, with glances elsewhere. In the forefront are the enormous differences between North and South in the shape of women's lives and the direction of change; the reader must often careen from Italy to England and back again. Just as prominent are the even greater disparities between the life of a rich woman and a poor one—in the same nation, or city, or even household. The fourteenth-century nun and the seventeenth-century *savante* have more in common than a merchant's wife and her children's nurse.

In addition to the great variety in women's lives, this book aims to explore the variety of words by which they are vividly illumined. Included here to recreate the rich texture of the past are women's words and men's words, the voices of the poet, notary, chronicler, and scholar, the witch's lament, the mother's plea, the silence of the sage, recluse, and prisoner. Contemporary voices are heard here, too, in the presentation of the most compelling interpretations—among the multitude to have reached library shelves in the past two decades—of the lives of women.

Much is dared here, but there are some tasks that could not be assumed. Eastern Europe and the rest of the world are neglected, as are female painters and musicians, and too little has been said of many others; poets and slaves alike have been slighted. The reader is asked to forgive the omissions which the constraints of time and space have required.

In addition, the reader is asked to indulge this author's particular perspective on the problem of the Renaissance woman. These pages accentuate the roles of mother and witch, the triad of virgin-matron-crone prefigured in the mythology of the ancients, the anxious and ferocious amazon, cells holy and book-lined, and the female community that developed from its germ in the walled convent to flower as the City of Ladies, the missing term in the constellation magnificently drawn by Saint Augustine, heir to Saint Monica's tears, of the City of Man and the City of God.

These themes are developed in three chapters which look at women in their usual and unusual settings. The first chapter looks at women in families: mothers, daughters, wives, widows, and workers. These were the roles in which most Renaissance women passed their lives. The second looks at women in the church: nuns, uncloistered holy women, saints, heretics, reformers and sectaries, witches. A significant fraction of Renaissance women committed themselves to such roles—or, in the case of the witch, were said to have done so. The third chapter considers the exceptional women who found some other place in Renaissance society for their energies and strivings: warriors, queens, and patronesses; scholars, writers, and visionaries. In closing, this book addresses the crucial question of the nature of the Renaissance for women—that provocative question that lay unasked and unanswered until late in this century.

The notes are numerous, but uncluttered. Full references are found in the "Works Cited" section. At the head of that section is an explanation of abbreviations. For the many quotations from Renaissance authors I have cited an English translation if one was available to me; where none is cited, the translation is my own.

I have been aided in the formulation of the ideas found here by many friends over thirty years: Mandy and Anne, Muriel and Lynn, Giovanna and Diana, Linda and Cyndee—too long a list to continue. My colleagues in the study of Renaissance women—Paul Oskar Kristeller, Patricia Labalme, and Albert Rabil, Jr.—have offered special insight. I await the corrections of other colleagues to the statements made in this report on research in progress, by its nature general and synthetic. My greatest debt is to my husband, who made truly heroic sacrifices during the period of most intensive labor on this project. I am grateful as well to the forbearance of my two sons, who inquired every day if I wasn't done yet; I hope they will someday understand what all of this is about. I must dedicate this book to my parents, who prepared me to write it, at whose dinner table each night conversation turned not to the use of the distaff or the choice of a milliner, but to the world of history, politics, and ideas, into which anyone might enter.

February 1990

I

❧

DAUGHTERS OF EVE
Women in the Family

Mother and Child

The Christian believer, marking the civilization of the West indelibly, divides all of time according to a single event—the birth of Jesus—and all of eternity according to another—Jesus' death and resurrection. At both moments a woman was present, and that woman was a mother. Joyfully she received word from the angel sent by God the Father that she had been impregnated by the bountiful Spirit who had also inseminated the whole of creation. Humbly she gave birth and dutifully she tended the child who grew in his Father's image and not hers. Sorrowfully she watched him die, mother and son alike tormented and alone. The *mater dolorosa* of exquisite beauty soon escaped from history, but not from the faith that would be called Catholic. Her God and husband restored her in triumph to the heavens, where, beside her son, crowned in glory, she listens to the pleas of sinners who trust in her forgiving love.

Devotion to Mary, the mother of God, grew as Europe grew.[1] She stood erect in stone on cathedral portals, gazed radiantly from sunlit windows, cradled her child on painted walls and panels, wept in four and five entwined voices in domed choirs. At the end of the Middle Ages and the beginning of the Renaissance, in stone and paint and glass, the mother of God smiled at her baby for the first time. The frequent and almost obsessive depiction of the concert of loving mother and unbounded child coincides with the birth of the explosive culture of the Renaissance.[2] Yet the mothers of the Renaissance not resident in paradise dwelt more in the shadow of the fallen Eve than the risen Mary, whose immaculate nature (officially so denominated from the sixteenth century) distanced her from the stain of sexuality that marked the ordinary woman. After God created Eve from the rib of Adam, Scripture teaches, she became curious about the one forbidden object in the perfect garden they had been given for leisure and communion (Gen. 2:15–3). Tempted by the diabolic serpent, she persuaded Adam to eat the prohibited fruit of that tree. Both were cast out, forever, from Eden, and from the presence of God. The sin of Adam, condemned to a life of sin and toil, lay in his act; his salvation would be wrought by the compensatory act of a different actor. The sin of Eve was bound up in her very nature. By nature sexual (where man was rational), upon her especially lay the sin of sexual intercourse, rendered sinful by the fall. She alone was sentenced to the pain which was the consequence of her sexual nature: the labor of motherhood. She alone, it was decreed, would forever both serve and love another: her husband and her master. Every woman was to be a daughter of Eve, whose primal sorrow would overwhelm even the virgin full of grace.

Most Renaissance women became mothers. Motherhood would define their lives and occupy most of their years. From their mid-twenties in most social groups, from adolescence in elite circles, they experienced a cycle of childbirth and nursing and childbirth again.[3] Poor women gave birth every twenty-four to thirty months. The intervals between births were governed by the period of lactation, which prevented further conception with some effectiveness. But when the child was weaned, a new conception could take place.

Wealthy women bore even more babies than poor ones. Since rich women did not nurse their own children (of which renunciation more later), they conceived again soon after each birth. The fertility of rich women in France has been termed "excessive," in England, "appallingly high."[4] High fertility was in the interest of the propertied family, whose ability to prevail "against the powerful forces of death" required at least one surviving male heir.[5] As in the case of the English Lady Margaret Denton Verney, as late as the seventeenth century, the wife's capacity to give birth to heirs was "her only indispensable contribution" to the family.[6]

Where fertility lagged, families died out. Unproductive marriages in sixteenth-century Venice threatened the survival of her ruling class and left citizen houses in fourteenth-century Florence, according to Dante, "vuote di famiglia," childless.[7] The dying protagonist of the Florentine humanist Leon Battista Alberti's *On the Family* was preoccupied with the same problem. For him, the marriage of his descendants was an urgent necessity if his own house—his reputation and his memorial—were to survive. "How many families do we see today in decadence and ruin! . . . Of all these families not only the magnificence and greatness but the very men, not only the men but the very names are shrunk away and gone. Their memory, almost every trace of them, is wiped out and obliterated."[8] The Venetian humanist Francesco Barbaro had the problem of houses *vuote di famiglia* in mind when he wrote in the margin of his copy of Aristotle's *Politics*, next to the philosopher's discussion of a law encouraging the begetting of children: "an excellent law, designed to replenish the city with citizens."[9] For this reason, both Alberti and Barbaro, in his elegant and widely read treatise *On Marriage*, saw the ability to procreate successfully as a preeminent concern in the choice of a wife.[10] Martin Luther spoke with characteristic clarity on the issue: "Even if they bear themselves weary, or bear themselves out . . . this is the purpose for which they exist."[11]

The need to preserve the family and conserve wealth thus compelled the women of the elite to be fruitful. In the sixteenth century, a wealthy Frenchwoman might rear six or seven children.[12] In the same country more than three centuries earlier, Isabelle of Aragon, the wife of King Philip III and the mother of Philip IV, "the Fair," gave birth in 1268, 1269, and 1270; in that last year she died, six months pregnant.[13] Henrietta Maria, the queen of King Charles I of England, was pregnant almost without intermission from 1628 to 1639.[14] Her contemporary, the Englishwoman Margaret Denton Verney bore twelve children over a twenty-eight-year period,[15] while the Florentine Alessandra Macinghi Strozzi, a descendent of the Alberti and Strozzi commercial dynasties of Florence, gave birth to eight children in the decade from 1426 to 1436.[16] From the fourteenth through the seventeenth century, the women of the noble Venetian Donato family may have achieved in each generation the average maximum biological fertility for the human female: twelve births.[17] Some Renaissance mothers surpassed this average to achieve staggering figures. The Florentine Antonia Masi, who died in 1459 at age fifty-seven, gave birth to thirty-six children; nine males survived her.[18] In fifteenth-century Venice, Magdalucia, the wife of the nobleman Francesco Marcello, gave birth to twenty-six children: nearly one per year for all the years of her fertility.[19]

To bear children is a woman's privilege and a woman's burden—both. In Italy and France, the woman who had just borne a child was celebrated and pampered. The Milanese canon Pietro Casola described the chamber of a new mother of the noble Dolfin family in Venice in 1494.[20] The room was hung with ornaments worth at least 2,000 ducats, and the female attendants wore jewels worth at least 100,000. Special decorative plates, commissioned by male admirers and supporters, honored the *trionfo* of the Florentine mother at the hour of birth, as they did at the marriage day.[21] The woman who gave birth, like a bride at her wedding, occupied for a passing moment a position of unparalleled honor. It was a badge of honor, likewise, to be pregnant. Piero della Francesca's frescoed *Madonna del Parto* points to her belly, in which she nurtures the future Christ, representing to her viewers the prestige enjoyed by the ordinary woman soon to bring forth life. When the Venetian nobleman and bishop Gregorio Correr spoke to Cecilia Gonzaga, the daughter of the ruler of Mantua, of the temptations in her own house that might distract her from her intention to take the veil, he mentioned the swelling bellies of her brothers' wives and the cries of their newborn infants, calling to her for nurture.[22] The wife of Francesco Datini, the renowned merchant of Prato about whose life a bonanza of records fortunately survives, longed for a child. Unable to give birth herself, she gave equal love to her husband's child by another woman.[23]

Even mothers who loved their children could dread childbirth. It was a fearful prospect, the particular punishment of God upon Eve for her duplicity in Eden: less than man's punishment, argued the fifteenth-century Veronese humanist Isotta Nogarola; worse than his, responded her male partner in a dialogue on the subject, because she bore two penalties: unending labor as well as the pain of childbirth.[24] From that latter malediction, wrote the Scots reformer John Knox a century later, "can neither art, nobility, policy, nor law made by man deliver womankind; but whosoever attaineth to that honor to be mother proveth in experience of the effect and strength of God's word." Nothing could save women from the torment of childbirth, a torment so great that it was acknowledged even by men. The archhumanist Erasmus knew the pain to be excruciating: what woman, asked Folly, "would ever yield to a man's advances if she either knew about or at least called to mind the

perilous labor of childbirth, the trials and tribulations of raising children?
. . . what woman who has once had this experience would ever consent
to go through it again if it were not for the divine influence of Lethe [for-
getfulness]?"[25] Joseph Swetnam conceded in his *Arraignment of Lewd, idle,
froward and unconstant women* in 1615 that women justly viewed childbearing with "great terror": "there is no disease that a man endureth that is
one half so grievous or painful as child-bearing to a woman."[26] Its intensity could serve as a measure of extreme pain, even for male patients.
"He is so cruelly ill," wrote the Florentine Isabella Guicciardini of the
parish priest, "that he would move the stones to sorrow, and he is often
heard to cry out like a woman in labor."[27] Oppressed by the fear of
painful childbirth and by the pain itself, women suffered. "If only God
had given some share to man; if only God had given him the childbearing," protested one medieval writer.[28] Both pregnancy and birth
overwhelmed the English mystic Margery Kempe, whose difficult labor
precipitated a six-month depression.[29] The diary of the seventeenth-
century clergyman Ralph Josselin is studded with references to his wife's
uncomfortable pregnancies: she was "faint and pained with her child,"
"exercised with qualms and weakness," "ill," "very ill," because "she
breeds with difficulty." The night before the third live birth, he prayed
for the woman "oppressed with feares that she should not doe well on
this child." At age forty-three, she delivered her last, "after many sad
pains, and sadder feares, in respect of the unkindliness of her labour."[30]

For many women, "unkindly" labor meant death: perhaps as many
as 10 percent of mothers died as a consequence of childbirth;[31] even the
more conservative estimate of 2.5 percent for England in the late Renaissance is five or six times higher than the rate recorded in the nineteenth-
century.[32] Tended by midwives trained in the school of custom, they
could not survive certain complicated births or bacterial infection, a
threat to rich and poor until well into the modern era. The high-born
English Lady Lowther died undelivered in 1648 as the result of antepar-
tum hemorrhage, untreated, though the evident onset of the rupture preceded her death by a full seven weeks.[33] The torment of the English Lady
Danby was recorded by her sister, writing in 1648: having already borne
nine children and miscarried six times, she underwent a sixteenth pregnancy and welcomed the death that followed two weeks later. A contemporary tomb in Middlesex, England, commemorates Lady Margaret
Leigh and her infant in her arms, who both died in the travail of birth,
together in death.[34] In the winter of 1774, puerperal fever swept an Edin-

burgh infirmary, infecting nearly all women within twenty-four hours of giving birth; every woman who fell sick died.[35] Guillaume Versoris lost three wives in the four-year space of 1523 to 1527: two within a month of giving birth, and a third probably during her confinement.[36] The mother of Agrippa d'Aubigné, their contemporary, suffered in giving birth "to such a degree that the doctors proposed the choice of death for the mother, or for the child. It was named Agrippa," and his mother was allowed to die.[37] Gregorio Dati noted, amid the lists of his accounts and of his children, the deaths of the first three of his four wives from illness or trauma related to birth. The litany may serve as a memorial for all the mothers of the past: Bandecca returned her soul to her creator in 1390, after a nine-month illness started by a miscarriage; Isabetta passed on to Paradise after the birth of an eighth child (1402), "and I shall have no more children by her to list here"; Ginevra, who bore Dati eleven children in fifteen years, died (not long before 1421) in childbirth after "lengthy suffering, which she bore with remarkable strength and patience."[38]

The mothers who survived often lived to face the death of the baby they had borne at such risk. Child mortality was a fact made relentless by epidemic disease, chronic malnutrition, and unrelieved filth. Infants, children, and adolescents succumbed to the plague, endemic in every century of the Renaissance, at a higher rate than adults, as well as to diarrhea, influenza, catarrh, tuberculosis, and starvation. The children of the poor (the class that suffered most from the effects of the plague and other infectious diseases) were especially vulnerable. Only 20 to 50 percent of western Europeans could hope to survive childhood.[39] Eight of nine children predeceased the fourteenth-century saint Dorothy of Montau, victims of the plague, freeing their mother for her career as an anchoress.[40] Three of Wibrandis Rosenblatt's four children died of the plague in the sixteenth century.[41] In seventeenth-century England, only two of the six children born to Sir Ralph and Lady Margaret Verney survived to adulthood.[42] In French Argenteuil, approximately 19 percent of infants born to wealthy families died, compared to 23 percent for the middle class and 26 percent for the poor.[43] In fifteenth-century Pistoia, nearly 18 percent of infants died between ages one and four, nearly 11 percent between age 5 and 9, and a little more than 11 percent between ages ten and fourteen.[44] In Florence in the same century, 45 percent of the children born to the families of the merchant class died before the age of twenty.[45] In Milan in 1470, 5 percent of newborns died within the first day of existence.[46] The same Dati who listed his past and present wives tracked the births and deaths of his children: of twenty births by his first three wives (not counting miscarriages and prebaptismal deaths), five remained alive in 1422; of six by his fourth wife, three had died by 1431.[47] Of the twenty-six children born to Magdalucia Marcello, thirteen survived to a "robust age."[48]

If some women could limit their attachment to these transitory beings, others knew grief. In the seventeenth century, the Duchess of Newcastle wrote of the irksomeness of having children: women are "troubled with their forwardnesse and untowardnesse, the care for their well being, the fear for their ill doing, the grief for their sicknesse and their unsufferable sorrow for their death."[49] Of Alessandra Macinghi Strozzi's five sons, only two survived after the death of the youngest, Matteo, in 1459. His death caused her to suffer, she wrote, "the greatest pain in my heart that I have ever experienced"; but she took comfort in the knowledge that he had received proper medical and clerical attention, and had been welcomed by God in heaven.[50] Apparitions of lost children sometimes came to bereaved mothers. The Spanish wool-carder's wife Francisca la Brava, a visionary examined and punished by the Inquisition in 1523, saw her dead son, in heaven, an angel.[51] The seventeenth-century Englishwoman Anne Bathurst saw her dead children rising to heaven: "I remembered Two little children, died one at fourteen weeks, the other at fourteen days end, and immediately as soon as I began to desire it, they came like two Bright Sparks, one after another, and entred into this great Light and became one with it."[52]

The apprehension of child death hovers over birth. The newborn child could have been viewed by some Renaissance mothers as an ephemeron in whom only a tentative affection could be invested. "Given the constant liability to sickness, pain or sudden death, the bonds that tied the family together could hardly be more durable than the lines of life itself."[53] The French Chevalier de La Tour Landry warned his daughters in the late fourteenth century not to rejoice too much in the birth of a child, or to celebrate it with too much pomp; God might be angered, and the child might die.[54] The reformer and heretic John Wycliffe advised coldly that mothers should be grateful for God's "great mercy" in taking a child from this world.[55] Infants who had died or were likely to do so (especially girls) were underreported in Venetian genealogies and Florentine tax records.[56] The tax declaration of a Tuscan father noted the presence of four children "ifino che Dio vorrà," "for as long as it pleases God."[57] The English mother's lullaby warned her child that he was but a guest in this hard and uncertain world.[58]

Sickness and destitution killed many babies, but so did anger and neglect. In peasant villages, swaddled infants were left unattended and helpless in the face of accidental cottage fires: one-third of fifty-eight infant deaths brought before the coroner in a fourteenth-century English sample perished in this way.[59] Unsupervised and active toddlers were prone to be drowned in wells, scalded by kettles, or crushed by passing horses. Children commonly slept in adult beds, and exhausted, unaware, drunken, hostile, or desperate mothers and fathers often rolled over and suffocated them. Such "overlaying" was so common an occurrence that contemporaries assumed and historians agree that in many cases the resultant death was no accident. From pulpits preachers exhorted and threatened parents, and in moral treatises scholars warned them, not to take in this way the lives of those whose needs threatened adult survival. A fourteenth-century English confessional manual instructs the priest to examine the consciences of husbands: "Hast thou also by hyre [his wife] I'layn / And so by-twene you they chyld I'slayn?"[60]

Every century prior to our own has known infanticide. In antiquity a normal and accepted form of population limitation (especially the population of females), infanticide was proscribed and abhorred in the Christian centuries.[61] It was nevertheless practiced, if rarely, in England and on the continent. The greatest concentration of infant murder was among the unmarried poor. Within stable peasant communities, illegitimate births were successfully avoided much of the time, if only by the remedy of marriage in the case of premature pregnancy.[62] When illegitimate births occurred, feudal arrangements taxed the women deemed guilty, and towns imprisoned or banished women who were convicted of fornication. These penalties were severe enough, but perhaps not as burdensome as the actual responsibility for an unwanted child—which was hers alone. Increased rates of illegitimacy, related in turn to urbanization, lie behind an upsurge of infant deaths in the later Renaissance. Many illegitimate babies were eventually abandoned and taken in by other households as foster children or servants, but others were killed by accident or neglect or intention: victims of the violence of mothers who were themselves victims.

Court judgments of women accused of infanticide in some cases show remarkable mildness. In England, where prosecutions were rare, defendants often pled insanity. The juries usually agreed, finding perpetrators "suffering from ague and frenzy," or "demented and vexed."[63] Women found to be insane were generally pardoned and released to the care of their families. This indulgence may reflect considerable understanding of mother-child hostility, an important component of female depression that emerges especially when mothers are isolated from wider family networks.[64] In Venice, as in England, there were few cases of infanticide—*pochissimi*—and these were generally decided in favor of the woman.[65] Spurts of judicial activity elsewhere, however, bear witness to the reality of willful infant death. In France, letters of remission from the fourteenth and fifteenth centuries testify to the murder of illegitimate infants by disgraced and frightened peasant mothers.[66] An ordinance of the German town of Freiburg in Breisgau from 1494 cautions midwives not to assist in the elimination of unwanted babies: they are "not to destroy any child, whether by doing too little or doing too much. . . . They are also not to use any gruesome or clumsy tools to damage or pull out the child, like long iron hooks or similar things."[67] If a woman was suspected of aborting or killing her child in the German towns, a thorough investigation followed: it was necessary to find and examine the corpses which were buried, often negligently, with the visible marks of the manner of death upon them.[68] Around 1500, the Bishop at Fiesole (near Florence) began to set specific punishments for cases of infant suffocation and, simultaneously, began to issue large numbers of absolutions for excommunications incurred by that act.[69] Two generations earlier, the outraged Fra Cherubino da Siena had complained of women who resisted motherhood: they attempted first not to become pregnant, but if they became pregnant, tried to abort, and if they could not abort, "then when the creature is born, they beat it, and would want to see it dead, so that they can be free to go freely about their business, here and there."[70] His countryman San Bernardino thundered: "Go to the Ponte Vecchio, there by the Arno, and put your ear to the ground and listen: you will hear a great lament. . . . Listen, and you will hear voices rising to heaven, crying, 'Vengeance! Vengeance! O God!' . . . What are these cries? They are the voices of the innocent babies thrown into your Arno and your privies or buried alive in your gardens and your stables, to avoid the world's shame, and sometimes without baptism."[71]

Though sometimes forgiven or overlooked, infanticide was nevertheless a crime—and one firmly linked to sex. Most infanticides were committed by women, and women were condemned for infanticide with increasing frequency in the Renaissance centuries.[72] The rage against infanticides recalls and is linked to the simultaneous rage against witches.[73] Infanticide was the major cause after witchcraft for the execution of Renaissance women, and many prosecuted witches were charged with infanticide. The burden of the vigilant prosecution of infanticide fell on the unmarried mother, who was presumed to be guilty of her infant's death, while the most likely victim of witch frenzy (as will be seen below) was both female and old. "The law and conscience of Europe . . . vented its force upon old women and unwed mothers."[74] And, in contrast to other offenses, women accused of infanticide or witchcraft were considered legally responsible for their crimes and bore the punishment for them. Otherwise, in the criminal law of many localities, "women did not exist": other offenses committed by women were to be for several more centuries legally the responsibility of their fathers or husbands.[75] The prosecution of women in these instances perversely marks the beginning, therefore, of the emergence of women as criminals and as legally responsible individuals.

For this original and distinctively female crime, the punishment was unequivocal and severe. Infanticide was punished by death: often death by a means (drowning, burning) far more painful than that typically used (hanging, decapitation) in the case of a male criminal.[76] In fifteenth-century Metz, the mother accused of infanticide was burned at a stake to which her guilty hand was nailed, while around her neck hung a placard bearing the image of her murdered child.[77] In sixteenth-century Nuremberg, the penalty for maternal infanticide was drowning; in 1580, a year in which the severed heads of three women convicted of maternal infanticide were nailed to the scaffold for public contemplation, the penalty was changed to beheading.[78] The city that pioneered this more humane remedy for infanticide executed fourteen women for that crime between 1578 and 1615, but only one witch. The Parlement of Rouen from the 1580s to 1606 prosecuted about as many cases of infanticide as witchcraft, but punished infanticide more severely.[79] Calvinist Geneva shows a much higher rate of execution for infanticide than for witchcraft: from 1590 to 1630, 9 women of 11 charged were executed for infanticide, compared to 19 women of 122 charged for witchcraft; for the next seventy years, 13 women of 20 tried were executed for infanticide, compared to only 1 of 30 suspects for witchcraft.[80]

Desperate mothers, then, sometimes destroyed the children they had borne in misfortune. More frequently, they abandoned them, in the hope that abandonment was a lesser sin than murder, or that some charitable stranger would allow the child to live.[81] Unthinkable to many of us who inhabit a century that has insisted on the parental responsibility to nurture, abandonment was understandably common in the premodern era: it was just about the only licit means of family limitation in an era when the poor faced the rigid limits of scarce resources and the wealthy adhered to equally rigid laws of inheritance. "How many infants," Boccaccio lamented in the *Corbaccio*, "are thrown into the arms of fortune! . . . How many are given over to the forests, how many to the wild animals and to the birds!"[82] Children left on street corners or church steps or thresholds of the urban houses of the rich would sometimes die, but more often were "found" and pressed into service as slaves, servants, prostitutes, or foster children. Large-scale abandonment must be assumed to explain (along with high rates of child mortality) the small dimensions of poor families, the large dimensions of wealthy ones, and the vast population of servants, some of them very young.[83] To this informal and tacit system of abandonment and charitable or self-serving recovery, the Italian cities led in presenting a modern and institutional solution: the foundling hospital.

Established since the eighth century in Italy, these institutions spread there and northwards from the fourteenth to the sixteenth century.[84] Where there was no hospital dedicated to the purpose, other civic institutions served: Montpellier hired 305 wet nurses during the fifteenth century to care in their own homes for a number of abandoned infants somewhat higher than that total.[85] Florence opened its famed Ospedale degli Innocenti in 1445, only one of several institutions dedicated to saving the unwanted children of its citizens. The opening of the Innocenti served to increase the total number of infants in institutional care in Florence: there was no end, it seems, to the flood of unwanted children. In the early sixteenth century, more than 900 children were in the care of the Innocenti (not counting those in other institutions), compared with a range of 60 to 150 during the first two decades of its operation.[86] Most of the foundlings were very young, not yet weaned: the children of female slaves or male clerics, or of the most destitute of country-dwellers in crisis times. Most of them were girls, more unwanted even than boys.[87]

The purpose of the foundling homes was to provide the humane care that natal families could not give. The humanist monk Ambrogio Traversari described the tending of charges at Santa Maria della Scala, which housed 200 infants: "Customarily they are first given over to wet-nurses for breast feeding. When they are weaned, they are diligently cared for within this institution. Boys are sent to learn their letters; Girls learn womanly things. When they later become adults, the boys learn a trade which will support them; the girls are married, with the institution providing a dowry."[88] Despite Traversari's optimism, the scant resources of such institutions were generally insufficient for the task of rearing orphaned children. The wet nursing of newborns had unsatisfactory results, as will be seen shortly. Those who survived infancy had only dim prospects for adulthood. At the Florentine Innocenti in the mid-quattrocento, cumulative death rates ranged from a little less to a little more than half—a wave of child death terrifying in itself, but mild if compared to the 90 percent sometimes reached in the foundling homes of eighteenth-century Paris, London, and St. Petersburg.

Abandoned children who were lucky were not enrolled in foundling homes, but taken into the homes of the rich. There they had relatively privileged childhoods—an exposure to the culture enjoyed by that class, and access, perhaps, to their tables—but began a life of service that they would continue when, still immature, they were sent out from their temporary families into the world of adulthood.[89] The children of the concubines of wealthy men and prelates were raised in similar conditions before Protestantism and Catholic Reform bore down on the practice. In fifteenth-century Florence, a young man's slave mistress and three children could be included in the same household as their father and his new wife.[90] But as the monogamous and tightly focused modern family emerged, illegitimate and "foster" children, relatives, and servants were excluded from the smaller space before the hearth.[91] They became, in many cases, the orphans tossed from desk to desk in the bureaucracy of recent centuries.

Whether within their families or abandoned to outsiders, those babies who survived were fed by breast, commonly for eighteen to twenty-four months: again, woman's specific task. Little else could be provided, and nothing better: human milk alone was sufficient to nourish and to ward off the diseases transmitted by other food and drink. In villages and in towns all over Europe, most adult women must have been nursing one or more babies most of the time: their own as well as those of others. Most women, and mostly poor women: for the women of the nobility and the patriciate, the ladies of the courts and cities of Renaissance Europe, declined to nurse their babies. The prevailing assumption is implied in the instruction of the fifteenth-century physician Paolo

Bagellardo: "if the infant is a child of the poorer class, let it be fed on its mother's milk."[92] There were exceptions, particularly in England after the turn of the seventeenth century; the wife of the Protestant pastor Ralph Josselin, for instance, nursed all of her children.[93] Among the large sample of mothers of the saints, however, who came predominantly from the higher social strata, only a few are noted by hagiographers as having nursed their own children.[94] The mother of Saint Catherine of Siena bore twenty-five children, but nursed only one: the future saint, whose twin sister was dispatched to a wet nurse and died, while the favored sibling enjoyed her mother's milk.[95]

The refusal of elite women to breast-feed flew in the face of an overwhelming body of advice from physicians, humanists, and priests, drawing from authorities as old and as honored as Aristotle and Plutarch: "Almost every writer on the subject points out the desirability of maternal suckling."[96] Francesco Barbaro declared it a mother's natural duty to feed her infant at her breast. It is the best food for the baby, he declared, and the best way to transmit parental qualities to offspring. "We beg and exhort the most noble women to follow this example of feeding her infant her own milk, for it is very important that an infant should be nourished by the same mother in whose womb and by whose blood he was conceived. No nourishment seems more proper, none more wholesome than that same nourishment of body that glowed with greatest life and heat in the womb and should thus be given as known and familiar food to newborn infants. The power of the mother's food most effectively lends itself to shaping the properties of body and mind to the character of the seed."[97] Maffeo Vegio considered the mother who did not suckle her own children a "monster."[98] Barbaro's and Vegio's contemporary Leon Battista Alberti agreed, as did the Spanish-born Juan Luis Vives a century later, in his famous work *The Instruction of a Christian Woman*: "the milk itself," he insists, "should be the mother's. . . . The mother thinks more seriously about her child if she has not only held it in her womb and given birth, but if also in its earliest infancy she holds continually in her arms, hears its cry, nurses it from her blood, . . . sees its first smile, and is the first to be delighted by the sounds of the babbling of its first attempt to talk."[99] Outside the humanist tradition, marriage manuals and hortatory sermons—Catholic and Protestant alike—presented the arguments for maternal nursing.[100] The preacher San Bernardino trumpeted to women listeners in the piazza that they fell into sin the day they put their babies out to nurse. The friar Cherubino da Siena

considered the outnursing of babies "a corrupt and abusive practice."[101]
Pediatric handbooks, with authority, recommended maternal nursing.
But patrician women did not nurse.

More than simple reluctance accounted for the avoidance of breast-
feeding by women from elite groups.[102] They may have been, as preaching friars charged, too self-indulgent to submit to the task. If they could
be spared the burden of nursing, at least some continuous months of
their fertile years could be enjoyed without the burdens of birth, pregnancy, or lactation. Husbands, moreover, played a role in the decision of
elite women not to nurse. They often did not approve of the appearance
of a nursing mother. In addition, nursing could discourage the high rate
of fertility desired in those circles. Lactation, having a known, if limited,
contraceptive effect, may have been avoided so that more children could
be conceived. In fact, sexual intercourse was both forbidden and feared
during lactation because it was universally thought that the milk would
become corrupted by intercourse or a new conception and kill the child.
Since the mother's milk was thought to be of the same substance as her
blood, and especially her menstrual blood, impressions of its whole-
someness and suitability were affected by the mother's sexual behavior.
A lactating woman, for these reasons, was off limits to her husband. He
may have rid himself of the obstacle by dismissing the baby.

For all these reasons, the children of the rich were fed from the
breasts of the poor: as the former were tied to "perpetual pregnancy,"
the latter were tied to "perpetual suckling."[103] Babies of the very
wealthiest (only in one of five of those families studied in affluent Florence for the period 1300–1530) were provided with a nurse who lived
with the household: these were the highest paid of all domestic servants.[104] The two elder sons of Isabelle of Aragon, Queen of France, in
turn heirs to the throne, each enjoyed the services of two such attendants,
who received two sous per day and an allotment of clothing.[105] The preeminent role of the chief nurse (*nutrix*) is indicated by Isabelle's will,
where she is called *mater*, "mother": justly, perhaps, for she performed a
mother's role. The assistant was termed *cunabularia*, or cradle rocker, and
charged with the second of the two principal remedies known to that age
and ours for the wailing infant. A single nurse cared at home for the
fifteenth-century Venetian infant Valerio Marcello, in whose arms and
not his mother's he first greeted his soldier father returned from the
Lombard wars: she tried to offer her breast but could not distract the
baby fascinated by clanking armor.[106]

More commonly, babies were sent from the cities of Italy, France, Germany, and England to the country within days of birth to be wet nursed by peasant women. Painstaking care went into the selection of a nurse. Guided by centuries of pediatric literature, parents considered the age, health, and character (for the latter was thought to be transmitted in the milk) of the candidate, the size of her breasts, and the consistency of the product. "It should be white, sweet to taste and free from any un-natural savour, and it is better that it should be too much than too little; and it should be of medium consistency, not too watery and not too thick": a drop placed on a fingernail should roll slightly but maintain its form.[107] The milk itself was subjected to such scrutiny because it was believed to have a more than just the material capacity to nourish: dis-tilled from the blood of its bearer, it was imbued with her character, and would, for better or for worse, shape the character of the nursling. This potent food was especially vulnerable to contamination and degenera-tion: from the wrong food or air, from too much worry, from lechery and especially, as has been seen, from pregnancy. If the nurse became preg-nant, the child was promptly taken away.

In Renaissance Florence, the arrangement for wet nursing was the father's responsibility and jealously guarded right.[108] His children were an asset to be protected, and he proceeded to perform his duties with his characteristic efficiency and competence. "It would take a long time to tell you how careful we fathers have to be about these things," lamented Alberti, "and how much trouble there is each time before one has found an honest, good, and competent nurse. . . . [and] how rare is a good nurse and how much in demand."[109] Most nurses were respectably mar-ried, and in the capital city of the Italian Renaissance, the wet-nursing contract was a masculine arrangement on both sides: the baby's father and the nurse's husband, or *balio*, arrived at a price: "hardly ever" is the mother mentioned, and the nurse herself is a "vague silhouette."[110] The same two men decided on the date of weaning, apparently on mercenary grounds: richer families allowed their babies longer at the costly breast than poorer ones, and boys overall fared better than girls.[111] The con-tract between parent and nurse (or father and *balio*) resembled in all re-gards a commercial one, as for a delivery of fish or a commission for a bauble. Salaries could be good: the rate of up to twenty florins annually to an in-house nurse in fifteenth-century Florence made her the highest-paid among domestic servants.[112] Wet nurses in European society (slaves excepted) only nursed for money.[113]

With all the fussing about the nurse's capacity to care for the child of a bourgeois or aristocratic family, little thought was given to the woman's own existence as mother, the precondition of her ability to nurse. Some nurses had such abundance of milk, perhaps, that the demands of caring for additional children were satisfactorily met: yet of instances of multiple nurslings we have scarcely a trace. Others had recently buried their own babies, or weaned them, or (lured by rich fees) handed them over to other nurses. Some nurses for the Strozzi, Busini, and Parenti families of Florence received advances on their salaries so that they could pay for the nursing of their own babies.[114] How might the servant or slave or hireling nurse have looked on the small creature she tended, dependent on her for life itself, yet her master or mistress nevertheless? The startling injustice of the system reached its maximum when the buyer watched for the death of one infant to favor the life of another.[115] A Florentine agent complained of a shortage of nurses due to the unanticipated recovery of their own natural babies. One prospect, with "fresh milk," was still good: "she promised that if her infant girl who is on the brink of death, died tonight, she will come [to me] after the burial."[116] In the same city, one woman abandoned her infant because "she could not feed her, and she wanted to hire herself out as a wet-nurse to be able to live"; another did likewise, finding it necessary "to hire out as a wet-nurse if she wanted to live, because she was dying of hunger."[117] The case of Elena Taliour of Skelton in fourteenth-century England was exceptional: asked to wet nurse the infant born to the gentry Rouclif family, she refused to set her own nursing son aside.[118] The disposition of those peasant children whose mothers accepted wet-nursing responsibilities for the wealthy is not nice to contemplate. Montaigne witnessed peasant children put to the teats of goats for nourishment: the goat-nurses came at the summoning wail of their charges, and the nurslings languished for lack of their own particular nurse. One child even faced death when he was separated from the goat for whom he had formed deep affection.[119]

In the hands of country wet nurses, many children died—more than those who would have died had they stayed in maternal care. Their deaths were due to a variety of causes: malnutrition, neglect, sickness. The nurse whose charge became ill was supposed to notify the family, but was often fearful of doing so. A fifteenth-century Venetian mother, informed of plague in the nurse's household, whisked the baby away to her own home and a live-in nurse.[120] But often the consequence of a nursing relationship was the return of a small corpse to the parents. Of 356 Tuscan nursing contracts for which the causes of termination are known, 62 (more than 17 percent) were due to the death of a baby in its nurse's care.[121] The Tuscan notary Ser Lapo Mazzei put fourteen children out to nurse the day after they were born; five survived. In the English town of Chesham, Buckinghamshire, between 1578 and 1601, 6 percent of all burials were of children in nurses' care.[122]

The child who survived disease and neglect frequently succumbed to the malign intentions of the nurse. Babies were not always wanted, and nurses often obliged by dispatching them. A classic method was overlaying: a death, as has been seen, that had the appearance of accident (and indeed often was accidental). Unwanted children also succumbed to other effects of neglect and abuse: starvation, exposure, and drugging. Of twenty-three children placed in the care of a Mrs. Poole in England in 1765, eighteen died within one month of life, two were discharged from her care as babies, and three remained, alive.[123]

The custom of exporting the babies of the upper classes to foster mothers for several years resulted in a toll of death and sadness over several centuries. The absence of maternal affection (or of any other kind) may have been a factor in infant deaths at the hands of nurses, just as the absence of consistent warmth from a single figure has a negative impact on infants and children today. Away in the country, children were seldom visited, although parents were advised by the writers of manuals to supervise their welfare. Lapo Mazzei had seen his son only once before when he came back "from his wet-nurse in the hills, the finest little curly badger that I have ever had."[124] Benvenuto Cellini visited one of his, a two-year-old, who cried when the treasured visitor attempted to leave: "he would not let me go, but held me with his little hands and a tempest of cries and tears."[125] Sometimes unvisited by parents, children were also handed from nurse to nurse. They were transferred if the child was not doing well, or if the nurse became pregnant or sick. A study of 318 Tuscan infants shows them at the breasts of 462 different wet nurses. Staying an average of only ten months with each nurse, about one-third were transferred at least to a second; some were transferred to a third, a fourth, and a fifth.[126] The physician Girolamo Cardano lost his first wet nurse in the first month of life and was soon sent off to a second; in her care, "my body wasted, while the belly grew hard and swollen," and he was transferred to a third, with whom he stayed until age three.[127] Stefano Guazzo seems to refer to his own abandonment in his *Civile con-*

versazione of 1581, in which a child reproaches his mother for having carried him only nine months in her womb before dispatching him to a nurse for two years.[128] A motherless child might be kept with nurses for years. The Florentine Giovanni Morelli relates that his father Pagolo (in the early trecento) was in the home of a brutal country nurse until age ten; he passed his still-rankling anger on to his son.[129]

Renaissance writers grieved for the lost intimacy of childhood. Literature abounds with images of the mothers' breasts that so many of the children of the age never knew. The Spanish saint Teresa, in her *Way of Perfection*, described the soul as "an infant still at its mother's breast," and the English poet Richard Crashaw likened heaven to a sea of milk where the hungry can suck their fill: "Milke all the way."[130] In visual images, too, the bond of mother and child was glorified. Portraits of adoring madonnas and chubby children depicted a relationship craved but rarely realized: a loving mother, a joyful and secure child. In the image "the child reigns supreme over the mother, the sole object of her love and attention," while in reality such a child "was probably lying swaddled and immobile, and often miserable and underfed, at the mercy of a wet-nurse miles away from its mother."[131] Writers and artists alike could have been conveying in this religious imagery "a secular fantasy of maternal intimacy"—as far from the truth as the veneration of Mary was from contemporary attitudes towards real women. The pain of childbirth, the despair of child death, the stress of poverty, the insecurity of wealth, and the ferocity of the law—all engulfed mother and child.

Yet many mothers did nurse, and others nurtured their children, and most—dare we guess?—may have loved their children with the sentiment we see today as commendable and necessary to their welfare. An English verse in which Mary laments her own loss depicts a mother holding and caressing her infant: "Your children you dance upon your knee / With laughing, kissing and merry cheer. / O woman, woman well is with thee," says Mary enviously, when her grown and crucified son lies "upon my knee, ta'en from a tree."[132] Some devoted "mothers" were not biological mothers at all, but the nurses and caretakers who affectionately tended the valued children of the rich and the abandoned children of the poor—like the "poor nursemaid" who raised the future Sienese priest Michelangelo del già Messer Domencio Santi, to whom, in recognition of her utter poverty and years of sacrifice, he left his property.[133]

Some women may have taken responsibility for the lives of children, ironically, by insisting on the prevention of births.[134] Among the poor, the "trigger of economic hardship" impelled mothers from as early as the thirteenth century to seek to limit births by the contraceptive measure of *coitus interruptus*.[135] A Florentine mother seems to have instructed her daughter in useful techniques of this sort, alluding in a letter to "the practices I mentioned to you when we talked together."[136] A Venetian girl, testifying about her father's incestuous assault, described the practice.[137] The fifteenth-century friar Cherubino da Siena clearly believed that some women, fearing pregnancy, attempted a means of intercourse that would avoid that consequence: they "assume a position such that they will not become pregnant."[138]

Many goals spurred men and women to such practices, but among them was the desire to enrich the lives of the children who were born by limiting nursling death and enhancing maternal care. The elite families who sent babies out to nurse had even more babies than those who did not, for the reasons we have seen: the positive spur to provide heirs to substantial wealth and the absence of the contraceptive effect of lactation. But the more babies they had, the more babies died. The "excessive" fertility of upper-class (especially urban) families was matched by the excessive mortality of their children: city-born babies died at twice the rate of country-born babies. Mothers and fathers discovered, in time, that contraception could save lives. Mothers who nursed their babies were spared both the fear of pregnancy and the commitment to mercenary wet nursing. The result was fewer babies, and thus fewer heirs, but also fewer victims of disease, abandonment, and dispassion. From the fourteenth century through the eighteenth, a growing number of parents kept death at bay by preventing birth.

If mothers waged a battle in this way against infant death, they were everywhere responsible for infant life. Until age seven, moralists from antiquity forward insisted, the child was charged to the mother's care. The Florentine Alberti recommended that quiet and tender mothers, rather than brusque and driven fathers, care for the littlest children: "So let the earliest period be spent entirely outside the father's arms. Let the child rest, let him sleep in his mother's lap."[139] The baby quickly outgrew his mother's lap, but continued to receive his share of the cultural heritage of his age primarily from his mother:[140] information about his social world, religious values, the world of work (concrete lessons here, if the child was a girl), and even, in elite circles, some reading, writing, and ideas. The Spanish humanist Juan Luis Vives, writing for the mother of the future queen Mary Tudor, his charge, described the fundamental role that women played in the education of their children: "so that they may know and love the same person as mother, nurse, and teacher, and learn more easily aided by their love for her who teaches them. . . . For the first voice the infant hears is its mother's, and attempts to form its first babbling to her speech; for at that age it can do nothing but imitate, and takes its first sense experiences, the first furnishings of mind from what it hears its mother say or sees her do; therefore, it is more in the mother's power to shape her child's character than anyone thinks."[141]

Protective mothers of the highest social strata continued to nurture and assist their children well into adolescence and even adulthood, promoting their achievements and fostering their ambitions. In seventeenth-century Siena, they were charged by dying husbands' wills to supervise the education of their children: one nobleman left his wife a free hand with all his property, trusting that she in turn would "carry out the responsibility for their dearest children, and . . . always retain with maternal affection the responsibility of educating their children, he beseeches her in the love of God to stay with the children, to educate, feed and clothe them . . . and to govern the household through divine and human laws."[142] In fourteenth-century Montpellier, mothers were present at the negotiation of commercial contracts undertaken by their sons.[143] In the quattrocento, noble Venetian widows arranged for the public registration of their adolescent sons in the rolls of the politically eligible and built networks of political advice and opportunity for them within their families when the paternal family had been distanced by death.[144] One Venetian nobleman, the cleric and humanist Jacopo Zeno, grieved deeply for the mother who had presided over his technical as well as his spiritual education.[145] Burgher women in Strasbourg publicly renounced the Anabaptist faith of their husbands in order to safeguard their children.[146] Renée de France, Duchess of Ferrara, resisted the pressures of inquisitors to return to orthodoxy until her children were taken away from her: she then succumbed, betraying the reform.[147] The powerful widows of royal and noble French families in the sixteenth century guarded the futures of their offspring: their inheritance, their safety, their salvation. One of these, Jeanne d'Albret, cousin of Renée, secured the climactic twin triumphs of her son's kingship and, in the Edict of Nantes, the safety of her coreligionists.[148] The mother of the sixteen-year-old Neapolitan Ottaviano Cesare, who fled home and school to join the Jesuits in 1553, refused to yield her child to the business of the other world.[149] She approached the founder and general of the order, Ignatius of Loyola himself, who fended her off with a series of letters and commands, complaining to his companions, "She is not the first mother of a monk, and the child belongs more to Jesus Christ than to the mother."[150] The relentless mother pursued the case over five years, enlisting on her side her high-placed husband, her Franciscan counselor, and Popes Julius III and Paul IV. She should concern herself with her daughters, the Jesuits retorted, and allow her son to hear the call of God. God listened to Ottaviano's mother: she won the case and in 1558 secured the release of her son from his Jesuit vows.

In volumes of letters, mothers exhorted their offspring to good conduct, wise spending, and high achievement. The maternal cares of the Florentine Alessandra Macinghi Strozzi, mother of eight, are uniquely well documented in seventy-two letters written between 1447 and 1471.[151] When her anti-Medicean husband (soon deceased) and elder sons were exiled from the city, she was left to rear her surviving children. She taught the children to read, fussed over their health and their diet, arranged the dowries of her daughters and the marriages of her sons, and guarded the family fortunes. Her desire, she wrote her sons Filippo and Lorenzo, was that on her deathbed "I should know that you had both taken that step which mothers desire, to see their sons married. . . . It's to this end I have sought to hold on to the little I have . . . , neglecting things which I could have done for the good of my soul and the souls of our deceased."[152] Not all sons heeded their mothers' advice. Nearly a century later, Wibrandis Rosenblatt wrote to her son, a theology student at the University of Marburg: "I haven't heard from you for some time, but I well know that if I had, the news would not have been comforting. You contrive always to be a cross to me. If only I might live to the day when I have good news from you. Then would I die of joy."[153] Elisabeth of Braunschweig, who lived to see her Lutheran cause triumph in her realm but her two children sworn to the enemy faith, wrote in a work of consolation for widows: "No one without the experience knows the anguish which children can cause and yet be loved."[154]

Of grander stature was the solicitous and ambitious Margaret Beaufort, descendant of the English Lancastrian line who spurred her son, the future Henry VII, first Tudor king of England, to high achievement and strict virtue.[155] This patroness and forerunner of the high-placed learned women of the Tudor age intrigued constantly to place on the throne of England her only child, born to her when she was fourteen. Mother and son exchanged letters revealing deep affection. In a letter granting his mother's wish about the disposition of her personal funds, Henry assured her that "not only in this, but in all other things that I may know should be to your honor and pleasure and weal of your soul, I shall be as glad to please you as any heart can desire it, and I know well that I am as much bounden so to do as any creature living, for the great and singular motherly love that it hath pleased you at all times to bear toward me."[156] Sending greetings from Calais on the day "that I did bring into this world my good and gracious prince, king, and only beloved son," Margaret called Henry her "only desired joy in this world."[157]

The epistles, handbooks, and diaries that mothers wrote to guide the children who no longer sucked at their breasts or nestled on their laps constitute the principal genre of secular female authorship prior to the modern age. It is a tradition that begins with the gemlike *Manual* of the Carolingian noblewoman Dhuoda written to her hostage son after 841.[158] More than five centuries later, the professional writer Christine de Pizan composed in 1377 for her fatherless child some *Moral Instructions: Les Enseignements moraux que je Christine donne à Jean de Castel mon fils.*[159] In the sixteenth century, Elisabeth of Braunschweig, Lutheran reformer and ruler of her region for five years, wrote two manuals for her children: a tract on government for her son and one on marriage for her daughter.[160] Early in the next, the English gentlewoman Elizabeth Grymeston detailed in a volume for her son, Bernye, wisdom on education, marriage, devotions, and death. It was the force of maternal love, she wrote, that compelled her to write: "My dearest sonne, there is nothing so strong as the force of love; there is no love so forcible as the love of an affectionate mother to hir naturall childe; there is no mother can either more affectionately shew hir nature, or more naturally manifest hir affection, than in advising hir children out of hir owne experience, to eschue evill, and encline them to do that which is good."[161] Elizabeth Joceline wrote her *Legacie* in 1622 to the child she still carried in her body and whose birth would cause her death. Upon this unborn baby she hoped to bestow promptly its inheritance: nothing "so poore . . . as the whole world," "the true reason I have so often kneeled to God for thee, is, that thou mightest bee an inheritour of the Kingdome of Heaven." "I thought," she explained, "there was some good office I might doe for my childe more than only to bring it forth."[162]

Serious and determined, these mothers exceeded the expectations of their age. They chose to fulfill the task of nurturing their children not at a minimum but to the maximum, transmitting to their offspring not only blood, not only milk, not only the faint memory of comfort, but also the vital knowledge that would foster survival in a world they knew to be hostile: knowledge communicable only through words and replicable only in ink. Motherhood was clearly a deep commitment for certain privileged women of the Renaissance, as it was the central task, for many years of their lives, for nearly all of them. With few exceptions, the women who were not mothers would take on that role in the future or had performed it in the past. Their lives unfolded according to the rhythm of sexual life—premarital, marital, postmarital.

While the bearers of ideas—preachers and theologians, philosophers and physicians, lawyers, humanists, and poets—defined men in terms of their worldly activity, they defined women in terms of their sexual role.[163] The male world could be schematized, using the feudal hierarchies of those who fought, prayed, and worked; or, as those traditional categories broke down on the threshold of the modern era, as judges, merchants, and lawyers, pilgrims and invalids, peasants and artisans, monks, friars, and prelates, noblemen and gentlemen. Women, with very few exceptions, were categorized in terms of their relations to the female ideal of virginity and nightmare of sexuality. Pride of place was given to virgins dedicated to God: the nuns and the religious. There followed married women (who could remain chaste within marriage if they obeyed their husbands and procreated legitimate children), widows (who had been contaminated by sexual experience), and girls (who would be thus contaminated in due course). These were the categories of female existence already defined by the fathers of the Church, lodged in handbooks and manuals by theologians, spread abroad in sermons by the preaching friars, and deposited in the social thought of the humanists. The fifteenth-century friar Cherubino da Siena expounds these categories as the three stages of life: "virginale, viduale e matrimoniale"—virginity, widowhood, and matrimony.[164] His contemporary, the Venetian humanist Giovanni Caldiera named wives and mothers, virgins (religious or bound for matrimony), and widows; he added two other female conditions—servant and prostitute—reflecting his clearer observation of social reality, but not differing in the approach of defining women in terms of their economic and sexual dependency on men.[165] In the sixteenth century, the humanist Juan Luis Vives devoted one book of his *The Instruction of a Christian Woman* to each of the three stages of a woman's life: youth until marriage, married domesticity, and widowhood.[166] Women workers were classed not by trade or level of skill, but in terms of their relatedness to a male patriarch or employer: wives and daughters, widows, maids (productive workers employed outside the family), and independent women workers, the illusory *femme seule*.[167] Women themselves, finally, defined their existence in terms of the periods before, during, and after marriage and childbirth.[168] The trajectory of their existence extended itself within the family—as daughters, wives, and widows, as workers and survivors.

Daughter, mother, widow; virgin, matron, crone: these were the possibilities that encircled the female sex. A very few, by an act of will or fortune, escaped the endless dance whose mode was set by sex and whose measure by years: a very few who, cheating nature, entered the service of God, and an even smaller number who joined the still lonelier pursuit of word, image, or power. Later chapters will consider such women, women who lived not with a family but in a convent, cell, or library. Here we will follow the cycle, defined by sexual status and imprinted by relation to property, that determined the lives of most women, rich or poor, as they traversed the stages that led to and from the vortex of motherhood. That cycle begins with the female infant.

Daughters

The daughters who made up roughly half of the babies born to Renaissance mothers often entered the world unwelcome. Dante noted the terror aroused in the father whose wife's travail yielded a baby girl: "Faceva, nascendo, ancor paura / la figlia al padre". The wife of the merchant Francesco Datini urged a friend to bring forth sons "because, as you well know, girls do not make families but rather 'unmake' them."[169] The greater joy that greeted the birth of a male is expressed in casual asides. Giovanni Morelli's exultation at his son's "having been born and being male and whole and well proportioned"[170] stands in contrast to his recommendation that a father should have children when still young, and in the course of moderate sexual relations; otherwise, he will ruin his own health and that of his wife, who "will only bear children with difficulty, and you will have females."[171] The German physician Eucharius Rösslin in his pediatric manual, the *Rose Garden (Den swangeren frawen und hebammen Roszgarten)*, urged the midwife to cheer the woman in labor with promises: "The midwife should also comfort the mother with the happy prospect of the birth of a boy."[172] The moment of viability in the womb for a female fetus was placed at four months, in contrast with that of a male fetus at forty days. "Male children are engendered of a more hot and dry seed, and women of a more cold and moist; for there is much less strength in cold than in heat, and likewise in moisture than in dry-nesse; and that is the cause why it will be longer before a girle is formed in the womb than a boy."[173] Considered sluggish even *in utero*, girls were generally regarded as the products of "inferior" conceptions.[174] Their perceived inferiority was matched by deficiencies in nurture. They were left ungreeted and unnoted: Morelli comments, for instance, on the births of "some females" between those of his uncle Dino and his father Bartolommeo,[175] and Lapo di Giovanni Niccolini consistently neglected the ritual welcome at the moment of birth (given for eight of ten boys) for all three of his daughters.[176] Girls were abandoned more frequently than boys; when abandoned and housed in a foundling home, they were more often sent out to nurse and more often died as a result.[177] Girls were more often the victims of infanticide, as mothers more often than fathers were the perpetrators.[178] If kept within the family, girls more of-ten went unnoticed in reports to the tax-collector, and their ages were more often misstated.[179] They slipped past genealogists as well: over the course of four centuries, genealogists list fifty-four males but only thirty-six females born to one noble Venetian clan, omitting the fifteen to sixteen girls who must have been born, but who lived and died un-noticed.[180] Girls were sent more frequently than boys out to the country to nurse (it was cheaper), were weaned sooner and more abruptly (to save money), and in time of famine were fed less and starved to death more, victims of decisions made by their parents when the time came to allocate scarce resources.[181] They were set at a younger age to tedious jobs, and they left the family at an earlier age to labor or to marry.[182] And they complained less: for this grim epic of the systematic undernurturing of girls is voiceless, told only by numbers tonelessly arrayed in columns and rows.

Sons were preferred to daughters because the former could increase, while the latter threatened, the patrimony. Their families were not pri-marily providers of education, nourishment, and cultural continuity, as they are imagined to be in the affluent West today, but producers and consumers of the goods of the earth.[183] Most families prior to the mod-ern era had to tend to economic concerns before all else. Poor families in city and country alike lived on the margin of subsistence, and wealthier families (including the very wealthiest) were vulnerable to natural disaster and social realignments, and were chronically anxious and insecure.

In this environment, children offered the possibilities of survival on the one hand, and of ruin on the other. Sons could continue to till the land or manage the business, but too many could divide the patrimony. Therefore, by the advent of the Renaissance centuries, all but one or two sons were normally excluded from the inheritance by such devices as primogeniture or entail. Daughters posed a persistent problem. Not only could they not take responsibility for the primary economic challenge—to conserve family wealth—but they threatened to consume it and alienate it. As children, they required food and clothing. As adults—and their maturity came frighteningly early—their labor or wealth profited others: the families of their husbands or their masters. By the dawn of the Renaissance, their marriage usually required (especially in the areas that bordered the Mediterranean) an enormous fee that strained the resources of even wealthy families: the dowry.

From the instant of her birth, the prospect of a dowry loomed large over the female: she represented potential loss rather than potential gain. A dowry granted by the bride's family to the groom's only gained ascendancy over the male bridal gift in the twelfth century, but it escalated throughout the succeeding centuries and peaked in the Renaissance.[184] In that era of unique cultural flowering, the matrimonial contract reached its extreme of monopolarity: the family of the bride surrendered daughter and dowry, cash as well as trousseau; the family of the husband assumed limited responsibility for the maintenance of wife and widow (more limited in the south than in the north) and provided a variety of gifts, real and symbolic.[185] Not only did the financial burden shift disproportionately to the bridal side, but the sums required spiralled upwards (especially among elite families) throughout the period. In Venice, the average patrician dowry increased from about 650 ducats in the middle of the fourteenth century to 1,000 by its end.[186] The escalation continued through the fifteenth century (the Senate called it "insupportable")[187] and into the following centuries, to culminate in enormous sums: in 1521, for example, as the master diarist Marino Sanuto reports, two famous lineages intersected when a sister (unnamed) of Gasparo Contarini married Marco Dandolo with a dowry of 8,000 ducats.[188] This, in spite of the Senate's 1505 decree setting a maximum dowry expenditure of 5,000![189] On an average, in fifteenth- and sixteenth-century Siena dowries increased more modestly, from about 370 to 663 florins (actually declining in real value, as did the wealth of the households providing them).[190] In fifteenth-century Florence, they reached a high of about 3,000 florins. In 1465, Alessandra Macinghi Strozzi belittled a dowry of 800 to 1,000 florins: a "mere artisan's," she sneered.[191] Dowry inflation may have reflected the decreased status of women: a reversal of the situation in the early Middle Ages, when all of Europe was a frontier and marriageable girls were in high demand as a remedy for demographic collapse.[192] As the European economy recovered and expanded, families with daughters needed to court reluctant husbands in a harsh and burdensome marriage market.

To manage the fearful cost of marrying a daughter, Florentine fathers had at their disposal a special institution: the *monte delle doti*, or "dowry mountain," an investment fund.[193] Investing a reasonable sum at his daughter's birth or in her early childhood—the average age was five years, one month[194]—a citizen could expect sufficient gain from a constantly reinvested yield to dower his daughter at an appropriate age. If the daughter died, the invested sum was lost. That risk was offset by peace of mind, since the fund lifted from the parent's shoulders the worry of compiling dower monies. Nearly one-fifth of the heads of Florentine households held investments in the *monte* in 1480; the highest percentage of participation was among the wealthiest one-quarter of the population.[195] The fund, indeed, appealed especially to elite families, from whom two-thirds of the investors derived.[196] Apparently, the goal of every family was to marry off its daughters promptly and confidently. Similarly, among the patrician families of Venice, when the obligation of the dowry exceeded a father's resources, mothers would contribute their own wealth to make up the dowries of daughters, nieces, and other female kin.[197]

Among poorer social groups, the provision of a dowry could strain family resources to impoverishment. If his two brothers had been able to marry two of his sisters, lamented the promiscuous priest Pierre Clergue of the Pyrenees village of Montaillou, his family would not have been ruined "because of the wealth carried away by those sisters as dowry."[198] As in elite families, dowry negotiations were the serious business of the peasant patriarch, and the specification in legal formulae of a dowry's components became a central requirement of the marriage.

Often a father was unwilling or unable to take on the task of providing a dowry for his daughter and she needed to provide one for herself. In northwestern Europe, the need to accumulate wealth preparatory to family formation generally encouraged late marriage ages, for both men and women.[199] Girls labored for years to scrape up a meager amount of capital, as did the daughters of eighteenth-century French peasants who carried with them the *livret* in which their employers recorded wages due less sums for food and clothing.[200] In fifteenth- and sixteenth-century Florence, girls were sent out at an early age as servants to patrons who took full responsibility for their keep and promised, after a set term of years, to release them with a dowry.[201] The provision of a dowry for a destitute orphan or foundling girl was a principal act of charity. In Bologna from the sixteenth century onward, the *Conservatorio* of Santa Maria del Baraccano helped to preserve the honor of poor families by housing female orphans and providing dowries for them at an early maturity.[202] In the same city, the *Casa del Soccorso* at San Paolo provided a home for female penitents: here the raped and the abused as well as the wayward found refuge and awaited some transformation of their circumstances—more often than not, upon the provision of a dowry, marriage.[203] Pious grants toward dowries for the poor accelerated in importance among the testators of Siena from the fourteenth through the fifteenth century. In the late quattrocento, "the dowry fund became the principal form of social charity, eclipsing all other donations to the poor."[204]

Among the other reasons for this trend is the simple one that, unless so funded, a poor girl could not marry: "Whoever takes a wife wants money," pronounced the realistic Alessandra Macinghi Strozzi.[205] Without a dowry, a girl could not marry in Renaissance Europe. And it was scarcely possible for a young woman not to marry. Social life did not include a category for the unmarried woman outside of the religious life; the women who chose that route inhabited an uncomfortable limbo. A few, the despair of their parents, may have passed the age of marriage and still remained under the paternal roof. In France and England, the rate of "permanent celibacy" for women was generally in the range of 7 to 10 percent.[206] In peasant Montaillou, it was zero: "not one woman in the parish was left a spinster for ever."[207] In Protestant England, in contrast, where monachation could not provide an alternative to marriage for wealthy daughters, the rate of spinsterdom was high: as high as 10 percent among nonelite women in the seventeenth century.[208] The spinster sister of Sir Ralph Verney (unwed at least until well past the usual age) lived under her brother's authority and on a short allowance. Unable to reciprocate the many favors for which she was pressed to ask, even at this late date and in a country relatively open to female independence, she was in "an untenable position."[209] In northern Europe, some women of the urban laboring class remained unwed. Such women appear among the surprisingly large class of women who were heads of households in German cities, for instance.[210] From the late fourteenth to the fifteenth century in Basel, Bern, Frankfurt, Friedburg in Hesse, Schwäbisch-Hall, and Trier, the percentage of female heads of households (of those who could be counted) ranged from 18 to 28 percent. These figures include the unmarried and unmarriageable, for men outnumbered women and other alternatives did not always suffice; but they also include the numerous group of widows. In London in 1319, such women (including wealthy *rentiers* and busy tradeswomen), accounted for 4 percent of the city's taxpayers.[211] In Italy, the semireligious life posed another alternative for unmarried daughters.[212] Such women could live at home in austerity, associated perhaps with a Third Order, and even wearing a habit. Very few lived independently. Those who did were not the never-married but the once-married, left independent by the death or desertion of their husbands.[213] In fifteenth-century Florence, unmarried women numbered only 70 of the 1,536 female heads of households recorded in the 1427 census: a minor fraction of a small fraction of all household heads.[214]

Since women's roles were defined by sexual and economic relationships to men, society made little place for the woman who was unattached to man or God. Moreover, unattached women were especially vulnerable to improper sexual advances, a matter of extraordinary gravity because of the value accorded to chastity in the economic and social system of the Renaissance. Chastity assured future husbands of the purity of their line, the legitimacy of their heirs, and the reputation of their family. Thus, the guarding of chastity was the primary business of the daughters of the Renaissance. Their honor consisted in the maintenance of their chastity; their fathers' honor consisted in their supervision of the chastity of their daughters and wives. "The sexual honor of a woman was not only hers, I would say not even primarily hers; it was tied to a calculus of honor more complex, which involved both the family and the men who dominated it. . . . The honor of an entire family and of the men responsible for it revolved about the conservation of a daughter's virginity."[215] For the peasants of Montaillou in the Pyrenees,[216] as for the patricians of urban Italy, the restraint of honor prevailed.

Accordingly, the daughter was kept at home and under close supervision. When caution failed, the consequences were terrible for the family. In 1383, Paolo Sassetti dismissed the death of his cousin Letta, who had become another man's concubine: "May the devil take her soul for she has brought shame and dishonor to our family."[217] Even slight infractions could damage honor. Marietta Strozzi, late in the fifteenth century, had taken part in a snowball fight with some young Florentines and brought suspicion of unchastity upon herself: "She has beauty and a good dowry," cautioned the brother of a would-be husband, "but there are drawbacks, which outweigh even these advantages. She was left very early without father and mother . . . and it would be no matter for surprise that there should be some stain."[218] If the daughter was "stained," the father could seek compensation from the responsible male directly, or in court. In fourteenth-century Venice, the Avogadori di Comun accused the man who had raped and abducted the daughter of the schoolmaster Guidono Frami: "He had sexual intercourse with her several times with great damage and loss of honor to the said Master Guidono."[219] In sixteenth-century Feltre, to the north, the father of Elena Cumano charged her seducer, Gian Battista Faceno, with having destroyed the honor of his family, "più che la vita caro," dearer than life.[220] The honor of a city, like that of a family, could be ruined by rape. The violation of chastity in wartime, prohibited by the custom of the day, added to the humiliation of the defeated. Breaking all tacit bonds of civilized behavior, the army of Duke Francesco Sforza undertook a mass rape of the women of Piacenza in 1447: wives, daughters, nuns. The rape of Piacenza, city and women both, caused massive economic and social disaster and provoked widespread outrage.[221]

Violated virginity and lost honor could be corrected, if not recovered, by a subsequent marriage obtained through moral and legal pressure or cash payment. Many Italian cities created institutions for penitent "fallen" women, where through their own labor and benefactions they could hope for marriage (or monachation) and reentry to mainstream urban society.[222] In peasant villages, young women might allow themselves to become pregnant to prove their fertility; such pregnancies, it was understood, were to be quickly followed, under the eye of neighbors and church, by a wedding.[223] French women in the eighteenth century who could no longer count on a village network to make suitors fulfill their responsibilities prudently insisted on a written promise of marriage, actionable in court.[224] In towns, legal authorities could compel the guilty party to pay due compensation to the victims of rape and seduction.[225] When the Venetian nobleman Francesco da Mosto broke into his neighbor's house in 1469 and enticed Alessandro Barbaro's daughter to intercourse with a promise of marriage, the Senate ruled that he must pay 1,500 ducats for her dowry and maintenance or marry her himself within the month, "in accordance with the custom of our fathers."[226] In contemporary Florence, the artisan's daughter Lusanna was lured into a relationship (sealed by a clandestine marriage, a promise, and a ring) with the patrician Giovanni. When he later denied the bond, she pursued the matter in court, and won.[227] Custom and the force of law in this manner converted many cases of fornication into licit matrimony, solidifying the families that were the building blocks of Renaissance society. But women without families who had been seduced or raped were left to defend themselves.[228] Such women were mostly from lower social orders and ill-equipped culturally to present their formal plaints. Even so, a settlement ordered by the court (or donated by a well-wisher) could maintain them in their unmarried and unmarriageable condition, or even overcome the fact of "sverginità," and procure a husband. These variations from the norm—fornication followed by matrimony or at least compensation for lost honor—do not disguise the fact that marriage was most efficiently and profitably negotiated for a woman whose chastity was intact: for chastity had cash value in a marriage transaction. Upon chastity, declared Samuel Johnson in the eighteenth century, "all the property in the world depends."[229]

From birth, then, daughters presented a double burden to their families: the preservation of their chastity and the provision of their dowries.[230] But while the potential loss of honor and drain on wealth threatened social and economic status, daughters nevertheless possessed value for Renaissance fathers. They promised biological continuity in a way that male offspring could not (for this reason Roman fathers may have preferred daughters, grandchildren, and even sons-in-laws to sons).[231] They offered, moreover, the possibility of advantageous alliance with other families (of greatest concern among the elite): women "might carry the blood of their ancestors into other houses and thus bind them to their own line."[232] So Marco Parenti congratulated Filippo di Matteo Strozzi on the birth of a girl; since he already had a boy, he should rejoice in a daughter, since through her he would make a fine alliance and derive advantage sooner (since she would marry younger than her brothers).[233] Through their daughters, fathers could be connected laterally to useful friends and vertically to future generations. These advantages, along with the liabilities of chastity and dowry, entered strongly into marriage negotiations. Daughters, locked at the midpoint between danger and hope, were pressured to conform to strategies for familial economic and social survival, at enormous cost to their autonomy and status. In contemporary terms, they were required to abjure, in effect, two "rights": the right to paternal property beyond the limit of the dowry, and the right to free sexual choice. Parents chose husbands for their daughters and negotiated property settlements largely without their participation.

In his *On Marriage*, the Venetian nobleman Francesco Barbaro offered advice that parents of daughters largely ignored. He argued that, in choosing a wife, some things mattered more than money: virtue, for one, and also nobility. "Virtue, therefore, should be considered first, because its power, its dignity is such that, if all other advantages are lacking, yet the marriage is desirable; and if they are present, they render it joyous."[234] While virtue is the preeminent requirement in a wife, he continues, nobility exalts the race: the best fruit produces the best seed. "For all men agree, that they may expect from excellent wives even more excellent offspring."[235] Wealth, however, should not be sought. Only poor and ignoble men seek wealthy wives, just as ignorant men buy bad books in splendid bindings; and there have been many great men "who as in other matters, so in their contempt for the wealth of their wives were also considered great, the story of whose excellence sparkles like the stars."[236] Marco Antonio Altieri agreed with Barbaro, writing in the next century of marriage as a device for the consolidation of the Roman patriciate. He condemned those of his peers who, "blinded by infamous and detestable avarice, only to acquire for themselves an abundance of gold, attached themselves at last to families of very low and sordid lineage."[237] Neither the standard of virtue nor that of blood figured prominently in most marriage arrangements, however: money was in reality a paramount concern. Marriage involved an exchange of goods, itemized in a contract and destined to pass into the husband's care upon achievement of the event.

With money issues so pressing, the needs, desires, and natures of the women who were the indispensable players in the marriage contract became subordinate concerns. For the seventeenth-century Puritan minister Ralph Josselin, the dowry allotment made for each daughter was the greatest expense he faced in the raising of his family. He "settled" five of his daughters through careful planning: dowries ranged from a generous portion of two hundred pounds (plus sixty pounds' worth of plate and "work") for the eldest, to almost nothing for the fourth, who was married young to a man who possessed little.[238] Amid such assessments of monetary value, the personality of the bride sometimes disappeared altogether. A letter of Alexander Denton's to his wealthy godfather Sir Ralph Verney in the seventeenth century mentions a marriage possibility but fails to note the name or charms of the young woman concerned: "When I was in London there was a proposal made to my aunt for me, to one that has six thousand pounds but it 'tis in land, half of it in present and half in reversion. The young lady is Mr [Herman's] daughter of Middleton Stoney. She was 15 years of age last St. James tide."[239] In Puritan Massachusetts, two gentlemen discussed the arrangements of their relative with equal directness: "The portion, as I understand, is about £200. If you be content therewith, I suppose the quality and person of the mayde will not give cause of dislike."[240] Alessandra Macinghi Strozzi referred brusquely to the future spouses of her sons as "merchandise" (*mercatanẓia*), and was pleased that she was able to send her own daughter (whose dowry amounted to 1,000 florins) off to a husband well equipped: "When she goes out of the house, she'll have more than 400 florins on her back."[241] Colder still was the list drawn up in the eighteenth century by a family steward of the Venetian Contarini to calculate the net return on marriage transactions from 1545–1736: one column showed dowries taken in by the marriages of males totaling 379,007 ducats; the other showed dowries spent in the marriages of females totaling 255,830: the bottom line was a net profit of 123,177 ducats, won by prudent matrimonial policy.[242]

In the period before the Reformation and the legislation of the Council of Trent, the marital act was not a pledge of love and fidelity but the approval of a marriage contract involving the mention of hard sums and real property, accomplished with a variety of ritual acts, and followed sooner or later by sexual consummation.[243] After this period, proper publicity and a church ceremony became required, placing a greater emphasis on the spousal relationship and less on the exchange of property. The rival churches that insisted on church weddings also argued throughout the era that marriage must be consensual: "Marriage signifies the conjunction of Christ and the Church which is made through the liberty of love," announced Juan de Torquemada in 1457, commenting on the jurist Gratian; "therefore, it cannot be made by coerced consent."[244] Clandestine marriages, the result of abduction or elopement, were honored reluctantly by the church, though families deplored them. In Avignon in 1546, the city council received a complaint that the young women of the town were marrying without parental consent, "which is a thing most wonderfully scandalous and injurious to the public well-being."[245] The German reformer Johannes Brenz fulminated against unregulated marriages: "When two young people secretly and without the knowledge and will of their parents, in the disobedience and ignorance of youth, as if intoxicated, wantonly and deceitfully, sometimes aided and abetted by a matchmaker, lying flattery, or other unreasonable means, join themselves together in marriage, who would not agree that such a union has been brought about by Satan and not by the Lord God?"[246]

In reality, even with the advance of the notion of consent, many young women (and men) were compelled against their will or preference to marry persons chosen for them by their families. Among the urban elite and the aristocratic lineages of France, girls were married so young that the decision was, self-evidently, one made by the family and not the individual. It was a civil offense in fourteenth-century Ghent for a woman to marry contrary to the wishes of her clan; in Spain of the *Reconquista* it could result in her disinheritance.[247] In fifteenth-century England, one of the daughters of the Paston family was imprisoned and beaten once or twice a week to curb her desire for a wayward marriage, while another was barred from the home and ostracized in society for her clandestine marriage to an unsuitable mate.[248] In England in the seventeenth century, former chief justice Sir Edward Coke forcibly abducted his daughter Francesca (and may have had her imprisoned and beaten) to compel her to consent to marry a mentally unbalanced brother of the Duke of Buckingham's: an opportune alliance was irresistible.[249] Pressure to marry prudently could be exerted from beyond the grave. An English father in 1558 willed a hundred pounds in dowry to each of his daughters; but the sum was to be reduced to sixty-six "if any . . . will not be advised by my executors, but of their own fantastical brain bestow themselves lightly upon a light person."[250] Another bequeathed his daughter some sheep and a husband in a single sentence of his 1599 will: "To my daughter Marjorie, LX sheep, and I bestow her in marriage upon Edward, son of Reynold Shaftoe."[251]

Pressure to marry the parental candidate was surely most fierce in elite circles, where only the most determined and fortunate of heiresses could hope to choose her own marital destiny. Those completely free of property, and thus of any basis for negotiations in the marriage market, clearly had the most freedom to choose.[252] But even among poorer families, family design and economic strictures dictated marriage partners. Those with a only a small patch of land made the best arrangements they could for their children. "To marry for love without land or chattels could assure nothing but a life of penury."[253] Peasant women seem to have accepted these decisions uncomplainingly in many cases: only three of eighty-four divorce cases in the diocese of Ely from 1374 to 1384 cite compulsion to marry as a complaint. But some did protest. A sixteenth-century Englishwoman had been threatened with loss of her inheritance if she did not marry a man she detested. Married to the objectionable suitor, she soon fled from him after a beating: "only for the fear of loss of my land I would never be with him an hour."[254] Francesca Coke left the obnoxious Villiers for a lover.

Wives

The wife who had married, willing or unwilling, had to develop a relationship with her husband negotiated between contradictory injunctions. On the one hand, she was expected to be a companion to her husband, but on the other, she was his subordinate and the object of restrictive regulations imposed by him and other male authorities.

The theme of companionship is sounded by the male theorists of marriage with unvarying enthusiasm: Catholics and Protestants alike shared the same vision of marriage and adopted the same priorities.[255] Marriage was to be a state of "unanimity," urged the Italian humanist Barbaro, where both partners shared one will. Conjugal love is "a pattern of perfect friendship," he continued, where all problems yield to discussion between husband and wife: "Let them openly discuss whatever is bothering them . . . , and let them feign nothing, dissemble nothing, and conceal nothing. Very often sorrow and trouble of mind are relieved by means of discussion and counsel that ought to be carried out in a friendly fashion with the husband."[256]

Alberti, the humanist author of *On the Family*, agreed: "If pleasure generates benevolence, marriage gives an abundance of all sorts of pleasure and delight: if intimacy increases good will, no one has so close and continued a familiarity with anyone as with his wife; if close bonds and a united will arise through the revelation and communication of your feelings and desires, there is no one to whom you have more opportunity to communicate fully and reveal your mind than to your own wife, your constant companion; if, finally, an honorable alliance leads to friendship, no relationship more entirely commands your reverence than the sacred tie of marriage."[257] For the preacher San Bernardino, there should prevail between man and wife "the most singular friendship in the world."[258] In fifteenth-century Bamberg, the German humanist and canon Albrecht von Eyb celebrated the joys of family, "where husband and wife are so drawn to one another by love and choice, and experience such friendship between themselves that what one wants, the other also chooses, and what one says, the other maintains in silence as if he had said it himself."[259] The arch-humanist Erasmus admonished all to recognize "that all things both stand and are maintained by the married couple, and without it all things would break apart, perish, and slip away."[260] His contemporary Vives celebrated true love: "Those who are united by an authentic and sincere love are two persons sharing a single soul, which is the natural effect of true love. . . . There prevails between them that holy and happy harmony which is the sweetest principle of matrimony."[261] The English Catholic Laurence Vaux defined matrimony as a sacrament "whereby man and woman joyned togather in marriage do enter into an undivided society or feloship of life" (its further purpose being the procreation and nurture of children and the avoidance of "filthy lust and incontinence").[262] The early reformers demonstrated their personal commitment to the ideal of marriage by taking wives in the first years of Protestantism: none with more alacrity than Luther himself.

God himself commanded spouses to love, thundered the American Puritan minister Benjamin Wadsworth: "How vile then are those who don't love their wives. . . . The indisputable Authority, the plain Command of the Great God, required Husbands and Wives, to have and manifest very great affection, love and kindness to one another. They should (out of Conscience to God) study and strive to render each other's life, easy, quiet and comfortable; to please, gratifie and oblige one another, as far as lawfully they can."[263] In a gentler tone, Thomas Hooker described a man's love for his wife: "He dreams of her in the night, hath her in his eye and apprehension when he awakes, museth on her as he sits at table, walks with her when he travels and parlies with her in each place where he comes. . . . she lies in his Bosom and his heart trusts in her, which forceth al to confess, that the stream of his affection, like a mighty current, runs with ful Tide and strength."[264]

The ideal of mutual love and support enjoined by the writers of books could be found to flourish in real marriages. English peasants' wills abound with expressions of concern and affection for spouses,[265] as do those of Venetian noblemen. Two-thirds of thirty-four husbands' wills written in Venice from 1402 to 1511 employ words of affection when mentioning wives: *dilecta, charissima, dilectissima consorte*.[266] In 1448, Jacopo Morosini confessed his great love for his wife, Cristina, "to whom I am altogether too obliged, for her admirable conduct, and also for all the cash—over and above her dowry—that I have received from her family."[267] Such feelings could be repaid in kind, as when Lucrezia Priuli left her husband a dwelling and 1,000 ducats in *Monte* shares; and Maddaluzza da Canal made her husband her universal heir (if she died childless) in recognition of his "excellent companionship."[268] Sometimes gratitude for services rendered, more than companionship and delight, was recorded in these wills. Thus the Sienese Andrea di Giovanni of Anciano confessed himself in a will of 1576 "cognizant of the love and benevolence which his most esteemed consort, donna Margherita, had brought him and her toil through her continuous assistance . . . in managing his properties, causing them to increase in value and to expand in size, desiring to acknowledge and to remunerate her for so many labors and to insure that after his death she should not be dispossessed by the heirs . . . and so as never to suffer from need or through any contingencies . . . he left her as *patrona* and *usufructaria* of all of his possessions."[269]

Earlier in the same century, in Nuremberg, Magdalena and Balthasar shared affection, business concerns, and hopes for their child, much as would a loving couple of our twentieth-century imagination.[270] On their first Christmas as betrothed spouses, Magdalena wrote her "honest, kind, dearest, closest bridegroom" from her garden, enclosing a flower, and "many hundred thousand sincere and friendly greetings and many happy and good wishes."[271] The correspondence that stretched from 1646 to 1648 between Sir Ralph and Lady Verney testifies likewise to an affectionate and trusting relationship. On his way to their house of exile in France, he wrote sorrowfully: "were I to meet thee there, I should ride night and day; for till now I never knew the sorrow of separation." She wrote to him from England: "and now my dear heart I must tell you if I had known what it had been to me to have parted so far from thee I should never have done it."[272] The Verneys were not unique: a student of seventeenth-century Englishwomen's diaries finds a "high proportion of happy unions."[273]

The imagery of happy conjugal union—in the visual arts as well as in letters—should not obscure the contradictions and tensions inherent in a Renaissance marriage.[274] A couple might love, but the husband was in charge. The family drew together, but the wife was excluded from the economic group that did not entirely coincide with the biological unit of mother, father, and children. The churches supported the domestic unit, but also undermined or invaded it and enhanced the role of its male guardian. The assertion and reassertion of male control over females in marriage during the Renaissance is an inescapable fact, however hard it is to reconcile that fact with other impressions of an age that rediscovered the meaning of liberty. The very age which elevated matrimony as a holy state—by the edicts of Trent within Catholicism, by the cultivation of family sentiment within Protestantism—strengthened, paradoxically, the authority of husband over wife and required her deeper submission.[275] Protestantism especially enhanced the role of the patriarch. It removed a third party—the priest or confessor—from the marital circle, encouraging intimacy and mutuality. Yet it was precisely in that closed circle of the Protestant marriage, it could be argued, that the power of the patriarch became overweening: he and he alone was commander of his wife, author of his children, priest, confessor, and pope, legate of the deity.[276] The Protestant William Gouge may have accurately summed up the scope of that authority and that submission in his *Of Domesticall Duties*: "the extent of wives' subjection doth stretch itself very far, even to all things."[277]

Still, patriarchs reigned before and beyond, as within, Protestantism in all the Renaissance centuries. Husbands exercised over their wives in private, and male authorities defended in public, a supremacy that was enhanced by age, backed by force, and rationalized in words. Most husbands were older than most wives, whether they both were married in their twenties, as was common in northern Europe, or half a generation separated an adolescent bride from her well-established husband, as in the Italian towns. Men could add to their greater stature their greater age and experience, mixing the role of father with that of husband and lending tremendous force to their summons to obedience. Such was the stance of the fourteenth-century author of the *Menagier de Paris*, who from the pulpit of his sixty years preached lessons in deportment and household management to his wife of fifteen.[278] "For many women have made great gain and come to great honour by their obedience, and others by their disobedience have been hindered and brought low."[279] Naming the duties of husband and wife respectively, the fifteenth-century friar Cherubino da Siena matched the former's supremacy to the latter's subordination: he owes her "instruzione, correzione, sostentazione": instruction, correction, maintenance; she owes him "timorazione, famulazione, ammonizione": fear, service, admonition.[280] A century later, the humanist and saint Thomas More, envisioning an ideal society committed to hard work, peace, and tolerance, also assumed the stark subordination of women to their husbands: "the one authoritarian feature in an otherwise egalitarian society."[281] The Strasbourg reformer Martin Bucer explained that the husband was to the wife as was the shepherd to the sheep,[282] while the Italian Orazio Lombardelli offered other analogues to his young bride: just as "the head adorns the body, the prince the city, the gem the ring, so the husband adorns the wife, and she should obey not only when he commands but when he doesn't."[283] The sixteenth-century Giovanni Mario Favini instructed wives to take note of Christ's act at Cana, whereby the institution of marriage was approved: when Jesus changed the water into "good wine," he wished "to signify that she, like water, an imperfect material compared to wine, must be wholly changed into the wine which is her husband: serving him, obeying him, subjecting herself totally to his will and to the nod of a good husband."[284] Like God ruling over creation, husbands were to rule and wives to obey, according to the seventeenth-century author of the *Bride Bush*, William Whately. He commanded: "If ever thou purpose to be a good wife, and to live comfortably, set down this with thyself: mine husband is my superior, my better; he hath authority and rule over me; nature hath given it to him . . . God hath given it to him."[285] The philosopher John Locke, pioneer of the Enlightenment, opposed the tyranny of husbands as much as that of kings; but within a marriage, woman was to cede authority to her husband, because he was, by nature, "abler and stronger."[286]

Other behaviors besides that of obedience were owed by women to the towering patriarchs of the Renaissance. The recommendations of the Dominican Umberto da Romans in the thirteenth century remained valid for the era: all women should appear "neither uncovered nor frivolous but chaste and clothed with modesty"; noblewomen should disdain "la gloria esteriore," outward splendor, and those of the middle classes "uno sfarzo superfluo," superfluous show; young girls should not be concerned with their beauty, nor nuns with their trinkets.[287] They should not wander about but remain quietly at home: the young girls with their parents, and the nuns in their *clausura*.[288] Late in the fourteenth century, Giovanni Dominici (another Dominican) advised women to allow their husbands to dictate "your ornaments, your food, your talk, your earnings and your prayers. . . . Go out of the house or stay in it, as he commands, and if he forbids it, do not visit even your father or mother or any of your kin."[289] A generation later, Barbaro described the bearing proper in a woman: "I therefore would like wives to evidence modesty at all times and in all places. They can do this if they will preserve an evenness and restraint in the movements of the eyes, in their walking, and in the movement of their bodies; for the wandering of the eyes, a hasty gait, and excessive movement of the hands and other parts of the body cannot be done without loss of dignity, and such actions are always joined to vanity and are signs of frivolity. Therefore, wives should take care that their faces, countenances, and gestures . . . be applied to the observance of decency. If they are observant in these matters, they will merit dignity and honor; but if they are negligent they will not be able to avoid censure and criticism." Laughter is to be eschewed: "This is a habit that is indecent in all persons, but it is especially hateful in a woman."[290] As for women who talk too much, "Loquacity cannot be sufficiently reproached in women, . . . nor can silence be sufficiently applauded."[291]

Thus injunctions of the preachers and the humanists alike restricted woman to the home, to silence, to plainness; they required a total flattening of her expressive will, her body, her voice, her ornament. It is in this context—as well as in that other and omnipresent one of traditional Christianity—that the restraints placed on sexual behavior must be understood. "Inordinately concerned" with such matters, the church through its professional spokesmen insisted increasingly during the Renaissance centuries on the correct channeling of sexual activity.[292] It was to occur only between married persons, and only for the sake of procreation: "in order to make a little boy or little girl who can be saved and fill a seat in Paradise," gently advised Fra Cherubino da Siena.[293] "Coitus is only permitted for the sake of offspring," pronounced the physician Bernard de Gordon.[294] In those proper circumstances, it could be demanded as a right by either spouse: it was the *debitum coniugalem*, or "conjugal debt," acknowledged by all moralists.[295] A wife must accede to her husband's sexual demands, admonished San Bernardino, a more famous contemporary, or she sins, and her mother still more, for not having taught her her duties: "It is like sending her off to sea with no biscuit."[296] The church's assumption was that neither the lusty male nor the lascivious female could long do without sexual contact, and should be free to indulge in it nearly at will. Such engagement was to occur only, however, at a proper time, in a proper place, and in the proper way.

Of these restrictions confessional manuals and marital guidebooks speak copiously. Cherubino's is typical. Times when intercourse was not licit included Sunday, Lent, the day of taking holy communion, during menstruation (given to women by God "to humble you," Cherubino explained), pregnancy ("or else you are worse than beasts"), and lactation.[297] Considering that an adult woman's life was largely engaged with the processes of pregnancy and birth (if not nursing), these strictures allowed only limited space for marital relations. Also limiting are the boundaries placed on the *way* in which intercourse should occur: it should not be too frequent (a risk to health), and it should be performed face to face, without the use of hands or mouth ("And you call this *holy matrimony?*"), without obscenity or visible nudity, nor violence or insult.[298] Ejaculation outside the body was deemed a sin, and was recognized by Cherubino as a method of birth control. As for place, Cherubino is explicit: "You must come together in those generative parts, ordained by God for that purpose, for generation," and if intercourse is achieved with any other organs, "always you sin most mortally; both you, woman who assents to him, and you, the man who performs the act. . . . Therefore, my daughter, you must not consent to so great a sin; rather let yourself be beaten, rather than be forced to do this. And if because you do not wish to consent to such a horrible evil, your husband batters you, give yourself [to that punishment] with good will; for you would die a martyr, and you would go surely to eternal life."[299] Far more than an improper mode, or way, of intercourse, this abuse of the principle of *place* outrages our adviser. Clearly the act of the male, such a sin's punishment and atonement was the female's burden. While proper sexual conduct was required of both men and women, compliance to its unyielding strictures was disproportionately women's responsibility.

Perhaps women bore that greater burden because they were seen as possessing a greater sexual appetite, one quite gross and uncontrollable: a construct of the philosophers, theologians, physicians, and writers of books. Their violent sexual passions disrupted the sexual order and were seen as an attack on the social order itself[300]—one source of the hostility toward any alteration of the normal sexual position in intercourse. At night, it was imagined, the insatiable woman pestered the harried husband: "Her husband being overcome by her flattering speech, partly hee yeeldeth to her request, although it be a griefe to him, for that he can hardly spare it out of his stocke; yet for quietnesse sake, hee doth promise what shee demandeth, partly because he would sleepe quietly in his Bed."[301] Like Chaucer's insatiable Wife of Bath, women exhausted multiple husbands *seriatim*, making the putative joys of marriage the "greatest torments, pains, sorrows, and sufferings to be found on earth, than which no others are worse or more continuous, except the cutting off of one's limbs."[302] Women seduced, manipulated, misled, and cheated. In cases of adultery, they were seen to bear greater guilt than men (while a man's adultery with an unmarried female was a crime that faded into nonexistence), and everywhere suffered the economic and legal consequences of conviction for that offense more than men. In some communities of the Spanish *Reconquista*, a husband was free to kill both offenders discovered in adultery, although he was not allowed to kill the male and forgive the female offender.[303] In France, a husband could without guilt kill his adulterous wife—and effectively appropriate her dower.[304] In Venice, a woman separated from her husband for adultery was unable to recover her dowry: one of the rare cases where that paternal inheritance was not guaranteed her.[305] Adultery was the most effective solvent, prejudicial to the wife, of the marriage tie.

Among the propertied, the polite, and in urban settings, marital breakdown would more often result in separation or (rarely, for bigamy or consanguinity) annulment. Forward-looking Protestants, such as Martin Bucer, conceded divorce where marital relations had become impossible, and many reformers permitted it in some cases of adultery or desertion.[306] In general, a husband remained liable to maintain a wife from whom he was separated. In fourteenth-century Ghent, separation especially among childless couples was common, as were complex settlements of the division of property made joint by the marriage.[307] In 1343, the Venetian patrician Caterina Morosini sued for separate maintenance, claiming to have been expelled from her house by "the cruelty, harshness, and wickedness" of her husband, who was compelled to provide her with thirty ducats a year.[308] Two centuries later, the wife of the British Earl of Sussex received 1,700 pounds a year for her own and her children's separate maintenance so that her husband could keep his mistress at hand.[309]

Among the poor, marriage⌐ ʰroke down in desertion. In the English city of Norwich in 1570, more than 8 percent of all women aged thirty-one to forty were deserted wives.[310] Such was the condition of the forty women abandoned by or separated from their husbands who appear, amid so many other persons tenuously connected to other households, in the 1427 Florentine *catasto*.[311] In the next centuries, there would burgeon in the Italian cities *case del soccorso* for penitent women, "fallen" not only into sin but also into the bad luck of desertion or abuse. These were the *malmaritate*, or "badly married," like the Bolognese Livia Tederisi who took refuge in the hostel at San Paolo because to return to her husband would be "to risk God's displeasure and her own life."[312]

While abuse could be the spur to marital breakdown, it could also transpire within the normal conjugal relationship. The husband elevated by age and stature often was taskmaster and policeman as well. When a woman failed in her real or imagined duties, she could be beaten, largely with impunity, and generally with the approval of the community.[313] In the peasant village of French Montaillou, "every married woman could expect a fair amount of beating at some time or other."[314] Most law codes acknowledged the husband's right to beat his wife—"Every master and head of a household may chastise his wife and family without anyone placing any impediment in his way," read one French code of 1404[315]—although excessive brutality was condemned in public opinion and actionable (when a defender could be found) in court. Even so, such brutality was often overlooked or dealt with leniently, as in fourteenth-century Ghent, where one domestic tyrant was imprisoned briefly not for having abused his wife, but for mismanagement of her funds.[316]

Gentler relations were increasingly urged during the late Renaissance, and the counterreality of a wife beating her husband became a commonplace of comic literature and popular ritual. Calvinists in Geneva and Puritans in America prosecuted men who beat their wives too harshly.[317] Since husband and wife are one, the Puritan William Gouge admonished, the man must not beat the woman; for none "but a frantic, furious, desperate wretch will beat himself."[318] Yet in practice domestic violence continued, with the woman as principal victim, ostensibly because wives required correction and husbands alone could provide it. Who but her husband should correct a wife? Just as a husband should have no contact with any woman but his wife, explained the Sienese friar Cherubino, she should be corrected by none but her husband—gently, at first, but then, if required, with blows. If nothing else works, "take up the stick, and beat her thoroughly."[319] San Bernardino showed how acceptable wife beating was when he reproved the ladies of Siena who dressed themselves and their daughters, he charged, like whores: "Were I your husband, I would give you such a mark with hands and feet that you would remember it for a long time!"[320] Beating is understood to be the responsible act of a teacher, a moral superior, in response to the failing of a woman. A man's rage was caused by a woman's fault: "Have you maintained a close union with your husband, suffering his shortcomings with patience and charity? . . . Have you not been sufficiently obliging towards him?" asked a French moralist in 1713.[321] The victims themselves were blamed for violence viewed as just.

While confessors, preachers, and theologians peered at the marriage relations and sexual activities of Renaissance couples, another group of male professionals began to intrude upon an exclusively female sphere: the business of birth. Up to the threshold of modernity, most European women were tended to, in obstetrical and gynecological matters alike, by midwives or female doctors. Modesty required it, and professionalized male physicians stood aside. A license granted to a female healer in Naples in 1321 by Charles, Duke of Calabria, explained that "it is better, out of consideration for morals and decency, for women rather than men to attend female patients"—even though it was considered "unusual and unseemly for women to appear among assemblies of men."[322] Among the women specialists in the condition and diseases of women were some highly trained in the male tradition. The twelfth-century Trotula, the archetypical female practitioner, may never have existed.[323] But it was believed that such a figure, the wife and mother of physicians, had been trained at the medical *studio* at Salerno in southern Italy close to the time of its origins. A gynecological-obstetrical handbook titled *Concerning the Disorders of Women (De mulierum passionibus)* circulated under her name in many manuscript versions and frequent sixteenth-century editions.[324] Much relied upon throughout the Renaissance centuries, it gave advice and pharmaceutical recipes for ordinary women's conditions and illnesses—for tumors and moles, for the preservation of chastity and the (contrived) demonstration of virginity, for genital irritation and unwanted pregnancy—as well as for maternal labor and the delivery of a child. The medical schools of Salerno and other Italian university centers would generate famous women healers of undoubted historicity. In Naples in 1321, Francesca, the wife of Matteo de Romana of Salerno, was licensed by the Royal Court to practice medicine after having been examined by members of the faculty of medicine and promising to abide by the traditions of the profession.[325] In 1390, at the university of Bologna, the daughter of a professor of moral philosophy and medicine carried on her father's mission after his death.[326] In 1422 and 1423, the noblewoman Costanza Calenda, the daughter of the dean of Salerno's faculty of medicine, appeared as a doctor of medicine at the university in Naples. The documents testifying to her existence as the first university-trained female professional in Western history were destroyed during World War II, but survive in modern copies which present her labeled by her rank and the names of her father, her husband, and her husband's mother: *Nobilis Mulier Costannella Calenda de Salerno filia Salvatoris uxor Baldassaris de Sancto Mango viri nobilis de Salerno filii nobilis mulieris Manselle Iscilliate.*[327] North of the Alps, women learned in medicine wrote prescriptive handbooks: the *Ertzneibüchlein* of Anna, the wife of the Elector of Saxony and daughter of Christian III of Denmark, and the *Six Books of Medicines and Artifices, Chosen for All Human Bodily Weaknesses and Illnesses* of the duchess Eleonore Marie Rosalie of Jaggersdorf and Troppau.[328] The Frenchwoman Louise Bourgeois, midwife to Marie de' Medici, Queen of France, published in 1609 her authoritative gynecological work, the fruit of her supervision of almost two thousand births.[329]

These exceptionally learned and privileged women aside, other women engaged in the care of women's health were trained by apprenticeship and experience. Male and female doctors alike appear in the citizen lists of towns: one-sixth of the entries under "doctor" in the Frankfurt tax lists from 1320 to 1500 were women.[330] The city of Nuremberg had a system of midwives, who were trained and certified to such a standard that they were sought by other towns and rulers.[331] Certainly they were prized by the women who benefited from their services. Louise Bourgeois described these women's devotion: "When their midwives died, the women went into deep mourning and prayed God not to send them children any longer."[332] From the fifteenth or sixteenth century, however, the competence of these professionals became suspect, and they were forced to defend themselves as benign and experienced healers. Katharine Carberiner defended to the Munich city council her modest competence: "I use my feminine skills, given by the grace of God, only when someone entreats me earnestly and never advertise myself, but only when someone has been left for lost, and they ask me many times. I do whatever I can possibly do out of Christian love and charity, using only simple and allowable means that should not be forbidden or proscribed in the least. Not one person who has come under my care has a complaint or grievance against me."[333] The Memmingen practitioner Elizabeth Heyssin declared in 1602 that her skill was given to her by "God in Heaven who gave me soul and body, reason and understanding, for which I have to thank him daily."[334] The city council responded: "Elizabeth Heyssin is to be allowed to treat external wounds and sores in the same manner that she has been doing up till now, but only on women and children when they request it of her. She should absolutely not handle new wounds, bloodletting, or setting bones and should behave and handle herself with all possible modesty." Lest she transmit her competence to heal to another generation of women, it added: "Her daughter, though, is to be totally forbidden from practicing any kind of medicine."[335]

At the same time that women's skills were devalued, those of professional male physicians, university-trained, were elevated. The extension of male expertise to women's bodies began in the Renaissance centuries. Their intervention launched a process that culminated in the eighteenth and nineteenth centuries with the ouster of the midwife from obstetrical practice. Laws were promulgated in cities and states to restrict more sharply the practice of medicine by those without proper training—a category that included nearly all women. In 1322, the masters of medicine charged the female practitioner Jacoba Felicie de Almania with endangering lives, as she practiced without formal university training. In spite of an eloquent and solid defense, she was debarred from medical practice and excommunicated by the church court.[336] In England in 1421, the university-trained masters of medicine petitioned parliament to proceed against members of the barber-surgeon's guild—especially women—who dared to practice medicine: they "make the gravest possible mistakes (thanks to their stupidity) and very oft kill their patients."[337] In the towns of western Europe, women healers joined in self-regulating guilds and were licensed to perform as "surgeons" (medical providers trained through practical apprenticeships) and midwives after being examined by male experts. They did so in France until King Charles VIII withdrew the right in 1485.[338] In Paris in 1560, a formal course of study was created for a clinic of midwifery that was imitated throughout Europe. The graduates of such programs were examined by physicians and practicing midwives, and themselves were licensed to practice.[339] Also graduates of such a system were the *ostetriche* who, late in the history of the Venetian republic, resisted the takeover of their profession by male, university-trained physicians, without success.[340]

Not only were women practitioners excluded by regulation from the medical profession, but male medical scholars began to establish the superiority of their theoretical knowledge in formal works. In Italy, the fifteenth-century academic physicians Giovanni Michele Savonarola and Antonio Guainerio began to write authoritatively about gynecological issues. The *De regimine pregnantium et noviter natorum usque ad septennium* of the former, based at the University of Padua, filled a powerful need by making gynecological information available to a wide public, including the midwives themselves: it circulated in the vernacular as well, as the *Trattato ginecologico-pediatrico*, addressed to the women of Ferrara.[341] Guainerio, a professor at the University of Pavia, provides in his *Tractatus de matricibus* an excellent picture of contemporary gynecological practice.[342] He employed a female assistant (an *obstetrix*) for many routine treatments—fumigation, purgation, bleeding—but also practiced himself, urging aggressive, often painful and disabling (though generally nonsurgical) treatment of female illnesses.[343] The German physician Eucharius Rösslin published in 1513 his *Rose Garden*, a guide for midwives and pregnant women, which, while assuming that women practitioners would actually attend births, provided the latest in male professional guidance.[344] In the next century, the English physician William Harvey, renowned for his explanation of the circulatory system, wrote a work on reproduction that charged midwives with ignorance and running "great risks of life."[345]

Thus, subject to the will of others in the management of her own body, as she was in her social relations, women's identities faded to anonymity within the marriage bond. Male control was matched by female insignificance. The patriarchal form of marriage was grounded in a fundamentally negative attitude towards women. Misogyny had always been a strong current in Western civilization, and in the Renaissance, the misogynous theme, far from diminishing, flourished with the intensity that otherwise characterized the age. In a torrent of books, poems, and pamphlets too vast to be recounted here, male authors attacked the female sex and the institution of marriage. The speakers were almost always men, who viewed women "as objects at once contemptible, terrifying, and tempting."[346] Attacks on women were backed by the apparatus of learned culture: philosophical, legal, theological, medical, resting on the authority of Scripture and the Fathers, Aristotle, Galen, and Thomas Aquinas.[347] Men were active, strong and hot and dry; women lethargic, weak and cold and wet. The woman's *hysteros*, or womb, wandered irra-

tionally in her body and caused, under stress and torment, "hysteria"—
that disease claimed at last to have been diagnosed and understood by a
male physician at the dawn of the present century. Her very presence
was malignant, and all things contaminated by contact with her body
when menstruating or pregnant were dangerous to men, as the natural
philosophers taught from the nasty thirteenth-century *De secretis
mulierum*.[348] Even looking at a woman "necessarily and ultimately cor-
rupts all mores," wrote Bernard de Gordon in the fourteenth century.[349]
Her unhappy inheritance from her mother Eve has already been recorded: the toil of work and the labor of birth; double, double, toil and trouble
(Shakespeare, *Macbeth* IV:1).

The vigor of the anti-feminist assault is a stark reminder that the
mutuality of man and wife was an ideal not universally enjoyed—and an
ideal at odds with others—during the Renaissance centuries, when
women's place in the family seems not to have gained, but rather to have
lost ground.[350] The moral power exercised by men over women was
matched by real power, as has been seen: legal, social, sexual, physical.
These powers in turn correlated to men's power over women's property.
This power was carefully guarded in the Renaissance centuries, and indeed extended itself, to the detriment of women's status. The paradox
that women could possess property (a promise of independence) yet not
control it (a denial of the same) is central to an understanding of wom-
en's place. That place was at the intersection of two lineages (the family
as defined by descent through male heads from a male ancestor), belonging to none.

Marriage was always exogamous in European society, and parents
normally transferred wealth to children of both sexes.[351] These two fundamental patterns in family structure meant that women played a key
role in the circulation of wealth. The dowry (or portion in England) they
were assigned represented their share—not always an equal one—of
family property. In some communities of northern Europe and in Spain,
where property was partible among heirs both male and female, the
dowry was a woman's fraction of the inheritance. In Italy and eventually
France, it was a settlement in lieu of inheritance. In either case, it constituted that fraction of the patrimony which was designated a woman's
own and excluded her from the rest. By the careful definition and assign-
ment of a dowry, fathers removed all further claims by daughters on
household property, so that the balance could descend through the males

who acquired their *dominium*. Her claims on the lineage ceased, but not theirs on her.[352]

When women married, they carried wealth out of the natal family to alien households. For the duration of her marriage, a woman retained title to her property. Husbands welcomed the wealth brought by wives into the marital household: it was theirs to use at the moment, and it would enrich their heirs in the future. When wives died, they transmitted their wealth to their fathers' descendants (who were also their husbands'). If a wife died childless, her dowry reverted to her natal family; the husband who had enjoyed its use was required to surrender it. At all times, therefore, dowry wealth belonged perfectly to daughters, but remained ineluctably in male control. Women conveyed wealth from fathers and husbands to heirs who belonged to families not their own. But these bearers of wealth were permitted neither to fully possess nor to dispose of that wealth.

The dowry, or personal and real property settled upon a woman at marriage, was not the only property she could possess. She could hold title to other wealth gained from non-dotal bequests—gifts of cash, property, or jewels—or her own labor. In her own right, especially among the wealthier classes in the fluid conditions of the Middle Ages and just prior to our period, women could acquire title to considerable property in land.[353] Women's power to dispose of their own wealth was, however, limited. Consider the case of the married daughter of the Florentine Giovanni di Marino Morosini. Her father, who had no sons and had already dowered her with 1,000 ducats, granted her in his 1397 will 10,000 ducats' worth of shares in the *monte*, the state investment fund.[354] She was to receive the interest on the investment during her lifetime, but the principal was to revert after her death to other heirs; it was not to leave the lineage. During her lifetime, both dowry and interest income would be managed by her husband.

The husband also managed property belonging to the conjugal family, held in most cases jointly by husband and wife though the situation varied among localities, classes, and generations. In the country, a wife had a right to her husband's real property. In the city, she could, alongside her husband, hold title to substantial wealth in merchandise and capital. Either spouse could be held responsible for the other's debts, wives were generally able to participate in decisions about the disposition of property, and women had a claim to be supported in widowhood on property that had been established during the spouse's lifetime. Yet, while a woman might hold property, the degree to which she could control it varied. Though she had the right to consent to the disposition of joint property, she had no power to do so herself. Thus in fourteenth-century Ghent, women possessed a great deal of property, mostly urban and rural real estate—but the principal owner was male; and they constituted a considerable percentage of those paying forced loans to the city—yet city officials identified their wealth by reference to their male kin.[355]

Within the marital household, its male head was empowered to dispose of all property: his own, his wife's, their joint property. While men were not empowered to alienate a woman's inheritance, they were able to make use of it during their lifetimes and count on it for the further enjoyment of their descendants. In England, husbands acquired absolute control of their wives' personal property and real estate: husband and wife became one person in law, "and that person was the husband."[356] In the same spirit, the Italian humanist Barbaro informs us that a woman's property mixed with her husband's is a perfect solution: "Just as when wine is mixed with water, where there is a greater proportion of water than wine, yet we call it wine, so we shall say that wealth and riches belong to the husband and not the wife, even if women provided the greater and worthier part; since I believe what matters is not who has brought more wealth to the marriage, but who more greatly benefits the family."[357] Barbaro's metaphor softens the reality that women's title to property did not make for status or authority, both of which remained completely in the hands of the husband. Her wealth, rather, increased the honor of his family.

Certainly husbands acted as though family property, shared or personal, was theirs. Italian husbands invested in shipping and manufacturing ventures with the dowries of their wives—a right also extended to her *mundualdus*, or guardian.[358] Husbands were considered responsible for dotal wealth, though they could not always be held to meet their responsibility. If a husband mismanaged a wife's dowry money, he could be sued for restitution. In Florence in the century following 1435, there were 460 cases in which women, during their marriages, petitioned for and received restitution of their dowries or the equivalent.[359] The records of fourteenth-century Ghent show that many husbands were tempted to overspend and waste a wife's dowry, and the alienation of real property was a problem women tried with some success to forestall.[360] If the husband died, his family was obliged to return the dowry: a cause of the ruin of families, lamented the Florentine Morelli. The widow's family often had to work hard to recover the sum they had settled on their daughter, but the law was clear; it was rightly theirs. On the death of his son Giovanni, laden with debt, Lapo di Giovanni Niccolini dei Sirigatti had to assume as a first obligation the repayment of the widow's dowry.[361]

The reality of male control over property is evident in the institution of guardianship. A daughter or widow without a father or husband would be assigned a guardian—a brother, an uncle, or any male at all— so that her property could be utilized; she alone was an insufficient instrument. The need was evident to jurists: "woman is of the weaker sex than the male . . . ," wrote Baldus Ubaldi shortly before the turn of the fourteenth century, "and the laws have less confidence in a woman"; he added, with a relevance clear to him if murky to us, "and [women] are more strictly required to preserve chastity and honesty than the male."[362] Guardians acted for the propertied women of fourteenth-century Ghent who were not responsible to a husband or father.[363] The Augsburg city councillors in 1578 ordered widows to report within one month of their husbands' deaths so that their property could be appraised and guardians appointed, "because so often out of stupidity and inexperience, especially in these difficult times, widows have diminished the estate of their children and even sunk into total poverty."[364] The institution of guardianship allowed women to act only at those rare moments when the protection of their rights or furtherance of their interests led them into the public realm, without disturbing the system of male dominance over all property.[365]

In the peasant's cottage and the artisan's home workshop, a woman's management skills and actual labor were as essential to the family economy as any property she might have brought to the household.[366] In Genoa, the artisan's wife won greater liberty than the nobleman's wife through her great value as a worker and transmitter of skills and property.[367] And the artisan husband contributed more in marriage gifts than did his noble counterpart, and was vastly more likely to bequeath property directly to his wife—who, moreover, was free (unlike the noblewoman) to take her children with her to a future remarriage. In this social milieu the marriage bond overshadowed the vertical ties of lineage, and patriarchal customs were weakened. The peasant or artisan wife, however, while she contributed to the patrimony, did not direct it: "Know that all you earn, is not yours, but his," thundered the preacher Giovanni Dominici late in the fourteenth century.[368] A wife's economic contribution to the family did not necessarily win her status and power, cautions one scholar: her task was assigned her by her husband, and women workers engaged in the household economy "were more like servants than partners."[369] Enhanced freedom within the family economy may have been no more than freedom to labor all the harder. But it allowed the artisan woman options in widowhood and in the planning of her children's future not open to women of the elite. It is in this social class where woman are most often encountered alone, by will or by necessity earning for themselves and their families and in full possession of their little property. Such independence was rare.

Women's economic position was highly ambiguous, therefore: empowered and powerless at once, they were "simultaneously independent legal persons (they owned property, inherited wealth, received wages, paid taxes) and dependent parts of a legal entity, the family, whose financial decisions they did not officially control."[370] While they held title to property, women did not make independent decisions about property—at least when there was much property at stake. Their economic frailty is reflected in their condition in law and in politics. Even economically independent women had few political rights, outside of those they possessed as members of families. Women figure less than men in the statute books of the day, normally entering the realm of public law only when, in lieu of men, they were required to pay taxes or perform services. Except as male surrogates, therefore, their participation in the public realm was weak, and their evaluation by that realm was low. As Henry de Bracton summed up in his thirteenth-century compilation of English law, "Women differ from men in many respects, for their position is inferior to that of men."[371]

The wealth a woman brought to her husband's family, water to be colored by wine, won her no honor. Her status derived not from the property she personally held, but from that of her husband, which cast its glow on her. A husband's aura adorned a woman even in death. In fifteenth-century Florence, when a married woman died, she was buried with the ornaments of her husband's rank. But if a woman died a widow, she was buried more modestly—indeed, anonymously—with only the pomp suited to her class.[372] In life or death, even a woman's clothing might not be hers, but rather her husband's. In Florence, it was understood that the *paterfamilias* had the responsibility of clothing two classes of persons within his household: servants (often female) and wives.[373] The wife's clothing, her *vestizione*, was even an element of the matrimonial contract. She brought, along with household linens, some items with her trousseau; he provided fine clothes and jewels for the nuptials. But these latter remained his, and while a generous spouse might assign them to his widow in his will, contingent on her remaining unmarried and chaste, he might also retain them for his household, or, even during the course of the marriage, sell them or rent them to others for the same festive purpose. Marco Parenti spent 700 florins to "dress" his new bride between 1447 and 1449; within three years, the finery given as a sign of his love had been liquidated.[374] Jewelry also was "given" to women by their wealthy husbands: it never ceased to be the property of the men, but worn by wives, illustrated the subordinate condition of those women. "Many ornaments are lent to wives which bring them pleasure and beauty, and bestow honor on their husbands," explained the Venetian humanist Giovanni Caldiera.[375] When Alessandra Macinghi Strozzi's son was about to marry, his mother knew the value of such trinkets: "Get the jewels ready, beautiful ones, we have found a wife. Being beautiful and belonging to Filippo Strozzi, she must have beautiful jewels, for just as you have won honor in other things, you cannot fall short in this."[376] When Elizabeth Stafford quarreled with the husband bestowed on her in a calculated match linking two of the most important families of Tudor England, he beat her, imprisoned her, "and took away all my jewels and all my apparel": these were his. She could have them back, he offered, as the price of a divorce.[377]

The material adornments of a woman's body were, then, expressions of the status of a related male: clothing, and even more jewelry, were signs of social standing. When San Bernardino of Siena urged decorum in female apparel, he instructed women to obey the framework imposed by class: "what is suitable for one, is not permitted to another."[378] Just as God distinguished hierarchies of angels, wrote the preacher Giacomo della Marca, "one more beautiful than another and each content in his condition," so such distinctions of status appear between stars, between animals, between flowers, and between men and women: each was to display his rank in his apparel, and demonstrate contentment with his lot.[379] The sumptuary law that Cardinal Bessarion, scholar and bibliophile, issued for Bologna in 1453 assigned different regulations to women according to their social status, as defined by that of their fathers or husbands: they possessed no standing of their own, but were the wives and daughters of jurists, artisans, and peasants.[380] Even women who appropriately reflected the wealth of their husbands could be criticized for too great display. The purpose of a wife's garb was to announce and to enhance the image of the husband; in excess, it announced only her own guilty pride. Everywhere during the Renaissance centuries, sumptuary legislation placed limits on the style, the quality, and the cost of female dress. So much for display, so little for the poor! lamented the moralists. But ironically, while sumptuary legislation bore down on women more heavily than on men, it was often the men who opposed such laws: it was the expression of their dignity in their wives' adornment which was threatened. In 1425, in the Venetian Senate—a body made up of proud and wealthy men—a law modestly limiting the value of the wool, silk, and gold that a wife could display in the first five years of matrimony passed, but only by two votes.[381]

If the standing a wife enjoyed in her social world was derived from that of her husband rather than from her own wealth, she did gain authority in her marital family through her family connections—just as an alliance with her husband's family was presumed to be of value to her natal family. A wife's father and brothers were important additions to the circle of her husband's friends, as were his to her male relatives. Wealthy families who could comfortably sustain high dowries aspired to build large networks of allied clans. In Genoa, such networks, essential in the settling of feuds, also served, in a calmer age, to bolster business interests.[382] In Venice, women were the agents who connected elite families and thereby helped effect "the relative intraclass harmony and stability that constituted one of the hallmarks of the Venetian patriciate during the Renaissance."[383] Of twenty-six marriages in the Mocenigo family in the fourteenth and fifteenth centuries, desirable linkages were established with twenty-one other families.[384] In the first half of the fifteenth century, the Morosinis made 240 marriages with 70 different clans.[385] In Florence at about the same time, carefully worked out matrimonial alliances could solidify a family's role in neighborhood and district.[386] Women were important, therefore, as a means of establishing or sustaining the social influence of their natal families, from which they had exited, amid their conjugal families, into which they were never wholly welcomed. As in the transmission of wealth, in the nucleations of family influence the woman was vehicle more than actor: she linked families together, just as she conveyed wealth across the boundaries of lineage.

What freedom was left to the married woman? Legally and economically subject to her husband, hemmed in by the strictures of male divines and experts, her body removed from female care to male scrutiny, clothed in the robes and jewels, hers and not hers, of her husband's social identity, the exiled daughter of one lineage and the dispossessed wife of another, one thing alone was in her power: she could make a will, and thereby dispose of her dowry. By this means, elite women could help construct a future for their children, the parallel in the economic world of the primary creativity of birth. Women's legal ability to make a will was in most places as clear as men's, and women who were privileged enough to possess property to bequeath enthusiastically assumed the responsibility of testation. Of fifty-seven wills left by the Venetian Mocenigo family, thirty-four were by women and only sixteen by men.[387] A sample of 305 wills of the Morosini family, nobles of the same city, shows that women's wills outnumber men's by nearly two to one, and that the proportion of women's wills to men's increases steadily from the early fourteenth through the mid-fifteenth century.[388] Women made these wills for the benefit of a large network: relatives (especially female), friends, churches, and pious causes.[389] But they often disposed the greatest bulk of their property, theirs at last, to their children or their children's children, or even their sisters' children. The claim of children upon a mother's property is honored by Roman law, which prevailed in many communities: if she died intestate, all her children, male and female, married and unmarried, were considered heirs. Caterina, the wife of Giovanni Mocenigo, her two sons having predeceased her but her husband still living, bequeathed legacies to the widow of one son (the caretaker of his sons) and the sons of the other, directing her wealth effectively downward to the male descendants of her father and husband alike.[390]

Though women bestowed their property upon sons preferentially, they made bequests to daughters and other women kin more often than did male testators. Of fifty wills of Morosini women from the period 1305–1450, twenty-eight married daughters (of forty mentioned) received bequests from their mothers.[391] The long-lived Ingoldise, widow of Simone Morosini, left her estate to a daughter of her sister, her granddaughter and her granddaughter's sons, and her grandson: descendants of three different patrician clans through the wombs of women from one family.[392] Sounding a modern note, the determined Sienese noblewoman Erminia Bellanti, testating in the seventeenth century, insisted that her property be divided equally between her eight sons and daughters "for the benefit of the family."[393]

Women testators could bestow their wealth not only upon children and favored relatives, but also upon pious causes: and with the impact of the Counter-Reformation, at least in the Italian city of Siena, their pious giving increased markedly.[394] Among the recipients of women's charitable bequests were a range of newly founded or regenerated institutions of special interest to women donors, such as hospices for poor women and religious confraternities now open to women. In the seventeenth century, women's pious gifts, having increased 35-fold from the previous century, exceeded those of men for the first time. The appeal of women's institutions to women testators during the same period is also revealed in their expressions of intent about the burial of their bodies.[395] These privileged women, who perhaps alone in this society had the power to choose the place of their burial, overwhelmingly preferred to lie in community with other women in churches or other ecclesiastical buildings rather than to be buried with their husbands, their fathers, or any other male members of their lineages. "Formerly the privilege of monastic orders alone, these sex-segregated tombs provided an alternative to the decisions of male executors, universal heirs, husbands and fathers as well as the past decisions of the male line."[396] Just as Renaissance women realized, on the edge of death, their financial independence, so too only in death do they seem to have realized female solidarity.

Widows

In dying, then, a wife at last acquired the property assigned her by her father, if only for the use of her children—someone else's heirs. But if her husband died first, a woman was sometimes able to acquire significant economic independence, particularly in the north of Europe and in the middle classes. In these instances, widows could dispose of wealth themselves, or bear it advantageously to second husbands: "No wife could attain the social freedom available to some widows."[397] In the artisan and merchant classes, she could expect to carry on her husband's trade, since it was really the family's trade, and she had no doubt contributed to its enhancement from the start. In some German towns, a widow was even able to carry on her husband's public office: jailor, tax collector, gatekeeper.[398] As the Renaissance centuries matured, however, widows' rights to succeed their husbands in trades were increasingly restricted. The time a woman was allowed to continue operating a shop was limited: to as much as one or two years, or as little as a few months.[399] After that time, she lost all rights unless she had remarried. A guildmaster's widow who married a journeyman made her new husband a master, even if she could not sustain the mastership in her own right. Not surprisingly, given the limitations of widows' rights and the opportunity for guild membership guildmasters' widows offered journeymen, remarriage was exceedingly common. In Genoa, for instance, the artisan widow usually remarried, seeking as a second husband either a master or even an apprentice of her own or her first husband's trade.[400] Remarriage was considered natural in an environment in which marriage was, far from "forever," likely to last no more than twenty years due to the late age of marriage of one or both partners and the early age of death.[401]

In some environments, such as those in which widows enjoyed rights to spousal property and an opportunity for investment, remarriage was discouraged by these not inconsiderable economic advantages of postmarital status. English law provided widows with the unequivocal right to at least one-third of their husbands' property for use in their lifetime (although only their portions, recovered by the husband's death, remained theirs absolutely). The provisions of a dead husband's will could be changed, as in seventeenth-century New England, if he had deprived his wife of her due—especially if she had "by her diligence and industry done her part in the getting of the Estate, and was otherwise well deserving."[402] A century earlier, a testator in England had expressed the same view—that she who had aided the increase of property should not be deprived of it: "As for all suche goodes whiche that I found with my wyfe, Cycely, my conscience will not geve eny porcion of it from her but utterly I geve itt unto her ageyne."[403] That property "given to her again" at her husband's death could confer rare independence upon a woman, as one lawyer advised a widow who contemplated divesting herself of her estate: "Therefore let me advise you, that is now a freed woman, a widow, that hath full power as any lord in the land, over your husband's estate, for the good of your children; . . . so you are the lady of all, and hath the possession of all, as your husband had; and for you to make over your estate to another man, you will become a mere servant, and your children mere servants to another man."[404] In fourteenth-century Montpellier, widows emerged as the most active group among women in commercial life. Cognizant of the advantages of widowhood, which freed them from the financial control of both father and husband, few remarried (only 7 of 132 for the sixty-year period prior to 1348).[405] Their countryman Brantôme recited the joys of widowhood: "To be out from under the domination of a husband seems to them paradise, and no wonder: they have the use of their own money, the management of the estate . . . everything passes through their hands. Instead of being servants, as before, they are in command; they can pursue their pleasures and enjoy companions who will do as they wish. [They remain widows] so as not to lose their position, dignity, advantages, wealth, status, and privileges."[406] As St. Jerome had described it centuries earlier, widowhood was an "occasion of freedom," the liberation from a physical and psychological enslavement to a husband.[407]

Not all widows found themselves so privileged. Some found themselves not freed and enfranchised by property, but victims of economic difficulty. Their wealth was vulnerable, as was all wealth, but more so because of lack of experience. Some inherited their husband's debts, the consequence of a husband's mismanagement, as a Mrs. Thornton complained: "It was a very pinching consideration to me that I was forced to enter the first conserne of my widdowed condition with bonds, debts, and ingagements for others, whereas I brought soe considerable a fortune, and never knew what debt was."[408] Those who remained on unencumbered property may have found it necessary, as their powers failed, to cede their wealth to the heir they had excluded (or even a stranger) in exchange for care and maintenance; or they might retire to a convent. Those without property were not only free to remarry, but indeed compelled to seek by that route a new means of subsistence. Disadvantaged in the marriage market by advanced age or lack of dowry, the unpropertied widow often faced years of solitude and poverty.

Among the elite of northern Italy, the death of a woman's husband left her in a particularly difficult predicament.[409] Husbands were usually considerably older than wives in urban settings, and such widely disparate ages meant that widows were numerous, and often young: in Tuscany, 10 percent of all women who reached age forty, 25 percent of all those who reached fifty, and 50 percent of those who reached sixty were widows.[410] Once the marital link was dissolved by death, a childless widow could be returned promptly to the authority and the house of her father or his male heirs. Indeed, propertied males often found "returned" to their houses not only daughters but also sisters, aunts, and cousins: any women of their lineage who, having once been married, could no longer claim spousal protection. Fathers sometimes provided in their wills for the eventual widowhood of their daughters. Thus the Venetian Marco Mocenigo (Maggiore), a testator in 1328, left his principal residence at S. Giovanni Grisostomo to his son Andrea, but to his daughter Costanza, already married, "if. . . she is widowed or cannot stay with her husband . . . , let her have for her housing for life her room in my aforesaid house in which I now live and the fireplace that is near that room, with the bed adorned with cover and linens as it now has and with it also one in the same room for her servant."[411] A widow's presence in the household of her father or his more or less distant relatives could be unwanted. She had left the family young, perhaps beautiful, equipped with her trousseau; she returned, perhaps, elderly, "tired and oppressed, like a stranger in her own house," her belongings worn with years and outlived hopes.[412]

The young widow did not always return to her father's house when she returned to his authority.[413] She could be a useful commodity to her natal family, who claimed "a perpetual right to the women's bodies and their fertility."[414] While sometimes allowed to remain with her minor children under the authority of their father's heirs or executors, a widow and her dowry alike could also be recovered—"extracted"[415]—and, as it were, and recycled: she could marry again, as advantageously to her natal family as before. The children, necessarily, were left behind: they were the property of their father's lineage. Such children, deprived not only of their mother but of the wealth her dowry brought to the family, often resented their mother's departure. The "cruel mother" of the Italian Renaissance received a full share of blame for decisions, made by her own relatives, that she was powerless to resist, and a full share of sorrow, we may guess, for the children she would not know or rear.

But a widow with young children was normally invited to remain in the marital household. The surviving adults of the household would need to accommodate the stranger in their midst—for once the conjugal tie was severed by fate, all relationship ceased—and the widow would be placed under the rule of an unrelated male patriarch. But these new authorities may well have rejoiced in her presence, for whatever else its significance, it conserved family wealth: a widow's dowry remained in the household where she dwelled. It was rare that, after her sons attained majority and her daughters were provided for (in part from her own dowry funds), she would choose to stay. The choice on the part of a young widow to stay with her children was a crucial one for them. Giovanni Rucellai wrote in his memoirs of his thankfulness for his mother, who was widowed at nineteen, already the mother of four: she "did not choose to abandon us and put up a strong resistance to remarrying against the wishes of her brothers and mother . . . and she lived to be more than eighty which was the greatest consolation to me."[416] In Genoa the noblewoman had little choice: tradition demanded that she remain with her marital clan, with her children and her dead husband's father, brothers, and cousins, achieving new authority and independence in widowhood, but enclosed nevertheless in the clumped stone houses of a complex that gave architectural expression to the solidarity of the patrilineage.[417]

If a widow stayed, she required maintenance—and many propertied husbands provided in their wills for the housing, food, and other requirements of their eventual widows. One Florentine guardian complained of the expenses he suffered "so that they [the widows in his charge] will not abandon their children."[418] But when a husband left no such provisions, a wife's right to this care was, in Italy, limited. According to a 1537 Venetian law, the widow of an intestate male was guaranteed the right (and this right only) to live in her husband's home until dowry obligations to her daughters or granddaughters were satisfied, or until her minor sons or grandsons reached the age of twelve.[419] One Florentine patriarch of the previous century grumpily declined to clothe, or even feed, his son's widow: "I am not the heir of my sons, and I am not liable for the clothing. . . . Note that the woman cannot ask for support from the husband's heirs."[420]

Whether a widow returned to her father's house or remained in the house of her husband in charge of his young children, it was better, moralists urged, that she not remarry. She should live quietly and responsibly, abjuring her former state and authority, neither dishonoring her spouse's memory, nor abandoning his children, nor threatening his patrimony. "You should behave like the Jewish women," San Bernardino advised, "who, when their husband dies, bury all their goods with him. If you used to wear headdresses with ornaments, pretend that you have buried them, and so with your clothes and all your other vanities. And bury your eyes, too, with him [your husband]; keep them modestly cast down."[421] The moralists' recommendation could have had economic motives. The pious austerity of the widow signified the nonrecovery of a dowry: her wealth continued to fructify the lineage of her husband after his death, as during his life.

Widows were numerous during the Renaissance: the survivors of marriages where women were young and men mature. Some benefited economically from the death of their spouses, or were able to bargain the fruits of their paternal endowments or first marriages into a second. When it was not preferable, according to family strategy, for them to remarry, widows retired to invisibility and subjection in their marital or natal households. They lost the status of a wife and often the authority of a mother. Left outside of those niches in which women enjoyed protection and respect, widows' economic and moral condition often deteriorated badly. "The poor widows, who followed their husbands in the funeral procession, like the servants and the objects dear to the deceased, were not the heroines of an inconsolable love, but the victims, perhaps not too resigned, of the logic of the law of property, of which it wished not the despoiling of even the ghosts of the dead."[422] Neither marriage nor widowhood had been instituted to benefit women. In Florence, the class of senior and impoverished single women was large. Women past the years of childbearing were, for most age brackets, more likely to be poor than men, and less likely to be rich.[423] Many who had not been laborers before, and in spite of the scant reward that female labor provided, were forced to seek jobs—though of what kind it is not clear, in an economy in which females were not free agents—in order to subsist.[424] Half of the women who sought assistance from the Ospedale dei Mendicanti were widows.[425] The impoverished Menica, age twenty-six, the widow of a mattress-maker and the mother of three children, stated her case: "she would be content if there were given her work to do for the maintenance of her family."[426]

The young woman who carried her dowry to an older husband, who bore his children and left them behind with his heirs, who took her dowry, married and bore children again, survived their minority, and became a widow in her second husband's house, belonged to no family constellation. She was a transient among male lineages, rooted nowhere. The widowed mother of the Florentine Lapo di Giovanni Niccolini dei Sirigatti—"a brave, dear and good woman"—never left the marital home to which she had come as a young woman; yet when she died in 1416, her son's scrupulous note of the event reveals that she had been a resident, but never a member of their household: she "came to [her] husband in the year of our Lord 1349, the first of October 1349, so that she remained in our house 67 years, 2 months, and 26 days."[427] Registered in the genealogies under the categories of *uscite* and *entrate*—those who had come forth and those who were admitted, for a time, to a privileged fellowship—women were "passing guests" in the male-headed house-holds of the Renaissance.[428]

Workers

The families that offered so little to and took so much from the women of the Renaissance were, nonetheless, their lifeline. Connection to a family could bestow social standing, economic security, a sense of pride, the possibility of children who might mirror their mother's nature, as well as their father's; disconnection could, and usually did, mean instability and loss of status. The family plays the same importance in the world of work. Just as most women were mothers, most were also workers: in all of history it has been woman's lot, as it was Eve's, not only to bear children, but also to work. When women labored with and for the family, their work benefited the whole family, but especially the worker herself, whose standing was enhanced by her unpaid productivity. When women labored outside of the family, they did so to the benefit of the families of others. No honor attended such work, and only very meager pay—and sometimes not even that—rewarded the toil of the female proletariat of the Renaissance.

In the country, wives and daughters and servants assisted in all farm tasks. Not excused from the heaviest fieldwork, women mowed, weeded, raked hay, pitched dung, sowed, harvested, and gleaned. They herded livestock, cared for poultry and gathered the eggs, milked cows and carted pails, planted and processed flax and hemp, which they washed, beat, spun, and wove to make shirts and table goods, sheared the sheep and spun and wove wool for cloaks and blankets, and tended the kitchen garden for herbs and vegetables which they then cooked. A fourteenth-century servant in rural England lamented: "I must learn to spin, to reke, to card, to knit, to wash buckets, and by hande, to brew, bake, make mault, reap, bind sheaves, weed in the garden, milke, serve hoggs, make cleane their houses, within doores make beddes, sweep filthy houses, rubbe dirty ragges, beat out old Coverlettes, draw up old holes: Then to the kitchen, turne the spit . . . ; then scour pottes, wash dishes, fetch in wood, make a fire, scalde milk pannes, wash the Charne and butter dishes, ring out a Cheese clote, set everything in good order."[429] Her sixteenth-century countryman Anthony Fitzherbert described a wife's responsibilities in his *Boke of Husbundry*: "It is a wyves occupation to wynowe all maner of cornes . . . to make heye, shere corne, and in tyme of nede to helpe her husbande to fyll the muck-wayne or donge-carte, dryve the ploughe, to loode heye, corne and such other."[430] The extent of the wife's labor can be estimated from the allotment of land to colonists: twice as much to the married as the unmarried—who but the wife would perform the labor on the additional land?[431] If a woman labored for pay, however, she was not viewed as the equal of the male: she was closer, in general, to half a man, as she was paid half as much. She was fed less, too. In Germany, female vineyard workers were to receive soup and vegetables for breakfast, milk and bread for lunch, and no supper; men, in contrast, were to receive soup and wine for breakfast; beer, vegetables, and meat for lunch; and vegetables and wine at night: an ample supply of both protein and alcohol.[432]

Even aristocratic women engaged in farm work at the managerial level if their husbands were away (as they often were, at war). They inspected crops, repaired mills, accounted for chickens and eggs, supervised the carding of wool and the winding of silk, and tasted, stored, and sold wine. Thus the seventeenth-century Countess of Warwick in England directed the dairy and henhouse and checked the annual accounts, while the Countess of Flanders, who in 1372 "had two great forges built which forge for her," supervised the operation of mines.[433] Such aristocratic managers continued a tradition as old as the Middle Ages, in which women's special skills were recognized and prized. These skills included all phases of farm work and textile production, as well as the command of numbers and letters necessary for effective management: the *muliebria opera.*[434]

City women, like their country counterparts, performed and supervised household work. In families sufficiently well endowed to have furniture, linens, tableware, and food supplies to sort and store, women were responsible for such tasks. The seasoned merchant Giannozzo Alberti, interlocutor in the Alberti's *On the Family*, introduced the young wife he had recently married to her new role by touring the household with her.[435] He showed her the proper places for grain, wine, wood, and tableware, which she was to manage; for his silver, tapestry, robes, and jewels, which he was to manage; and for his records and ledgers, which she was not to touch. Alberti's contemporary San Bernardino assigns similar duties to a diligent wife: "She takes care of the granary and keeps it clean, she takes care of the oil-jars. . . . She sees to the salted meat. . . . She sees to the spinning and the weaving. She sells the bran, and with the proceeds gets the sheets out of pawn. She looks after the wine barrels, and notes whether they have broken hoops or if one of them is leaking. She sees to the whole house."[436] Fra Cherubino da Siena advised his reader to "govern well everything in the house, so that they are not lost, so that they are not thrown here and there. Your husband perhaps exhausts himself, on sea or on land, or with some other responsibility or task of his, to earn a living; it is not good that then, because of your poor guardianship, it is dissipated. Therefore govern the whole house well, and all the housekeeping both of kitchen and bedrooms, of clothing and linens, and the cellar, checking on the wine and the grain, and other things much more precious, with good housewifery. And have ready in your house shirts and tablecloths and robes and sheets and other things you require, necessary for your husband, your children, the servants and slaves, both male and female, that all be well provided, and also with good discretion, so that they are not encouraged to ruin and waste things."[437] The role in domestic management prescribed for women by Italian quattrocento authors also appears in Protestant advice books in the sixteenth and seventeenth centuries. A husband's duties were performed in the world beyond the house: to get goods, money, provisions; deal with many men; and travel, converse, and dress for such occasions. A woman's duties were confined within the smaller circuit of household walls: to gather and save and arrange and rearrange and account for goods, spend nothing, say nothing, and dress to be attractive to her husband.

Domestic management was only one of the responsibilities of most town women of the artisan and merchant classes. They were also tradeswomen with a great variety of skills, enrolled in a range of craft guilds both in England and on the continent. "They were butchers, chandlers, ironmongers, net-makers, shoe-makers, glovers, girdlers, haberdashers, purse-makers, cap-makers, skinners, bookbinders, gilders, painters, silk-weavers and embroiderers, spicers, smiths and goldsmiths."[438] They entered these trades as laborers themselves, after an apprenticeship (arranged by a father or his surrogate) with a female adept, or gained entry as the wife, daughter, or widow of a master. In Frankfurt, from 1320 to 1500, women participated in no fewer than 201 occupations; of these, they monopolized 65 kinds of work, predominated in 17, and equaled men in numbers in 38.[439] In the city and suburbs of Leiden, they were important workers in the process of dying and finishing drapery, a heavy cloth of English wool.[440] In Cologne, the crafts of yarnspinning, goldspinning, and silkweaving appealed especially to women, who, as guildmembers, operated "as independent, highly skilled artisans with their own shops, their own apprentices, and their own materials."[441] In Munich women worked as "weavers, seamstresses, dyers, veilmakers, silk embroiderers, glove knitters, bag makers, nappers, bag and glove embroiderers, and spinsters."[442] In fifteenth-century Strasbourg, women are listed in the capacities of blacksmith, goldsmith, wagoner, grain dealer, gardener, tailor, and cooper.[443] More than one-third of the weavers in that city appearing in a partial list of 1,434 were women.[444] In fourteenth-century Ghent, women figured significantly among the money changers, moneylenders, hostelers, and wholesale cloth buyers, as well as in many other trades and business transactions.[445] In sixteenth-century Geneva, they made pins, carded silk, wove taffeta, embroidered with gold and silver thread, and crafted watch chains. One female manufacturer and merchant of gilded decorations became in the seventeenth century the "most successful Genevan entrepreneur of her generation"; no others approached her.[446] In late thirteenth-century Paris, women worked in eighty-six of the hundred occupations listed by Etienne Boileau, author of the *Livre des métiers*; and of these, six are occupations monopolized by female guilds.[447] According to Boileau, women silk spinsters were permitted to supervise apprentices (although the nature and number of these employees was strictly limited). Husband and wife teams of cotton and silk lacemakers could hire twice as many apprentices as the husband alone, but widows of glass-cutters and gem-workers, themselves allowed to continue working at their husband's trade, were not permitted apprentices for fear that the skill was too delicate and dangerous to be taught by a female.[448]

In fourteenth-century Montpellier, girls were apprenticed as early as age twelve to men and women masters in a variety of trades, especially those in the textile-finishing industry, such as gold spinning.[449] Only 9 percent of the girls of Lyon were formally apprenticed, and these were channeled to textile production, small metal work, and provisioning, but many learned their skills in their families, in domestic service, or in small training schools (which also functioned as workshops) and contributed actively to the city's economy.[450] A 1561 agreement among the master silk weavers, wimple makers, and button makers gives clear notice of how most girls of the merchant class learned their trade: it assumed that the "father can show [his art] to his daughter and the brother to his sister."[451] Some women trained by such methods became independent artisans, especially in the textile and clothing trades, making gloves and wimples, linen and silk cloth. In sixteenth-century Lyons, one gold-smith's wife produced wimples, and a shoemaker lived well on the profits from his wife's linen shop.[452] In these roles women prospered, and won the respect of their families and friends—but no public role in the guild structure or place in the processions of the masters of their craft.[453] Guildsmen and city councils jealously restricted rights to the immediate female relatives of masters and workers. Daughters of leather belt makers could continue the trade taught them by their fathers after they married, but were forbidden to teach the craft to apprentices, or even to their husbands.[454] A Bristol (England) law of 1461 barred the hiring of wives, daughters, and other women from the weaving trade to prevent male unemployment, but excepted those wives already working along-side their husbands.[455]

Surely the most privileged female worker of the Renaissance was the wife or widow, or even the daughter, of a guild master in one of the northern European cities.[456] In the same home to which they were priv-ileged to be confined, such women engaged in the kind of skilled, pro-ductive, and high-status work that yielded the fruit of considerable self-esteem. In this family manufactory, they often supervised other workers as well—daughters, apprentices, journeymen—and so gained habits of authority. Theoretically barred by law from buying and selling goods, or lending, borrowing, or donating money without the approval of hus-band or guardian, in fact many women circumvented such regulations. And, working in the home, they could also tend to household needs and to the rearing of their children. In northern Europe, including France and England but particularly in the German and Flemish cities, women even became guild members, either by succeeding their deceased husbands or in their own right, and upon marriage they could transfer that invaluable membership to husbands who practiced the same trade.

Rich or poor, women spun thread and wove cloth: descendants of Andromache, who supervised her handmaidens' work while Hector war-red, and Penelope, who wove daily as she awaited the return of Odys-seus. Textile production has been, through most of civilization, characteristically women's work. From the Middle Ages, women "had exerted a virtual monopoly over the processes of cloth production," housed separately on the great manors in all-female workshops.[457] In time, they dominated the newer industry of silk production. Their work-manship was seen at all levels: winding and spinning, weaving, washing and dying, sewing, trimming and embroidering. The humanist Jacob Wimpheling praised Margaret, the daughter of Duke Louis of Bavaria and the wife of Phillip, the elector of Palatine, by describing her sedulous work as a clothworker: "She was active during her whole life with feminine occupations, consisting mainly of spinning and weaving of wool and silk, sewing and all sorts of embroidery, which she did together with her entire female retinue."[458] At one end of the ladder of social status and economic well-being, the practitioners of this woman's work were (setting aside the leisured noblewomen) the guildswomen of Europe. The occupations that were most frequently all-female, or that contained predominantly female workers, were those of the spinners, weavers, and decorators of fine garments, silken and golden. They made and finished and trimmed cloth, and produced veils, hats, purses, and belts. At the other end, in homes and shops, they were the uprooted, those no longer protected by the family shell: the day laborer, the undowered daughter forced into dependency, the unmarried "spinster" (whose English appellation derives from the craft which was her necessary occupation), the widow. They worked for wages, in a parlor, in a shop, in a garret, alone. Even their leisure was committed to the task: in quiet moments, "women spun, knitted or sewed."[459] When a Frankfurt household was liquidated for debt in 1595, "and everything was sold down to the last spoon," the destitute widow was left her spinning wheel: a means of support and a mark of her sex.[460] Consider the widow, who sustained her family or made her own way with her labor: the widowed mother of the Englishman William Stout lived with first one son, then another, spinning until within four months of her death in 1716 at age eighty-four.[461] As daughter, as wife, as widow, without thought of retirement, she had spun.

Though women's involvement in textile production was perduring, the level at which they were permitted to participate shifted downwards as cloth production became increasingly organized and taken over by male supervisors and workers.[462] Skilled work became the province of the male-exclusive guilds of weavers and cloth cutters, and women were left the carding and spinning, the early stages of the process, or the production of rougher cloth or clothing products intended for female use. The restrictions that precipitated this process begin as early as the fourteenth century and intensified over the next three centuries; nor were they limited to the textile trades. The opportunities previously so rich for widows and wives of guild masters were limited, and those for unrelated women workers within the guilds or independent women outside of them were considerably reduced. In exceptional cases, women petitioners of city councils could win exemptions from the rules. These were granted if the woman was sufficiently poor or desperate: "so that women's individual pleas are filled with statements stressing their age, poverty, number of dependent children (some of whom are usually sickly or still nursing), sick husbands and war losses."[463] Such exceptions were too few and too half-hearted to improve the condition of the working woman; they only document the increased humiliation of the female worker and depression of the value of her labor. So successful were these measures that by the last years of the Renaissance, only a few women appeared on the rolls of the guildmasters. Those who worked performed low-status tasks: they boiled flax or unwound precious fiber from the carcasses of silkworms or performed other such unpleasant tasks; or they spun, as their numbers increased, for ever lower wages.

At the same time that women were excluded from those aspects of production that yielded higher-status work, in some settings economic modernization and political reorganization meant the displacement of the domestic workshop as the center of production and a shift to a system more closely resembling modern industrial production, enmeshed in a network of long-distance trade.[464] This shift in the structure of production also had a negative impact on the valuation of women's work. A woman who worked as part of a family unit, whether as a household manager or a tradeswoman, enjoyed a relatively high economic and social status. Women who worked adrift from their families enjoyed none of these benefits. The enhanced position of women in the world of work depended, therefore, on their being able to work at home: they thrived when workplace and household were one. As long as the craftsman or trader was an individual whose place of business and place of residence were the same and whose own economic status was assured by his ties to guild structure or the urban patriciate, his wife or widow had access to public economic life. Women suffered when, in the latter two centuries of the Renaissance (particularly in some areas of England and Flanders), such conditions shifted in favor of larger economic units organized outside of the home. New legal restrictions were devised to prevent women's owning or transferring property or benefiting from guild association.

Not only in the guild-managed manufactories but also in other elements of medieval productive life, a woman's participation depended on her role in a family and her position in the sexually determined cycle of virgin-mother-crone. Her place in that cycle determined her availability to labor for a surplus beyond absolute necessity, and her rootedness in the home steered her toward trades mirroring the pursuits of her daily life. It does not surprise us, then, to find women engaged in retailing eggs and cheeses, flour and butter and beer, as well as the eternal spinning, sewing, and trimming. The English village alewife used household tools and experience to brew ale for her family, one of the two staples—the other being bread—of the peasant diet.[465] When time permitted, however, between episodes of childbearing and other requirements of her position, she produced a surplus for the market as well. Thus the alewife floated into and out of the category of tradeswoman as her domestic status permitted, and as the family's needs and requirements ordered; a man would have been (would have had to be) a tradesman or not been one, defined fixedly by his occupational category. While the woman's role remained unfixed, it was significant. Fully one-fourth of the identified women in the English village of Brigstock during the six decades preceding 1348 paid ale fines, indicating their participation in brewing for the marketplace.[466] Elsewhere in Europe, also, women's work applied itself outside of the male-dominated guilds. Such was the case in Montpellier, in southern France, where in the period 1293–1348, of 197 transactions in silk and wool cloth, women participated in a total of only 13 (6.6 percent); but with their dowry wealth, mostly as widows, they could buy and sell agricultural commodities, invest in long distance trade, and profit from real estate sales.[467] In Lyon, wives of artisans participated in their husbands' trades more or less according to location (at home or elsewhere), the nature of the work (too heavy? too dangerous?), and the place at which they stood in the cycle of their own lives.[468] In Nuremberg, Magdalena Behaim was her husband's "distributor, bookkeeper, and collection agency," in charge of billing peasant customers, and often exhorted to keep more exact records.[469] The businesswomen of Ghent frequently served as surrogates for their kinsmen.[470]

In Italy, women participated in the public world of money as they did in the north. At upper levels of society, wealthy women could invest in business ventures, or extend small loans at interest to kinsmen so engaged.[471] They initially played a role, too, in textile production and guild organization. At the turn of the fourteenth century, a Sienese statute concerning the wool merchants' guild bears witness to the active participation of women in the trade: it forbade members to pay a spinster until work was completed, and ordered guild consuls to see that all weavers, "male and female," kept their combs well set.[472] Such openness to female labor steadily decreased as the Renaissance period progressed. Even where women were admitted to guilds, restrictions abounded. Earlier than in Flanders, Germany, or France, women were barred in Italy from high-prestige occupations. Restrictions from the fifteenth century resulted in exclusion by the sixteenth. Whereas in the towns of northern Europe women could work at crafts and in shops, as peddlers or market vendors, in Italy they were increasingly barred from such public pursuits. The records of the Venetian parish of San Polo at the end of the sixteenth century, for example, show women workers represented only sparsely in productive trades. Of 584 productive workers (who constituted 70 percent of the heads of families of that parish), some 250 were women; the overwhelming majority of these (245) were *massare*, domestic servants or charwomen.[473] The handful of women who, in the generation previous, appeared as "fornera" or "murera" or "sartora" were most likely the widows of tradesmen. The goal of protecting women's honor—in itself, an economic concern, since successful marriage depended upon demonstrated chastity—required in southern Europe their isolation. Arcangela Tarabotti complained late in the cinquecento of the relative scarcity of roles for women in Italian public life compared with the north: "In how many cities do they perform tasks that with us are performed only by men? In France and in Germany and in many areas of the north, women govern their households, manage the accounts, keep inventories of merchandise, and even high-born ladies go to the public market-places to perform family business, enjoying that liberty and exercising that free will which they were given by the Giver of all goods without those limitations and obstructions, not to mention abuse and punishment, which are customary in our cities."[474]

The situation in well-studied Florence and its *contado* warrants a closer look.[475] Although records of women's participation are slim for the earliest periods, by the fifteenth century they had clearly entered the marketplace. By late in the sixteenth century, women workers were active employees in silk and wool manufactories. By the early seventeenth, they constituted more than half of all weavers and almost half of all wool workers, not counting the countrywomen who, as always, spun. By the second half of that century, they had come to predominate in many aspects of the process of silk manufacture. By that time, as many as 73 percent of the women of working age in Florence were participants in the work force. They participated, however, not as the peers of men, but as an underpaid army of low-level laborers. Women were concentrated in the wool and silk trades, while men sought employment in the newer and more diverse luxury trades. The sexual segregation of labor reflects differences in levels of skill and remuneration. Within the process of textile production, men dominated in the more highly skilled and better-paid tasks, women in jobs requiring less skill and paying a lesser reward. Women had free access to the less-prestigious Linaiuoli, but could not gain entry to the greater guilds, such as the Arte di Calimala. A female weaver of plain silk could expect to earn, in the early seventeenth century, one-third to one-fourth of the wage of a skilled male weaver of luxury cloth. The jobs women were permitted to do were further limited by the fact that women worked mostly at home: they could spin and weave within the household and as they tended to children; but they could not clean, comb, or card wool, jobs performed in the workshop.

At the same time that Tuscan women were excluded from the city luxury crafts, some of them found a role in the country in sericulture, the major breakthrough in Tuscan agricultural production of this era.[476] They kept silkworms, wound raw and wove finished silk, and performed other tasks specific to the farmhouse apart from the city economy. It was largely their labor that accounts for the enormous increase in the proportion of locally produced raw silk consumed by the Florentine silk cloth industry: from 12.5 percent in 1590 to about 75 percent in the 1650s. To some extent, these pursuits, in which women performed useful and beneficial service, compensate for their inability to perform high-paid city labor. But they were also pursuits less productive of self-esteem and wealth. Poor country women tending to sericulture can scarcely be compared to the substantial female partners and heirs of northern craftsmen in the textile industries.

The processes were complex, then, that led to the exclusion of women from high-status trades requiring skilled labor and providing commensurate rewards. While much about these processes remains to be unravelled, that they attained their effect is clear: by the end of the Renaissance centuries, women were excluded from high-level productive work: "it was only as wage-earners that women were extensively employed in the textile trades."[477] Wives of the wealthy ceased to perform productive work: "it would hardly win us respect," commented the crusty Giannozzo of Alberti's *On the Family*, well ahead of his time, "if our wife busied herself among the men in the marketplace, out in the public eye."[478] The wives and daughters of artisans worked on a small scale at home, where they could divide their work day between the demands of their craft and the care of their family and house. Or they entered the labor market as individuals, to take on the tedious and repetitive tasks that fed the skilled male weavers and finishers their thread and cloth. Their low wages can be measured by this fact: at home, they had been able to feed and clothe their families and themselves with their unpaid labor; in the shops, their wages were insufficient for maintenance. Thus far was their labor devalued and their status depressed. Women of this condition merged with the ranks of the day laborers, wage workers, and domestic servants who had left their families or been sent out by them to earn their bread as best they could.

Women without families: who and what and where were they? In childhood, in adolescence, in age, they were often poor, and made up a large fraction of all the poor.[479] They rarely, as we have seen, lived alone; and only a fraction, as the next chapter will show, could resort to convents or female religious communities. They could find refuge— especially in Roman Catholic areas, from the sixteenth century onwards, under the influence of the Counter-Reformation—in one of the many charitable hospices established for needy women left outside of the family system of support: in Italy, the houses of *convertite, derelitte, malmaritate, penitente, abandonnate, fanciulle sperse*; the orphaned, the widowed, the disabled, the abandoned.[480] Here—where they may have constituted a small factory of female proletarians—they waited for benefactions that would lead to marriage or the convent, or for work. Widowed, they came with their children. Children themselves, they were taken in by foundling homes and hospitals, and soon sent out to work—like the eighteen little girls of Lyon dispatched in 1557 to work as chambermaids and silk-winders.[481]

Poor women everywhere swelled the ranks of servants or laborers in household services—little distinction was made between hard labor outside and the multitude of tasks within the walls of the home or institution where they labored. More women were employed as household servants than in any other role in late thirteenth-century Paris (25 percent of all designated occupations, nearly four times as many as the next largest).[482] Of the approximately one-half of one percent of the 7,000 female heads of household in Tuscany in 1427 whose occupations are known, nearly half were servants; the next three largest occupational groups were "uncloistered religious," "dependent of a religious house," and "beggar" or "pauper."[483] These women who cared for the homes, possessions, and persons of others left their own homes in town or, more often, in the country, sometime between ages eight and twelve, and worked in the homes of others for pay and keep, or only keep, and perhaps the promise of a dowry.[484] As rootless wage workers, they were likely to slide down the *cursus dishonorum*, the ladder of dishonor, that led from labor to mendicancy to prostitution. Their wages (if they received any) were one-half, two-thirds, two-fifths—it varied, but it was always a fraction—of what men earned.[485] They swelled the population of households (which counted servants, foster children, and miscellaneous "Inwohner" [co-residents] as parts of the whole).[486] Too poor to pay poll or property taxes, they formed an often uncounted, but large number of the town's residents. A rare census in Florence in 1552 identified 8,890 servants (in a population of about 100,000), two-thirds of them women,[487] while in the German towns the servant population, male and female, mounted to 15 to 20 percent of the whole.[488]

Supervised by the matrons of burgher households, servants applied themselves to the variety of tasks required by the household as both a productive and a domestic entity. As much the property as they were the labor force of the elite, they were available for exploitation, watched over by the patron saint of servant girls: Zita of Lucca, who entered service at age twelve; her sign was a ring of household keys.[489] More to the point, they were watched over by the woman of the household, as is seen in the advice given by the author of the *Menagier de Paris* to his wife. After the servants have completed their day's work, he commands, they should be allowed time and space for sleep: "And make you certain beforehand that each hath, at a distance from his bed, a candlestick with a large foot wherein to put his candle, and that they have been wisely taught how to extinguish it with mouth or hand before getting into bed, and by no means with their shirts. And do you also have them admonished and told, each separately, what he must begin to do on the morrow, and how each must rise up on the morrow morn and set to work on his own task, and let each be informed thereon. And . . . if one of your servants fall ill, do you yourself take thought for him full lovingly and kindly, and visit him and think of him or her very carefully, seeking to bring about his cure."[490] According to the Venetian nobleman Barbaro, wives not only should instruct servants with words, but also by action demonstrate the required task, correcting their mistakes without anger.[491] Just as a general disposes his legions, or a captain his crew, a wife should separate and organize the servants' tasks. Moreover, she should feed them so as to "satisfy both their human needs and reward their constant labor," and should clothe servants "comfortably as befits the season, climate, and place."[492]

Food was in fact provided to servants, forming part of the reward for their labor; the cost of clothing was generally deducted from wages. The wages of the female domestic were low; in many communities they worked for maintenance alone. In fourteenth- to fifteenth-century Florence, where there was considerable amelioration of the female servant's condition in the aftermath of the plague (1400–60), her wages were still lower than those of male servants or unskilled male laborers, and of that aristocrat of domestic service, the resident wet nurse of the well-heeled upper-class family.[493] Thereafter and into the sixteenth century, the condition of female servants deteriorated further: men competed more successfully with women for fewer available posts, and the terms of employment worsened.[494]

As in the towns, servants comprised an important fraction of the rural labor force. In some communities of fourteenth-century England, the proportion of servants (male and female) in the population may have reached about 40 percent. Two and three centuries later, that figure may have climbed to about 60 percent.[495] In eighteenth-century France, where most work was agricultural, daughters of smallholders or agricultural day laborers, few of whom could afford to maintain their own families, constituted the largest social category of women.[496] Female day laborers, they were in early adolescence set loose from their families to wander from job to job in search of miserable pay. If lucky, they worked on large peasant farms, acquiring the skills that would serve a peasant husband, or as servants in bourgeois and noble households. Otherwise, they streamed to towns to work for shopkeepers or craftsmen or larger textile manufactories. Wherever they worked, their wages were less than men's: women's pay was never meant to support life, and barely did. They accounted for their meager recompense in a little notebook, accumulating a dowry with the narrow attention a miser gives to his heaps of gold. They learned a trade and hoarded their wages, hoping that years of underpaid labor would result in a combination of capital and skills that could purchase a husband.

Although some labored as servants for a lifetime (both before and after marriage), for others, male and female, the years of service were temporary: an initiation for children into the world of married adulthood. In Florence before the plague and after the middle third of the fifteenth century, many young girls lived a "preconjugal purgatory," awaiting a husband while serving a master.[497] Indeed, so many were still children that the social categories of childhood and service overlap in ways nearly incomprehensible today. The word for "boy" was equivalent in several modern languages (as also in ancient Greek, Latin, Arabic, and Syriac) to that for servant.[498] An adolescent could as naturally work for others as for his or her own family, if the latter had more need of pay than of labor, and many passed those years in the service of others. The children of even upper-class households were expected to wait on their elders at table. A fifteenth-century Italian visitor—who could have been no stranger to the labor potential of children—was surprised at English custom, where even upper-class children circulated as servants in cognate households: "The want of affection in the English is strongly manifested towards their children; for after having kept them at home till they arrive at the age of seven or nine years at the utmost, they put them out, both males and females, to hard service in the houses of other people . . . and few are born who are exempted from this fate, for everyone, however rich he may be, sends away his children in to the houses of others, whilst he, in return, receives those of strangers into his own."[499] The children of the poor as well as of the rich were taken in by substantial families: was their status that of foster child or exploited laborer? In Florence, children aged three to seventeen constituted 39 to 44 percent of the population of the households of the wealthiest quartile—more than twice as many as in the poorest.[500] Clearly the wealthy absorbed the children of others, in one role or other, for a significant portion of those children's preadult years. Later, they exited from these families as they had entered, their social position unknown, but lesser, than it had been when they resided with their privileged hosts.

Alongside the servants in urban households, especially in the south of Europe, one or two slaves might also labor—like the servants, more often female than male.[501] In fifteenth-century Florence, they numbered perhaps one-tenth of all domestic servants. Female slaves shared with female domestic servants, although to a heightened degree, the condition of being isolated from their natal families in a society where family was the most frequent and reliable source of status and protection. Their career possibilities depended upon the households in which they served, which often denied them chastity and marriage alike, the two main routes to female honor.

Female laborers, slave or free, were especially vulnerable to sexual exploitation by members of the family they served and by outsiders. When Sir Ralph Verney required a new maid, his uncle provided him with one, and sent written assurance that she would serve more than one intended function: "Because you writ me word that you were in love with Dirty Sluts, I took great care to fit you with a Joan that may be as good as my Lady [Verney's wife] in the dark, and I hope I have fitted you a pennyworth."[502] In the next century, that of the childhood of the English novel, the experience of such Joans would be encapsulated in the life of Richardson's Pamela, who triumphed over her seducer in the manner that fiction allows. Infants of slaves accounted for a large fraction of the babies brought to Florence's foundling hospitals—many of them no doubt fathered by the heads of the households in which the mothers resided, or by his sons or friends or associates.[503] Among the girls registered in that city's dowry *monte* were the illegitimate daughters of servants or slaves, a meager future thereby assured for them by the high-status householders who were their fathers or their fathers' kin.[504] Willem Plucroese of Ghent inflicted on his servant Merkin "disgrace through force and violence by which her honor is greatly diminished."[505] She was a minor, and he was fined more severely than in most cases of injury to children, but still lightly; it was not considered a great offense to rape one of the servant class.

The female worker had to contend not only with her employer, however, but also with the large numbers of male laborers, apprentices, and journeymen found in the towns. These men, being unsupplied with the wealth that would make marriage possible, sought sexual contact by other means: often by rape, generally (the evidence here is French) gang rape by groups of males of one female. In Dijon from 1436 to 1486, 80 percent of recorded rapes were of this type.[506] There was a standard plot: "the rapists caught the woman at home, during the night; they began by calling her a prostitute and by making a racket; then they broke down the door, caught the woman, brought her outside, beat her, raped her, and often tried to force her to accept some money. Because of the noise, the neighbors could not help listening to what happened; they observed it through the chinks in their shutters; but four times out of five, they did nothing about it."[507] In 1516, Jeanne Jacquet, a twenty-year-old woman who lived with her mother and stepfather, was victimized this way in a village of the diocese of Troyes: "Everyone within was in bed. The mother, upon hearing the noise, roused her daughter, and had her climb to the attic. During this time, the companions were breaking down the door. Jean Benoît, Claude Ruynel, and the servant came into the house and began looking for Jeanne. They looked in the bed, in the bread-bin, in the oven and when they failed to find her, they climbed to the attic where they discovered her. They dragged her down, pulled her outside and took her to a garden where they raped her, one after the other."[508]

In Venice, the dynamics of rape reflected the hierarchical patterns of that society.[509] Servants and slaves were the women most frequently victimized, and the victimizers were higher-status males, often noblemen, who could wield authority in lieu of a weapon in compelling compliance to their wishes. The prosecution of such cases (whose victims were mostly unmarriageable women whose male relatives made no claims of damaged honor) "reveals a continuing low evaluation of the crime," and confronts us with the "grim reality that stalks the history of male-female relations in the West."[510] How remote from the experience of such women, committed to labor and exploitation at once by families who could not offer them nurture or refuge, was the world of carefully guarded chastity and hoarded dowry in which the daughters of the patriciate or nobility lived!

For some poor women, one alternative to unpaid exploitation was paid prostitution: the commerce of their bodies being, like the labor of their hands, a form of women's work.[511] Tolerated in the Middle Ages, prostitution was accepted and actually institutionalized from the early fourteenth century. In Italy, Venice opened a public brothel in 1360, Florence in 1403, and Siena in 1421.[512] In Germany, Frankfurt led the way in 1396, Nuremberg had joined by 1400, Munich by 1433, Memmingen by 1454, and Strasbourg by 1469.[513] In Southern France, Dijon opened its "Great House" in 1385 and added a second one, refurbished, early in the next century.[514] Toulouse operated its own municipal brothel from 1363 or 1372. As late as 1608, the Dominicans of Perpignan assisted in fund-raising for that town's municipal brothel.[515]

So commonplace was prostitution that it was managed in much the same way as other urban institutions. Like the members of guilds, prostitutes claimed a special section of the city for their activities. From here, they were not to leave to wander abroad in other districts, but neither could they be expelled. They flourished, and reached considerable numbers: in Lyon before 1480 some seventy to eighty prostitutes could be found, and in Dijon, in a population of less than 10,000, there were more than a hundred.[516] By the middle of the fifteenth century, authorized prostitution was the rule in most sections of Europe, and prostitutes themselves had acquired a certain status. They were protected by the laws and treated as practitioners of a recognized profession—although they were required to wear distinctive clothing (and were fined when they did not), and were universally despised by the authors of moral treatises. Their clients did not despise them: these included churchmen and university students, apprentices and journeymen, servants and their employers' sons, pilgrims and transients—any who were unmarried, whose marriages were postponed, whose wives were absent or unavailable, if pregnant or lactating, and others.

But by the mid-sixteenth century, the institution was in retreat. In the fifteenth century, the prudish humanist Giovanni Caldiera had denounced the brothels as "wolfdens" (*lupanaria*), because their inhabitants were more savage than wolves, killing both body and soul.[517] His view would soon become the norm. Fear of the plague, venereal disease, and crime, and the newly repressive moral strictures of Protestant and Catholic reform, had transformed the prostitute from an urban worker into a despised species. The official brothels underwent a wave of closings equivalent to the wave in which they had arrived. After this, while prostitution did not disappear, "it became more expensive, more dangerous, and more shameful."[518] The monarchs of the great new secular states pursued the criminalization of brothel keeping and prostitution as part of a strategy for the increased consolidation of power; the rape of a prostitute, in sixteenth-century France, ceased to be a crime.[519] Ironically, the legal isolation of the prostitute coincided both with a general deterioration of women's legal condition, and with a devalorization of her role in the home.

Although institutionalized prostitution declined in much of Europe in the later Renaissance, it flourished in the lush cities of Italy. Largely for this reason, the humanist Roger Ascham urged that innocent English boys not be exposed to the immoral customs of Italians, which he excoriated at length in his influential *Schoolmaster* (published posthumously in 1570).[520] Protestants accused Rome, above all, for this vice among others; consider the accusations made against Pope Julius II by Erasmus (in the person of St. Peter, barring the gates of Paradise) in the *Julius exclusus.*[521] There was some substance to these protests. A population of nearly 12,000 prostitutes made up a robust fraction of the 100,000 residents of Venice in 1500. In the slums off the Rialto bridge lived the common whores. In splendid apartments lived the "honored courtesans," elegantly dressed, skilled poets and musicians, who entertained gallant travelers and Venetian patricians (many of these latter celibate out of patrimonial interest and especially reliant upon courtesans). The courtesan "was richly attired and she lived in a respectable street; she . . . did not even keep a private bordello but received her admirers and paid 'visits' to important personages. . . . nothing in her bearing set her apart from a woman of estate. . . . Far from being 'common to all,' she was mistress or concubine to only a few, confounding the comfortable categories of traditional typology."[522] In her behavior, dress, and style of life this "intellectual courtesan" mimicked the nobility. She lived in richly furnished apartments, like Julia Lombardo, whose residence included three large bedrooms, a receiving room, a maid's room, and overflowing storerooms.[523] The chests kept in her bedroom were filled with items that "would have made a handsome trousseau for any patrician bride": linens, rugs, clothing, shoes, gloves, stockings, purses, sleeves, and sixty-four fine white blouses, or *camicie*. The 1570 *Catalogue of All the Principal and Most Honored Courtesans of Venice* (giving addresses, prices and procurers) listed 215. Of them, two were among Italy's leading women poets: Gaspara Stampa and Veronica Franco. The latter, whose own mother had introduced her to the profession,[524] eventually retired (when nearly sixty) to found an asylum for poor prostitutes.

Curiously, the high-caste courtesan, with her luxurious apparel and apartments, her poetic skill, her literary coterie, her lute and her lapdog, resembled the patrician's or nobleman's wife who, over the Renaissance centuries, was increasingly distanced from the world of work. As public life became more complex, as household and hearth receded from the center of economic and political life, elite women occupied a "shrinking circle" of occupation.[525] As early as the fourteenth century, Francesco da Barberino viewed the sewing and spinning of the patrician's or professional's daughter as mere make-work: it was done to chase away the tedium of her isolation.[526] By the seventeenth century, it was not respectable for a woman of the elite classes to work: her menfolk would be shamed. Facing vast hours of leisure, she engaged in the kind of repetitive and useless tasks (needlework and knitting, parties and visiting, card games and gossip) that could without appearance or taint of industry fill that vacuity.[527] Her job was to reflect her husband's honor, dimmed if the work of her needle was for use or sale, enhanced if for decoration. As upper-caste women lost their productive role in the European family, some critics would charge (as did the English authors

Daniel Defoe and Mary Wollstonecraft) that they became a kind of legal prostitute. Otherwise, for those of the comfortable classes, the dignity of work rescued women from the shame of concubinage; and for the poor, the burden of work approximated a slavery of which concubinage was but one face.

2

❦

DAUGHTERS OF MARY
Women and the Church

Convent Walls

The men of medieval Christendom availed themselves of an institution unknown to antiquity, to Asia, or to Islam for the control of a surplus female population: the convent.[1] In Greece and Rome, fathers were free, in most cases, to raise as many daughters as they wished. Roman fathers often chose to raise two, upon whom they doted. The others were left to die or, abandoned, to descend into families of lesser social status, or into slavery or prostitution. Fathers did not raise all their sons, either, since in superfluous quantity they too could drain family resources: but they raised more sons than daughters. Possessors and producers of family wealth, as has been seen in the previous chapter, males were preferred to females, its alienators and consumers. Wealth descended, via the male, in the paternal line: patrimony indeed. Via the female, it left one family constellation and traveled to another. While daughters well placed in marriage to peers or superiors could enhance a man's social standing, too many daughters endangered patrimony. Prudent fathers had few options in their quest to secure wealth: infanticide was forbidden, abandonment discouraged, adoption (as a legal mechanism) unknown. But supernumerary daughters could be prevented from alienating their fathers' resources if they were contained in a place reserved especially for the pursuit of celibacy: the nunnery. The system worked for much of the history of the West.

During the early Middle Ages, girls and widows were delegated to convents that were created in large numbers.[2] Many entered as young children, "oblates" offered, with an emolument, to religious communities.[3] "Oblation" became a satisfactory means for the management of family resources. Gifts made upon entrance enriched the monastic foundations, which had reserves of manpower and managers to guard their wealth effectively. Families reaped the benefit of having given a child to the service of God, and small children were assured careful supervision and a secure if unchosen future. Thus the male Benedictine foundations were stocked, along with the female; but girls were more often oblates than boys. Mature mothers and wives and sisters, too, in need of asylum or widowed early and frequently during an age of chronic violence, enjoyed the security and status that resided within the convent walls. In the central Middle Ages, the Benedictine double monasteries directed by abbesses with the assistance of trained monks gave way to new foundations, coincident with the flowering of alternative forms of male religious communities: in turn, Augustinian canons, Cistercian monks, Dominican and Franciscan friars. But convents continued to be founded, as they had been before, in ever greater variety to fulfill an enduring need. By the Renaissance centuries, convents in cities—serving burgeoning and diverse populations—were added to those endowed with vast agrarian resources during the Middle Ages.

Whether belonging to a traditional order or a new one, whether ancient or modern, convents served the elite of their community: royalty and old nobility in the case of the first Benedictine foundations; lesser nobles, magnates, burghers, and patricians in the expanding social milieu of the Renaissance. The abbey at Fontrevault was populated almost entirely by women from that realm's most lofty families. From the fourteenth through sixteenth centuries, the approximately three hundred nuns who resided in three Cistercian cloisters in the vicinity of German Marburg came overwhelmingly from the patriciate or nobility.[4] The daughters of wealthy dowry-fund depositors in fifteenth-century Florence were more likely to become nuns than daughters of the poor: the average deposit for future nuns was 435 florins, compared to 417 for the far more numerous group of future wives.[5] In sixteenth-century Florence, as many as half of the women of some elite families resided in convents, and in a seventeenth-century Venetian noble clan, one out of three daughters was persuaded to "monacar" rather than "maritar."[6] Women of lesser social standing lived in convents as servants or workers, but the nuns themselves were recruited almost exclusively from wealthy and respected lineages. For these were the groups that possessed inheritable property that needed to be defended against the awesome fertility of excess daughters. And these were the groups that could most successfully claim the privilege of a humane and useful asylum for girls to be removed from the cycle of reproduction and for women whose reproductive duties had ended: the "desolate" mothers—the meaning of *relicta*, Latin for widow.

In Renaissance Italy, then, most of the women who lived within convent walls were patricians, and a significant fraction of elite women (if only a small fraction of all women) lived within convent walls. In Venice especially, the convent was a solution for the father with more daughters than he could dower. The practice peaked in the mid-seventeenth century, when nearly 3,000 nuns were registered in that city—some 3 percent of the whole population.[7] Their numbers must have climbed higher still in the settecento, as 3,789 former nuns received state pensions in 1815. In the last year of the Republic, there were thirty-seven convents in Venice: fifteen Augustinian, ten Benedictine, eight Franciscan, two Dominican, one Carmelite, and one Servite. These had developed over centuries: the Augustinian, for instance, developed continually from 1187—when Santa Maria degli Angeli was founded on the island of Murano as the result of a noblewoman's gift of vast property—into the settecento.[8] Small cities like Arezzo, Pistoia, Cortona, and Prato could boast of between ten and twenty female convents each. In Florence, female convents increased from five in the mid-trecento to forty-seven in 1552, while the number of nuns in each soared to approximately seventy-three from approximately fifteen a generation after the Black Death. In all, including the lower-class *conversae* who served as quasi-religious servants in each foundation, the numbers of female religious dropped from 500 in 1336 to 440 in 1428–29, reflecting the inroads of the plague, but swelled thenceforth to 3,419, an increase of more than sevenfold, by the same terminal year of 1552. This absolute increase mirrors an increase in the proportion of the female religious relative to the population of all women: 1.2 percent, 2.25 percent, and 13 percent (including *conversae*), in 1336, 1428–29, and 1552 respectively.[9] The surge in the sixteenth century relates to the upward pressure on marital dowries, which caused elite families to consign their daughters to convents rather than allow them, at lower expense, to marry downwards. Late in the seventeenth century, in Milan, one-half to three-fourths of the daughters of noble families were placed in convents: among them the four Arconati daughters whose father had them painted in the family portrait still young and nubile and wearing the elegant clothes they had already been made to forswear forever.[10]

In northern Europe, female monasticism in the traditional orders, having climbed through the thirteenth century, declined in the following two centuries.[11] Convents were closed down, and the rolls diminished in those that endured. In England, the nunneries both lost population and waned in moral commitment and intellectual verve during the fourteenth and fifteenth centuries, well in advance of the Protestant Reformation. While 3,500 women resided in English convents in 1350, only 1,900 remained (in thirteen fewer houses) in 1534, when the process that led to the dissolution of all such foundations had begun.[12] London, in contrast to Florence, had a population of 220 nuns in around 1500; nuns comprised only a fraction of one percent (.11 percent) of that city's female population in 1540.[13] In Germany, where the Cistercians had 255 female to 75 male foundations, the number of nuns also suffered some erosion.[14] The nuns at the Cistercian cloisters of German Caldern and Georgenberg, for instance, lagged from the late fourteenth century.[15] But female monasticism, at least in the fourteenth century, thrived in Germany, the home of mystics and their followers such as the disciples of those epitomes of fourteenth-century male spirituality, Meister Eckhart and Heinrich Tauler.[16] In pre-Reformation Strasbourg, the population of nuns had shrunk from 300 (in five convents) in 1237 to 140 (in nine) in 1450. In 1480, there were eight convents (five strictly reserved for members of the nobility or urban patriciate), many of which housed only ten to fifteen nuns. Moribund, perhaps, these nunneries nevertheless fulfilled for prudently managed families the role for which they were intended: to house females for whom there was no other convenient role. At the attempted closing of the Strasbourg nunneries, as at the unequivocal suppression of the Venetian ones, dazed nuns were returned to fathers, brothers, and sons, who became responsible once more for housing and support.[17]

The convents of Renaissance Europe sometimes deteriorated in morale as they did in numbers. As in male monasteries, incomes that had sustained a hundred residents now served as few as ten, and all evidence of austerity vanished. The luxurious conditions enjoyed by some of the Strasbourg nuns, for instance, infuriated townsfolk and fueled the spirit of reform.[18] Christine de Pizan, visiting her daughter's nunnery at

Poissy, dined on silver and gold plate, toured the establishment, and chatted for hours with her child, constrained by no burdensome limits.[19] Worse than such unnoticed luxuries, from the point of view of ecclesiastical discipline, was the failure to observe the rules of claustration. In some of the laxer convents, nuns went about the city or entertained visitors: male visitors, and with entertainments that the rule of chastity forbade. The stories of conventual frivolity told by Boccaccio in his *Decameron* and Marguerite d'Angoulême in her *Heptaméron* were not without a realistic basis. The illicit sexual behavior charged to nuns could amount to more than peccadillos. They could, in sum, amount to a gross defiance of principle, threatening to the public welfare. The biographer of San Carlo Borromeo chided the "excessive openness" of these houses, where "any layman could enter . . . and the nuns depart as they pleased."[20] A 1537 report "For the Reform of the Church" complained of the many nunneries in which "there are performed public sacrileges with the greatest possible shame to all."[21] In the next year, the city councillors of Milan requested that the Pope do something about a Benedictine house so corrupt that, far from being virgins pledged to God, the nuns "had become and were held to be lay prostitutes."[22] Nowhere, perhaps, did the problem of conventual misbehavior exceed that in Venice.

Preaching in that city's basilica of San Marco in 1497, the observant friar Timoteo da Lucca charged that the nunneries proudly displayed to the visitor to Venice were "not convents but whorehouses and public bordellos."[23] A few years later the chronicler Girolamo Priuli found his city's convents a conspicuous scandal: called "open convents," they were "public bordellos and public whorehouses."[24] Statistical evidence supports, though does not prove, these charges.[25] In the fourteenth and fifteenth centuries, thirty-three convents were involved in one or more prosecutions for fornication with nuns. Nine of these had between ten and fifty-two prosecutions. Scandalous above all was the Benedictine convent of Sant' Angelo di Contorta, populated by women of Venice's most lustrous families. Between 1401 and 1487, it faced fifty-two prosecutions for sex crimes. Its records tell tales of "dissolute deeds" performed at picnic outings and in convent cells, of illegitimate births, of jealous rages, of fugitive lovers. These involved not only noble nuns but also two abbesses, who shared their favors with aristocrats and *popolani* alike. The Pope closed down Sant' Angelo in 1474, but other convents not quite so conspicuous in their misdeeds remained.

If some late medieval nuns relished ample rations, enjoyed domestic service, conversed gladly with foreign visitors, played the lute and embroidered elegantly, entertained their lovers openly and gave birth covertly, one reason is surely that they had never entered the convent walls to seek spiritual things. They had been placed there because they could not or would not marry and they could not be left free. The history of female monachation is at least in part the history of female imprisonment. Deep in the Middle Ages, Peter the Venerable had called the newly founded Cluniac convent of Marcigny a "glorious prison."[26] In 1420, a Venetian law lamented the many noble girls who "are imprisoned in monasteries with just tears and complaints."[27] The contemporary humanist Giovanni Caldiera admired the nuns who served God *ut mortue mundo* ("as though dead to the world").[28] In 1523, the celebrated Erasmus described in two of his *Colloquies* the fate of the *virgo misogamos* ("The Girl Who Didn't Want to Marry"), who sought what she viewed as the independence and stimulation of the convent, and the *virgo poenitens* ("The Repentant Girl")—the same girl who, after twelve days of life behind walls, prevailed upon her parents to release her.[29] Her friend Eubulus had reproved her for her original inclination: "Now you intend to surrender your freedom voluntarily and become a slave"; and congratulated her when she reconsidered: "It's well for you to back out quickly before committing yourself to perpetual servitude."[30] Eubulus's remarks convey the sentiments of Erasmus, who had himself fled the slavery, as he saw it, of monasticism. Brantôme's estimation of the institution was about the same: How have you sinned so greatly, exclaimed one of his *Dames Galantes*, that your penance is to be sealed up alive in a tomb![31] The prisoners sought what comfort they could.

The ten or so generations of Renaissance nuns included many who were claustrated unwillingly, coerced as children (as young as five or six; nine was normal in Italy) by family will and need. But the complaints of only a handful come down to us, expressing what many voiceless women may have felt. "My mother wished me to become a nun / To fatten the dowry of my sister / And I to obey my Mama / Cut my hair and became one," laments one girl in a folk song. "Mother don't make me a nun; that I don't desire; . . . I would go quite mad if I was forced to fast / and go to Vespers and Eventide and sing at all hours."[32] Some of the young women who were sent unwilling to the cloister subsequently fled. When Charlotte de Bourbon, daughter of one of the great Catholic families of France, was forced in 1559, at the age of twelve or thirteen, to profess conventual vows, she also filed a witnessed deposition of protest. Four or five years later, weeping, she was installed as abbess, and swallowed her responses to the presiding prelate. In 1571 she left for a new country, a new religion, and a husband—William the Silent, organizer of the Dutch Republic.[33]

Caterina di messer Vieri di Donatino d'Arezzo, 160 years earlier, had resisted the conventual life to which she had been pledged at age eleven by her recently widowed mother.[34] A few years thereafter, she fled from the convent and her vocation, hoping to marry. Literate, on the model of several learned females of the age, she wrote in 1399 of her flight and her aspirations to the statesman and humanist Coluccio Salutati, chancellor of Florence. She had reason to expect encouragement. Salutati was a pioneer spirit of the Renaissance, and one of the first to value the active life of the layman equally with or more highly than the contemplative life of the monk. His stern response must have been a disappointment. He wished to recall her "to the road of salvation," which God would succeed in summoning her to if she had not become "entirely abandoned . . . to perverted ideas." The decision that others had made for her, she was to follow earnestly, crushing the pitiful first flowers of that learning in which she prided herself. Fortune and her mother had given her to God, Salutati wrote, as a bride of Christ: "Had you sincerely followed this rule of life as your vow demands, and, laying aside the trifles probably learned with your natural genius in the convent, had you devoted yourself to love of God with all your heart, all your soul, and all your powers as is fitting and as we are commanded—had you done these things you would not have left the cloister. You would not have wandered over the earth, moved by unfulfilled desires, notorious, ridiculed, and despised."[35] As for the marriage she intended, it could not be legitimate: her true and prior husband was Jesus. "Worse than incest, more serious than debauchery is the marriage that you so ardently desire. Although you call it marriage, you cover a crime with this name. You are not able to be the legitimate wife of another. When you embrace this man . . . , you will know that you embrace not your husband but a fornicator, an adulterer."[36] She embraced him, nevertheless, and in 1403 accomplished what she sought by papal act: the annulment of the childhood vows and the legitimation of her children.

Salutati's letter to Caterina di Vieri can be paired with the same author's letter to the Bolognese chancellor, Pellegrino Zambeccari.[37] The latter, depressed over a recent love affair, was on the point of becoming a monk. Salutati dissuaded him. The contemplative life was good, but the

active life was productive and blessed as well. If he was sure of his vocation, Zambeccari should proceed; but if was acting merely to escape from
despair, he should stay in the world. Two letters, two messages: to the
learned colleague, the need for an authentic religious vocation, and the
nearly equal merit of productive life in the world; to the uprooted female,
the stone wall of convention, a vacuum of choice, the poison of contempt
and condemnation. The alternative of an active life was possible, and
thus desirable, for the male, but unthinkable for the female. An editorial
comment (written in 1978) would perhaps be modified today (1991) in
view of more than a decade's investigation of the historical condition of
women: Salutati's discouragement of Zambeccari's intention to undertake religious vows and his virtually simultaneous insistence that
Caterina resume them "has nothing to do with Caterina's sex."[38]

Escape was not an option for most unwilling nuns. A few of them
have left written works that bear witness to their distress, as flight testified to that of their sisters.[39] Nuns made up a great fraction of educated
women, and cloistered women were disproportionately literate: it was a
commonplace of advice books that young girls should not be taught to
read or write unless they were destined to be nuns. Finding in the convents the leisure to study and write, women composed works largely in
the vernacular, devotional in type. Among these were the moral plays or
sacre rappresentazioni written for the many festivals of the Church, and
performed elaborately for the convent community by the nuns themselves. These plays constituted one of the few genres in which claustrated women could, if obliquely, express themselves.

One such play, the *Amor di virtu*, is a protest against the conventual
imprisonment of women in the guise of a devotional drama. It was written in the mid-sixteenth century by the Florentine nun Beatrice del Sera
(1515–86), of the Dominican convent of San Niccolò in Prato. Its images
of rock, wall, and tower represent the cloister in which women are unwillingly confined. Women were not born for happiness, one player
complains, but to be made prisoners, slaves, and subjects. The heroine is
eventually saved from prison. Its author, in contrast, continued to grieve
for the freedom snatched from her at an early age and awaited an eternal
reward for her patience. "Whence I, poor and alone in the rock, put my
hopes in the good of my future life."[40] In the meantime, she could address the microcosmic world of her fellow prisoners, from which whis-
pers reached the larger world of male culture without ever modifying its
hostility.

Like Beatrice del Sera, the Venetian nun Arcangela Tarabotti never was to escape from the *sasso*, "rock."[41] But in contrast to del Sera, she was able to address the male world directly and boldly. In a series of treatises and letters written during her thirty-two years of unwilling claustration, she defended the female sex, protested against forced monachation, and—before Locke, before Rousseau, before the American or French Revolutions—called for liberty. Born in 1604, sent to the convent of S. Anna as a child, Tarabotti became a nun in 1620. She dedicated her solitude to her own education (to the extent possible in a convent library, to which "female prisons," as she said wryly, "not all the books written by men arrive")[42] and to a lifelong reflection on her condition. Before 1644, she had begun her principal work, which she would revise repeatedly and knew would never be published in her lifetime. It appeared in 1654, two years after her death. Entitled *La semplicità ingannata*, or *Simplicity Betrayed* (originally *Tirannia paterna*, or *Paternal Tyranny*), it laments the fateful act by which fathers, to horde their wealth, enclose their daughters in nunneries. Thus she makes the critical event of her own life the fulcrum of a critique of her society, and the springboard for an original vision of female equality and freedom.

Only the nun who has chosen her vocation can truly achieve the perfection that is the presumed goal of the conventual life, Tarabotti wrote. The coerced nun is the victim of paternal greed and selfishness. "It is well known that the majority of nuns cannot attain perfection because they are forced to the religious life by the force exerted by their fathers and kin. . . . Most of them are not moved . . . by the call of the Gospel . . . ; and surely God has shown himself to hate any act which is not born of a voluntary disposition. . . . Only those who are willing nuns, even if against the will of their relatives, like Clare of Assisi and Catherine of Siena, who renounce the world even if they must be buried behind holy walls; but men imprison others so as not to bear expense and so as to be able to surround themselves with every sort of luxury, delicacy, and superabundant vanity, even in order to have more means of satiating their vile desires with swollen whores, to dissipate their wealth at the games, drowning themselves in the consummation of every one of their unjust desires."[43] You fathers who confine your daughters in convents, Tarabotti charged, are crueller than Nero or Diocletian: "More than the worst tyrants in the world . . . , you deserve eternal torments, because they, cruelly torturing and tormenting the bodies of the holy martyrs, did not at all harm their souls, so that howsoever many drops of blood spilled from their wounds, all were transformed into the shining rubies of the crown of glory."[44] The imperial tyrants assisted, unknowing, in the martyrs' realization of God's glory. The father is the greater criminal because he violates free will.

Consider, Tarabotti implored her public, the plight of the tender and beautiful child forced into a conventual life. "It seems to me, when I see one of these unfortunate girls so betrayed by their own fathers, that I see that which happens to the little song bird, which in its pure simplicity, there between the leaves of the trees or along the banks of rivers, goes with sweet murmur and with gentle harmony stroking the ear and consoling the heart of he who hears it, when there comes a sly net and it is caught and deprived of its dear liberty. In the same way these unhappy girls, born under an unfortunate star, pass the years of their innocent girlhood, and with a tongue tinged with milk singing pretty lovesongs, and with their tender limbs forming graceful movements, please the ear and delight the soul of the base fathers who, deceitful, weaving nets of deception, think of nothing but to remove them from sight as soon as possible and so bury them alive in cloisters for the whole of their lives, bound with indissoluble knots."[45]

This innocent child is forced to cut her hair, her most beautiful ornament and a sign of her original liberty; for a shaved head has always been an emblem of slavery.[46] She is forced to wear a habit, obey a rule, and eat and live exactly like her fellows, when the fundamental rule of creation is glorious diversity. "Variety and dissimilitude alone, in men as in their activities, as in the beasts, birds, fish, plants, flowers, and fruits, arouse wonder in the human intelligence and make evident to our eyes divine omnipotence. Why then do you wish to oppose the works of the Most Just by desiring that many women all wear the same dress, live in the same habitation, eat the same meals and do the same things; while the Lord of Lords reveals how miraculous is his infinite wisdom when he creates all things each different from the other?"[47] The regimentation of conventual life, moreover, is without surcease. Marriage can at times end in divorce, or more often with the death of a spouse; "why must nuns be condemned, by an unappealable decree, by the sacrament of their vow to observances that are eternally irrevocable? Only your ambition, oh deceitful man, and your overweening arrogance, without any requirement of the supreme will, condemn against their inclination the innocent creatures of your flesh to the hell of the convent . . . ."[48] Over the gate of hell is inscribed the warning "Abandon all hope, you who enter here"; the same should appear over the convent gate, with the additional eloquent verses: "The torments of death surround me; the torments of hell surround me."[49]

In this "monastic inferno," women denied hope do not become saints, but rebels. They may violate their vows of chastity, flee the convent, dishonor the family.[50] They may seek to educate themselves, but are denied all access to the disciplines that make men great: philosophy, law, theology. Instead, an ignorant woman teaches them their ABC's— "I who know can easily testify to this"—and if they lift a pen, they are reproved and forced to take up needle and distaff again.[51] Nevertheless, some transcend the convent walls and succeed in lifting their voices. "Even in this heavy tedium and in a compelled lethargy there are still women who, with only the liveliness of an uncultivated intellect, without schools or the skill of any expert in this world, produce marvellous forays of spirit that could astonish the most lofty spirits alive."[52] As does Tarabotti.

This unrelenting author charges not only fathers, but also the city that represents their accumulated power, with the confinement of innocent girls. Too many girls were a threat to the noble houses, which might impoverish themselves with the provision of too many dowries.[53] It would be better to kill young male babies, allowing one only per family to survive, than to bury young girls alive. As innocents, they would fly promptly to heaven and join the angels; "but the nuns seized and buried alive will mostly descend into that abyss of horrors to find their tortured fathers, for whom to look upon their daughters' faces will be a greater martyrdom than all the afflictions of hell, as with a thousand blasphemies they curse the hour of their own, but even more of their children's birth."[54]

The parents who acted from the barefaced economic motivation that Tarabotti understood so well were not always so cruel as that furious victim alleged. There were those who were proud of their daughters, and appreciated the spiritual fruit of their prayers. In time, more parents respected their daughters' freedom. In the same city in which Tarabotti wrote, a few fathers and some mothers left some scope for the vocational choice of their children in their wills. Still, "it was a rare father who would or could go against the perceived family interest to satisfy a daughter's choice of adult life."[55] Late in the sixteenth century, the nobleman Marco Giustiniani (brother-in-law of the doge Leonardo Donà) ordered in his will that the management of his daughters' inheritance should be delegated to his wife "until they are married or in convents according to their wishes."[56] The seventeenth-century French bishop Claude Joly rebuked parents who compelled their daughters' monachation: "Must you so harshly ill-treat this daughter, that you compel her to hasten into a convent, for which she has no vocation whatsoever, so that she surrenders her legitimate portion of the inheritance in favour of those whom you prefer?"[57] By the eighteenth century, the practice was in decline. The playwright Carlo Goldoni described in his memoirs the decision made concerning his niece and ward, who was being educated in a convent. When she described herself as being "in chains," he realized "that she was not fond of the convent."[58] She was released, and married instead. But she lived in the century that saw the victory, in Catholic France, of the principle of liberty for which Tarabotti longed. By the law of the victorious Revolution exported in the person of Napoleon, convents were reorganized, rationalized, and suppressed, and testators were constrained to leave wealth to daughters as to sons.[59]

That was a new age, however, while the age of the Renaissance was continuous, in terms of the patrimonial concerns of the elite, with the medieval era, when the institution of the convent as a repository for unneeded daughters began. The system of forced claustration, even though it affected a small number of European women in the Renaissance centuries, was in some ways as cynical and as cruel as Tarabotti argued. Many parents disposed of their daughters pitilessly. An English father of the Protestant seventeenth century dispatched his unwanted daughters to continental nunneries. Desolate, they wrote begging for letters expressing interest and affection. He replied that, in the absence of urgent matters, he found an annual communication quite sufficient.[60] An Umbrian father who made his will in 1374 left his daughter, a nun at the Franciscan convent of Monteluce in Perugia, the "ridicola somma" of 20 soldi (a few pennies!), stipulating that she was not to ask for more. If she did, the legacy would be invalidated. The usufruct of two little fields, which she was to have for life, was to revert upon her death to her brother, universal heir.[61] Even mothers dispatched their offspring to conventual isolation with indifference. When her daughters (Ippolita and Paola) entered convents, Isabella d'Este expressed satisfaction: Jesus was likely to prove a docile son-in-law.[62] Caterina di Vieri, Charlotte de Bourbon, Arcangela Tarabotti, and hundreds of other coerced nuns were the victims of parents acting out of a kind of greed, there is no way around it; it was a greed so profoundly rooted in their social world as to be immune from moral scrutiny. These women would have recognized the intonation of the fifteenth-century Florentine document concerning fathers' claustration of daughters, who were thereby rendered effectually dead: *tamquam vere mortua.*[63]

Determined Nuns

Not dead, however, but fully alive, were those for whom the convent was a positive choice for God and a triumphant negation of the labyrinth of familial relationships. This positive choice required the renunciation not only of family, but also of sexuality. Of the vows taken by those who dedicated themselves to Jesus in all the Christian centuries through the Renaissance—poverty, chastity, obedience—none was more important for women than the vow of chastity. Where woman's principal function, as male contemporaries saw it, was to reproduce, her principal role to mother, and her principal sin to lust, her supreme virtue was chastity, and especially a state of virginity, a repudiation of all other descriptors.[64] As a virgin, wrote the theologian Jean Gerson, chancellor of the University of Paris, at the turn of the fifteenth century, "You sing a new song. You will be singled out and crowned with a divine crown in paradise. You can be consecrated in holy church, and wear the gold ring as a sign of your excellences and incorruption. You are the most beautiful part of holy church and merit the hundredfold fruit . . . . You are queen of the earth and heaven by the ardent song of contemplation."[65] This one virtue (a special virtue to be achieved by women) exceeds all the others, declared the Spanish humanist Juan Luis Vives in the sixteenth century: "The virginity of which I speak is the integrity of the mind extended to the body: it is total existence, lacking any corruption or contagion. There is no kind of life more like the life which is lived in heaven than this life of virginity. There, every law of the flesh lifted, we shall be like angels of God."[66]

By the observance of chastity, a woman was removed from the cycles of sexuality and birth and freed from the negative image of seductress. The whole weight of male authority posed her alternatives and beckoned her to choose: Aristotle, the philosopher, described her wandering womb, her instability, her lesser role in the generation of a child, her subordinate standing in the social order; Jerome, the saint, offered her authority, dignity, transcendent power. The ideal of chastity was uniquely prized in Roman Catholic theology and eloquently championed from pulpits. It appealed to women to whom other socially valued goals were unavailable. They could not normally achieve great wealth or great power in their own right, or develop the most esteemed craft or artistic or intellectual skills; but chastity, achieved by negation alone, was a summit for which they could strive. The crown of virginity would become at the end of time the crown of joy, as the 144,000 virgins gathered around the risen Christ. Accordingly, women denied their bodies in order to gain the consummation of union with the divine. Self-denial became the path by which many women hoped to gain an eminence that the secular world would not permit them. In chastity, a triumph of denial, women could find a fulfillment parallel to or greater than that of the esteemed wife and mother in secular society.

The positive value of virginity was rearticulated and restated through the centuries. Angela Merici, the founder of the Company of Saint Ursula, reminded her followers how the noblest women envied them their virginity: "empresses, queens, and duchesses . . . would wish to be considered one of the least of your handmaids, esteeming your condition so much more worthy, so much better than their own."[67] Diego Pérez de Valdivia, in his handbook for Spanish *beatas*, put the case even more strongly: "Zeal for holy chastity and virginity makes a weak young woman or woman of whatever sort stronger than many men, and than the whole world, and than all hell; and when men see such extreme energy and force, they are afraid and jump back dismayed."[68]

Just as conventual women could perform the role of "bride" apart from the secular world and its dangers, they could engage in productive work without presenting the economic and social threats that their secular sisters did. They could care for the poor, the sick, the insane, the abandoned children; and if they did not, who else would? What a rich bounty of self-esteem the laboring nun could harvest from the performance of these vital tasks! They could teach, transmitting to future generations the culture of their ancestors as surely and richly as biological mothers did when they talked to their babies. If their interests were intellectual, they could write devotional works, translate saints' lives from Latin into the vernacular for the benefit of less-cultivated companions, even compose religious verse and drama. From the privileged security of the cloistered community they could preach, prophesy, or write letters to the great and powerful. A very few ruled over their own communities as abbesses or prioresses, attaining an equivalent of male supervisory power nowhere else possible for them in their society. Not surprisingly, many women consciously and passionately chose virginity—many women even of the highest social classes, at the risk of punishment or exile, at the cost of solitude and self-denial. The convents, as communities of virgins, whatever their limits, were, of those settings available, the one most favorable to female autonomy and self-expression. Female monasticism was the institution that offered the greatest scope for autonomy and dignity to the women of Christian Europe.[69]

Many women sought peace and dignity in the cloister. As a child, Cecilia Gonzaga, the daughter of Gianfrancesco Gonzaga, Marquis of Mantua, and pupil of the humanist Vittorino da Feltre, yearned for the holy life.[70] She dreaded the marriage planned for her by her father to Oddantonio di Montefeltro, the heir to the dukedom of Urbino (subsequently assassinated). Gonzaga attempted to force Cecilia with blows and threats. Even after marriage plans were abandoned, he refused to allow her to pursue her unchanged goals. The papal notary Gregorio Correr, a former co-student of Cecilia's, wrote to encourage her in her decision, noting the entrapments that surrounded her in her home as impediments to the spiritual life: a devoted nurse, lavish banquets and entertainments, objects of beauty, the pregnancies and births of her brothers' wives. She should implore her father, he urged, with this speech: "I ask you, father, in the name of your concern, if you have any, for my salvation . . . , do not let your daughter remain in peril for so long among the sirens of the world. . . . If you had pledged me to a mortal husband far across the seas, then you certainly would have sent me to a remote land and would never see your daughter again. Now because I hasten to a heavenly spouse, it displeases you to be separated from me by mere walls and partitions. . . . You have the consolations of this life: wife, sons, daughters-in-law, grandsons. My other sister you gave to the world, and she has left you (for she has died) a sweet little grandson. Why, among so many dear loved ones, am I alone desired? Why am I held back against my will? Why is a tiny cell begrudged me, and the meagre table of the humble family of Christ?"[71] Having resisted her pleas at every turn, her father finally conceded her wish by his testament. Freed by the patriarch's death in 1444, Cecilia took refuge in the Franciscan convent of Santa Croce in Mantua, together with her mother, who founded it.

Like Paola Malatesta Gonzaga, Cecilia's mother, Queen Sancia, the wife of King Robert the Wise of Naples, had yearned during her married years for a "little cell." She had promoted the cause of the Spiritual Franciscans with lavish donations and spirited defiance of the Pope. After King Robert had died, his widow entered a house of the order of St. Clare in 1344. She died herself a year later and her holy remains, like a saint's, were reported to be without blemish or odor.[72] Two centuries later, Sor Isabella Roser retired to a convent after death put an end to married life. From Barcelona she wrote Ignatius Loyola, the founder of the Jesuit order. Her husband had died, her children had found positions, her wealth had been distributed to them and to worthy causes—to fund a hospital, to dower a relative's daughter—and now, having entered the cloister of Holy Jerusalem, she had finally found peace. "We are 52 nuns here, and there reigns among us so much love and blessedness, that one can only give thanks to our Lord God."[73]

Costanza Barbaro was the eldest of four daughters of the Venetian statesman and humanist Francesco Barbaro.[74] Her devoted father had given her an education in the new humanist program of the study of classical and Christian antiquity. By June 1440, when she could have been no more than twenty years old, Costanza had resolved upon the life of a nun—no doubt, in part, so that she would have the opportunity to continue her studies. She entered the convent of Santa Maria degli Angeli, on the island of Murano—one of the oldest Augustinian foundations in Venice. Her sister Ginevra joined her there before 1448, and a third sister, Lucrezia, entered the convent of Santa Chiara on the same island before 1453. Only the fourth sister, Paola, married (in 1453). In the case of the wealthy Barbaros, no shortage of funds could explain the rejection of marriage opportunities by three of four daughters; in the sixteenth and seventeenth centuries, the strapped Leonardo Donà would marry off two of his three daughters. Costanza, at least, and likely her two sisters as well, were nuns by choice.

Her father was not altogether happy with Costanza's decision. He was pious, but he believed in marriage (as we have seen), and he would miss his daughter's company and the possibility of grandchildren. His friend Leonardo Giustiniani, another learned nobleman, a poet and the brother of Venice's own saint and first patriarch, Lorenzo, tried to cheer him. The convent was as productive as the family, prayers as productive as children: "this blow should be borne with equanimity, since it may be hoped that she can profit the republic as much by uttering prayers as by bearing children."[75] Barbaro remained in contact with this daughter who was to be fertile in prayers only, and addressed to her in 1447 a consolatory letter on the death of a female relative.[76] In closing, he sent greetings and asked for spiritual aid: "May he who watches over Israel preserve you in body and spirit. To your Mother Superior, who is the head of the convent, and to the virgins who serve God together with you, commend me, and aid me with your prayers."[77]

How far removed we are from Tarabotti's world of oppression and rage! Here the convent is viewed as a sweet and harmonious refuge for motivated and productive women. Such it was for many, for whom the walls enclosed a small cosmos, for whom the tiny windows facing always inward gave access to a chosen peace. The blessed Camilla (Sister Battista) da Varano found just such tranquillity in the convent of St. Clare in Urbino, which she entered in 1481: "I found the sweetest singing of pious prayers, the beauty of good examples, secret chambers of divine grace and heavenly gifts."[78] More than a century before, the anguish felt by Agnes, who had been compelled to leave the convent of San Damiano, was expressed in a letter to her natal sister Clare (later sainted). It suggests the closeness felt by committed nuns to their communities: "Know then, Mother, that in my body and soul there is great distress and overwhelming sorrow, and I am oppressed above measure and tormented and almost unable to speak, because I am separated in body from you and from my other Sisters with whom I had thought to live and to die in this world. This distress had indeed a beginning, but it knows no end; never does it know surcease, but always gains increase; it has risen upon me recently, but gives no promise of decline; it is always near me and never desires to be apart from me. I used to believe that those who shared in one life and converse in heaven would share alike in death and life on earth, and that one sepulchre would enclose those who are one and equal by nature. But I see I am deceived; I am straitened, I am forlorn, I am in tribulation on every side."[79]

Secure in their female communities, engaged in the task of prayer unquestioningly valued by their contemporaries, skeptical of other forms of women's work, many nuns feared nothing more than a change in their condition. But with the advent of Protestantism, earnest male reformers set out to liberate the nuns from their convents. Martin Luther himself led the way, opening up the convent doors in his city of Wittenberg, and espousing the former nun Katharina von Bora.[80] Only "blind and mad" bishops and abbots, he asserted in his 1523 pamphlet "Why Nuns May Leave Cloisters with God's Blessing," would condemn young girls to waste away in cloisters, for "a woman is not created to be a virgin, but to conceive and bear children."[81] "Let the poor virgins be unbound," anonymous Lutherans wrote in a 1524 pamphlet. "Let them stay in the cloister only so long as they freely choose, and when one wishes no longer to remain, let her follow the example of her friends, take a husband, and serve her neighbors in the world."[82] Such liberty was not easily granted. The nobleman's daughter Florentina of Ober Weimar, who was placed in a convent at age six and confirmed at age eleven, discovered at age fourteen her lack of true vocation. When she appealed to Luther for help, she was imprisoned, beaten, and humiliated by order of her superiors before her eventual escape.[83]

The challenge of the convents was confronted, city by city, throughout the early Reformation. As we have seen, not all nuns wished to be freed. Loyal to the old church, they wanted no part in a new order in which the right to marry loomed large as an obligation; for these women, an unwanted one. At least one convent in Strasbourg refused to disband. Patiently the sisters listened to the fiery pastors sent to announce to them their liberty. They forbore when they could not hear mass or confess. But they would not go home, as the city leaders requested them to do.[84] Here, as throughout Protestant lands, determined sisters remained in their convents until death, sometimes sole residents of the moribund institution in which they had sought salvation.[85] In Geneva and in Nuremberg, the sites of the two cases which follow, eager reformers encountered similar resistance from nuns who didn't want to go (or leave) home.

Sister Jeanne de Jussie, a nun of the order of St. Claire who lived in a Geneva convent during the years just before the Reformation, left a narrative of her experience as a loyal Catholic in a time of transition: *Le Levain du Calvinisme, ou Commencement de l'hérèsie de Genève*, which chronicled the years 1526 to 1535.[86] For her, women more than men were gifted to withstand the assault on the sacramental Church and the inversion of Catholicism's valuation of virginity. Catholic wives of "heretic" husbands persisted in the faith, she noted with approval. Some "martyrs" were beaten and imprisoned by their husbands. Refusing to attend Protestant services, they escaped from their houses to attend mass. They armed themselves and their children, ready to attack Protestant wives as male Catholics attacked Protestant men. The Clarissas, meanwhile, stayed firm, even when Protestant men ransacked their convent and reformers of both sexes attempted to persuade them to abandon their vocation. In 1534 they barred the door in the face of a Lutheran woman who explained the errors, as she saw it, of the conventual ideal. A former abbess, now a married Protestant, exhorted them: "If only you knew that it is good to be with a handsome husband, and how agreeable it is to God. I lived for a long time in that darkness and hypocrisy where you are, but God alone made me understand the abuse of my pitiful life, and I came to the true light of truth. . . . Thanks to God alone, I already have five handsome children, and I live salutarily."[87] The nuns spat at her. Only one of all the sisters of St. Clare was "perverted," de Jussie reported proudly. She herself, with her companions, left Geneva in 1535 to relocate to Annecy in France, of which foundation she was eventually made abbess.

Caritas (born Barbara) Pirckheimer, daughter of one of the proudest patrician dynasties of Nuremberg, was the abbess of a convent in that city (also of the order of St. Claire) during the turbulent years of the unfolding Reformation.[88] In that capacity, she guided a community of about sixty women, managed considerable property, dealt directly with city officials, enhanced the convent library, and ran its Latin school for girls. Her *Denkwürdigkeiten*, or *Memoirs*, of 1524–28 record her heroic defense of the convent during those years, when Nuremberg underwent the process of reform. In 1525, the city council ordered her to free the sisters of their vows, and ordered the nuns to doff their habits and leave the cloister. The convent's property was to be inventoried, and the former nuns, if they did not have adequate familial resources, were to be granted allowances for material support. Her "children," Pirckheimer replied, were bound by vows to the Almighty, not to her, and she had no power to loose them. Only one member of the community deserted willingly to Protestantism. Some Protestant families wanted their daughters released. The daughters preferred to stay.

Pirckheimer described the dramatic removal from the convent of three young women by their mothers, converts to the Reform. "Then the wicked wives ran inside like wild she-wolves. . . . The wives then bade the children come out with kind words, saying that if they did not do so willingly, they would pull them out forcibly. . . . The mothers told the children that it was their duty according to God's commandment to obey them, that they wanted them out because they wanted to save their souls from hell, that their daughters were sitting in the maul of the devil, and that they could not suffer this on their consciences. The children cried that they did not want to leave the pious, holy convent, that they were absolutely not in hell, but if they broke out of it they would descend into the abyss of hell, and that they would demand from them their souls on the Day of Judgment before the Strict Judge."[89] The women were twenty-three, twenty, and nineteen years old, and had joined the order at ages fourteen (the first two) and thirteen.[90] The mothers who reclaimed them had to separate them from their surrogate mother, the abbess, who could not resist but would not assist in the process. One daughter protested: "You are a mother of my flesh, but not of my spirit, because you did not give me my soul. For this reason it is not my duty to obey in these matters which go against my soul. . . . Each mother argued with her daughter, for a while promising her much and for a while threatening her. But the children wept and screamed incessantly; the battle lasted a long time, and Katharina Ebner spoke so courageously and steadfastly, proved all her words with the Holy Scripture, captured them all with her words, and told them how much they acted against the Holy Gospel. The men outside might have said after this that they never in all their living days had heard anything like it: she had talked without interruption for absolutely an entire hour, and without a wasted word—rather so very meaningfully that each word weighed a pound."[91] In the end, the three young women were dragged out of the convent and brought home, after years of separation, to the families which had given being to flesh but not soul.

The convent was a more satisfactory home for these women than the homes the reformers promised them, just as the convent in Catholic regions remained for many a desirable refuge and goal. Not all who wished to do so could enter a convent, however, and win the status and the tranquility that it afforded. It was available only for the privileged and the few. Almost without exception, the convents were peopled with the women of the feudal nobility and urban patriciate. The family who gave a daughter to a convent gave a gift as well, of property or money, beyond the means of all but the wealthiest—even if it was a lesser gift than was given to the man who married another daughter. These gifts were essential, because the convent required sufficient property to be able to support its nuns (who performed no productive labor). In addition, there were not enough convents to house the women who wished to join them. Many were overcrowded, in spite of episcopal and papal pronouncements limiting the size of conventual communities to such a number as could be realistically maintained by its endowment. Yet, from the Middle Ages and into the Renaissance, the church acted to limit rather than open up more such refuges for women. Where women came together in groups outside of the framework of conventual institutions, because the convents were too few and the groups too many, the church acted to constrain them. The process of continued resistance to the expansion of conventual organization and the continued constriction of possibilities for female aggregation is curious to behold.[92]

The most splendid years of female monasticism were the early ones. In the first Benedictine convents of the Middle Ages the nuns enjoyed great autonomy, and nobly born abbesses wielded considerable power. As the Anglo-Saxon abbess Liona explained, "the calm and order of the cloister was a space for women," and meant "freedom, not constraint."[93] But eventually, that freedom would fall to successive papal decisions and new male monastic energies. The double monasteries vanished, where an abbess ruled and a community of monks provided the services that only they, as males capable of ordination, could provide. The Cluniac reform included no plan for women, and only one convent was created in its wake: that at Marcigny, for the wives left behind by newly converted monks. In the high Middle Ages, women reached out again to form conventual establishments that would, in a new and richer way, satisfy spiritual needs. In so doing, they were following the lead of men, who had diverged from the mainstream of Benedictine monasticism after the eleventh century to form new orders: notably the Premonstratensians and Cistercians, dedicated, although in different ways, to active service. When women attempted to form convents parallel in mission to the male foundations, their efforts were discouraged and canalized. By 1150, more than ten thousand women lived in Premonstratensian nunneries. The general chapter of the order was provoked to decree that it would receive no more, and one abbot explained why: "recognizing that the wickedness of women is greater than all the other wickedness of the world . . . , we will on no account receive any more sisters to the increase of our perdition, but will avoid them like poisonous animals."[94] In 1198, Pope Innocent III, backing the order, dedicated a bull (the *De non recipiendis sororibus*) to the exclusion of females from the Premonstratensian mission.

Beginning in that same century, and again without the official invitation of the order's leadership, many communities of women began to appear in Spain and Portugal, Flanders and Germany, Switzerland and Hungary, living under the Cistercian rule. Multiplying "like the stars in the sky,"[95] they grew in number (though not always in wealth) to equal the male monasteries—in frontier areas to exceed them—and everywhere to impose on them for pastoral care. Especially in Spain, they grew in authority and eminence, housing the daughters of the highest nobility. But the aggressive, expansionist, and austere Cistercians were, of all orders of monks, the most hostile to women, whose "high-pitched tinkling" they urged their robust baritone choirs never to imitate.[96] In 1228, the general chapter of the order acted to choke off new foundations and to subject existing communities to strict enclosure and burdensome regulation (and deprivation) of sacramental services. The aristocratic abbesses of the foundations protested and resisted. Male discipline in the end prevailed. As male monasticism became more adventurous, more extroverted, more productive, female monasticism became more introverted, more powerless, and more dependent. As the church hardened its institutional structure, it permitted women, viewed as undisciplined and disruptive, fewer opportunities. Nevertheless, groups of nuns continued to shelter under Cistercian wings.[97]

This pattern repeated itself with the creation of the mendicant orders, Franciscan and Dominican, in the thirteenth century. Outcroppings of an increasingly urbanized society, these orders were, even more than the Augustinians or Cistercians, oriented toward Christian action in the world. As soon as they were founded, the friars found that groups of women wished to organize themselves according to the same principles of active service in modern settings. Francis's companion Clare of Assisi, converted by the saint in 1212, organized immediately thereafter a community at San Damiano (which she ruled until her death in 1253) devoted to the ideal of spiritual poverty.[98] Dominic himself sponsored the foundation of a community of female Dominicans at Prouille. Dominican foundations for women subsequently spread, especially in Germany.[99] But papal legislation insisted that the new nuns be incorporated (a problem for the Franciscans), served by male confessors, priests, and advisers, attached to existing male orders, and enclosed. An exception was Clare's own community at San Damiano, which in 1215 or 1216 was granted by Pope Innocent III the *privilegium paupertatis*; but it had to accept enclosure, as Clare herself, guided by Francis, probably wished.[100] The mendicant orders still resisted the female foundations altogether, wanting no responsibility for the pastoral care of women. Francis complained: "God has taken away our wives, and now the devil gives us sisters."[101] Between pressures from above to force the foundations to conformity, and resistance from the orders themselves, the nature of female participation in the mendicant orders was shaped so that women were not true partners to the males. Dominican convents and convents of *clarisse* grew to resemble the enclosed and contemplative foundations of traditional monasticism—just like the two convents of the order of St. Clare in Geneva and Nuremberg where Jeanne de Jussie and Caritas Pirckheimer lived. Once again a new frontier had opened; once again, women were turned back from its dangerous luxuriance.

Options for women seeking the dignity of virginity, the haven of female community, and the challenge of a disciplined spiritual life narrowed further after 1215, when a Lateran Council prohibited the formation of any new religious orders. This action effectively closed the door on the possibility of a women's order, organized independently and not linked organizationally to a men's. Within existing convents, new restrictions were imposed. Their residents were to be protected from the outside world, and also to be denied awareness of the world about them. Pope Boniface VIII's bull *Periculoso* of 1293 forbade them to leave without a bishop's permission. Their good works could only be works of contemplation, not action: they could not go forth, as did the friars, to serve the poor or the sick or the ignorant. The nuns were placed under everstricter male supervision, their communities visited and investigated by conscientious bishops or fact-gathering committees with each wave of reform.[102] In a church with a jealously male priesthood, nuns were dependent on male clerics to function: only male priests could perform the mass, or hear confession. Nuns were free to pray, or study, in their little cells, and they were free from the entangling demands of families. But they were not free to seek God in any but the prescribed way, nor to serve their neighbor, nor to imitate Christ.

Holy Women

The official church's ingrained anti-female bias seems to have made it insensible of women's need for more open forms of ministry and association. From the thirteenth through the seventeenth centuries, women increasingly made their own way regardless: "they found their own space and boundaries of autonomy, however limited these were."[103] They explored new forms of aggregation for the purpose of living a holy life outside of the framework of the monastic establishment. They thus created new opportunities for women to enjoy the same freedom of spiritual expression within a communal life as men had already claimed. And these opportunities, too, were taken away, often as soon as they appeared.

The most characteristic movement of female communitarian life in the early Renaissance is that of the Beguines.[104] Groups of women (sometimes men, but mostly women), drawn together by no male leader, associating under no formal rule, linked in no network of cities or nationalities, would pool property, share a residence or live at home, work together, pledge themselves to chastity and poverty, worship communally, and perform charitable acts. Initially they were viewed as heretics, and their very name, "Beguine," derived from the name of the "Albigensians," recently extinguished in the south of France. Living by the "work of their hands," they posed a different model of voluntary poverty, an important counterpart to the mendicants, as the philosopher Robert Grosseteste observed.[105] They created effectual families, parallel at once to the natal families they had known and the organized "families" of the male or female monastery, ruled by "fathers" or "mothers," and inhabited by "brothers" or "sisters." Beginning in the thirteenth century in Belgium and Germany, communities of Beguines formed in the next two centuries southward to the Alps and eastward to Bohemia. In 1243, Matthew of Paris interrupted his chronicle of world events to note the new development: the women had multiplied so quickly in the area around Cologne that now two thousand dwelled there.[106] In 1250, he remarked yet again on their growth: "In Germany there has arisen an innumerable multitude of celibate women who call themselves Beguines: a thousand or more of them live in Cologne alone."[107]

The Beguines of Cologne continued to grow rapidly into the early years of the fourteenth century. As they became established, the women created more formal convents (always the tendency, encouraged by ecclesiastical supervisors), which continued to be founded up to the dawn of the fifteenth century. By that time, these convents totaled 169, and had incorporated Cologne's whole Beguine population of approximately 1,500. These, in a citizen population of about 20,000, amounted to 7.5 percent of the whole!—far beyond the percentage of traditional nuns we have seen in Venice or London or even in Florence for any period but the extraordinary mid-sixteenth century. The women workers who lived in such unstructured communities, outside the normal patterns of conventual aggregation, were far more numerous than the cloistered daughters of the nobility. In Strasbourg, the mushrooming of the Beguines followed a similar timetable.[108] The largest growth in the number of

Beguines and associated holy women occurred in the four decades prior to 1318, when the restrictive legislation of the Council of Vienne was published. That event "ended completely the claims of women living alone in the world to a beguine life."[109] Thereafter, most of those who professed the vows of the Beguine were moved into communities under adjacent male monastic supervision, as the decree required. The number of formally pledged Beguines diminished rapidly from this point—only two are in evidence for the whole of the fifteenth century—while the number of women living a related holy life continued to grow, including the matrons and widows who could not consecrate themselves to virginity as the Beguines did, and who remained with their families. The Beguine ideal of unmarried women consecrating themselves to virginity, study, and service crested early in the fourteenth century and, frustrated by new regulations, subsided in the fifteenth.[110] It would reappear in different guise.

The Beguine movement is largely associated with northern towns, where it later merged with the *devotio moderna* or "new devotion" launched by Gerhard Groote. Groote turned his own house into a home for sisters of the Common Life in 1374. Like the Beguines, these women (who numbered several hundred at the peak of the movement) made informal vows of chastity, wore simple clothes, worked with their hands, and professed the imitation of Christ.[111] As late as 1520, the artist Albrecht Dürer observed a procession in Antwerp of "all the guilds and trades, each man dressed according to his rank and most richly. . . . The procession also included a large troop of widows, who keep themselves by the work of their hands and live by a special rule. They were dressed in white linen from head to foot—a moving thing to see."[112] If not Beguines by name, these women belonged to a community of the same type and professing the same goal. Like this one, communities resembling those of the Beguines, lacking precise denomination, developed in the other areas of continental Europe. In Spain flourished the *beatas*, who took informal vows of chastity (and claimed exemption from sexual passions), dedicating themselves to charitable work and visionary piety.[113] In Italy, where many such informal aggregates emerged in the thirteenth through fifteenth centuries, the women participants could be called Beguines, or otherwise *mantellate*, *bizzocale*, or *pinzochere*. In the regions of Umbria and Tuscany, the florescence of such female devotional communities was so great that papal and episcopal regulation could neither encompass nor regulate it. A single decade at the end of the thirteenth

century saw the birth of thirteen such organizations in the city and suburbs of Spoleto alone. While many women gathered in associations such
as these, others lived as *incarcerate* or *recluse*, solitary penitents, an-
chorites, oblates, sometimes accompanied by one or two companions.
Along with the reputation of holiness, contemporaries suspected these
women of the usual evils: unchastity and heresy.[114]

The beguinages resembled other communities of those living a holy
life. They looked, for instance, like the thirteenth-century communities
of the *umiliati*, pious laypersons dedicated to caritative work centered in
Milan. They resembled even more closely the groups of laywomen (and
men) who surrounded male Franciscan and Dominican establishments
as "third orders." The Dominican tertiaries, whose members took vows
but lived an extraconventual life, were graced by the participation of
Saint Catherine of Siena (Caterina Benincasa), among others; the Franciscan tertiaries by Angela of Foligno and Angela Merici. By definition
such groups lay outside the symmetrical framework of male and female
mendicant establishments, themselves only gradually formalized as the
fifteenth century approached: the establishments of female Franciscans
who professed the order of St. Clare were not yet, in this early period,
formally cloistered. As diverse and variable in form as the communities
in which women congregated for spiritual reasons were, women were
still not admitted to the public expressions of piety engaged in by male
members of town confraternities: female piety was to be expressed in
private acts.

Who were these women who in persistent and mounting numbers
from the Middle Ages through the Renaissance sought to live a holy life?
Nuns, Beguines, *clarisse, mulieres sanctae*, tertiaries, oblates, saints, they
came from substantial families: noble, patrician, bourgeois.[115] A few
poor sisters were cared for, and as a relic of medieval social organization,
the traditional nunneries housed many *conversae*, semireligious servants
from humble origins. But these were exceptions, as were a few saints—
like Margaret of Cortona, attached to the Franciscans, conspicuous for
her poor origins. Daughters and widows of brewers and cloth merchants, landowners, and city councillors, these women had much to lose
when they thrust away wealth and status and sought labor, poverty, and
isolation. Their action bespeaks a profound rejection of the social world
of their origins. "These women . . . wished not only to be poor but to
live with the poor. Against the natural order of society they deliberately
chose to deny their noble or rich background and turned instead to a way

of life scorned by those they had known."[116] This same social impulse seems to energize groups of European women, in whatever the landscape that they chose for the creation of community, or of solitude.

Opportunities for female piety were sought out with great enthusiasm, resulting in "an extreme diffusion of female penitence," of which the large number of saints and uncanonized *mulieres sanctae* were only a small reflection.[117] Increasingly, the religious lives of women resisted definition, as the lives of the solitary penitent (living at home, in the open, or in a cell) and the small community (gathered in a house, in the wild, in a convent) melded. The fourteenth-century holy woman Filippa Mareri of Reati, for instance, lived these various lives successively. Resisting her powerful family's plans for a splendid marriage, she retreated to a cell in her house to pursue her own spiritual goals. In time she left her house, accompanied by other women of similar mind, and established, amid some rocky caves on the hills overlooking a family-owned fortress, a community of women—only one of many in the area. Eventually, her brother made peace with his renegade sister and resettled the whole community, more properly, he must have felt, next to a church.[118] The fifteenth-century Roman saint Francesca Bussi de' Ponziani also began her holy life in isolation: in a retreat—*eremo*—in the garden of the house she shared with her husband. Later, having agreed with her cooperative spouse to live in continence, she joined—still living in her own home—a congregation of other women dedicated to caritative service in the streets of her city.[119]

The blending of forms of female communitarian life in early Renaissance Italy is revealed in the history of the beguinage (or *oratorio*, or *mansione*) of Corpus Domini in Ferrara.[120] It was launched in 1406 by Bernardina Sedazzari, a widow and former nun, who committed to its foundation the small but sufficient sum of 200 ducats given her by a wealthy aunt and other female friends. Her original goal, formally stated in an extant notarial act, was to found a cloistered community under the rule of Saint Augustine. "Bernardina's original intentions are worth noting because, as later events would show, she seems to have made every effort to avoid realizing them."[121] Instead of the formal establishment envisioned, Corpus Domini emerged under Sedazzari's leadership as an unstructured community of pious laywomen living in an ordinary house a life of religious worship, domestic work, and charitable activity. Among its famous members was the future abbess and saint Caterina Vegri.

The founder of Corpus Domini died soon after making her will in 1425. By that instrument she had bequeathed to one of the other residents, Lucia Mascheroni (who had been reared in the beguinage) the task of maintaining the community according to its original spirit. By now the residents of Corpus Domini had won recognition as pious workers for the reformed church promoted by important spiritual leaders of the Northern Italian quattrocento. It had also grown larger, in property and in numbers. Another resident and the young girls in her following split away in 1426 from the original foundation, purchased a new house in the same city, and began a new community, formally aggregated to the Augustinian order in 1429. With fifteen nuns, the new Sant' Agostino was not much larger than Corpus Domini had been at first, nor much differently housed. But it had crossed a delicate line and gained proper ecclesiastical definition, along with which came male clerical supervision. The new nuns gave their vows to the famous Venetian reformer Ludovico Barbo, abbot of Santa Giustina in Padua, later Bishop of Treviso. By 1461, Sant' Agostino had spawned a new Augustinian convent in Verona and had been entrusted with the reform of two others in Ferrara. It had become rich, and its resemblance to a traditional convent was complete: its members now included many members of the Ferrarese patriciate.

Meanwhile, the original Corpus Domini, against the will of Mascheroni, who attempted loyally to carry out its founder's wishes, had been "captured" by a wealthy patrician matron, Verde Pio da Carpi. Along with her bequests, which permitted the rebuilding of the house, Verde Pio arranged, by interceding directly with the pope, for the formal incorporation of the community. She invited nuns from the famous convent of Corpus Christi in Mantua—founded by the noblewoman Paola Malatesta Gonzaga, the widow of the Marchese of Mantua and the mother of the erudite Cecilia, already discussed—to join the Ferrarese group, which was to be organized as nuns of the order of St. Clare. By 1432, the transformation was complete. Caterina Vegri, the community's most famous alumna, became herself a *clarissa*. Under her influence, the convent of Corpus Domini in Ferrara gained renown as a nucleus of Franciscan reform. On the basis of her work there, she was called to Bologna to form and head as abbess a new Corpus Domini, formally committed from the first to the Franciscan order. Thus from the modest family of *pinzochere* who shared a small house were born at least three convents, one Augustinian and two Franciscan, and several others were renewed in the spirit of reform by its stellar example.

A century later, Angela Merici, later sainted, established a new order for noncloistered women.[122] An offshoot of the male Confraternity of Divine Love, Merici's order reflected the reformist spirit of her own day: the evangelism of the pre-Tridentine era, not too different, in its focus on the individual's state of grace and its resistance to clerical intrusion, from the contemporary early Protestantism. Merici's urgent and clearly focused goal was to involve women living in the world in community service, teaching, and curing. Young girls of at least twelve, having obtained the permission of their families, were to dedicate themselves to prayer and charitable work, living without constraining vows as "consecrated virgins" within their homes: "Each one must conserve her holy virginity, not doing this because of a vow resulting from human direction, but voluntarily making a sacrifice of her own heart to God: because virginity . . . is the sister of all the angels."[123] When gathered together, the "figliole," daughters, were subject to the gentle leadership of the "madri," or mothers, mature matrons and widows who dedicated themselves to the responsibilities of administration and education. The community envisioned closely resembled the models of the spiritual life preferred by many women over the previous three centuries: the Beguines, the *clarisse*, the third orders.

Merici's order was founded in Brescia in 1535 and named the Company of St. Ursula, after the legendary British princess martyred, while en route to her wedding, along with her 11,000 virgin companions. Its members took an informal vow of virginity and met twice a month—at first in the very Ospedale degli Incurabili founded by the Confraternity next to which they eventually established their own base. They lived at home with their families or, if they were without workable family ties, were placed in reliable families as housekeepers or governesses. Merici envisioned a democratic society of women in which differences of social class would be erased in shared labor and circumstances. The poor were welcome, and the social gulf between aristocratic "sisters" and unpropertied *conversae* was avoided from the start. Members wore no special habit and had no formal roles beyond those of "mother" and "daughter," mirroring the familial relationship that best avoided Tarabotti's "paternal tyranny." This was not to be another order of nuns, but a vital alternative to the convent. Christ Himself had founded the Company, according to Merici, and wished it to be as it was and not confined by the rule of claustration that had overtaken so many of its predecessors.

After Merici's death in 1540, clerical pressures were exerted to enclose the "daughters" of St. Ursula. Merici's secretary and confidant, the priest Gabriele Cozzano, attempted to adhere to the legacy she had clearly defined in her *Regola, Ricordi*, and *Testamento*. "First of all," he wrote in his defense of the Ursulines against their opponents, "the Church in its Primitive, Golden state was without cloisters and convents. . . . Today in these years so close to the Antichrist and the End of the World, we are renewing the Primitive Church's ways, coming full circle. We cover ourselves with the Holy Spirit and virtue, and not with cloisters."[124] Cozzano's views are scarcely distinguishable from those of the reformers at some points here, and reach into a tradition of Renaissance spirituality so distinct from the mainstream that he quotes only one of all the philosophers: Nicholas of Cusa. He said further: "Some say that Religious life is greater than life in the Company of St. Ursula. This is false because God introduced this Company into the Church. It is wrong to see only exteriorly. The way of the Company is a way of dignity—the life of St. Martha, of the first flowers—the martyrs of the Primitive Church and of the Madonna. According to the people who state falsehoods, only those in a cloister have a better life. What about uncloistered St. Ursula and her Companions?"[125]

The laywomen who were Merici's followers imitated and demanded respect for the laywomen martyrs whose descendants they desired to be. In Brescia, its home, the Company of St. Ursula was, in fact, exempt from the rule of enclosure—by the same kind of exceptionalism that allowed Saint Clare alone, of all the heads of *clarisse*, to observe Francis's rule of apostolic poverty.[126] The Company survived as a society of laywomen engaged in charitable work from 1535 until 1810. But elsewhere, the communities of women that had been built on Merici's original foundation were forced to accept the same reduction to enclosure as had so many independent female communities. Pope Pius V ordered in 1566 the strict cloistering of all professed nuns, and Pope Paul V ruled in 1612 specifically that the order of the Ursulines be cloistered under the Augustinian rule. Thenceforth, the Ursulines pursued their mission to educate young girls; but they did so behind walls.[127]

The church's insistence on claustration and on male direction of female religious life had begun centuries earlier. Peter Abelard had lectured Héloise on the need for the strict isolation of women; the

Cistercians had insisted on it; the Beguines were instructed to observe it by the Council of Vienne in 1312. The requirement became even more determined after the challenge of Protestantism and the Council of Trent.[128] The former movement had mightily challenged the authority of priesthood and sacrament, and the latter had acted to restore it. One result was the enlargement of the confessor role to that of spiritual director. The docility to their advisers displayed by Jeanne de Chantal, who, with Francis of Sales, founded the Visitation Order, and by Louise de Marillac, a disciple of Vincent de Paul and the founder of the Daughters of Charity in 1633, qualifies their leadership in a noticeable way. In a second national setting, they had followed the example of Angela Merici and established a space where women could pursue an "active apostolate" of teaching, consoling, feeding, and healing. Once again, though, the issue of enclosure was pressing. While the piety of Jeanne de Chantal was not in doubt, the Archbishop of Lyons observed in 1615, the daily visiting of her followers might become an opportunity for idleness and dissipation. His view prevailed, and the Visitation Order became a traditional cloistered order and ceased to visit. Louise de Marillac and the Daughters of Charity were able to survive as a visiting order doing hospital work, but at the cost of accepting a status less than that of the "religious." The lesser social origins of the Daughters of Charity may explain why the church establishment permitted them to remain uncloistered. On the whole, the church's logic was pure: women who had professed simple or private vows of chastity before Trent must now profess solemn ones; and all those who professed solemn vows required cloister to guard their intentions. The Spanish saint Teresa of Avila gave voice to the spirit of Trent when she lamented that "a convent of unenclosed nuns seems to me a place of very great peril, and more like a road to hell for those bent on wickedness than a remedy for their weaknesses."[129] Where once a few women religious had escaped enclosure to pursue spiritual objectives in the world (increasingly, the goal of pious men), now claustration was to be total and without exception.

The fate of the Ursulines and the daughters of the Visitation also befell the effort launched by the English recusant Mary Ward at about the time these other movements capitulated to enclosure.[130] Learned herself in Latin and inspired by the example of the English Jesuit college at St. Omer, she attempted and briefly succeeded in establishing (from 1609) a European network of schools under the leadership of lay female teachers: the Institute of the Blessed Virgin Mary. She and her companions described their objective to Pope Paul V in 1616: "As the sadly afflicted state of England, our native country stands greatly in need of spiritual labourers, . . . it seems that the female sex should and can . . . undertake something more than ordinary . . . , we also desire . . . to devote ourselves according to our slender capacity to the performance of those works of Christian charity towards our neighbour that cannot be undertaken in convents."[131] Like Merici's "daughters," the women workers in Ward's order were to be unenclosed, leading "a mixed kind of life," such as that taught by Christ to his disciples, and led by his mother and other holy virgins. They wished to live as a community, without closure or full habit, to elect their own "mother general," and to be exempt from the supervision of the secular clergy. This structure, of course, was closely modeled on the recently formed Jesuit order, which recognized no male superior but the Pope. The Institute opened houses, from 1616 to 1628, in Liège, Cologne, Trier, Rome, Naples, Munich, Vienna, and Prague. By 1631, it had three hundred members, with some of the schools (some free day schools open to the poor) enrolling as many as five hundred pupils. The curriculum included, beyond needlework and music, religion, Latin and Greek (as well as French and local vernaculars), and mathematics, and the girls performed (like their brothers under the tutelage of the humanists) Latin plays. Ward and her coworkers traveled ceaselessly, conferred with princes and cardinals, and raised funds (to the envy of their enemies).

Their plans, however, met with the opposition of the official Church, now irretrievably opposed to organizational innovations in female religious life. Ward's opponents—the most bitter among them were the English Jesuits and secular clergy—appealed to the pope, complaining of her aggressive posture in spiritual matters. Indeed, she had dared to conceive of a newly prominent role for women in the Church. She admitted male preeminence in some functions—heading a family, heading the church, administering sacraments, preaching in public assemblies; "but in all other things, wherein are we so inferior to other creatures," she asked, "that they should term us 'but women'? For what think you of this word, 'but women'? but as if we were in all things inferior to some other creature which I suppose to be a man! Which I dare to be bold to say is a lie."[132] In working together, Ward and her sisters had gained an invigorated presence and self-image, quite the reverse of the passivity and silence imposed by convent walls. Ward appealed to Pope Urban VIII in 1624, unsuccessfully. Her order was suppressed in 1631, "demonstrating how abhorrent was the idea of a public and independent role for women in the Counter-Reformation church."[133] Three hundred sisters were sent home to England by the Bull of Suppression, and Ward was imprisoned by the Munich Inquisition, denounced as a heretic and schismatic.

A pattern of astonishing continuity greets the eye of the observer of female devotional movements over centuries—the fourteenth through the seventeenth—that saw such diverse forms of religious life. Pious women, committed to the strict observance of orthodox doctrine and to the performance of useful caritative works, joined hands. They joined, for the most part, spontaneously, although they also cared for young women in their communities who could not have made adult commitments to the communitarian life. They lived simply, avoiding the costs as well as the rigors of conventual life. They brought their own property to these ventures, and their willingness to labor. They were not of the highest social classes, to whom a convent was more often available. But they were frequently from substantial families who had nurtured for their daughters quite different expectations. In due course, the informal communities in which these women lived, which inhabited the spaces between the limbs of the gigantic armature of the late medieval and early modern Church, came under the scrutiny of the male clerical establishment. The founders and bearers of a culture of lay female piety were commended for their good intentions and told to step aside. They were to be organized according to one of the rules available for nuns. They were to wear a habit. Their voluntary chastity was to be enforced with bars and vows. They were to cease the production of marketable goods. They were to educate only children, within the confines of the walls. They were to evacuate the streets filled with need and to look only inward. Their convents were walled islands amid the urban maelstrom of the new age, and their experience was to have nothing to do with it. Women could not be entrusted with the present moment, nor with the imitation of Christ.

Ironically, this recurrent pattern of increased restriction of female piety and reclaustration of female communities, which can be tracked from the Middle Ages to the brink of the modern world, coincides with the florescence of a male piety fully empowered to find new forms of expression: Franciscan and Dominican, Protestant and Jesuit. Saint Filippo Neri, for instance, in his struggle to overcome all trace of carnal desire, "did not wrestle with his sexual demons in the stillness of the cloister or by escaping to the mountains." Like many Catholic Reformation saints, continuing the tradition launched in the thirteenth century by the mendicants, "he fought and won his spiritual battle in the streets."[134] Those streets were barred to women. The arms and branches of the church provided ample room for new adventures of the mind and spirit. But they were jealously guarded for the same sex that also headed states, waged war, learned Greek, hoarded money, and propounded theory. More than a few women resisted the male monopoly on life and thought. Some found that heresy promised more than orthodoxy to female initiative.

Women were attracted to the deeply as well as the marginally heretical movements of the early Renaissance (as too, in its last centuries, they were attracted to the radical versions of Protestantism).[135] They had previously been active participants in Cathar and Albigensian groups in the high Middle Ages. In the south of France, heretics especially appealed to the superabundant daughters of the minor nobility, teaching them to read scripture and offering them "an ideology which made sense of their plight"—the fundamental sinfulness of the world, of the parents who brought them into it, of the marriages they would never know. It was in order to attract daughters of the nobility away from charismatic Cathar leaders that Dominic founded the first convent of his order at Prouille in 1206.[136] Suffering a disadvantage in the marriage market, women outnumbered men in many of the cities of the late Middle Ages: in Bologna and Nuremberg, in Basel and Verona. This social pressure, which also attracted many women to the life of the beguinage, lured them into heresy. The heresiarchs often addressed themselves directly to women—"O bona femina," "Good women," they might begin—whose concerns were not only spiritual and intellectual growth but also asylum from the ruthless demands and bleak opportunities of family life. They gave support "to one of the most pitiful groups in the medieval world— unmarried and unmarriageable women."[137] The Albigensians struck a particular nerve in their hatred of marriage, which was, in their view, an obstacle to salvation. "These girls learned that the marriage they could not have was a heinous sin, and that their families and the Church which abandoned them included the worst of sinners. Their very parents were more pernicious than and deserved to be punished as thieves and murderers; their own existence upon earth was proof of the evil of those who conceived and bore them. It would be hard to find in history an example of a deeper alienation."[138]

In contrast to the Albigensian appeal to women, female Lollardy from the fourteenth century operated within the family, and adherents converted their husbands, servants, and children. Supporters of John Wycliffe, the English Lollards (like the Waldensians or *valdesi* elsewhere) awakened the suspicions of the established church against the lay study of the Gospel.[139] The Lollard Anna Palmer, a Northampton anchoress, did not ease those suspicions when, brought before ecclesiastical officers in 1393, she labeled the bishop and his clerks as Antichrist and his disciples.[140] In 1511, when Lollards in several parts of England joined in the "great abjuration," more than one-third of the suspects in Coventry were women.[141] Detailed confessions from 1521 show women in the Chilterns "teaching lollardy, acquiring lollard books, learning lollard tracts by heart and demonstrating their dislike of catholic ceremonies."[142] Some were martyrs: the eighty-year-old Joan Boughton, for instance, who in 1494 held (it was charged) eight of Wycliffe's opinions, and possibly soon after her daughter as well: Lady Young, the wife of a former mayor of London.[143] There were no Lollards in Venice, but something of the same infection existed in the currents of pre-Tridentine evangelism: one woman was brought before the Inquisition in 1548 for having the Bible read aloud to her on Sunday mornings.[144] The Spanish *beatas* dared, like the English Lollards, to read from the New Testament and to preach. Some were implicated with the heretical *alumbrados*; the *beata* Isabel de la Cruz was an *alumbrado* leader. Prosecutions of these and other *beatas* spurted in the sixteenth and seventeenth centuries. Their most common punishment was to be imprisoned in a house or hospital under the direction of a male confessor assigned "to redirect their spiritual lives into the safe boundaries of official orthodoxy"— precisely the relationship to the established church that it was their purpose to avoid.[145]

Women were also involved in heretical groups whose behavior involved more extreme expression: notably as adherents of the Spiritual Franciscans and of the movement of the Free Spirit, groups that believed that divine grace could create a state that placed the subject above all human authority.[146] Associated with these (and with the Joachimites) may be the Guglielmites, who flourished in late thirteenth-century Milan.[147] Worshippers of the prophetess Guglielma (who had died in 1279) as the female incarnation of the Holy Spirit, their organization was headed by a female pope, and their female priests alone could perform the new sacraments of an *ecclesia spiritualis* that had, at last, arrived.[148] Not "a spiritual aberration but rather . . . a specific fulfillment of thirteenth-century enthusiastic aspirations," the sect is surely notable for its quest for high-status ecclesiastical roles for women.[149] In France in 1325, a follower of the Spiritual Franciscans was burned for believing that she (as Guglielma's followers believed of their champion) bore the Holy Spirit. In her recorded testimony, Na Prous Boneta claimed special Christ-like, salvationary gifts: "Likewise, the Lord God shall give two things to every person who believes in the words of Na Prous; that is, he will forgive the sins of the believing person, and he will give him the Holy Spirit. Likewise, he who created the world redeemed me, and shall renew it. Likewise God sent his Son to a virgin to redeem human nature, and the Son of God sent the Holy Spirit to another virgin for redeeming human nature; saying that God gave her to understand clearly that she is the virgin to whom God sent the Holy Spirit to redeem human nature."[150] In 1434, as late as the age of John Hus and on the brink of the great witch-hunt, a vagabond woman was tried in Regensburg for similar beliefs that she claimed were the fruit of divine revelation: she could not sin, she held, but was more blessed than the Apostles, and was not subject to the pope. After "her limbs were sufficiently humiliated," she recanted.[151]

Most dangerous to the orthodox church were those committed visionaries, considered heretics, who wrote books that spread their beliefs. The Beguine Marguerite Porete from Hainaut gave sophisticated expression in more than sixty thousand words to some distinctly heretical notions of the Freedom of the Spirit and was burned at the stake around 1310.[152] Excerpts from her book, *The Mirror of Simple Souls*, were forwarded by a Dominican Inquisitor to a board of examiners at the University of Paris. They found much to condemn in her notions (among others) of the annihilation of the soul in mystical experience and its identification with the divine: "Now this soul is a blank, because it sees its nothingness by fullness of divine knowledge, which makes it a blank, makes it a void. . . . Now the Soul is fallen from love into nothingness, and without this nothingness it cannot be at all. This fall is such a deep fall, if it be rightly fallen, that the Soul cannot arise from this abyss." In a still higher state, "God by his divine majesty sees himself in the Soul, and this purifies the Soul so that it seems that nothing exists except God himself, who is and therefore everything else exists, and that what truly is is God himself; and therefore the Soul sees only itself, because one who sees what is sees only God, God who sees himself in this very Soul by means of his divine majesty."[153]

The boundaries between God and the self, in Porete's vision, are richly blurred. For Porete, however, the soul liberated in God was not above moral law. Other believers in the freedom of the spirit thought it was. Around 1400, Mary of Valenciennes shocked the learned prelate Jean Gerson, then chancellor of the University of Paris, with her book on divine love: it was frightening precisely because it was subtly argued and well written.[154] Composed in the vernacular, and thus widely available to the masses, it preached that those who had reached the perfection of divine love were no longer bound by moral precepts. Here the heresy of Free Spirit appears to give license to sexual immorality, a reputation for which its followers shared with the Guglielmites and other alleged heretics (and, as will be seen, witches). Women who adopted radical notions of forgiving grace cast off (or were accused of doing so) all shackles of sexual regulation. Since in this area above all, women, more than others, were limited in traditional society, it is not surprising that some marginal and rebellious spirits among them accepted the promise of sexual liberation. It may be more surprising that so many women who pursued a spiritual life in the Renaissance centuries clung to orthodoxy, while their rich and fascinating experience stretched to the limit allowed by traditional Christian imagery. "Rebellion in the context of obedience, the vocation of a saint, provided more space for women than did sectarian protest."[155]

Female Sanctity

Women engaged in the pilgrimage of the spirit with great earnestness in the Renaissance centuries. As consolers and healers, as tireless penitents and unrelenting ascetics, they ministered to their fellows and evoked wonder. As visionaries they explored the realms of religious experience which unfolded from the high Middle Ages to the edge of the modern era, especially rich in possibility for a female subject. More than a thousand years after Christ, his followers discovered a loving God who was both father and mother, an incarnate Christ, both body and spirit, a compassionate Mary, both virgin and mother, and with these they sought indissoluble union. God as a loving mother, Christ as a passionate spouse, the host as the vital body of the Lord, the child as the deity held in one's arms, the family of saints as sisters and brothers and mothers and fathers—these were the vibrant and satisfying images that dwelt in the silence of prayer and contemplation. In these experiences of union and relationship, sometimes felt with an overwhelming passion incomprehensible to the depleted twentieth-century onlooker, many women found fulfillment and dignity not otherwise available to them in a world in which the family served objects other than love.

Yet the family often entered into the imagery of the holy life. At the turn of the fourteenth century, Marguerite of Oignt compared Jesus to her own mother: "The mother who bore me labored in delivering me for one day or one night but you, my sweet and lovely Lord, labored for me for more than thirty years. Ah, my sweet and lovely Lord, with what love you labored for me and bore me through your whole life. But when the time approached for you to be delivered, your labor pains were so great that your holy sweat was like great drops of blood that came out from your body and fell on the earth. . . . Ah! Sweet Lord Jesus Christ, who ever saw a mother suffer such a birth!"[156] Although men as well as women understood the sacrificial love of Jesus for humanity as a mother's love, it is striking to hear women relate to a male God in terms of female experience and emotion.[157] The fourteenth-century Englishwoman Julian of Norwich, more than any other Renaissance mystic, felt the power of God as mother as well as father.[158] "And thus in our making God almighty is our kindly Father, and God-all-wisdom is our kindly Mother, with the love and the goodness of the Holy Ghost, which is all one God, one Lord."[159] It is precisely in our bodily existence that we experience the Motherhood of God, and it is Christ, the second person of the Trinity, who is our Mother, and his acts are the mother's acts of mercy. Although our nature "is whole in each person of the Trinity, which is one God," yet "our sensuality is only in the second person, Christ Jesus, in whom is the Father and the Holy Ghost."[160]. Jesus is the mother of our substance and the merciful tender of our physical needs: "our mother in kind in our substantial making, in whom we be grounded and rooted, and . . . our mother of mercy in our sensual taking." Thus our mother works in us in various ways, "in whom our parts are kept unparted; for in our mother Christ we profit and increase, and in mercy he reforms and restores us, and by the virtue of his passion, his death and his uprising joined us to our substance. Thus our mother works in mercy to all his beloved children which be to him close and obedient."[161] Jesus began his life in a mother's womb, and then took on the job of mother to us all. Just as our mothers bore us in pain, every one, so he suffered all for our benefit, and would gladly have suffered more. Our mothers feed us with the milk of their breasts, but Jesus feeds us with his body in the host. Jesus our mother protects us in the strife of good against evil and is therefore the essence of love. Our being is from him, "where the ground of motherhood begins, with all the sweet keeping of love that endlessly follows."[162]

Where the love of God that transported Julian was understood as a mother's love, others experienced a mother's love for the infant Jesus. The Flemish Beguine Marie d'Oignies recalled "that for three or more days she held Him close to her so that He nestled between her breasts like a baby, and she hid Him there lest He be seen by others. Sometimes she kissed him as though He were a little child and sometimes she held Him on her lap as if He were a gentle lamb."[163] In the fifteenth century, Saint Catherine of Bologna (Caterina Vegri) received in her arms and bosom the Infant Jesus from those of Mary.[164] Caterina de' Ricci, as a young girl, prepared herself spiritually for Christmas by identifying with Mary's motherhood: she said 275 paternosters "in reverence for that number of days which my Jesus rested in the womb of the most holy Mother."[165] The contemporary English holy woman Margery Kempe experienced the love of Christ as alternately a father's and a husband's. Once, in the depths of depression, she was visited by the healing Jesus: "In the likeness of a man, most seemly, most beauteous and most amiable that ever might be seen, clad in a mantle of purple silk, sitting upon her bedside, looking upon her with man's eyes so blessed a face that she was strengthened in all her spirit, and said to her these words: 'Daughter, why hast thou forsaken me, and I forsook never thee?' And anon, as He said these words, she saw verily how the air opened as bright as any lightning. And he rose up into the air, not right hastily and quickly, but fair and easily, so that she might well behold Him in the air till it was closed again."[166] At another time Christ invited her to be wife and daughter at once, as he would be son and husband: "Take me to thee as thy wedded husband, as thy dear worthy darling, and as thy sweet son, for I will be loved as a son should be loved by the mother and I will that thou lovest Me, daughter, as a good wife ought to love her husband."[167] To these blended roles of wife and daughter Kempe—a woman who had herself borne fourteen children—would add that of mother in her relations with the people she consoled and cared for. She would make them, as Jesus commanded, her children.

More common among holy women than the experience of God as mother or even father was this sensual experience of Christ—possibly encouraged by the eucharistic principle of the real presence of Jesus in bread that was tangibly incorporated into the body. Besides innumerable reports of eucharistic visions, many reports have come to us of physical, even erotic, encounters with Christ. Seventy-seven saints were brides of Christ, of whom fifty-two (twenty Franciscans and thirty-two Dominicans) received wedding rings and forty-three also received the stigmata, sharing in the wounds of the crucified.[168] Among the brides of Christ was the patient Bridget of Sweden, whom Jesus visited after the death of her husband and claimed for his own: "I have chosen you and gathered you to me as my bride, so that I may reveal to you my secrets, as it pleases me. You also, since you are rightly mine, since upon the death of your husband you assigned your will to my power, since also, his being dead, you have wished and begged to become a pauper for me, and to give me all things. . . . You therefore, my bride, if there is nothing except me that you desire, if you despise all things for me, not only children and parents, but also honors and wealth, I shall give you a most precious and sweet reward: not gold and silver do I give you for your reward but me myself as husband, I who am king of glory."[169]

More dramatic is the spiritual marriage that was experienced by Saint Catherine of Siena, the woman about whom more is known than any other in fourteenth-century Italy.[170] In the presence of the Virgin Mary, John the Evangelist, Saints Paul and Dominic, and King David, bearing the Psalter, Christ "with his own right hand took Catherine's right, and having a golden ring adorned with four most precious pearls and a very rich diamond, put it on Catherine's ring finger, saying these words: 'Behold I betrothe you to me in a faith which will endure from this moment forward forever immutable, until the glorious wedding in heaven, in perfect conjunction with me, in eternal marriage, when face to face you shall be allowed to see me and enjoy me entirely."[171] The love Catherine bore her spouse was so great that once her heart, overburdened, stopped. Jesus came to her and, opening his side, gave her his own heart, replacing in his own body her restored one, *lucido e rubicondo*, resplendent and aglow.[172] Catherine's experiences of Christ included those of absolute union. As she described it: "Many times my body was raised up from the earth for the perfect union of the soul with God, as if a heavy body had become light. But it is not that its own heaviness was taken away, but because the union that the soul had made with God is more perfect than the union between the soul and the body; and thus the strength of that spirit, united with mine, lifted up from the earth the heaviness of the body."[173]

Such experiences of rapture became a common feature of the profile of the Renaissance saint. The Roman saint Francesca Bussa de' Ponziani early in the next century was said to experience ecstasies and visions following the eucharistic act: "She remained rapt for two or three hours or more in a state of complete immobility, and insensible to such an extent, that if anyone touched her, she was not aware of it, so deeply was she absorbed in a union of infinite love with her divine Spouse."[174] Nearly a century later, Saint Catherine of Genoa (Caterina Fieschi Adorno) underwent in her long final "supernatural" illness a series of exhausting experiences: explosions of the fire of infinite love that racked her body and caused her to think the city was in flames; a ray of light that extended directly from her heart to God; a vision of paradise culminating in the extension of her body to form the sign of a cross: "and as she suffered crucifixion within, so she appeared without."[175] Fire piercing her heart and exploding around her and the sensation of furnace-high heat also afflicted the fourteenth-century German saint Dorothy of Montau.[176] The Franciscan holy woman Magdalena Beutler of Freiburg in 1430 suffered a mystical death (as she had accurately foretold) that was witnessed by a crowd, assembled for the purpose, that included at least seventeen of the city's governors.[177] Found apparently lifeless before the altar of her convent choir and exhorted to speak, she replied, barely audible, "My body is dead but my heart still lives." A night and a day and more she remained in this state until, having heard the recitation of the Passion, she cried out that her foot pained her, "and her foot was shown to those who stood by. Then a wound broke out on her foot, from which fresh blood ran out on to the ground, and the same thing happened to her hands."[178] She had descended into death and returned, was the conclusion of all observers, and had been blessed with the stigmata of the crucified Jesus.

The most famous visions and ecstasies of a Renaissance woman, perhaps, are those of the sixteenth-century Spanish Saint Teresa of Avila, who described them eloquently. "There grew a love of God within me," she writes, "that I did not know who had planted it there. It was entirely supernatural; I had made no efforts to obtain it. I found myself dying of the desire to see God, and I knew no way of seeking that other life except through death. This love came to me in mighty impulses which . . . robbed me of all power of action. Nothing gave me satisfaction, and I could not contain myself; I really felt as if my soul were being torn from me."[179] These impulses are uncontrollable and come unexpectedly, as though the worshipper is thrown into the burning fire of his own desire. "The soul makes no effort to feel the pain caused it by the Lord's presence, but is pierced to the depths of its entrails, or sometimes to the heart, by an arrow, so that it does not know what is wrong or what it desires. . . . It is impossible to describe or explain the way in which God wounds the soul, or the very great pain He inflicts on it, so that it hardly knows what it is doing. But this is so sweet a pain that no delight in the whole world can be more pleasing. The soul . . . would be glad always to be dying of this ill. . . . The entire body contracts; neither foot nor arm can be moved. If one is standing at the time, one falls into a sitting position as though transported, and cannot even take a breath. One only utters a few slight moans, not aloud, for that is impossible, but inwardly, out of pain."[180] In such a state, the saint was blessed with an especially mighty vision of an angel, depicted unforgettably in the marble of Bernini: "In his hands I saw a great golden spear, and at the iron tip there appeared to be a point of fire. This he plunged into my heart several times so that it penetrated to my entrails. When he pulled it out, I felt that he took them with it, and left me utterly consumed by the great love of God. The pain was so severe that it made me utter several moans. The sweetness caused by this intense pain is so extreme that one cannot possibly wish it to cease, nor is one's soul then content with anything but God."[181]

The mystical experiences of the Renaissance holy women were impressive to their contemporaries as proofs of sanctity, but so were their acts of penitence and ascetic observance. Repetitious prayer, endless genuflections, the wearing of hair shirts and other instruments of bodily mortification, sleeplessness, weeping and howling, self-mutilation, isolation, chronic illness produced by these austerities and by mental strife, and above all, self-starvation were the actions performed and the conditions suffered by the practitioners of the Christian life.[182] Colomba da Rieti wore, beneath her hair shirt, chains adorned with sharp points around her hips and across her breast. These so scarred and abused her body that three would-be rapists were deterred from their object and converted to awed reverence.[183] Elena of Udine wore a wreath of iron barbs on her head to remind her of the Lord's passion, and tied a thick cord around her neck so that, in imitation of Christ, she might be dragged about.[184] Francesca Bussa de' Ponziani whipped herself with a cord studded with iron pins until her blood gushed out. The same saint burned her genitals with hot candle wax or molten lard, wounding her-

self so that she could not move without feeling intolerable pain, thus en-
suring the loss of pleasure associated with the sexual intercourse
required of her married condition.[185] Margaret of Cortona, who before
her conversion was the mistress of a petty central Italian lord, had been
graced with enviable and sparkling beauty; this she sought to despoil
when, a penitent, she procured in her cell a razor with which to mutilate
her nose and upper lip.[186] Marie d'Oignies and Margery Kempe were
beset with uncontrollable weeping, and the blessed Angela of Foligno
with wild and uncontrollable screaming.[187] Dorothy of Montau passed
her nights not in sleep but in spiritual exercises, in imitation of Christ:
"shuffling about on her knees, crawling, arching her body in the air with
her forehead and feet on the floor, joining her hands in front of herself in
the form of a cross, falling on her face with her hands behind her back is if
they were bound."[188] Umiliana de' Cerchi sequestered herself in the
tower of her noble father's house; Smiralda (Eustochia Calafato of Messina) did so in a small cell in hers, built for her by the family, "where she
prayed night and day, never letting herself be seen by them or conversing
with them"; Colomba da Rieti did so in her room, upon the floor of
which (when she ran away) she left the abandoned vestment of a Dominican tertiary, folded cruciform; Catherine of Siena did so in her room,
or rather the "interior cell" of her heart, which her confessor had urged
her to "build" for herself to pursue her holy goals.[189]

Disfigured by pox and shorn hair, her flesh bitten by the chain she
had tied, while still immature, around her hips, this last Catherine ate
meagerly, and very nearly what she claimed: nothing. From adolescence,
she touched only water, bread, and raw herbs. Ten years later, she could
only chew the herbs before spitting them out. Her stomach could retain
"not even a bean," and at thirty-three, she died of starvation.[190] Saint
Catherine did incorporate in the stomach that would take no nourishment the noxious solids and fluids that presented themselves in her work
of giving: joyfully she drank the pus that exuded from the cancerous sores
on the breast of one of her patients.[191] The blessed Angela of Foligno
drank the water in which she had bathed a leper's rotting flesh,[192] and
Caterina Fieschi Adorno, nearly two hundred years later, did the same:
"She went and tended all the wounds and abscesses, and when her stomach heaved with nausea, she took in her mouth the pieces of flesh that she
had cleaned."[193] Though she survived to a good old age, the Genoese
Catherine fasted with Jesus in her visionary world one Lenten season,
ate during the three days of celebration, then fasted again, being unable

to retain food, another forty days.[194] The bread she required, the bread she would eat, was another bread. As she said in her *Treatise on Purgatory* (recorded by an amanuensis), if there were in all the world only one bread "which could satisfy the hunger of all creatures, just to see it alone would be satisfying. Thus, man by nature, if he is sound, has the instinct to eat it. And if he does not eat it and is neither sick nor dead, the hunger always increases. Knowing that this bread alone can satisfy him, he remains in intolerable pain."[195]

Fasting to extreme is the characteristic ascetic act of the Renaissance holy woman. Male saints might give up "money, property, and progeny; women gave up food."[196] These adepts of the spiritual life exceeded the injunctions to austerity found in Christian literature: theorists Greek and Roman, ancient and medieval, urged moderation—as did the confessors assigned to counsel their charges. Yet young virgins and widowed matrons alike might fast for cycles of forty days, or three times a week, or daily, with chronic physiological effects. Their bodies might in time reject all food, or the pattern of severe fasting might include either deliberate or spontaneous vomiting. Fasters often described their state by saying that they "could not" eat. They might eat only the Eucharist, or only eggs, or seven seeds for Christ's seven wounds, or bitter herbs for his suffering, or only food contaminated by loathsome objects, or nothing whatever. Regular digestion and menstruation ceased, but other products of the body—bits of skin, bone and entrails—could emanate sweet odors or work miracles. The body would become wasted (in some instances, as for Catherine of Siena and Colomba da Rieti, to the point of death), so that the chosen virginity of the holy woman consecrated to God would be enhanced by the asexual body achieved through self-starvation. Though only a handful of cases were this extreme, many women nevertheless engaged conscientiously in rigorous fasting practices: a striking 30 percent of all Italian holy women from the thirteenth to the seventeenth centuries, concentrated among the adherents of mendicant orders who fostered the resurgent female spirituality of these centuries.[197]

Beyond the well-known spiritual benefits thought to accrue from such bodily discipline, women apparently sought other goods from this behavior. The Eucharist was food. Abstention from ordinary food was the due preparation for the eucharistic act, the ingestion of the body of Christ, often accompanied by the ecstatic experience of union with him, perceived in some cases as perfect food.[198] But why did the imagery of eating, for women in particular, become central in Christ mysticism? Food purchase, preparation, and consumption was the central business of the familial environment from which consecrated women had come: to reject food was to affirm the vocation of holiness. Food may have loomed larger as a symbol in an epoch in which large numbers lived perpetually on the edge of starvation than it does in the West today, where superabundance poses a greater threat to well-being. Such a greater valuation of food would enhance any meaning its avoidance might have had to seekers of God. The consumption of food, finally, is one element of human existence that each controls for himself or herself—as the residents of northern Irish prisons or Chinese protestors in Tiananmen Square have understood. It requires no clerical intervention, and indeed avoids it. If one is powerless in all other regards (as, with respect to the *saeculum*, holy women might quite plausibly have perceived themselves), one still has power in this: not to eat, but to love. The discovery and empowerment of self that women found in the holy life could be mirrored in the flesh by the mastery of food, a link in the chain that made women slaves.

Women starved themselves and fed others. Penitence and service went hand in hand in an urban environment where, as was not the case in the cloister, the needy thronged and accepted, demanded, self-sacrifice. Saint Francesca Bussa de' Ponziani of Rome, with her sister-in-law Vannozza, tended the poor and sick in the streets of her city: "the more their poverty grew, to the same extent Francesca and Vannozza multiplied their services."[199] Their husbands took away the keys to the *granaio* and stored there in reserve what was needed for their families, selling the rest, fearful that their wives' uncontrollable generosity would leave them unprovisioned. Holy women tended to others not only with food but also with other kinds of service. They healed the sick, taught the young, inspired, and consoled. Marie d'Oignies spent her energies in a leprosarium, Catherine of Siena and Catherine of Genoa spent theirs in hospitals in their cities, Margaret of Cortona spent hers in the hospital for poor women she founded in her city, Jeanne de Chantal and the daughters of the Visitation spent theirs in seventeenth-century Paris. The scholar Giovanni Francesco Pico della Mirandola, nephew of the more famous philosopher Pico, revered for years the "deformed, subliterate, anorexic" holy woman Caterina de' Racconigi, who healed members of his family at the family castle.[200] Angela Merici and Mary Ward, already met in these pages, established networks of schools. Catherine of

Siena journeyed to console a condemned man, who then walked "like a gentle lamb" to his execution, at which "place of judgment" his last words were only "Jesus" and "Catherine." She delighted in the blood that spattered her garments: "When he was at rest, my soul so rested in peace and quiet, in such a fragrance of blood, that I couldn't bear to remove from me the blood that had fallen on me from him."[201]

Women served also by preaching and prophesying—missions which made them vulnerable to collision with official limitations on female action. Women, the pseudo-Pauline epistle enjoined, were to listen and not teach (1 Tim. 2:11–12) and the rule had been adopted as official policy. Jean Gerson warned: "every teaching of women, especially that expressed in solemn word or writing, is to be held suspect, unless it has been diligently examined, and much more than the teaching of men."[202] Many consecrated women whose attempts to teach doctrine aroused the notice of the authorities were cautioned. It was for daring to preach that the female practitioners labeled heretics by the church were often convicted. Censors pursued others whose offense fell short of heresy. One Seville *beata*, who often gave public reading and comment on the New Testament, when questioned by inquisitors, challenged the Pauline prohibition on female preaching, without consequence; but others brought before the Inquisition were penanced in 1624 for having presumed to direct male clerics as their "spiritual sons."[203]

A few holy women of exceptional charismatic power, it is true, were able to exercise considerable authority in the public realm. Saint Catherine of Siena exercised authority effectively as *mamma* to a "family" of disciples, whom she addressed as "sons" and instructed in matters of the spirit.[204] She harangued leaders of orders, cities, and states in her labors for the reform of the church. Bridget of Sweden, her contemporary and the other female arch-saint of the fourteenth century, chastised the king himself for his worldliness.[205] In the most famous episodes of their triumphal careers, Catherine and Bridget separately predicted the Great Schism of the church, pleaded for its restoration, and unreservedly rebuked the popes who presided over the bleeding community of the faithful. Their efforts helped bring Gregory XI from Avignon to Rome and to bolster the unstable Urban VI. Bridget thereafter established herself in Rome, persistent in her desire to attain papal approval for a new order of nuns, eventually attained in 1370: the Bridgettine, which flourished in the fifteenth century with its simple, austere, but reasonable rule, securely under female leadership.[206]

Catherine of Siena was a dervish of admonition and advice. She rebuked the English mercenary captain John Hawkwood for having worked so long in the Devil's service, and urged him, instead, to take up the cause of Crusade: "Now my soul wants you to change your course and enlist instead in the service and cross of Christ crucified, you and all your followers and companies."[207] She lectured Giovanna of Anjou, Queen of Naples, for her arrogance, and recommended to her, instead, the role of servant: "And no one, however powerful, or wealthy, or well-born, can evade the duty of serving this sweet Lord Jesus."[208] Pardon me, Daddy (*Babbo*), Catherine wrote to the flaccid Pope Gregory XI, for "what I have said to you and am saying; I am constrained by the Sweet Primal Truth to say it. His will, father is this. . . . It demands that you execute justice on the abundance of many iniquities committed by those who are fed and pastured in the garden of the Holy Church. . . . Since He has given you authority and you have assumed it, you should use your virtue and power; and if you are not willing to use it, it would be better for you to resign what you have assumed."[209] Catherine's ideal was a standard to which she was prepared to hold all the possessors of power and glory: "a bulwark of personal integrity and autonomy over against church and world."[210]

Evidently, these holy women whose lives were marked by pain and supernatural experience, by deprivation and sacrificial service, earned (like none of their sex except a very few daughters of monarchs) unparalleled stature.[211] In pre-Tridentine Italy, "divine madri" or "holy mothers" won the attention of male hierarchies for their prophecies about pope and church.[212] Holy women inspired learned men to write their lives—not just semiliterate confessors and followers, but scholars like Francesco Giorgi, author of *On the Harmony of the Whole World*, who wrote the life of the Venetian visionary Chiara Bugni (d. 1514), or Pietro Barozzi, noted bishop of Padua and author of works of theology, devotion, philosophy, and political science, who wrote the life of the blessed Eustochio (d. 1469), holy virgin of Barozzi's generation and city.[213] Giovanni Francesco Pico, already noted as an admirer of Caterina de' Racconigi, wrote her *Life*, and the high-placed Cardinal Federigo Borromeo wrote that of Caterina Vannini (d. 1606).[214] The early Beguine Marie d'Oignies so impressed the formidable cleric and cardinal Jacques de Vitry that not only did he accompany her in awe and write her life, but he proceeded for the rest of his career to be a protector and proponent of the *mulieres sanctae* who had begun to sprout so abundantly in the fertile soil of Flanders and Italy.[215] Raymond of Capua, the confessor of Catherine of Siena who wrote the *Legenda* of her life that would circulate widely in Latin and in vernacular translations, became the Master General of the Dominican Order.

Not only learned and prominent persons, but crowds of the faithful were awed by holy women. Such a crowd observed Catherine of Siena in Rome, as she promoted with her austerities the cause of the whole church. Citizens of Freiburg, the governors as well as the governed, stood about as Magdalena Beutler received the wounds of Christ. In the last decade of the twentieth century, worshippers still come to revere, in Bologna, the incorrupt body of their Saint Catherine (Caterina Vegri); in Brescia, the undamaged body of their Angela Merici. Of the Bolognese saint's preserved corpse, her contemporary Fra Girolamo Savonarola would write:

> From a thousand directions the people run
> To see your body, on the strength of only rumor.
> Although you are dead, your body seems alive
> And seems to recall your soul.
> Everyone who sees it is amazed
> And filled with wonder does it homage.[216]

Everywhere in these centuries female worshippers of God aroused awe for their heroic asceticism, their unstinting service, their otherworldly visions, their inner power. These are surely the heroines of the Renaissance, the daughters of Mary both virgin and fertile, *dolorosa* in giving birth and in beholding her child's torture and slaughter. The daughters of Mary were also the lovers of Jesus, who exchanged, in the moments of vision when they became united to his body and his blood, their femininity for his masculinity, their passivity for his activity: "the feminine, the all-nurturing blood, is discovered to be the origin of the efficacy of the sacrifice of Christ," and "the hierarchy of male dominance is subverted."[217] In such visions the female sex is validated and empowered to act in the world. Thus women transcended the utter passivity of the chastity, silence, and obedience imposed on them more absolutely than on male lovers of God to embrace the profound experience of divine illumination and to enjoy the high reputation awarded, in their world, above all to the holy.

So great was the stature that holiness conferred that many women sought stature by feigning holiness or were accused of doing so. Churchmen worked hard to rout out fraudulent saints. Women were to be investigated with special diligence, the prelate Jean Gerson had urged, "because they are easily seduced."[218] An eminent theologian and famed proponent of conciliarism, Gerson specialized in the important matter of testing the validity of visionary experience. He authored two books on the subject—the *De distinctione verarum visionum a falsis* and the *De probatione spirituum*. Invited to help decide, during the Council of Constance in 1415, on the reliability of the visions of Saint Bridget of Sweden, he was unimpressed; but he thought favorably, when asked in 1429, about those of Joan d'Arc. The examiners of the latter hinged on the issue of false sanctity: were the spirits to which she had such free access from God or the devil? In both cases, other experts disagreed with Gerson; Bridget was canonized, Joan burned.[219]

The ecstasies experienced by the seventeenth-century nun Benedetta Carlini of Pescia had "put her in the category of privileged women."[220] In due course, her claims to sanctity would awaken the skepticism of authorities and subject her to lengthy examination and life-long punishment. Ecclesiastical officials denounced the "vanity and falsity of her ecstasies," and revealed the marks of the stigmata (which she had renewed herself, with a needle) to be "the work of the devil." Not the least of the charges was that she had pretended to be an angel so as to seduce one sister into performing with her "the most immodest acts."[221] Carlini spent thirty-five years in prison, until released by death and dressed again in the habit of a nun. Her treatment mirrored that assigned two generations earlier to the Lisbon visionary and nun María de la Visitación. Graced with the stigmata, she had been consulted by the mighty on quite serious matters until her fraudulence was uncovered. For her crime, she was condemned to perpetual imprisonment, unbreakable silence, twice-weekly flogging, and humiliations in feeding and treatment by her fellows.[222] Saint Teresa of Avila's frequent visions of the glorified Christ were doubted by her confessors. One advised her to make the sign of the Cross and snap her fingers at the intrusive vision. "Many," she wrote, "were the reproaches and trials that I suffered when I spoke of this, and many were my fears and persecutions. They felt so certain of my being possessed by a devil that some of them wanted to exorcise me."[223] Late in Carlini's century, Orsola Giuliani (Saint Veronica) was pestered to revise her autobiography repeatedly and advised to keep a detailed diary for thirty-three years by confessors who doubted the validity of her visions; her extant manuscripts total more than twenty-two thousand pages, and could not satisfactorily resolve the question.[224] Of fourteen *beatas* brought before the Inquisition in Seville from 1480 to 1650, eight were charged with (among other things), false visions, false revelations, false prophesies, false ecstasies.[225] The *beata* María de las Dolores Lopez was hanged and burned, successively, in the same city, midway between the American and the French struggles for the inalienable rights of man, denounced by her confessor as a pseudo-saint. In that late year of 1781, a blind autodidact, she was the first and last *mistificatrice* to be executed by any Mediterranean Inquisition.[226]

Real and feigned, validated or discredited, holiness in women surged in the Renaissance centuries, in numbers and in the consciousness of the holy and their worshippers. This age of commercial aggression and mental strife was an age of female sanctity. "The realm of the holy . . . was populated with female figures": the saints, the virginal Mary, and God our mother.[227] God was reachable (according to males as well as females: witness Bernard of Clairvaux) by love rather than reason. Women seekers of the divine could thrive in this environment of affective spirituality "which expressed itself in images of growth, nurture and feeding and love, erotic and filial."[228] These were "particularly fertile times for female religious leaders."[229] The counts suggest a swelling of female sanctity in the Renaissance. One scholar finds 260 Italian holy women (not only saints, but also those known as "blessed" or "vener-able") active from 1200 to the present; of these, 152 died in the four-teenth through seventeenth centuries. Another finds the percentage of women among the saints rising from just under 10 percent around 1100, to 15 percent around 1250, to 24 percent by 1300, to 29 percent for the fifteenth century.[230] Another compares male to female sums (the males were always more numerous), noting the twofold increase in the propor-tion of women in the early Renaissance. At the same time, the require-ments for sanctity became tougher; only 87 saints of the 3,276 for all of Christian history to the end of 1500 emerged during the last 150 years of that epoch. During the whole of that span, there were slightly more than five male saints to each female; but after the mid-fourteenth century, there were only about two and a half.[231] From 1305 through 1500, writes another authority, women pulled ahead of men among lay saints (al-though men still predominated when clerics—who were mostly male—were included): about 55 percent of those canonized.[232] In no other period from the time of Christ until the eve of the Reformation did wom-en weigh so greatly in the balance of sanctity.

The Family and the Holy

Not all Renaissance saints were women, but sainthood became in these years a feminine endeavor—for the sound reasons, no doubt, that we have seen (as well as for the assuredly true reason the saints themselves gave: the profound sinfulness of the world). The status that could be gained by a female saint, virginal or celibate, exceeded that which could be gained by a mother of children, a wife of men, or a daughter of a patriarch. Sanctity offered an honorable refuge from the anonymity and subservience of life in the family. Would-be saints determinedly fled their fathers, husbands, and suitors. Cecilia Gonzaga, who avoided a husband; Isabella Roser, who survived hers and disposed of her children; and the young nuns in the care of Caritas Pirckheimer, who resisted the order of a reforming town council to return to their families, have already been encountered. They were not merely willing, but determined, nuns who wish to release themselves from earthly ties. Sor Isabella's fifty-two sisters, enclosed and guarded, clearly formed a family more satisfactory than the one she had left behind. The examples can be amply multiplied. Although traditional nuns were often placed in convents by the will of their fathers, women pursuing the holy life, particularly in its nontraditional forms (and it is precisely these that flourished during the Renaissance), more frequently did so in spite of families or in their absence. The holy women of the Renaissance were more often married or widowed than in earlier periods, so that their spiritual mission had to struggle with their sexual role. Female holiness was closely related to the rupture of the ordinary female condition of familial existence.[233]

In the thirteenth century, Marie d'Oignies, from a wealthy family, married at fourteen but later separated voluntarily from her husband, who followed her lead in serving the leper colonies of Flanders. Christine of Stomeln ran away from an impending marriage, and at age twelve sought to join the Beguines of Cologne.[234] The main concern of the parents of Ivetta of Huy was that she should marry well; left a widow with three children after five years of an unsatisfactory marriage, she turned to the religious life. Ludgard of Aywières was permitted (by her mother's intervention) to enter a convent at age twelve rather than be committed to a worldly marriage.[235] Jacques de Vitry defined four types of religious women in the area of Liège with a twist on the usual categories of female social status: they were first, the "holy virgins," brides of Christ, pledged to poverty having rejected the riches of their parents;

second, the holy matrons, who lived with and guarded for the heavenly bridegroom the chastity of the virgins; third, the widows, who through prayer, ascetic acts, and works of mercy attempted to please Christ even more than they had once pleased their husbands; and fourth, those with husbands still living who were pledged to continence. Marriage, in this contemporary description, is rejected by those who have outlived it, by those who seek to avoid it, and by those who are still, while inwardly free, officially bound by it.[236]

The leitmotif of the flight from marriage and family is encountered in Italy as well as the north. Umiliana de' Cerchi, who hadn't wanted to marry in the first place, was widowed while still young, sent back childless to her father's house, deprived of her dowry first by her husband's family and then by her father, and resisted a second marriage planned by that patriarch, preferring, she told her hostile brethren, to walk into a roaring fire.[237] When Saint Clare was converted by Saint Francis to the *vita apostolica*, the well-born young woman was seventeen, attractive, and marriageable. It was her chosen alternative to what would have been a substantial marriage.[238] Her sister Agnes ran away to join Clare's community of female followers of Francis and was very nearly abducted with main force by male relatives. Her body became mysteriously heavy (as though, the would-be abductors said, she had eaten lead all night) and could not be removed.[239] The brothers of Saint Chiara Gambacorta had more success. Married at seven and widowed at fifteen, Chiara was forcibly removed from the convent where she had taken refuge and imprisoned in her house until she would agree to remarry. She resisted, and at last her father permitted her to become a Dominican nun, and promised to build her a convent.[240]

Catherine of Siena, Colomba da Rieti, Orsola Giuliani (Saint Veronica)—all fought their families to win freedom from marriage obligations. Still more common was the story of Maria (Sturion) da Venezia, who went dutifully to a husband at age fifteen but returned happily the next year to her natal home (the husband having gone off) to experience a conversion and undertake a holy life of mild austerity and charitable work in the Dominican orbit.[241] What to others appeared to be the harsh deprivation of the consecrated life "became for the saint a liberating transformation of family contest into eternal triumph."[242] For some, perhaps, the alternative to family was not even the lofty prize of eternal salvation, but the more modern and familiar one of personal liberation. At the end of the seventeenth century, the Mexican nun Sor Juana Inés de la

Cruz, whose prodigious intellectual talents went unaccompanied by the more usual spiritual gifts, found serenity in a convent cell equipped with her scientific and musical instruments and her own splendid library. She explained to a prying bishop why she had sought the shelter of those walls: "I became a religious because, although I knew that that estate entailed things very repugnant to my temperament . . ., it was, given the total aversion which I felt toward matrimony, the least unsuitable and the most honorable I could choose."[243]

If married or otherwise engaged in sexual ties, holy women could be what seems to modern eyes quite uninvolved with their families. Bridget of Sweden, married against her will at age thirteen and mother subsequently of eight children, prayed in advance of each coition that the act would be procreative and free from sin; as soon as was possible—when she reached age forty—she and her husband agreed to a mutual vow of chastity.[244] Marie d'Oignies, Margery Kempe, Francesca Bussa de' Ponziani, and Caterina Fieschi Adorno all made arrangements with their husbands to live continent lives, in the same household or in the same service of God. Margery Kempe, the daughter of the most politically prominent burgess in the town of Lynn, was married unsatisfactorily to one of the town's solid businessmen.[245] Her first pregnancy and birth were marked by exceptional and intolerable pain and were followed by severe illness, and, after an unsatisfactory session with her priestly adviser, a total nervous breakdown. The story of "this creature's" dark depression (as Kempe refers to herself throughout) begins with the second sentence of her *Book*: "And after she had conceived, she was belaboured with great accesses [illnesses] till the child was born and then, what with the labour she had in childbirthing and the sickness going before, she despaired of her life, weening [believing] she might not live."[246] Immediately following an awkward confession leaving Kempe unclear about the state of her soul, "this creature went out of her mind and was wondrously vexed and laboured with spirits for half a year, eight weeks and odd days."[247] Demons thronged, bidding her to deny God and friends. She thought often of suicide, and frequently punished her body with nails and teeth. Jesus appeared to her with comforting words, and Kempe came to her senses again. Thereafter, she decided "that she was bound to God and that she would be His servant."[248] The crisis that led her to embark on her spiritual quest was caused by childbirth, and the quest could not be pursued in truth until burdens of children and husband were put aside. That release did not occur immediately. Her subsequent pregnancies, which led to the births of fourteen children, drove her to physical collapse and mental despair. She and her husband agreed to cease sexual relations, after twenty years of marriage, in 1413; the bargain was that Margery would agree to overlook Friday's fast, bartering food for sex.[249] Kempe nursed her husband in his last years, and the imagery of nurture and home comforts adorns her spiritual writings. Within the family shell, she absented herself from the family.

Francesca Bussa de' Ponziani observed within her well-stocked household the discipline of the saint and experienced the visions and ecstasies of sainthood. While still appearing to carry out family obligations to the letter, her real commitment was elsewhere. She greeted the death of her son Evangelista (at age seven) with unusual equanimity, and shortly afterwards had a vision of the impending death of her younger daughter, Agnese. An angel announced to the mother that the little one would soon join the angels in heaven who were made by the souls of innocent children. Following the vision, Bussa treated her with special love and respect, "no longer as her daughter, but like a bride destined to Jesus Christ, giving thanks to God that he had deigned to call her to himself."[250] And indeed, soon afterward, Agnese did die, in her fifth year. So detached was this mother from her children that she escorted them to the door of death.

The death of an unwanted husband was a relief for several holy women. The German Dorothy of Montau (1347–94) married at sixteen, bore nine children, and survived her brutal and abusive husband to live as an anchoress, walled off in a cell in the cathedral at Marienwerder.[251] The Genoese Saint Catherine was driven to suicidal desolation by the persecution of her worthless husband. With his early death, she won her postponed freedom.[252] Margaret of Cortona, who must have mourned the sudden loss of her noble lover, undertook the life of a recluse and abandoned to acquaintances their illegitimate child (who embraced, once grown, the career of a Franciscan tertiary). Angela of Foligno was simply relieved by the deaths of her entire immediate family. "And as this time, God willing, it happened that my mother, who was a great impediment for me, died; and within a short time after this my husband and all my children were dead. And since I had embarked on the aforesaid path and had prayed God that they would die, I felt great consolation at their deaths. And I thought that from then on, after God had done these things for me, that my heart would always be within God's heart, and God's heart always within mine."[253]

The suggestion has been made and often repeated that the large involvement of women in religious activity beginning in the thirteenth and fourteenth centuries was due to the disproportionately great number of nubile but unmarried, widowed, or unmarriageable women.[254] This demographic explanation is persuasive: women lived longer on the average than men in this violent era, and certainly many could not, as we have seen, be dowered by overburdened families. Both processes resulted in a superfluity of women, who could in turn find a dignified refuge from such demographic pressures in the religious life. But the assumption underlying this explanation is that more women would have married if they could have. How then are we to understand the numerous cases of women who escaped from marriage, from sexuality, from domestic responsibility, from the torments of engagement through the flesh, to the far less toilsome engagements of the spirit? Another explanation might be that women sought dignity and autonomy, and in the landscape of late medieval and Renaissance culture, those commodities were made available to women only in one of the many, all strenuous, forms of the holy life. More than twice as many women as men seemed to suffer from conflicts relating to sexuality.[255] These women were fleeing, it seems, not only the social values enshrined in their families, but also from the families themselves: they were struggling "against the familial order in general" for personal salvation.[256] Medieval heresies appealed to those (especially women) who sensed hostility to the families that could not care for them, and thus alienation from the prevailing culture.[257] Renaissance holiness seems to have had the same appeal. Women could find in the convent or the beguinage or in a little cell not only the freedom to pursue their goals in dignity, but also the freedom from those forces that rendered their condition "dismal":[258] the risks and burdens of family existence, whose very basis was the sexual relations from which virginity, if it offered nothing else, meant release. For if daughters were a growing problem for the families of the Renaissance who had to maintain and dower them, as a wise observer has remarked, families were a growing problem for daughters, who had to endure the strategies in which they were always pawns and never principals.[259]

Women and the Reform

With Protestantism, the landscape changed. For those women whose fathers and husbands and cities and hearts embraced Reform, the option of life in a female community dedicated to sanctity disappeared. Reformers rejected the celibate standard of traditional Catholicism, the bulwark of the clerical orders that were a principal target of their activism. They valued marriage with a new conviction, and as former priests rushed out to court wives, they urged all women to form productive marital ties.[260] Martin Luther opened the convents and himself married a former nun. He condemned "all who despise the female sex," and announced that women possessed one good that "covers and conceals" all their weaknesses: "the womb and birth."[261] Barrenness, not childbearing, was a curse, and sexual union he saw as "an honorable pleasure."[262] A wife brought many good things to a man: "the blessing of the Lord, children, community of all things and other things so good that they might overwhelm a man."[263] John Calvin, too, found in the Old Testament authority for a reevaluation of marriage as a companionable and honorable state. Wives must show obedience to their husbands, he cautioned, but the family regime was to be "more that of a society than of a kingdom."[264] For Martin Bucer, marriage was central to a society under God.[265] Catholicism had posed two goods for women: the greater one of fruitful virginity, the lesser one of procreative marriage. Protestantism posed only one: the latter. For woman en masse, the Reformation above all else was a revolution in the nature of her responsibility to the family. Women who wished to pursue the spiritual life would do so, ideally, amid household hubbub, the homely clank of pots and pans.

And many of these were needed to feed the eight or nine children of Wibrandis Rosenblatt, widowed in 1532 by the reformer Oecolampadius, in 1541 by the reformer Wolfgang Capito, and in 1550 by the reformer Martin Bucer.[266] The important work of these men was given a foundation of joy and labor by this tireless woman. The Italian refugee Pietro Vermigli described the hospitality he received in Bucer's house in 1542, the consequence of Wibrandis's efforts although the hostess is wholly unacknowledged: "It is like a hostel," he reported, with ample food and godly observances.[267] Katharine Zell, the daughter of a Strasbourg carpenter and the wife of the former priest and Protestant pastor Matthias Zell, also thrived in this new social environment as a homemaker (though not as a mother) and a companion in intellectual and pastoral work.[268] She was challenged to take a public stand nearly from the very start of their union. When her husband's decision to marry was challenged by the representatives of the old church, she defended his right to do so and her own to speak forth on the issue in a competent treatise that marshalled both economic and theological arguments.[269] Childless, she toiled during her marriage and as a widow to care for visitors, prisoners, lepers—all those in need, and in large numbers. For a year and a half following the suppression of the Peasant's War, she managed the care and feeding of three thousand refugees, including the wives and children of the slaughtered. Toward the end of her life, she summed up her work in a letter to the "entire citizenry" of Strasbourg. "That I learned to understand and helped to acknowledge the Gospel I shall let God declare. That I married my pious husband and for this endured slander and lies, God knows. The work which I carried on both in the house and out is known both by those who already rest in God and those who are still living, how I helped to establish the Gospel, took in the exiled, comforted the homeless refugees, furthered the church, preaching and the schools, God will remember even if the world may forget or did not notice . . . I honored, cherished and sheltered many great, learned men, with care, work and expense . . . I listened to their conversation and their preaching, I read their books and their letters and they were glad to receive mine . . . and I must express how fond I was of all the old, great learned men and founders of the Church of Christ, how much I enjoyed listening to their talk of holy things and how my heart was joyful in these things."[270]

As in the case of Katherine Zell, in some marriages it was possible for women to live a rich spiritual life in defiance of the old Church's claim that the flesh was an impediment to the spirit. Together, husband and wife could read Scripture, spiting the old priestly order.[271] Even outside of the companionate marriage, Protestantism afforded an independence to some women that was not available in Catholicism: and women who had acquired some independence found it an attractive option. But not all women entered the reform led by a husband: some entered first, or on their own initiative, reflecting "in a new sphere the scope and independence that the women's lives had already had."[272] For those whose abilities and interests inclined them to intellectual endeavors, Protestantism was attractive because it encouraged the reading of Scripture and the comprehension of abstract theological concepts previously closed not only to women, but also to the laity. And how wonderful it must have been for women, for the first time in European history, to sing religious song in medley with male voices.[273]

More frequently, however, Protestantism resulted in a "social demotion" for women.[274] It unseated the priest and the confessor as the governor of the female conscience and replaced him with the patriarch. That patriarch possessed, as he always had, social and economic control of the family, but he now gained the power of the keys. It was he who read the gospel, decided innocence or guilt, and mediated with God. Within their own families, women were secondary citizens—and families they had to have. Protestant theory distrusted single women and female communities alike. Since Protestants doubted that women could remain celibate, women in both those alternative situations were subject to the suspicion of whoredom. Under these circumstances, women could hardly act together to advance their condition. They had the more pressing problem of survival to face. The option of the convent was denied to those who didn't wish to marry. More women appear to have married in Protestant England than in, for instance, Catholic Italy. In the seventeenth century, in the classes below the elite, perhaps 10 percent of all mature women were spinsters. In the late sixteenth, more than 95 percent of peers' daughters who survived to adulthood married, but that figure dropped considerably by 1700 to 75 percent. Pressures for marriage were severe, as the condition of not being married had become censured and difficult.[275]

Protestantism limited choices, and closed off that one in particular which, at the cost of abnegation of the flesh, had for some purchased dignity and solitude. The possibility of freedom of conscience remained (as it did for Catholics, once Protestantism posed itself as an alternative), but for that freedom (and this hasn't changed), man or woman could pay a fearsome price. Martyrs accumulated on both sides, indeed on all sides, as radical sects added to the complexity of confessional struggle. Among these sufferers were many women. Of the 275 Protestants who suffered under England's Queen Mary, 55 were female, and nearly all of them were poor (elite Protestants fled to the Continent to avoid persecution); in contrast, only three of the 189 Catholics who suffered under Mary's sister and successor, Elizabeth, were women—largely because her persecution targeted clergymen or missionaries, necessarily male.[276]

In the sects and cults of radical Protestantism, more than in the sober burger life of the mainstream cities, women found possibilities of spirit exceeding those that had been allowed by the patterns of Catholic sanctity. The attraction of radical Protestantism resembled that of the old heresies. Central to one branch of Anabaptist thinking was the principle of antinomianism: those whom God had saved were released from the laws of men. The doctrine appealed to many women in the sixteenth century, as had earlier versions of it in Albigensian and Free Spirit heresies in the thirteenth and fourteenth centuries. Margarette Prüss, a printer's daughter and twice married to a printer, was able to diffuse Anabaptist literature in Strasbourg through her press, and allowed her daughter's marriage to the Spiritualist Sebastian Franck.[277] In the same city, the Anabaptist prophets Ursula Jost and Barbara Rabstock had considerable influence.[278] In Antwerp, however, execution was the fate of the Anabaptist Elisabeth Munstdorp in 1573. She left a testamentary letter to her infant daughter, urging her not to be ashamed of her parents (Elisabeth's husband had already died), and to follow God and thereby receive the crown of eternal life: "this crown I wish you and the crucified, bleeding, naked, despised, rejected and slain Jesus Christ for your bridegroom."[279] This daughter of a radical reforming sectary was inspired to the same mystical fulfillment as desired by contemporary Catholic saints.

It was not merely for their beliefs that some women sectaries were persecuted, but for their daring to teach: an activity, when performed by women, that neither Catholic nor Protestant males could accept. Anne Hutchinson of the Massachusetts Bay Colony dared to teach theological doctrine, sometimes to as many as sixty or eighty visitors at a time, male and female, in her own small parlor. The male Puritan establishment disapproved. Brought before the General Court, she defended the public role she had played, citing Scripture and faring well in the war of wits against her male clerical accusers. Only when she professed to have had a direct revelation from God, thereby claiming an extrascriptural communication of religious truth, did her defence collapse. "We do not mean to discourse with those of your sex," Governor Winthrop rebuked her during the inquiry.[280] Charged with antinomianism, she was banished from the Boston church and forced to leave Massachusetts, one of the first of those colonies dedicated to the principle of religious freedom. The young English noblewoman Anne Askew, who would be crippled by torture and then executed in 1546 for her denial that the Eucharist was the real body of Christ, was first examined on her right to speak. She frustrated her examiners with her knowledge of Scripture and, to their fury, added some qualifying notes of her own to the text of the statement of faith they compelled her to sign.[281] Elizabeth Dirks, the wife of the Anabaptist Menno Simons, was seized in Holland in 1549. The discovery in her home of a Latin testament caused one of her captors to call out: "We've got the right one. We've caught the teacher." In prison, she was examined. Since she would swear no oath but only, elusively, quote the Gospel in response to questions, the accusation was repeated: "Now we see you are a teacher because you make yourself equal to Christ." In the course of her interrogation, she taught her Catholic examiners about baptism, grace, and the priesthood of Christ alone. She was tied in a sack and drowned.[282]

Anabaptists generally eliminated distinctions based on sex, and their priesthood could include women. Quaker women, with the approval of their leaders, sought to preach and teach.[283] Of the 300 female visionaries who took advantage of the Lord Protector Cromwell's policy of freedom to worship, preach, and publish in England, 220 were Quakers.[284] Men and women had been created equally in the image of God, such women claimed, and though subjected to men as a result of the Fall, as a consequence of Christ's restoration, women were once again raised to equality with men. Aware of the God within, and possessing a spark of divine life, they were empowered as much as men, they argued, to communicate their faith. The secular authorities did not agree. In 1653 two Quaker women went to Cambridge to speak forth the word of God to the students and professors who considered themselves the bastion of orthodox Christianity. The Mayor of Cambridge had them whipped; they were the first Quakers to be so treated. Two others challenged Oxford, where they were attacked by a crowd of students: there "they suffered by the black tribe of scholars—for they dragged them first through a dirty pool, afterwards had them to a pump, and holding their mouths to the pump, endeavored to pump water thereinto with other shameful abuses."[285]The principle that women as much as men should be allowed to discourse in public, which had always been opposed by Catholic and Protestant alike, was central to the Quaker philosophy. George Fox, the founder of the Quaker community known properly as the Society of Friends, staunchly defended women's right to receive the Spirit and to speak from its power. He married Margaret Fell, who argued the point in print in 1666: *Women's Speaking, Justified, Proved, and Allowed of by the Scriptures.*[286] The inner light empowered women as much as men—if only because they were equally "weak" and "naked" before God—and to it alone they would be obedient.

Such obedience to the inner voice of conscience in spite of the external authority of worldly power enabled some extraordinary women to become true knights of the Protestant revolution. In France, where they were forbidden by law to inherit the throne, a few high-ranking noblewomen played key roles in the wars of religion between the old church and Calvin's new one: "representatives of the most privileged class and the less privileged sex."[287] Jeanne d'Albret is the most remarkable of these: she was the daughter of the evangelical proto-reformer Marguerite d'Angoulême (herself the sister of the king of France) and the mother of the Henri de Navarre who would think Paris worth a mass and become the fourth French monarch of that name. D'Albret established Calvinism in her province, which she controlled as widowed regent for her son, and took part in the political and military maneuvers that mark the history of that nation in the sixteenth century. Militant in her defense of her faith, she would not (like Renée de France later) consent to the cold-blooded slaughter of her opponents. She is one of only three sixteenth-century monarchs who never martyred anyone for his faith.[288] Marguerite had willed a reformer's mission to her daughter, as Jacqueline de Longwy, Duchess of Montpensier, and Charlotte de Laval, wife of the Huguenot leader Gaspard de Coligny, had bequeathed Protestant loyalty to theirs: respectively, Charlotte de Bourbon and Louise de Coligny, who fled dangerous France for the Protestant Netherlands, where they became in turn the third and fourth wives of William of Orange.[289]

The same self-determined spirit that empowered Jeanne d'Albret and others of her ilk guided Protestant sympathizers in Italy to profound and dangerous commitments of conscience. Renée de France, daughter of King Louis XII, would have been king, as she put it, if she had had a beard.[290] Instead, her brother-in-law ascended the throne and she was married, as part of the usual dynastic strategies, to Ercole d'Este, Duke of Ferrara, and thus exiled, as she saw it, to Italy. In her childhood, Renée had dwelled in the happy circle of Marguerite d'Angoulême. Her inclinations were Protestant, and from the year she met John Calvin, in 1536, until his death in 1564, Calvin wrote her letters attempting to bolster these inclinations. At the Ferrarese court (as it was generally known) she sheltered evangelicals and proto-reformers of the sort that flourished in France and northern Italy during the dawn of the Reformation. Among the "heretics" who had gathered there by 1536 were Clément Marot and Calvin himself, and Renée's personal secretary was a known heretic. Her circle also included Olimpia Morata, daughter of the court physician Pellegrino Morata and companion to Renée's own daughter, who was to flee with a young German physician to a life of witness in the north. To have so prominent a protectress of the heterodox in so prominent a court as Ferrara was intolerable in the inquisitorial climate that prevailed on the eve of the Council of Trent. Examiners launched a campaign to pressure this duchess of royal blood to affirm her orthodoxy. The French king dispatched to Ferrara a French inquisitor whose special mission was to harness the runaway princess. From Geneva, Calvin dispatched a Protestant minister to inspire her to steadfastness. Threatened with the loss of her ancestral lands, she was kept under house arrest and her children were taken away. Finally, pressured beyond endurance, in 1554 she summoned the inquisitor and announced that she was ready to hear mass. Her "conversion" to Catholic orthodoxy was surely a superficial accommodation to events. As soon as she was freed by her husband's death from her obligations to the people of Ferrara, she returned to France (in 1558) and to the reformed faith. A Calvinist pastor at her side, she protected the Huguenot victims of the armies of her daughter's husband, the Duke of Guise, leader of the Catholic party.

Humanists of the Italian Renaissance such as Lorenzo Valla and philosophers such as Giovanni Pico della Mirandola and Marsilio Ficino had set in motion currents of ideas that anticipated and blended with those of the early reformers north of the Alps. Conscientious churchmen, among them the highly cultivated who had imbued these traditions, were committed to the reform of the church whose many abuses had become intolerable by the late quattrocento. Gasparo Contarini, Gian Matteo Giberti, Jacopo Sadoleto, and the leaders of the Oratory of Divine Love made up a circle that was the locus of a body of commitments and values called "evangelical." These inspired many productive movements within the Catholic reformation (Angela Merici's order, for instance), as well as activity that would come to be labeled heretical. In the period prior to the establishment of the Roman Inquisition in 1542, followers of these evangelical notions, women as well as men, did not think of themselves as Protestants or heretics but as genuine Christians, pure and simple. Vittoria Colonna, one of the century's finest poets, a Neoplatonist in the tradition of Marsilio Ficino, a correspondent of Michelangelo's, entertained in conventual seclusion (so much in the pattern of the saints of her age!) proto-reform doctrines.[291] Influenced by Bernardino Ochino, the Capuchin who influenced so many evangelicals, she reveals in a series of sonnets that she had adopted evangelical notions of the justification by faith and the theology of Christ crucified. More practically, she had learned from Ochino the course of witness in the world, of living a holy life without joining an order or following a rule: "she lived in convents, but she did not take the veil."[292] At Rome and then Viterbo, she was the center of an evangelical circle that entertained dangerous notions during the last moments of such liberty in Italy. In the shadow of the Spanish monarchy, however, on the eve of Trent, the Inquisition came to Rome, and the Reform's first growth in Italy was struck down. Some died and many fled, as did Ochino. Just before his flight to the north, he sent from Florence a last letter to Vittoria Colonna, examining his options.[293] Ochino had counted on her support, or at least her tacit understanding, but the spiritual mission Colonna had shaped for herself evidently did not include the risk of implication as a heretic. She passed the letter, unopened, to her intimate, Cardinal Reginald Pole, a reformer but a staunch Catholic, a victim himself of the Protestant regime in England. From Pole, it reached the hands of the inquisitors. Colonna herself was believed to be a secret believer, an "accomplice of heretics," but avoided prosecution and died, neither Protestant nor Catholic, just in time to avoid a final commitment.[294]

Other refugees were women. Isabella Bresegna, plucked from the inquisitors by Giulia Gonzaga (of whom more below), resettled in Switzerland; there she in turn was a friend to compatriots and coreligionists—Bernardino Ochino, Pier Paolo Vergerio the younger, and Celio Secondo Curione—and protector of other refugees. When she followed her conscience north, she left her husband and son behind her, importunate for her return.[295] Olimpia Morata, raised at the court of Ferrara under Renée de France, fled to Germany with her Lutheran husband and courageously witnessed her devotion to the new faith in the siege of Schweinfurt.[296] She would die as a consequence of her harsh experience in escaping from that cataclysm. The first edition of her works was dedicated to Bresegna, who had like Morata risked everything to persevere in her faith.

There now remained in Italy few committed evangelicals, male or female. The Tridentine reformation absorbed the energy of many former evangelicals, and those who could not accommodate themselves to the old church generally preferred not to stay and be burned. Giulia Gonzaga, however, took that risk.[297] Daughter of the ruling clan of Mantua, she married Vespasiano Colonna at age fourteen and was widowed two years later. In a villa halfway between Rome and Naples, she became the center of a literary circle. Under the influence especially of the protoreformer Juan de Valdés (already expelled from his native Spain as a heretic), she became a determined evangelical.[298] At the same time, in the pattern of Catholic sanctity, she dedicated herself to perpetual chastity and joined the *clarisse* at San Francesco delle Monache in Naples, living attached to a convent while retaining full personal liberty. Valdés wrote for her in 1536 his *Alfabeto cristiano*, a primer of evangelical doctrine, and his translation of the Gospel of Matthew.[299] After Valdés died in 1541, she became the leader of the *valdesiani*, which she remained for twenty-five years. Willing to confront the reality that Colonna had let slip past her eyes, not acting, for the remainder of her life Gonzaga stayed just barely clear of the inquisitors' net. From the south of Italy, she promoted the escape of others (including Bresegna) to safer lands and funneled money northwards. In 1566, Pietro Carnesecchi, a friend and member of the circle of Valdés who had once escaped the Inquisition, was beheaded and burned in Rome. His interrogators asked specifically whether Gonzaga had possessed or distributed books by Valdés.[300] After his death there were found among his letters many from Gonzaga. But she had already died, on 19 April. If she had not, Pope Pius V announced when he learned of the incriminating evidence, "She would have been burned alive."[301]

The Great Witch-Hunt

Many women were burned alive in the fires of the Renaissance, those centuries that constitute the first phase of the European age of reason. Heretics were burned by the orthodox, martyrs by opponents of any and all faiths, witches by their judges, women by men. For the great European witch-hunt was tantamount to a war waged by men, under the generalship of the learned and the powerful, upon women. In their hunt for quarries of the female sex, Protestants and Catholics found common ground: each feared the other, but in unison they hated women who ate boiled babies, spit on crucifixes, flew on broomsticks, and prostituted themselves to the devil. Scarcely a person who has inherited the civilization of Europe believes, today, in witchcraft. But for centuries, "while Leonardo painted, Palestrina composed, and Shakespeare wrote," witches burned.[302]

Not so many burned, really: about 60,000, of 110,000 prosecuted, over two or three centuries.[303] From the standpoint of numbers, it was a queer and obscure cataclysm compared to the holocaustal millions who died in the concentration camps of central and eastern Europe during this century's Second World War. But the cataclysm swells to a greater dimension if the nature of the victim is considered: she (for the victims were mostly if not exclusively female, just as the concentration camp typically, if not unexceptionally, murdered Jews) was indistinguishable by any mark or sign from the wife and the mother of the hangman and the judge. Each one destroyed was in herself a holocaust and a reproach to the civilization of the Renaissance. Furthermore, if the holocaust of the witch-hunt seems small in relation to that of our own century, it is enormous in relation to the opposite phenomenon: female holiness. During the years the witch-hunt claimed 60,000 victims, all of Europe contained a few hundred holy women.[304] Condemned witches outnumbered recognized saints and near-saints by something like a hundred to one. If the Renaissance was an age of uniquely feminine sanctity, it was much more so an age of exceptional brutality to women. So bright burn the fires that consumed the witches of Europe that they cast special light on the condition of the Renaissance woman.

The witch-hunt was born in the medieval Alps and centered in the Empire; it peaked in the sixteenth and seventeenth centuries and rallied in a last frenzy in late seventeenth-century New England before disappearing during the Enlightenment. Exceptional variety characterizes the era of the witch-hunt. It was not a continuous phenomenon, but a period of centuries in which "witchcraft" was punishable by death and was so punished as a consequence of thousands of separate hunts. In some places and years, many suffered that penalty. There are communities that experienced local and intense witch hatred. In the six years between 1587 and 1593, twenty-two villages in the territory of Trier burned 368 accused witches, while Ellwangen executed 310 in 1611–13, and Bamberg 600 from 1623 to 1633.[305] An eyewitness of the Trier hunt notes those who "gloried in the multitude of the stakes, at each of which a human being had been given to the flames."[306] During such panics, when residents must have had the impression of the massive presence of dangerous witches, the chase and trial and execution were "a cleansing operation."[307]

Confessional differences had little effect on the rate of witch fever. Differing on crucial points of doctrine, Catholics and Protestants nevertheless shared the same witch beliefs and fears of the devil. They burned witches of both creeds, and paused in the persecution of their co-religionists to arm themselves against practitioners of a rival faith.[308] There are both Catholic and Protestant areas where accused witches suffered harsh persecution, and where they did not. In the German south-west, Catholics held nearly twice as many witch trials as Protestants and burned nearly four times as many victims. Between the two, at least 3,229 persons were executed for witchcraft between 1561 and 1670.[309] In the same period, Catholic Italy knew only minor anti-witch frenzy. Prot-estant Scotland pursued witches with diligence from 1563 into the sev-enteenth century, accusing 3,000 and executing 1,337.[310] At the same time, Protestant England's mild prosecutions dwindled after 1650, and soon after Cromwell's armies and administrators put an end to the witch-hunt in Scotland, from whence they wrote home tales about ungodly torture and slack rules of evidence.[311] Witch suspects were more harshly treated in the Protestant than in the Catholic areas of French Switzerland.[312] In Calvin's Geneva, exceptionally, there was little inter-est in the fantasies of witchcraft, seen as minor deviations from theologi-cal correctness. A mere 21 percent of Geneva's accused witches met with death.[313]

Although regional variations are many, a picture can be constructed of the accused witch. The "typical" witch was poor, uneducated, sharp-tongued, and old, but above all, female.[314] In colonial New England, where female witch suspects outnumbered males by four to one, the ac-cused witch was typically married and a mother of children (though fewer than the average).[315] She was often known for her "assaultive speech" and was likely to be over forty (as were about 80 percent of those whose ages are known).[316] On the ladder of social status, she stood at the bottom (nearly 80 percent, again, of those classifiable).[317] In England 93 percent and in Scotland 80 percent of accused witches were female; in both countries most were poor, quarrelsome, and disliked.[318] In the Jura region on the French-Swiss border, women ranged from 58 percent to 95 percent of the total of accused witches, averaging 76 per-cent. More were married than widowed, but not by much, and the mean ages ranged from 60 to 65: they were old.[319] In southwestern Germany before 1627, 87 percent of those executed for witchcraft in the large hunts were women; the figure fell to 76 percent after that date.[320] In Ger-man Langedorf in 1492, "witch" and "woman" were nearly coter-minous: a search for witch suspects garnered the whole female population of the town but two.[321] And just as most witches were wom-en, the crime for which women were most often condemned was witch-craft: from 1480 to 1700, more women were killed for witchcraft than for any other crime.[322]

The makers of European thought helped forge the witchcraft charge.[323] Scholastic theology clarified the place of the devil in the cosmic system and added to the ingredients of the witchcraft charge the important element of intercourse between the female witches and the male Satan. For Thomas Aquinas, in all cases of magic a contract was to be assumed between the practitioner and the devil. As a result, all witchcraft was seen as demonic, and suspects could no longer be easily dismissed as innocent lunatics.[324] Diabolism became tied to magic, creating the witch, whose miraculous powers derived from her relationship with the devil. Humanist practitioners of "natural" magic carefully distinguished their benign activities from the "black" magic of the witch. Humanists, the shapers of the new intellectual program of the Renaissance, could believe in witches. The Italian humanist Giovanni Francesco Pico della Mirandola described characteristic witch practices in his elegant dialogue *Witch (Strix)* in 1523.[325] Although one of the erudite interlocutors was skeptical, another believed firmly in the malevolence of the woman servant of the devil who also participated in the conversation; a third, the spokesman, apparently, for the author himself, urged cautious attention to the phenomenon of witchcraft. The latter two persuaded the skeptic, who had turned "believer" by the end of the conversation: no longer will he think those crimes to be fantasies which are attested to by "all the ancients and moderns, among them the poets, the orators, the stoics, the jurists, the philosophers, the theologians, men of good sense, soldiers, and peasants."[326] The German Ulrich Molitur published his *De lamiis et pythonicis mulieribus* in 1488 (one of the first illustrated statements of the witch belief), the Frenchman Nicolas Rémy his *Daemonalatrie* in 1595, the Italian Stefano Guazzo his *Compendium maleficarum* in 1608: all broadcast witch mythology, introducing the growing literate public to sabbats, orgies, and pacts with the devil. Learned Dominicans and learned Jesuits pursued witches in Catholic Europe, and the erudite Puritan Cotton Mather spread the witchcraft belief in North America. The Protestant King James of Scotland, and soon England, director of the most famous English translation of the Bible, called in 1597 for the extirpation of witchcraft in his *Daemonologie*. The celebrated French jurist, historian, and political philosopher Jean Bodin had much to say about witches, too, in his *Démonomanie des sorciers* of 1580: why they were mostly women (fifty females to each male, by his count); why regular legal procedures could be suspended in their examination (witchcraft was a "special case," a *crimen exceptum*). He explained that "proof of such evil is so obscure and difficult that not one out of a million witches would be accused or punished if regular legal procedure were followed."[327]

The intelligentsia included a few defenders of the victims of the witch-hunt as well. Erasmus and Heinrich Cornelius Agrippa von Nettesheim steered away from witchcraft belief, and Pietro Pomponazzi denied the reality of witches along with that of the devil. Andrea Alciati lamented abuses in witch trials, and the essayist Michel de Montaigne insisted that there be "sharp and luminous evidence" for witchcraft accusations: "It is putting a very high price on one's conjectures to roast a man alive for them."[328] But neither of the latter disbelieved in witches. The physician Johann Weyer's *De praestigiis daemonum* of 1563 posed a more fundamental challenge to witch belief.[329] The devil was so powerful that he did not require the assistance of witches, argued this student of Agrippa, like his teacher both an occultist and a defender of women. Instead, that demon deluded foolish old women afflicted by melancholia, causing them to believe that they had magical powers. "Since witches are usually old women of melancholic nature and small brains," he wrote, "there is no doubt that the devil easily affects and deceives their minds by illusions and apparitions that so bewilder them that they confess to actions that they are very far from having committed."[330] Without denying diabolic power, Weyer attacked the notion of the devil's pact that was the linchpin of witch prosecutions, and paved the way for psychological explanations of the witch belief. Weyer's follower in England, Reginald Scot, was so shocked by witch trials in his own Kent and nearby Essex, it seems, that he put his hobby aside—raising hops—to write *The Discoverie of Witchcraft* in 1584.[331] How absurd, he argued, that the devil should make use of "a toothless, old impotent and unweldie woman."[332] Here he used Weyer's arguments and his own experience of legal procedure to refute Bodin and other "witchmongers." It was Scot's work that provoked the royal *Daemonologie* some years later; the king may have cast Scot's *Discoverie* on the fire.

Following the learned (skeptics aside), who attached diabolism to magic to define the activity of the witch, the jurists associated sorcery with heresy in defining her crime. The Renaissance association of heresy with witchcraft had its roots in the medieval persecutions of the Cathars and Albigensians.[333] In the French Jura region, the words for heretic (*herege*) and Waldensian (*vaudois*) were synonyms for the word witch.[334] From such heretics as the Cathars, Albigensians, and Waldensians the witches' accusers knew about antisacramental acts. These involved the embrace of the devil and the repudiation of Christ, central features of the witchcraft charge. The Cathars had highlighted the power of the devil in the world, paving the way "for the assimilation of heresy to witchcraft."[335] Their followers met secretly in small groups, and participation in such secret meetings, reached by magical night flights, often on broomstick, was an earmark of the Renaissance witch. The Cathars were also believed to engage in orgies at such meetings, as were the later witches, whose orgiastic sessions were called, adding a dose of anti-Semitism, "sabbats," demonic sabbaths.

The fourteenth-century Inquisition projected upon the witch phenomenon the deliberate system it had used in its pursuit of the Albigensians. It assumed there must be, and therefore found, a highly organized Europeanwide cult of devil-worshippers. The meetings which must have occurred, in their thinking, were identified with the witches' sabbat.[336] This diabolistic component of witchcraft belief, the notion that the witch had entered into a pact with the devil, met with him regularly—arriving, broom-propelled, by air—and performed his service, was central to the Renaissance notion of witchcraft. Witches flew to their sabbats on broomsticks, smeared with magical grease to enable flight. There they made obeisance to the devil, spit on the cross, desecrated the Eucharist, renounced God and salvation, danced naked, murdered infants and ate them as well, and engaged in sexual acts with each other and their master, whose semen was icy cold.

The engraftment of witchcraft on heresy gave the European witch-hunt its unique proportions and consequences. The witchcraft charge was a compound of the milder offense of sorcery attached to the heinous one of heresy. As a crime against religion, heresy carried the penalty of burning, whereas sorcery, a civil offense, carried the penalty of hanging. (England, where witchcraft prosecution was mild and torture illegal, was an exception.[337]) Prosecution became the responsibility in most areas of the secular arm, and the secular machinery of state helped establish the existence of witches where, in its absence, none might have been found. Thus the witch-hunt was not a spontaneous outburst of folkish fears, but "a phenomenon essentially imposed on the powerless by the powerful."[338] The secular governments, outfitted with new rules of procedure and instruments of torture after the thirteenth century, took to the task.[339] The two Dominican inquisitors Heinrich Krämer (Latin Institoris) and Jacob Sprenger, busy hunters of witches in southern Germany, had issued by 1486 their *Malleus maleficarum*. This handbook for prosecutors on the proper examination and sentencing of witches emphasized the diabolic pact and aroused secular governments to participate in its extirpation. It would appear in fourteen editions between 1487 and 1520, putting enough copies in circulation for every judge to have his own.[340] The 1532 *Constitutio criminalis carolina*, the criminal code issued by the Holy Roman Emperor Charles V, established parameters for the witch-hunt in much of central Europe: it established regulations for the use of torture and called for burning as a penalty for the condemned.[341] In Scotland, the legal establishment self-consciously honed its apparatus on accused witches, coincident with the establishment of a new political regime.[342] An intricate set of procedures was devised to test a suspect for witchery, the most famous being the search for the devil's mark—the physical sign left somewhere (anywhere) on the body of the woman by her seducer.[343] The inquiry required disrobing the suspect and pricking her with a special device, of which there were many, elaborately designed; all were essentially stilettos. The Scots were expert prickers (a male occupation), and also explored a fruitful method of torture: sleep deprivation, which would promote, in a remarkably short period, disorientation and hallucination.

The torture of the alleged witch was one of the innovations of the modern judicial system, and great faith was placed in it.[344] Torture prepared the accused for a fresh examination. The victim would be asked not whether she was a witch, but for how long she had been one, and by what intermediary, and with which demonic master, and by what perverse sexual act, leaving what mark, and by what means she had flown to the orgiastic encounter.[345] And if she denied she had done any of these things, she was tortured again until she answered the questions to the satisfaction of the examiners. If torture did not elicit confession, she was tortured again, and repeatedly, until she either confessed to witchcraft or made plain her "guilt" by her "obstinacy." Once condemned by her own testimony, the victim was usually punished by death, generally by burning—the penalty by which women more than men had always suffered. Her estate would be confiscated to help pay the expenses of her trial. In some cases, her property was inventoried even before the trial began!—a practice leading to inevitable corruption in procedures prescribed with cautious legalism. But the condemned witch was usually a poor woman, and the public coffers profited precious little by the confiscation of her mite.[346]

Witch confessions were closely related to the use of torture and to the learned tradition at the same time. Up to the point in a trial when torture was applied, the charges would center on *maleficia*, magical acts of harming; thereafter, the diabolistic element would surface, pernicious. The confessions from all parts of Europe have a remarkable sameness: so many naked dancing women, so many orgiastic sabbats, so many slaughtered infants and brooms rubbed with bat's blood and toad's excrement. Surely the judges themselves, their expectations of witch behavior shaped by what was read in books, conveyed to the examiners and torturers what the suspect needed to confess. "For this reason it is valid to claim that torture in a certain sense 'created' witchcraft."[347] The high success rate of witchcraft trials is likely due to a gross disregard for the guidelines regulating the use of torture: torture was applied repeatedly, and confessions thus elicited were used in fresh accusations. Certainly it created confessions: 95 percent of tortured suspects confessed and were convicted, while in England, where torture was not used, the rate fell to below 50 percent.

Although most victims protested innocence until torture produced the expected admissions, some women believed they were witches and willingly accused themselves. Finding the "tyranny of the devil" intolerable, sixteen-year-old Maria Ostertag of Ellwangen confessed that, to ease her hunger, she had allowed her aunt to seduce her into witchcraft. She displayed the devil's mark on her right shoulder and incriminated thirty-four others as witches. Struck by her repentant posture, the judges permitted her the privilege of death by the sword, which she suffered on 21 August 1613.[348] Not all cases of self-accusation had so harsh a result. Caterina de Bono of Quiliano, in the Italian *savonese* region, presented herself to two local ecclesiastical gentlemen on 4 May 1608, and announced she was a witch.[349] A local witch, she said, had lured her into witchery when she was eight years old. The witch introduced her to a handsome young man dressed in black, who watched as Caterina stamped on the cross and renounced God. He then caressed, then sodomized her. From that moment, she and a number of associates (whom she named) practiced witchcraft, bringing harm to her neighbors, their farm animals, and their children. Asked how many children she had harmed, she replied: "Between dead and harmed more than fifty; . . . of which a dozen are dead."[350] Caterina's examiners appear not to have believed her confession: in part, perhaps, because the numbers of accomplices and dead babies were too many for the tiny village! She was never prosecuted; the secretaries and auditors were pledged to silence: "Thus Quiliano . . . lost out on its witch."[351]

While some secular states pursued witches with relish, the Inquisition declined to participate too strenuously in the hunt. From the sixteenth century, the Inquisition presided in witch cases only in Spain and Italy. These regions accounted for fewer than 10 percent of the witch prosecutions of Europe, and with the exception of the Italian Alpine zone (which resembled on this issue regions to the north) scarcely three hundred executions for witchcraft occurred in the Mediterranean states.[352] The infamous Spanish Inquisition only intervened with secular prosecutions of witches late in the fifteenth century, and by 1522 had limited its involvement.[353] In an outbreak of witch hysteria in the Basque region in 1610–12, the diligent inquisitor Alonso de Salazar Frias declined to prosecute. In what must be regarded as a breakthrough for rational principles of justice, he concluded that there was no concrete evidence of witchery at all: "I have not found the slightest evidence from which to infer that a single act of witchcraft has really occurred." People must not be burned, even if they willingly accuse themselves, in the absence of any trace of a crime having been committed, he declared. No more edicts should be published, moreover, since in the "diseased state of the public mind" they only have harmful effects: "I deduce the importance of silence and reserve from the experience that there were neither witches nor bewitched until they were talked and written about."[354]

Italian witches were few, but Italian women were suspected and sometimes convicted of other church-related "crimes" that might have been viewed as witchcraft by a different administration.[355] Sicilian records from 1540 to 1572 show women as prominent offenders, among the "crimes" pursued by the Inquisition, as Judaizers (50 percent! but here the records stop at 1549), bigamists (39 percent), and practitioners of illicit magic (29 percent). From 1564 through 1740 in Naples, women constituted 34 percent of those examined for the crime of illicit magic. In the Friuli, women were targeted as practitioners of love magic and various spells, and of "therapeutic" magic (here they outnumber men), in the period 1596 through 1685. In a pattern more typical of northern Europe, however, they were also present in overwhelming proportions among suspected witches: nearly five women to each male suspect for the period 1506–1610, and six for each in the period 1611 to 1670. The Friuli, too, was the site of what may have been the only group of accused witches in Europe related to an ancient fertility cult.[356] Overall, in Italy traditional forms of witchcraft persisted—healing, love magic, and divination—and the "modern" witch, seduced by the devil, was rare.

Women under the Inquisition suffered fewer charges of witchcraft in part because the religious examiners' main concern was not to find evidence of pacts with the devil but to establish correct belief. The symptoms of witch activity closely resembled those of false sanctity—an issue, as has been seen already, of great concern to the church. Some saints were very nearly witches, according to contemporary definitions, and the experiences of some witches were quite like those of saints.[357] Candidates for sanctity and suspected witches shared many of the same experiences: ecstasies and out-of-body sensations and demonic visitations (caused in both cases in part by undernourishment, perhaps in part by hallucinogens). Both saints and witches gave themselves to a master—God or Satan—and received charismatic gifts. "The witch, through a special relationship with the Devil, performs impious miracles; the saint, through a special relationship with God, performs pious miracles."[358] The vision of Jesus that either could receive could be either divine or demonic. The Eucharist had special significance for both: as an object of adoration or defilement. Thus Catherine of Siena was suspected of demonic possession, and Francesca Bussa de' Ponziani and Umiliana de' Cerchi were liable to the charge, given their experience of frequent diabolic dream visions.[359] An autopsy was performed on the body of the blessed Colomba da Rieti in 1501 to determine whether she was saint or witch, and Caterina de' Racconigi, the saint befriended by Giovanni Francesco Pico della Mirandola, was suspected of witchcraft.[360] If these are the threads that bind together saint and witch, what is the line that separates them? It appears to be sociological: the women of the aristocratic, patriciate, merchant, and even upper-artisan classes who became saints rarely figure as witches. Witches were overwhelmingly poor peasants, defenseless in their villages against spiteful neighbors and unprotected by the culture of the learned and powerful.

Witches could as easily be confused with healers as they were with saints. In the village setting, the woman who was consulted for pregnancy (and abortion and contraception), headache, and childhood illness had a certain power: it was perceived as benign as long as her healing was effective, but as menacing when it was not.[361] Presumed witchcraft activities, in fact, closely resembled the normal activities of housewifery: the witch, like the wife, brewed and baked and counseled and cured, cared for children and assisted at childbirth. The midwife, especially, was vulnerable to a witchcraft charge; the dead babies of whom there were such a sad abundance could be seen as victims of her curse. Part one, question eleven of the *Malleus maleficarum* is entitled: "That Witches who are Midwives in Various Ways Kill the Child Conceived in the Womb, and Procure an Abortion; or if they do not this Offer New-Born Children to Devils."[362] The midwife in witch belief becomes the cannibalizer of infants, just as the healer becomes a malefactor, a causer of harm, as in the following cases. Matteuccia di Francesco was charged with "enchanting" many times and in many ways, from 1426 until 1428, when her therapeutic exercises were stopped, "those who were suffering in their bodies, heads or other parts of their bodies."[363] She smeared them with oils, prescribed remedies, performed rituals involving their belts and vests or wax dolls in theirs or their lovers' images. She acquired some meat and fat from the body of a man who had drowned in the Tiber, and cooked it and skimmed the oil, which she used "to cure people's pains and wounds."[364] "Not content with these things and adding evil to evil"[365] she helped a priest's concubine regain her partner's love and prevent his daily beatings, attempted to cure a paralytic by transferring his affliction to a passerby, and sucked the blood of many children "as it is her usual custom."[366] The one day of 20 March 1428 saw her trial, her condemnation, and her execution, all recorded in detail by notaries and witnessed by responsible persons.

A century later, Bellezza Orsini cured her neighbors with the sign of the cross, resolved rifts between husband and wife, and resolved problems of unrequited love.[367] Accused of witchcraft in 1528, she denied all charges at first, but under pressure began gradually to admit to peccadilloes. Then, as was the usual procedure at this point in the investigation, she was shown the instruments of torture. Terrified, she begged for a quick death: "Kill me quickly, don't rack me, don't make me die in torment."[368] Confessions to more serious crimes followed. Fearful of torture, she attempted suicide in her cell (as did many accused witches, and their deaths should rightly be added to the toll of the executed). Her son came to court to halt the proceedings: he initiated an appeal to a higher court. But Orsini was tortured repeatedly, each session eliciting more horrible litanies of crime. Before long, she described how she and confederates chopped up and stewed an unbaptized infant: "When we begin, we take a creature who was born dead, or a heathen, who had not been baptized, and we dig it up from where it was buried, . . . and we take a knife and cut off the head, and then we cut it up and put all of it in the kettle, and we set it to boil so that it all separates, and then we stir it two or three times and put it in a pot with oil, and then we bury it well sealed beneath the ground for forty days."[369] They then anointed themselves with the mixture and were soon rewarded with a visit from the devil himself, handsome and lecherous. These revelations were still insufficient, and Bellezza was tortured again. She eventually confessed to having practiced witchery for thirty-three years (an increase from the one year to which she had first admitted). She was then allowed to return to her cell to await sentence. Once again, she attempted to kill herself, this time with success: "with a nail or key she struck herself in the throat with two thrusts with a tremendously abundant effusion of blood, and remained as though half dead. . . . when interrogated [she] said that tempted by a diabolic spirit she had wished to kill herself and thought of nothing other than to vanish and flee from this world."[370] Thus the village healer became the village demon. Her powers made her dangerous, her poverty left her defenseless, her sex made her hateful.

The war against women that the witch-hunt embodied resembled other wars in human history, in which the enemy was wholly identified with evil. Many of the charges characteristically brought against witches were ancient: "The Syrians brought them against the Jews, the Romans against the Christians, and the Christians against the Gnostics" and eventually against heretics and again, Jews.[371] What is distinctive here, however, is that evil is linked not to a people or to a creed, but to a sex. The notion of "witch" and the notion of "woman" nearly merged: the Latin word for witch—*malefica*—is a female noun. Women were witches because they were "more wanton, more weak, and more wicked than men."[372] Something essential in Christianity encouraged the formulation of woman-as-evil. Every woman shared with the devil himself the distinction of posing the opposite pole to the masculine, rational God.[373] Even the ordinary woman was a descendant of the irresponsible and seductive Eve (the "ultimate witch"), inclined to "carnal abominations": "All witchcraft comes from carnal lust," wrote Krämer and Sprenger, "which is in woman insatiable."[374] As King James wrote, it is demonstrated that woman is more likely than man to be entrapped by the devil "by the Serpents deceiving of Eve at the beginning, which makes him the homelier with that sex ever since."[375] Throughout Christian Europe, women were suspect. In the witch-hunt of the Renaissance centuries, as one scholar has put it, the distinctive misogyny of the European tradition turned "lethal."[376]

Only with the advent of the age of reason would the witch-hunt cease. At the end of our period, voices of reason would first be heard from the wielders of power. Queen Christina of Sweden put an end to witch-hunting where she could and claimed, after her 1647 abdication, that she had limited the death penalty to proven cases of murder.[377] William Penn queried a defendant tried by a Quaker jury in colonial Pennsylvania: "'Art thou a witch? Hast thou ridden through the air on a broomstick?'" She admitted that she had. She had every right to do so, Penn responded cordially. She was set free.[378]

3

❦

VIRGO ET VIRAGO

Women and High Culture

Women of Might, Power, and Influence

On the stake that supported the burning corpse of the peasant Joan of Arc, who had donned armor and rallied a king, a placard bore the names that the people of the Renaissance gave to the women they hated: heretic, liar, sorceress.[1] The mystery of that hatred has preoccupied the many tellers of the tale of the life of this patron saint of France. Their answers cannot be recounted here, but without simplifying too much they can be summed up in this way: she was hated because she did what men did, and triumphantly. The men who planted stakes over the face of Europe would not tolerate such a transgression of the order they imagined to be natural. In the age of emblems, Joan of Arc is an emblem of the Renaissance women who attempted to partake in the civilization of the Renaissance: not as bearers of children or worshippers of God, but as forgers of its cultural forms. These women did not share her fate, but a few of them understood it.

Foremost among these women, in the records that that age has left us, are those who had no choice about the role they played. Like Joan, they bore arms, or wielded powers still more formidable. They were the queens and female rulers who ruled as the surrogates of their absent husbands, dead fathers, and immature sons. Extraordinary in their personal strengths and achievements, they have left no residue: their capital passed through the male line of descent and not to female heirs—at least not in the centuries of which we speak. But as women who held command, even if briefly and without issue, they deserve our attention.

In Italy later in the same century that Joan illumined with her strength, Caterina Sforza posed a more traditional but still boldly independent figure.[2] The illegitimate granddaughter of Francesco Sforza, who was in turn the illegitimate usurper of the dynasty of the Visconti in Milan, Caterina was propelled into the political maelstrom of quattrocento Italy by her marriage to Girolamo Riario, nephew of Pope Sixtus IV. After her husband's assassination in 1488, she fiercely defended her family's interests and the cities of Imola and Forlì. Greatly outnumbered by her besiegers, she defended Forlì against the enemy who held her six children hostage. Twelve years later, she again commanded the defense of those same walls, was defeated, possibly raped, and was brought captive to Rome by Cesare Borgia.

While Sforza, like Joan of Arc, assumed a military role, she secured no power; few women, even of the most exalted noble and royal families, ever did. Two major exceptions were the Italian-born Catherine de'Medici, who as the widow of France's King Henri II was the regent for his successors, François II and Charles IX, and Elizabeth, daughter of the Tudor kings of England. Both molded a Renaissance identity for a female sovereign that expressed the ambiguity of their roles. The former adopted for herself the emblem of Artemisia (the type of armed-and-chaste maiden to be considered at greater length below), who was known for her dutiful remembrance of her predeceased husband, Mausolus.[3] Wielding this device, Catherine de' Medici could both act assertively and demonstrate piety to the male rulers between whom she transmitted power. The more independent and bolder Elizabeth was a master builder of her public image and presented herself to her subjects in a variety of feminine identities: Astraea, Deborah, Diana.[4] At the same time, to win support in moments of crisis for the unprecedented phenomenon of a female monarch, she projected androgynous images of her role (man-woman, queen-king, mother-son), and haughtily referred to herself as "prince," with the body of a woman and the heart of a king. She defied the identification of her sex with instability and incompetence. In 1601, the elderly Elizabeth asked Parliament in her Golden Speech: "Shall I ascribe anything to myself and my sexly weakness? I were not worthy to live then";[5] "my sex," she said a few weeks before her death, "cannot diminish my prestige."[6] Had she married, she might have borne an heir. But had she married, she would have fallen under the influence

of a male consort. Instead, a complete dyad in herself, she took no husband and declared herself married to England. Her heroic virginity, more
in the pattern of the great saints than of a modern woman, set her apart
from the other women of her realm who continued to marry and dwell
within the family. Her sexual nature was exceptional, just as her kingly
authority was anomalous. In and of herself, she insisted on her right to
rule, and was the only woman to hold sovereign power during the
Renaissance.

Much of the culture of the late sixteenth-century Tudor court
revolved around this manlike virgin whose name still identifies it:
Elizabethan. Subtly, the poets, playwrights, and scholars of the age
commented on the prodigy among them. Foremost among these commentators was William Shakespeare; in the androgynous heroines of his
comedies can be found versions of the monarch, sharp-witted and exalted beyond nature.[7] These female characters, played by boys dressed
as women who often dressed as boys to create beings of thoroughly confused sexuality, charmed and entranced like the queen herself. The
Shakespearean genius also understood how deeply the phenomenon of a
queen-king violated the natural order. In the seemingly lighthearted
"Midsummer Night's Dream" he spoke about the abnormality of a political order ruled by a woman when the Amazon Hippolyta was wedded at
the last to the lawful male wielder of power.[8] Like Joan of Arc, Elizabeth
was perceived (and perceived herself) as an Amazon, and deep in the
consciousness of the age she dominated was the discomfiture caused by
an armed maiden, a rational female, an emotional force unlimited by natural order.

The phenomenon of enthroned women like Catherine and Elizabeth
provoked controversy about the legitimacy of female rule.[9] No one was
more outspoken than the Presbyterian John Knox, who charged in his
First Blast of the Trumpet Against the Monstrous Regiment of Women of 1558
that "it is more than a monster in nature that a woman shall reign and
have empire above man." "To promote a woman to bear rule, above any
realm, nation, or city, is repugnant to nature, contumely to God, . . . and,
finally, it is the subversion of good order, of all equity and justice."[10]
When a woman rules, the blind lead the sighted, the sick the robust, "the
foolish, mad and frenetic" the discreet and sober. "For their sight in civil
regiment is but blindness, their counsel foolishment, and judgment
frenzy."[11] Woman's attempt to rule is an act of treason: "For that woman
reigneth above man, she hath obteined it by treason and conspiracy com-

mitted against God. . . . [Men] must study to repress her inordinate pride and tyranny to the uttermost of their power."[12] God could occasionally choose a woman to rule, John Aylmer wrote a year later, refuting Knox; but most women were "fond, folish, wanton flibbergibbes, tatlers, triflers, wavering witles, without counsell, feable, careless, rashe proude," and so on.[13]

Most defenders of female rule in the sixteenth century could not transcend the problem of gender. While Knox was driven to fury by the accession of Mary Tudor to power, the behavior of her successor Elizabeth the Great enraged the French Catholic political theorist Jean Bodin. In the sixth book of his *Six Books of the Republic*, Bodin explored thoroughly the emotional dimension of female rule. A woman's sexual nature would surely, he claimed, interfere with her effectiveness as ruler.[14] As Giovanni Correr, the Venetian ambassador to France, said of another Queen Mary, the unfortunate monarch of Scotland, "to govern states is not the business of women."[15] Other Venetian ambassadors to the court of Elizabeth's successors were more impressed: that queen by her exceptional wisdom and skill had "advanced the female condition itself," and "overcome the distinction of sexes."[16] Male observers thus viewed the sex of the female monarch as an impediment to rule or considered it obliterated, overlooking it altogether, as though the woman was no woman. Spenser simply made his monarch an exception to the otherwise universal rule of female subordination: "vertuous women" know, he wrote, that they are born "to base humilitie," unless God intervenes to raise them "to lawful soveraintie" (*Faerie Queene* 5.5.25).

Although this problem was agonizing for the few women who ruled, there were only a handful who had to face it: it was rare for a woman to inherit power as did these English queens. It required, in fact, the timely death of all power-eligible males. Most women in the ruling classes did not rule, but only shared some of the prerogatives of sovereignty. In the vibrant artistic and intellectual climate of the Renaissance, particularly in Italy, this meant that they exercised the power of patronage. Women who did not rule or direct with their armies the forces of destruction could wield their authority and wealth to shape thought and culture.

Wherever courts existed as centers of wealth, artistic activity, and discourse, opportunities abounded for intelligent women to perform in the role of patroness of the arts and culture. In France, Anne of Brittany, Queen of Charles VIII, commissioned the translation of Boccaccio's *Concerning Famous Women* (*De claris mulieribus*), and filled her court with educated women and discussions of platonic love.[17] The same king's sister-in-law Louise of Savoy tutored the future king François I and his sister, Marguerite, according to the principles of Italian humanism. The latter—Marguerite d'Angoulême, later of Navarre—was the director of cultural matters at her brother's royal court and the protector of a circle of learned men.[18] Influenced by the evangelism of Lefèvre d'Etaples and Guillaume Budé, guided in matters of spirit by the bishop Guillaume Briçonnet, she was at the center of currents of proto-reform. An original thinker herself, her collection of stories, the *Heptaméron*, raised questions about the troubled roles of women in a man's world. From this court circle of active patronesses and educators there derived other women of some power and influence: among them the Calvinist Jeanne d'Albret, Marguerite's daughter and the mother of the future king Henry IV, a valiant fighter for her family and religion; and Renée, the heir of Louis XII who was bypassed in favor of her male cousin François I and made wife instead to the Duke of Ferrara, who chose as a companion for her own daughter the adolescent Italian humanist Olimpia Morata.[19]

In Spain the formidable Isabella guided religious reform and intellectual life, while in England, her learned daughter Catherine of Aragon, King Henry VIII's first queen, was surrounded by the leading humanists of the era. It was for her that Erasmus wrote his *Institution of Christian Matrimony (Christiani matrimonii institutio)* and Juan Luis Vives his *Instruction of a Christian Woman (Institutio foeminae christianae)* and other works. She sought Vives as a tutor for her own daughter, the future queen Mary Tudor.[20] A generation earlier, the proto-figure of the royal patroness and learned woman in England was Margaret Beaufort, Countess of Richmond, already noted as the mother of that country's first Tudor monarch.[21] At the courts of Edward IV and Richard III, she had surrounded herself with minstrels and learned men, supported the art of printing (then in its early stages), endowed professorships of divinity at Oxford and Cambridge (where she founded two colleges), supervised the education of her son and grandchildren, and herself translated from the Latin the devotional *The Mirror of Gold of the Sinful Soul*.

In Italy, where courts and cities and talented men clustered, opportunities abounded for the cultivated woman to help shape the culture of the Renaissance. Notable among such patronesses was Isabella d'Este, daughter of the rulers of Ferrara, sister of Beatrice, who was to play a similar but paler role in Milan, and of Alfonso, Ferrante, Ippolito, and Sigismondo, whom she was to rival in fame.[22] Trained by Battista

Guarini, the pedagogue son of the great humanist Guarino Veronese, she had mastered Greek and Latin, the signs of serious scholarship, alongside such skills as lute-playing, dance, and witty conversation. Married to the ruler of Mantua, she presided at that court over festivities and performances, artists, musicians and scholars, libraries filled with elegant volumes; she lived surrounded everywhere by statues, ornate boxes, clocks, marbles, lutes, dishes, gowns, playing cards decorated with paintings, jewels, and gold. Ariosto, Bernardo da Bibbiena, and Gian Giorgio Trissino were among those she favored. She studied maps and astrology and had frequent chats with the ducal librarian, Pellegrino Prisciano. Her *Studiolo* and *Grotta*, brilliantly ornamented rooms in the ducal palace, were her glorious monuments. For these and other projects, she designed the allegorical schemes, consulting with her humanist advisers. Ruling briefly when her husband was taken captive during the wars that shook Italy after the invasion of the forces of France, Spain, and Empire, she was repaid with anger for her bold assumption of authority. Her great capacity was left to express itself in patronage.

Also dislodged from the limited tenure of sovereignty was the wealthy Venetian noblewoman Caterina Cornaro.[23] Born to an ancient Venetian noble family with interests in the eastern Mediterranean—her own mother was from a Greek royal family—Cornaro was married in 1472, at age eighteen, to the King of Cyprus, James II. Her city was concerned with her royal marriage from the start: the island of Cyprus was strategically important, and the Serenissima was jealous of its citizens' involvement in consequential foreign affairs. Venetian concern was justified, for Cornaro became queen of Cyprus a year later, after her husband's sudden death, and held unstable sway, racked by conspiracies, for sixteen years. When Cornaro was tempted by a marriage into the Neapolitan royal house, Venice exerted its authority mightily to force her to abdicate the Cypriot throne. A Neapolitan connection would have meant the alienation of Cyprus from Venetian control. The legate dispatched to the island and charged to persuade her to step down was none other than her brother. He came with offers of an annual salary of 8,000 ducats and a small fiefdom on the Venetian terra firma: she would win fame for herself, he promised, and be known forever as Queen of Cyprus, if she donated her husband's island to her *patria*. Thus compensated by fame and wealth, Cornaro left her rich island kingdom for the miniature one at Asolo. In that court she reigned as queen over a coterie of *letterati*: not the least of them Pietro Bembo, who memorialized the activities over which

Cornaro presided in the Arcadian dialogue *Gli Asolani*. Published in 1505 by Aldo Manuzio in Venice, ten years after the conversations that sparked Bembo's imagination had taken place, it circulated in twenty-two editions, Italian as well as Spanish and French. Perhaps more significantly, it influenced the even more famous and complex dialogue of Baldassare Castiglione, commemorating a court presided over by another patroness of letters.

Cornaro's court as described by Bembo prefigures the one in Urbino which Castiglione described. There two women—the Duchess, Elisabetta Gonzaga, and her companion, Emilia Pia—guided and inspired the discussions of proper behavior for both sexes that made up the age's principal handbook of aristocratic values, circulated in some hundred editions and translated into all the major vernaculars: *The Book of the Courtier (Il libro del cortigiano)*. For both sexes, that behavior is sharply defined by the phenomenon of the court: men were not to be too boisterous; women were to be occasions of beauty and delight. No court "however great, can have adornment or splendor or gaiety in it without ladies"; in the same way, no courtier can "be graceful or pleasing or brave, or do any gallant deed of chivalry, unless he is moved by the society and by the love and charm of ladies."[24] "Who learns to dance gracefully for any reason except to please women? Who devotes himself to the sweetness of music for any other reason? Who attempts to compose verses . . . unless to express sentiments inspired by women?"[25]

The virtues that women had to possess to inspire these male achievements were manifold. The courtly lady shares some virtues possessed also by the gentleman—she should be well born, naturally graceful, well mannered, clever, prudent, and capable—but also others which are distinctively hers.[26] If married, she should be a good manager of her husband's "property and house and children," and possess "all qualities that are requisite in a good mother."[27] Beauty is a necessity for her, though not for her male counterpart: "for truly that woman lacks much who lacks beauty."[28] Above all, she must be charming: "she will be able to entertain graciously every kind of man with agreeable and comely conversation suited to the time and place and to the station of the person with whom she speaks, joining to serene and modest manners, and to that comeliness that ought to inform all her actions, a quick vivacity of spirit whereby she will show herself a stranger to all boorishness; but with such a kind manner as to cause her to be thought no less chaste, prudent, and gentle than she is agreeable, witty, and discreet."[29] The qualities the court lady possesses are distinct from those of the courtier she is set to amuse: "above all . . . in her ways, manners, words, gestures, and bearing, a woman ought to be very unlike a man; for just as he must show a certain solid and sturdy manliness, so it is seemly for a woman to have a soft and delicate tenderness, with an air of womanly sweetness in her every movement, which, in her going and staying, and in whatever she says, shall always make her appear the woman without any resemblance to a man."[30] Unlike the queen who bears the power and the glory of the males who otherwise occupy her throne, according to Giuliano de' Medici, Castiglione's spokesman by no means hostile to the female sex, the aristocratic lady must be taught to be something other than a man. The same was true of her humbler counterpart in the bourgeois or artisan classes.

The Schooling of Women

Poor women, like poor men, received no formal education whatsoever, although many men and some women were trained in certain crafts. Middle- and upper-class women were initiated in a particular female culture, however, in which they were taught to perform household functions and pursued a regimen stressing needlework and spinning, silence and obedience. Reading was useful, but should be limited to good books: devotional works and the sounder titles by Dante, Petrarch, and Boccaccio.[31] The goals of education for these women were twofold: first, to guide the young woman to develop those traits of character most suited to patriarchal marriages; second, to train her in those skills most useful in the domestic economy.

A more substantial curriculum was outlined in the *Instruction of a Christian Woman*, published in 1523 by the Spanish humanist Juan Luis Vives, a vast and comprehensive summary of the advice of the humanists on that subject.[32] A volume nearly as popular as the contemporary *Book of the Courtier*, it circulated in forty editions and was translated into English, Dutch, French, German, Spanish, and Italian. Those cities where the education of women is neglected, Vives warned, alluding to Aristotle, Xenophon, and Plato, "are deprived of the greater part of happiness."[33] Young girls should be taught to read so that, rescued from ignorance, they can approach some of the most serious authors of their civilization: the gospels; the Acts of the Apostles and epistles of the New Testament and historical and moral books of the Old Testament; the saints Cyprian, Jerome, Augustine, Ambrose, John Chrysostom, Hilary, and Gregory; also Boethius, Fulgentius, Tertullian, even Plato, Cicero, and Seneca.[34] Vives's list includes some Christian authors traditionally read by literate women, but also some secular philosophers and orators normally outside of their purview: such texts were necessarily to be read in Latin. This bold humanist, therefore, who during his career would also challenge the scholastic monopoly of university education and argue the responsibility of the lay state in the relief of the poor, opened the door to the serious education of women.

At the same time, Vives seems to close the door he opens. Though women are to acquire literacy at a high level, the scope and purpose of their learning is sharply limited. He intimates what Jean Jacques Rousseau would state with characteristic succinctness nearly three centuries later at the dawn of the modern era: "She ought to learn many things, but only such as are of use to her to know."[35] Women are to avoid secular poetry and romances: Boccaccio and other authors, for instance, who according to Vives were "otiose, lazy, without humanity, given to vices and deceit."[36] And domestic skills must not be neglected: "The little girl should also learn, together with her letters, to spin with her hands both wool and linen, two arts which that famous golden age and that epoch of innocence taught to posterity, most useful in the domestic economy."[37] The women of antiquity—Persian, Greek, and Roman, he continued, were producers of cloth and won great honor thereby. Clearly, though Vives added the dimension of Latin literacy to the traditional curriculum for the training of the middle- or upper-class daughter, he did not abandon its original format.

The education Vives prescribed for the young woman of the Renaissance was not one that would cultivate her mind, but one that would encourage her obedience to familiar duties and virtues. Men must do many things in the world, and so must be broadly educated; but only a little learning is required of women.[38] He makes the point explicit: while she is to be introduced to literary studies, "her studies should be in those works which shape morals and virtue; the studies of wisdom which teach the best and most holy manner of life. I recommend that she not be concerned with rhetoric; a woman doesn't need that; that which a woman needs is probity and prudence; it is not unbecoming for a woman to be silent; what is foul and abominable is to be wayward and behave badly. . . . When she learns to read, put in her hands those books which improve morals, and when she learns to write, do not give her base verses . . . , but some grave saying or some little passage, wise and holy, taken from Sacred Letters or from the writings of the philosophers, which when written over many times adhere more fixedly in the mind."[39] Ignorance of such precepts are and have always been the ruin of women: "most of the vices of women in this our age and in ages past . . . are the products of ignorance, since they never read nor heard those excellent sayings and monitions of the Holy Fathers about chastity, about obedience, about silence, women's adornments and treasures."[40] If women's treasures are chastity, silence, and obedience, chastity ranks highest of all: "chastity is woman's particular concern; when she is clearly taught about this, she is sufficiently instructed."[41]

Two and a half centuries later, the framer of Europe's economic liberalism, Adam Smith, still admired this aspect of female education: women are taught what it is useful for them to know, "and they are taught nothing else." Every element of their education has a clear purpose: "either to improve the natural attractions of their person, or to form their mind to reserve, to modesty, to chastity, and to economy; to render them both likely to become the mistresses of a family, and to behave properly when they have become such."[42] In all the settings of female education—in a girl's own house or someone else's, in school or the convent, these were the necessary and sufficient components of female education: admonitions to be chaste, silent, and obedient,[43] and the acquisition of textile and other housekeeping skills. The former ideals were ancient, as previous chapters have shown, and fundamental both to the maintenance of the patriarchal family and to the value system of established Christianity. The latter arts, too, were fundamental, whether a girl were destined for paid labor outside of the home or unpaid labor within it. Women's mastery of these skills had equipped them for a near-monopoly of the trades associated with the production of cloth and the manufacture of clothing, as has been seen, until the largely male guild structure intruded on that sphere in the course of the Renaissance centuries.[44]

Training in needlework and spinning accordingly played a conspicuous role in the education of girls. Early in the fourteenth century, Francesco da Barberino praised such activities over reading: the daughters of merchants have to learn many household tasks and should not bother with reading; daughters of the working classes should know how to sew and spin, to cook and care for other household members.[45] A generation later, Paolo da Certaldo urged householders to keep a close eye on the females in his house, making sure they always have work to do to prevent idleness—perilous to all, but especially to women. A daughter should be trained to sew, not to read (suitable only for future nuns), and to bake bread, clean chickens, make beds, weave, embroider, and mend socks. Thus she is prepared for her future role as wife, "and will not look a fool and it will not be said that she came out of the woods; and you won't be cursed for having raised her that way."[46] A century later, the Sienese saint Bernardino recommended the same curriculum: teach your daughters to spin and to sew, he urged the mothers in his audience.[47] A 1599 report to the Augsburg city council explained why few girls were sent to school: "The children must be soon sent out to work, especially the daughters, who can expect only very little time in school . . . they must also learn sewing and be used in running the household."[48] As late as the early years of the eighteenth century, Madame de Maintenon advised that middle-class students be provided with middle-class information: how to run the household, how to behave with husband, children, and servants, how to cultivate the virtues appropriate to that class, and by no means to consider the enrichment of their minds.[49] Most little girls dislike reading and writing, remarked the pedagogue Jean Jacques Rousseau, ever-solicitous to develop the potential of the "natural" child, "but exhibit the greatest pleasure in learning the use of a needle."[50]

While many women of the elite classes received a traditional education at home consisting of a combination of character-training and needlecraft, the same setting also provided for some the means of literacy—first reading, then writing—in the vernacular. The fifteenth-century English lady Margery Paston knew how to write her name (just barely), though she used amanuenses for her letters. The Paston daughters learned to read at home or in the households of other aristocratic families—the English more than others having the custom of circulating their young children among families of the same social standing.[51] Paston's Florentine contemporary Alessandra Macinghi Strozzi, author of so many expressive and informative letters to her children, commanded only an ordinary vernacular permeated with everyday locutions and proverbial wisdom—and this in the central sanctum of the Italian Renaissance.[52] In sixteenth-century France, among the elite families in the major towns, girls studied French, Italian, music, and arithmetic with tutors, and might go on to organize a fashionable salon for the discussion of new ideas.[53] Their freedom had been more restricted in an earlier age. The queens of France, noted the author of the fourteenth-century handbook entitled *Goodman of Paris*, were able to read letters: but only "such as be by the hand of their husband, . . . and those read they all alone, and for the others they call company and bid them to be read by others before them, and say often that they know not how to read letter or writing, save that of their husband; and this they do by wise teaching and full well, that they may be far even from whisper and suspicion, for there is no fear of the deed itself."[54] Even the perusal of a letter could be construed as an act of unchastity.

Some girls went to schools where they learned the fundamentals of reading and writing (in the vernacular only) and arithmetic. In Florence in 1338, Giovanni Villani reported, 8,000 to 10,000 boys and girls from age six to thirteen learned to read in elementary schools. Subsequently, the boys alone—from 1,000 to 1,200 of them—proceeded to schools where calculation, required for business, was taught; another 550 to 600 went to schools that taught logic and Latin, required for university training.[55] The figures, suggesting that as many as 37 percent to 45 percent of all children from six to fifteen attended school, are surely exaggerated, and camouflage the reality that no more than one in ten of the elementary students were female.[56] Nevertheless, the municipal schools of Florence were actively educating their young, and even some of their young women. In 1304 in the same city, a married schoolmistress (*doctrix puerorum*), taught Latin: the reading of the Psalms, the grammar book called *Donatus*, and the preparation of rudimentary notarial acts.[57] Throughout the flourishing towns of Italy, in fact, from the fourteenth through the seventeenth century, women teachers joined men in the elementary education of the young, amounting to as many as 10 percent of the total number of pedagogues in any given place or year. Often they were paid less than men, and though some taught Latin grammar to boys, many others taught reading in the vernacular and even sewing and cooking to girls, usually in a household school rather than a formal one; almost never did a girl attend an independent school taught by a male teacher. Thus Ursa ran a girls school in Venice in 1409, and Lucia left a will in 1413 making specific bequests to girls, her pupils: *sue discipule*. A regulation of religious conformity in Turin in 1566 was explicitly to apply to *le maestre*, "the mistresses" who taught little girls to read and sew. Veronese records show three female teachers of girls: Onorata, Tadea, and Maddalena, in 1465, 1469, and 1555 respectively; the same documents note a total of twenty-one female pedagogues, aged eighteen to eighty-seven, active in that city from 1382 to 1595. Every one of these *maestre* had herself learned to read, indicating an ongoing current of female education at the elementary level.

Schoolmistresses and schools for girls are found beyond the Alps as well. Tax records from thirteenth- and fourteenth-century Paris mention schoolmistresses (from shopkeeping and artisan backgrounds) as well as masters of mixed "little schools," though these were segregated by sex in 1357: "a woman should teach only girls," instructed the chartulary.[58] In French Lyon, from the 1490s to the 1560s there were five schoolmistresses to eighty-seven schoolmasters (who could teach boys only)![59] In London in 1390, the orphan daughter of a candle-maker, ward of a broiderer, attended an elementary school from age eight until she was married, at age thirteen.[60] In the same city, the Merchant Taylor's School was established in 1561 and provided elementary education for girls.[61] Other "dame schools" in England were established to teach reading, religion, and the arts of spinning and weaving.[62] Their place was taken in the later centuries of our era by the charity schools, which taught large numbers of girls spinning, knitting, sewing, and religion.[63] Boys and girls gathered together, sometimes in schools run by Beguines, in some cities of northern Europe. In fifteenth-century Flanders, the chronicler Froissart learned Latin in a mixed school, and recalls falling in love with one of the girls.[64] In 1535, the town ordinances of Ypres, based on recommendations of the humanist Juan Luis Vives, provided for the protection and education of orphaned and abandoned children. Girls were to be trained in the usual household skills—they were destined, most of them, for domestic service, as in the foundling homes of France and Italy—but also, if they were capable, in reading and writing.[65]

A few German cities—Speyer, Bern, Regensburg, Mainz, Zurich and Frankfurt—had schools as early as the fourteenth century, and soon afterwards they were joined by Augsburg, Nuremberg, and others. The town of Emmerich in 1445 arranged for two or more women teachers for girls.[66] Frankfurt in 1600 had twenty small "house schools," about half of them taught by women. In such schools, *Lehrfrauen* taught little girls in their homes how to read and write, supporting themselves with modest stipends and, as a supplement, additional jobs of spinning and sewing.[67] Although they were self-sufficient in this way, they were to some extent supported by city councils, as they were also regulated by them: required to be citizens, of good character, and, after the Reformation, of the proper religious persuasion. The city of Arnstadt provided one teacher with an apartment which, she complained, had deteriorated to such an extent "that bugs and worms slither in and can freely creep in and out, so that the children are always screaming and terrified."[68] In Überlingen in 1456, one *Lehrfrau* was so respected, a male teacher complained, that "some people in this city have decided to have their boys learn German as well and have sent them to her. She has understood that this has brought difficulties to me and my school. So I request that she be ordered to pay me three schillings per year for every boy that she teaches, because my own income has been diminished, and that she give this to me without stalling or objections."[69] His plea was granted.

Perhaps the strongest force for women's elementary education lay in Protestantism. If all believers were to make their own peace with God, it was argued, and God spoke in Scripture, then all must learn to read. Luther had hoped that schools for girls would be established, where Scripture might be read for an hour daily either in German or in Latin.[70] In 1533, Elsa von Kaunitz established such a school in the reformer's own town of Wittenberg. Philip Melanchthon, the executor of Luther's pedagogical program, ordered that schools be set up for girls (staffed by women teachers) which they would attend for one or two hours a day for one or two years.[71] By 1528, Johann Agricola had written a catechism for another school: *One Hundred and Fifty-Six Questions for Young Children in the German School for Girls in Eisleben*.[72] In Calvinist Geneva, it was ordered in 1536 that all children attend school, and separate girls' schools were established at the elementary (but none at the secondary) level after 1541.[73]

In Strasbourg, the reformer Martin Bucer likewise called for the establishment of public schools in all parishes, where girls as well as boys might be taught to read. By the end of the sixteenth century, princely or municipal decrees had called for the establishment of girls' schools in Hamburg, Lübeck, Bremen, Pomerania, Schleswig-Holstein, and Württemberg; in the last state, elementary school was made obligatory for all children in 1649.[74] The impulse for women's education remained strong in the German states well into the seventeenth and later centuries. Protestantism had its impact elsewhere. Under King Gustavus Adolphus, Sweden instituted a system of universal education. It was boasted in 1637 that every peasant child in that kingdom could read and write; before the king died, he had left explicit instructions for the education both holy and humanistic of his six-year-old daughter and successor, Christina.[75] In England, the richest fruit of Protestant education for girls was found in the Quaker schools: fifteen boarding schools had been established by 1671, of which two were for girls only and two for both sexes.[76]

The goals of these schools were limited. Girls were to be instructed so as to fulfill their domestic and religious duties, not so as to attain a general education. The reformer Johann Bugenhagen stated these objectives succinctly: "From such girls who have laid hold of God's word there will come useful, skillful, happy, friendly, obedient, God-fearing, not superstitious and self-willed housewives, who can control their servants and train their children in obedience and to respect them and to reverence God."[77] Beginning in 1587, a prize was to be awarded each year to the best student at the girls' schools of Memmingen—the "queen"— who would win such distinction for her "Great diligence and application in learning her catechism, modesty, obedience, and excellent penmanship."[78] Goals were further specified in 1643: "The main thing is for the girls to learn Christian teachings and religion, together with the explanation of these as it is given in the Christian catechism, and to recite this obediently not only in school, but also in church or wherever else it is requested of them."[79] Minimally instructed, the graduates of this and other such schools returned to their homes and to their spinning.

The convents of Europe also provided an education to some girls of the upper classes: at a steep price, to day students and boarders not destined for the religious life as well as to novices.[80] Here, isolated from the world (*in serbanza*, "put aside"), they learned enough Latin to recite their prayers, the trivium and music, some passages from Scripture and the Fathers, and needlework and its companion arts: chastity, silence, and obedience. Convent schooling expanded in the Counter-Reformation, which spurred some educational ventures for women designed to insulate them from the evils of humanism, laxity, and Protestantism. In Brescia, Angela Merici launched a program of Christian education that spread throughout northern Italy, to Belgium, France, the Netherlands, and Catholic Germany, and continued to have great influence into the seventeenth century.[81] In 1617, the Pope authorized the bishops of France to erect Ursuline convents, which were all pledged to the task of female education. In some locations, the education offered by the Ursulines was elementary only, with minimal instruction in reading and writing. At the school of Faubourg St. Jacques in Paris in the seventeenth century, learning beyond reading, writing, arithmetic, a little Latin, and needlework was discouraged: in 1665 one child who attempted to pursue her Latin studies was prohibited from doing so.[82] In some aristocratic Ursuline boarding schools, however, girls received a secondary education including Latin, Italian, geography, composition, and, always, religious training. Other Counter-Reformation schools followed a similar pattern: those established in the seventeenth century by Mary Ward, for instance, and by the Jansenists at Port-Royal, under the leadership of Jacqueline Pascal (the philosopher's sister).[83] There all learned to read, and they read only holy books.

The Quest for Knowledge

In this patchwork of convent schools, neighborhood schools, household schools, and municipal schools, taught by schoolmistresses who were also laundresses or seamstresses, mothers or nuns, a few girls of even the artisan classes and the petty bourgeoisie began to learn to read and write and figure. They were not normally taught Latin, the gateway to a broad literary education and any advanced subject matter, and major goals were the cultivation of sexual morality, silence, and deference; appropriately they were called "little schools," for little was taught. Nevertheless, it was by such steps that many women at the edge of our own era would eventually gain a level of education equal to that attained by most men. In German towns city women would show a high level of basic literacy before the end of the Renaissance.[84] By the end of the eighteenth century, the German states had acquired the highest male literacy rate in Europe—over 95 percent; female literacy, in these territories where school was mandated for girls as well as boys, could have been nearly as high.[85] In Lyon in the 1560s and 1570s, 28 percent of women named in contracts were able to sign their own names. They were all from families of merchants and publishers, or at worst surgeons and goldsmiths; literacy had not yet extended to women of the artisan classes (although it had to the men), nor to either sex of the working poor.[86] By 1690, nearly 14 percent of all French women could sign their marriage contracts.[87] In Venice in 1587, approximately 12 to 13 percent of all girls (as opposed to about 33 percent of all boys) achieved literacy, at least in the vernacular, including "almost all females of the nobility and the majority of wives and daughters of professional men and merchants."[88] Among the (limited) London merchant class around 1500, if women did not quite receive the same education as men, it appears "that it was quite commonly within their reach."[89] In England at the end of our period, one woman for each four men would be literate; in London, it was five women to seven men.[90]

By the fourteenth century, not only had many women of the elite achieved a basic education, but they had also begun to develop a positive taste for reading vernacular books.[91] The first of these were prayer books and other devotional works, of which the most famous though the most rare are the splendidly illuminated books of hours that are still the showpieces of our museums and libraries. The perusal of pious literature was not too distant, for the first modern generations of female readers, from its auditory reception: perhaps the preaching of sermons in the vernacular, particularly to women, from the thirteenth century forward encouraged the vernacular culture of the Renaissance.[92] While women continued throughout the era to read pious books written in their own language or translated from the Latin, they became avid consumers of other works as well. They read advice books about housewifery or childbirth (such as Rösslin's *Rose Garden*, encountered in the first chapter), and stories, poems, and notorious romances by authors Vives had spurned as "otiose" (such as Boccaccio, whose *Decameron* is addressed to an audience of "dear ladies"). As the patrons, purchasers, consumers, and distributors of books in the vernacular, these women exercised considerable influence in the cultural niche they occupied—even though it was one considered less than and certainly separate from that of the learned, who favored heftier books, in Latin.

One index of the depth of female involvement in vernacular reading is the number of books they owned. A remarkable 186 European laywomen from the fourteenth and fifteenth centuries have been identified as book owners. Of these, the majority (117) owned but one book, although fourteen owned at least fifty, and one—the Frenchwoman Gabrielle de la Tour—owned two hundred manuscripts in 1474.[93] These are the slim but significant beginnings, in an age when books were rare, expensive, and handwritten, of the accelerating contact of women with the written word. The women who owned books also gave them away, and women's wills frequently bequeath beloved volumes to heirs who could not necessarily read; but perhaps they could. In a 1395 will, Lady Alice West left her daughter-in-law "all my books of Latin, English and French,"[94] and four years later Eleanor de Bohun, Duchess of Gloucester, left a French *Golden Legend* (containing saints' lives) to one daughter and a "Book of Psalms" and other "Devotions" to another.[95] A century later the pattern was still in place: Cicely, Duchess of York, left to her granddaughter in 1495 a *Life of Catherine of Siena*, a *Life of Matilda*, and a *Golden Legend*, in which she might read about the holy women who were the revered models of female behavior well into the heart of the Renaissance.[96]

A few women with exceptional resources deliberately shaped their collections. Mahaut, Countess of Artois, ordered thirty books for her library in the thirty years from 1300 to 1330, as well as a reading desk for her own use.[97] Early in the sixteenth century, Anne of Brittany, who survived her two husbands, Charles VIII and Louis XII, both kings of France, inherited the volumes that they had bought and stolen from Italy during their campaigns, and commissioned some more to be made to enrich her collection.[98] A generation earlier, the English royal widow Margaret Beaufort and the Italian duchess Isabella d'Este dealt respectively with the famous early printers William Caxton (supervising the first book to be published in English in 1476) and Aldo Manuzio. Isabella admonished the Venetian printer in 1505 for the high price of volumes he had sent: "When you print any more, at a fair price and on finer paper, with more careful corrections, we shall be glad to see them."[99]

The trickle of vernacular books that came to the hands of women readers became a flood in the centuries that followed as the printing press multiplied the copies of each edition. In England from 1475 to 1640, 163 titles were produced specifically for women, of whom 800 were explicitly named.[100] More than half were "how-to" books of housewifery, midwifery, needlework, and comportment, dominating the field in all but one of sixteen decades. Another 25 percent consisted of books for recreational reading: the romances considered so obnoxious by the Latinists, as well as light history and biography (including biographies of women). Other titles were connected with the controversy about women's nature, of which more later. Devotional titles were few because these were generally not designed specifically for women, although women were ceaselessly enjoined to read them. Overall, the production of vernacular works for Englishwomen accelerated abruptly after 1570: only twenty-four appeared in the first century of printing, while eighty-five (more than half) appeared between 1573 and 1602, with the remaining fifty-four published through 1640.[101] From 1570 through 1640, assuming a press run of 1,500 and counting multiple editions, there were printed perhaps 400,000 volumes targeted for a female audience.

The triumph of the vernacular among laywomen is matched by their distance from Latin, the language of the powerful and their advisers. Latin had been throughout the Middle Ages the property of the more talented of the privileged residents of Europe's convents. Indeed, the tradition of female literacy began in the communities of nuns and holy women, where the root of the modern female intellectual experience is also found. The convent, for all that it was limited to women of the elite and only very few of those, and despite its decline and increasing restrictiveness during the Renaissance centuries, remained the main locus for female learning throughout this era: "religious schools produced virtually all the great intellectual women of the Middle Ages."[102] Nuns knew at least their prayers in Latin; some could understand sermons as well, and the books recited over meals; some could read; some were chosen to recite or to correct the Latin diction of the reciter; some copied the books themselves, or illustrated the manuscript pages. In the convents founded by Bridget of Sweden, as an indication, each nun was to have the books necessary for divine service: "but by no means any more."[103]

No one objected to this education achieved by some nuns, for it was holy and they were cloistered. From their number, and from those who shared their culture without formal claustration, come the great scholars and mystics and *mulieres sanctae*, holy women, of the medieval and Renaissance centuries. Many lived before our period: the very earliest, from the tenth century, was Hrotswitha of Gandersheim, whose works were first edited for print by the sixteenth-century humanist and poet, Conrad Celtis.[104] From the twelfth and thirteenth centuries, foremost among many were Héloise and Hildegard of Bingen, and the three nuns of Helfta: Mechthild von Hackeborn, Saint Gertrude (called the Great), and Mechthild of Magdeburg. By the next century, the age of the great female scholars was well over, and their successors were probably "none too proficient."[105] The author of an early fifteenth-century English version of Benedict's *Rule* explained himself: "Monks and learned men may know the rule in Latin . . . ; it is for the purpose of making it intelligible to women who learnt no Latin in their youth that it is here set into English that they may easily learn it."[106] Nevertheless, in isolation and obscurity, women of the convents and the beguinages read the books available to them and yearned for more.

A seventeenth-century list of works recommended for the residents of a beguinage includes Thomas à Kempis's *The Imitation of Christ*, writings of the mystic Johannes Tauler, sermons of Saint Bernard, treatises of Ambrose, and letters of Jerome.[107] In the fifteenth century, Gregorio Correr urged the noblewoman Cecilia Gonzaga, a humanist trained by Vittorino da Feltre and skilled in Greek as well as Latin, to engage in the kind of studious pursuits that could benefit her sister nuns—and only them; for laywomen did not read such works, and men, lay and cleric alike, read Latin. "A bride of Christ should read only sacred volumes and ecclesiastical writers. Therefore dismiss your beloved Virgil. . . . Take up instead the Psalter, instead of Cicero, the Gospel. . . . You have the writings of the saints, in which you may delight, upon which you may nourish your soul. Read these. Moreover, . . . [you should] gather the better passages, and translate them into the mother tongue for the instruction of the unlettered virgins."[108] At least some of the nuns of the Venetian convent of Santa Croce knew their letters. For their library and at their request, the humanist bishop Ermolao Barbaro (the Elder) prepared a translation from Eusebius's Greek of the life of Saint Athanasius, whose body had recently been brought to rest in their keeping.[109] Arcangela Tarabotti, the reluctant nun of the sixteenth century whose protests were heard in the last chapter, taught herself to read in such a female community, while Beatrice della Sera composed plays.[110] In the mid-fifteenth century Clarissa Leonard, a Beguine at Malines, had been instructed in her twofold duty: "to learn the Psalter and sew." Yet at her death an examination of her belongings turned up a tightly closed box full of little books the hermit had written, unknown to any, by herself.[111]

The fourteenth and later centuries abound with thoughtful and forceful holy women, whose words, written down by themselves or others, won wider audiences; some have already been heard from. Their achievement informs us not only of the revelations which they wanted to communicate, but also of the possible fruits of serious female education. Few of the holy women could write, but they had long experience by oral transmission of passages from scripture and the Fathers from their years in church and convent. Thus equipped, "miraculously" they preached and expounded, claiming the authority of the unlettered who had been seized by God.[112] They could compose mentally in their own languages or even in Latin, and dictate to an amanuensis.[113] From this semiliteracy we have many of the great works of spiritual leaders (including the heretics!) of the Renaissance: notable among them Margery Kempe and

Julian of Norwich, Catherine of Siena and Bridget of Sweden, among others. For Bridget, the condition of semiliteracy was insufficient. She insisted on studying Latin herself, which she began doing in 1350 upon her move to Rome at age forty-seven, and continued until the end of her life.[114] The text of her *Revelations* she personally supervised, establishing to her satisfaction that the words conveyed her true experience in the Latin that would make them acceptable to the world. She had written down in her own tongue and by her own hand the words God had given her, and had them translated into Latin by her confessors. She then listened to the Latin, comparing it to her own autograph, "so that," as the text of the canonization proceedings of 1379–80 reads, "not one word was added or subtracted, but was exactly what she had heard and seen in the divine vision." Sometimes she dictated in an ecstatic trance "as if she was reading from a book; and then the confessor dictated these words in Latin to the scribe, and he wrote them down there in her presence. When the words had been written down she wished to hear them and she listened very carefully and attentively."[115] So the sainted Bridget struggled to bring her insight to the public in the language which she well knew to be the code of the learned and the powerful. Soon women with no claim to sanctity would want to seize hold of that powerful instrument.

If women received the education that men did, wrote the first free-lance author among womankind, the Italo-French Christine de Pizan, they could do anything that men did. "If it were customary to send daughters to school like sons, and if they were then taught the natural sciences, they would learn as thoroughly and understand the subtleties of all the arts and sciences as well as sons. Indeed maybe they would understand them better . . . for . . . just as women have more delicate bodies than men, . . . so do they have minds that are freer and sharper."[116] In cinquecento Venice, Modesta da Pozzo, employing the nom de plume Moderata Fonte—moderate fountain? a river held in check?—for the literary labors of her short lifetime, also claimed women's capacity and right to be educated. In the fourth canto of the thirteen *Canti del Floridoro,* a verse romance otherwise quite unrevolutionary, she states the case.

> In letters, and in every undertaking that man does and speaks of,
>   women have also produced and continue to produce such good
>   fruit that they have no need whatever to envy men. . . .
> Gold which lies hidden in the mine does not cease to be gold,

although entombed; and when it is brought out, and worked, it is as rich and beautiful as all other gold.

If when a girl is born to a father he were to set her alongside his son to an equal task, she would be inferior to her brother in neither grand or small tasks, nor unequal; or if he sent her off with him to the army, or to learn the liberal arts; it is because she has been raised for other things that she is not respected for her learning.[117]

Fonte had sound experience of the equality or superiority of women, given the opportunity, in the realm of learning. She had acquired her own education by entreating her brother, upon his return from school, to teach her the things he had learned.[118]

Fonte's contemporary, Louise Labé of Lyon, the daughter of a rope-maker and one of the few women of her social class to be educated, regretted that she had not attained the level of learning she would have liked and argued the advantages of education for women. "Since the time has come," she wrote her friend, Mademoiselle Clémence de Bourges, "when men's harsh laws no longer prevent women from applying themselves to the arts and sciences, I believe that those of us with the ability to do so should employ in study this noble freedom which our sex has so long desired; and thereby show men how they have wronged us by depriving us of the benefits and honor that we might have enjoyed from study. And if any of us excel to that degree that she can express her thoughts in writing, let her do so proudly and not resist the glory that she will win, greater than that won by necklaces, rings and fine fashions. For these are ours only because we have used them, but the honor which we win through study is truly ours."[119]

In 1622, Marie de Gournay, adopted daughter and literary executor of Michel de Montaigne, pointed to the need for education as the critical element in attaining *The Equality of Men and Women* (*L'Egalité des hommes et des femmes*), as she named the work she dedicated to the queen of France.[120] Sixteen years later, the Dutch-born Anne Marie van Schurmann would sum up such aspirations by publishing her Latin treatise advocating female education: *On the Capacity of the Female Mind for Learning* (*De capacitate ingenii muliebris ad scientias*). Her modest demands, which did not threaten the traditional definition of roles for women, were widely read in French (1646) and English (1673) translations, in which the work's title became less direct and challenging: *Whether it is Necessary for Women to be Educated or Not; The Learned Maid; Or, Whether a Maid may be a Scholar?*[121] Although van Schurmann envisioned female education only for the rich, leisured and pious like herself, she makes some truly startling claims about learning. As it was for this polymath herself, with competence in most modern languages and several ancient ones, she claimed that learning was divorced from both salon and seat of power, and was an end in itself and equally suitable to both sexes. Three of her theses read thus: "Arts and sciences are fitting for those who by nature desire them"; "Whatever perfects and adorns human understanding is fitting to a Christian woman"; "Whatever fills the human mind with uncommon and honest delight is fitting for a Christian woman."[122]

In England in the last two Renaissance centuries, women lamented their exclusion from the classroom and championed their capacity for learning. The male monopoly on learning had been "devised by men in order to secure their own continued domination" complained such works as *The Woman's Sharpe Revenge* of 1640 and Hannah Wolley's *The Gentlewoman's Companion* of 1675.[123] The linguist and royal governess Bathsua Makin wrote in 1673 of the need for women to receive a solid classical education in her *Essay to Revive the Antient Education of Gentlewomen in Religion, Manners, Arts and Tongues.*[124] The teacher of several women of the nobility and even royalty, she recommended a curriculum that included the serious study of languages, ancient and modern, in which she saw the possibility of spiritual liberation for women. "Let Women be Fools," she warned, "and then you may easily make them Slaves."[125] It is an index of women's enslavement that Makin found it necessary in publishing her work to suppress her name and present herself as a male. While these and other critics deplored the state of women's education, they envisioned only a better preparation of that sex for the roles still seen as primary: companionable wife and effective mother. As late as Mary Astell's 1694 *Serious Proposal to the Ladies* urging the higher education of that sex, only a domestic career was envisioned: men will still "enjoy their Prerogatives for us, we mean not to intrench on any of their Lawful Privileges"; "We pretend not that Women sho'd teach in the Church, or usurp Authority where it is not allow'd them; permit us only to understand our *own* duty."[126]

In the ferment of the early Reformation in Germany, some women seized the initiative to employ the learning they had managed to acquire. Katherine Zell, wife of the Strasbourg reformer, spoke of her early attraction not only to the new religion, but also to the circles of its learned adherents: "Ever since I was ten years old I have been a student and a sort of church mother," she wrote in a letter to the hard-liner Ludwig Rabus of Memmingen, "much given to attending sermons. I have loved and frequented the company of learned men, and I conversed much with them, not about dancing, masquerades, and worldly pleasures but about the kingdom of God."[127] Argula von Grumbach, born to the not inconsiderable noble family of the Hohenstaufen, was drawn to the same exciting milieu. She challenged the faculty of the University of Ingolstadt to a debate—in German, as she had no Latin—about the charges of heresy laid against a young professor: "You seek to destroy all of Luther's works. In that case you will have to destroy the New Testament, which he has translated. In the German writings of Luther and Melanchthon I have found nothing heretical. . . . I would be willing to come and dispute with you in Germany and you won't need to use Luther's translation of the Bible. You can use the [Catholic] one written 31 years ago."[128]

So bold a challenge to the male learned order assembled in its university fortress, though exceptional, signals the mood of defiance exhibited by some women proponents of female education in the Renaissance centuries. Since the "old" education was to be discarded for the "new" to be undertaken, it is not surprising that the symbols of the instruments of the socialization of women are explicitly rejected. Woman's traditional education had consisted of textile crafts; so needles and spindles and such presented themselves to a new generation of intellectually independent women as emblems of subjugation. The French poet Louise Labé urged women to raise their thoughts above such implements, "to lift their minds a little beyond their distaffs and their spindles."[129] Another, Catherine des Roches, more ambivalent, addressed her spindle affectionately:

> With you at my side, dear, I feel much more secure
> Than with paper and ink arrayed all around me.

She would love it forever, she promised, and hold it in one hand while she wielded, in the other, her pen.[130] The Ferrarese humanist and Protestant convert Olimpia Morata wrote—in Greek!—of her self-transformation:

> I, a woman, have dropped the symbols of my sex,
> Yarn, shuttle, basket, thread,

I love but the flowered Parnassus with the choirs of joy
Other women seek after what they choose
These only are my pride and my delight.[131]

Male admirers employed the same imagery, as did Angelo Poliziano, one of the giants of quattrocento literature, in his eulogy for the Venetian Cassandra Fedele: in this age when "it is rare even for men to excel in letters, you are the only maiden living who picks up a book instead of wool, a quill instead of rouge, a pen instead of a needle, and who rather than powdering her face, covers paper with ink."[132]

Desiderius Erasmus, the foremost humanist of the next century, recommended that the distaff and spindle, commonly women's tools, be put aside for a higher goal. The well-born train their daughters to work silk and weave tapestries, but "it would be better if they taught them to study, for study busies the whole soul. . . . It is not only a weapon against idleness but also a means of impressing the best precepts upon a girl's mind and of leading her to virtue."[133]

These words are from his work entitled *The Institution of Christian Matrimony*, dedicated in 1526 to Catherine of Aragon, whose own marriage was soon to meet with dissolution.[134] An earlier letter to the reformer Guillaume Budé had first made the point: "I do not necessarily reject the advice of those who would provide for their daughter's virtue through handiwork. Yet there is nothing that more occupies the attention of a young girl than study. Hence this is the occupation that best protects the mind from dangerous idleness, from which the best precepts are derived, the mind trained and attracted to virtue. . . . Nor do I see why husbands should fear that their wives would be less obedient if they are learned. . . . In short, in my judgment, nothing is more intractable than ignorance."[135] Erasmus clearly is no feminist: he urges education for women not so that they may profit themselves or the world but because study is more effective than needlework in chasing away idleness, preserving virginity, and enhancing matrimonial relationships. All his pedagogical works are explicitly concerned with the education of boys. Nevertheless, he recognized women's capacity to learn the same subjects as boys, and greatly admired the learned women of his day: above all Margaret Roper, the daughter of his friend Thomas More, and the probable model for the learned lady who disputes and confutes an abbot in one of his popular colloquies.[136]

A contemporary of Erasmus's joined and exceeded him in admiring female accomplishment: the German physician and humanist Heinrich Cornelius Agrippa von Nettesheim. His generous and forward-looking *On the Nobility and Excellence of Women*, dedicated to Margaret of Burgundy in 1529, made an extraordinary proposal for the full equality of the sexes. The only differences between man and woman were in biological constitution, Agrippa maintained, defying the conventional notion of the inherently distinct natures of the sexes. "In everything else they are the same. Woman does not have a soul of a different sex from that which animates man. Both received a soul which is absolutely the same and of an equal condition. Women and men were equally endowed with the gifts of spirit, reason and the use of words; they were created for the same end, and the sexual difference between them will not confer a different destiny."[137] Agrippa's work dominates the later works that similarly argued the equality of women against traditional authorities. It circulated widely in its original form and within a generation was copied and more broadly diffused by the Italian Ludovico Domenichi and the Englishman Thomas Bercher (Barker), among others.[138] It animates the angry polemic against the Aristotelian and Platonic traditions of the Venetian feminist Lucrezia Marinelli, who stooped to borrow sound arguments from a male supporter.[139]

In this radical claim of spiritual equality and merely physiological differentiation, Agrippa distinguishes his position from that of eulogists of women in the tradition of the poet and scholar Giovanni Boccaccio.[140] Boccaccio's *Concerning Famous Women* parades 106 notable women from Old Testament through medieval times and helped make all readers aware of a sex normally forgotten in letters. Employing the same zeal and skill that he used in the composition of another encyclopedia, his *On the Genealogy of the Gods (De genealogia deorum)*, Boccaccio ransacked the classical corpus for notable female figures: Livy and Ovid, Pliny and Valerius Maximus, Josephus, Suetonius and Tactius, Hyginus, Servius and Lactantius.[141] He should not be blamed, perhaps, for the harm he unintentionally inflicted upon women with this set of portraits laden with misogynist elements. Most of the women he portrayed epitomized those traditional virtues of chastity, silence, and obedience; their example, in fact, reinforced the patriarchal view of a woman's role. Those few he depicted who were active and productive in the public realm (such fearsome figures as Zenobia, Penthesilea, Artemisia, Semiramis, Hippolyta, Camilla, and the like) had violated female sexual norms in some way, for which transgressions they were duly punished: dragged in chains, mar-

tyred, humiliated. Their example, however tantalizing to new generations of women who yearned to burst out of their chains, could also serve
the cause of female oppression.

The work of Boccaccio paved the way for a rash of catalogues of
illustrious women of the biblical, classical, Christian, and local past:
among them Filippo da Bergamo's (*Of Illustrious Women*), Brantôme's
(*The Lives of Illustrious Women*), Pierre Le Moyne's (*The Gallerie of Heroic
Women*) or Pietro Paolo de Ribera's (*The Immortal Triumphs and Heroic
Enterprises of Eight Hundred and Forty-Five Women*).[142] A case in point is the
In Praise of Women (*De laudibus mulierum*) of the humanist Bartolomeo
Goggio, addressed to Eleanora of Aragon, Duchess of Ferrara.[143] That
energetic patroness, who gathered about her learned men and a considerable library, and raised the two Este daughters who would garner
even greater fame, Isabella and Beatrice, must have engendered in her
entourage an atmosphere favorable to female achievement. For Goggio
went very far in his praise of her sex. "I have been able, most illustrious
and most excellent Madam," he wrote to Eleanora, "to narrate the deeds
of innumerable women of the greatest worth, so as to make manifest
their virtues, and [to show] that one may say that in every respect they
have been far superior to men."[144] In spite of his enthusiasm, Goggio's
work was to have no public beyond his patroness and her circle; it survives in a single manuscript, in the Ferrarese dialect. Such catalogues of
illustrious women, which repeatedly rehearsed stories from biblical and
classical antiquity as well as the more recent past, were unable to provide
the reconceptualization of women's role found in, more than any other,
the work of Agrippa. The parades of exceptional women left no legacy
for the ordinary woman, or women as a sex. Their proliferation is notable, however, in an age nearly obsessed with the task of defining the
proper role of women.

The claims for female excellence made by Agrippa had a more direct
descendant in the English Sir Thomas Elyot's *Defense of Good Women*,
dedicated to the English King Henry VIII's fourth wife, Anne of
Cleves.[145] In this dialogue justifying both women's participation in civic
life and prowess in arms, the Roman characters Candidus and Caninus
debated the proposition that woman was the equal of man in her capacity
for reason. The argument was settled after the appearance of the pagan
warrior queen Zenobia, widow of Odenatus, king of Palmyra, one of
those militant figures who appear among Boccaccio's heroines and those
of his followers. Here she comes forth to urge education for women,

claiming that her own training in moral philosophy prepared her for the role of wife, mother, and queen. A regent for her sons, she was thrust into the public arena to make speeches, establish laws, conquer and defend her territory, and rule so benignly that former enemies willingly accepted her authority: "[I] added moche more to myne Empire, not soo moche by force, as by renoume of juste and politike governaunce, whiche all men had in such admyration, that dyverse of our said enemies . . . chose . . . to remayne in our subjection than to retourne to theyr owne countryey."[146]

Were these masculine defenders of female mental capacity primed to positive attitudes because of their relation to female patrons? Elyot wrote for Anne of Cleves; Juan Luis Vives and Erasmus for Catherine of Aragon, Agrippa for Margaret of Burgundy, Boccaccio his *Concerning Famous Women* to the Florentine Andrea Acciaiuoli, and Goggio his *In Praise of Women* to Eleanora of Aragon, Duchess of Ferrara. Perhaps they shaped laudatory views to conform to the inclination of the listener who had commissioned them, or perhaps, thinking well of women, they addressed their writings to influential paragons of that sex.

While that question may be unanswerable, one small group of men at least sincerely believed in the female capacity for advanced education. They are the fathers of learned women whose actions themselves testified to their high estimation of their daughters' intelligence. The fathers of the humanists Laura Cereta and Alessandra Scala (respectively a physician and the humanist chancellor of Florence) were their daughters' instructors in Latin literature, while the fathers of Cassandra Fedele and Olimpia Morata (a Venetian state secretary and a humanist, respectively), men of considerable erudition themselves, provided their daughters with excellent tutors.[147] Not a learned man, but a prince, the father of Cecilia Gonzaga sent his daughter to the famous school of the pedagogue Vittorino da Feltre, alongside her brothers. The proud fathers of Cataruzza Caldiera and Costanza Barbaro, both Venetian humanists, the former also a physician and the latter a leading statesmen, wrote fine Latin works on serious subjects for their offspring. Late in the sixteenth century, Lucrezia Marinelli lived unwed for the first fifty years of her life, absorbing the resources of her father's library and vast knowledge, while the orphans Modesta da Pozzo and Irene da Spilimbergo were nearly as well served by the libraries of their male guardians.[148] Forerunner of all these, Christine de Pizan, the daughter of the physician and court astrologer to King Charles V, was guided by her father, as the personification of Rectitude recalls to her in the *City of Ladies*: "Your father, who was a natural philosopher, was not of the opinion that women grow worse by becoming educated. On the contrary, as you know he took great pleasure from seeing your interest in learning." It was her mother who tried to hold her back from the perilous pursuit of letters: "Your mother, however, who held the usual feminine ideas on the matter, wanted you to spend your time spinning, like other women, and prevented you from making more progress and going deeper into science and learning in your childhood."[149]

Mothers who had themselves been raised in observance of traditional limits on female education were unable to direct their daughters to higher achievement. The anonymous author of the English *Northern Mother's Blessing* of 1420 confirms that the girls "were limited to such narrow and unlettered goals as humility, silence, obedience and chastity."[150] Two seventeenth-century mothers who left didactic works to their children—Dorothy Leigh and Elizabeth Joceline—in discussing the matter of education sketched quite different ambitions for sons than daughters: professional goals for the former, more modest ones for the latter. Joceline wrote that if her yet unborn child proved to be a daughter, "I desire her bringing up may bee learning the Bible, as my sisters doe, good housewifery, writing, and good workes: other learning a woman needs not." Learning for a woman was a risky thing, she warned, unless accompanied by wisdom and humility. But, she addressed her husband, "If thou desirest a learned daughter, I pray God give her a wise and religious heart, that she may use it to his glory, thy comfort, and her owne salvation."[151]

Most fathers did not desire a learned daughter: those who supervised or encouraged their daughters' education were rare. Reading was seen as a useful skill, but it threatened the order of the household. Learning in women engendered lax housekeeping and marital discord, according to the French Calvinist Agrippa d'Aubigné, disapproving of his daughters' quest for an education comparable to their brothers.[152] In 1687, his compatriot Fénelon urged in his *Treatise on the Education of Girls* that (rich) men teach their daughters to read and write, but did not find it necessary for them to learn Latin as boys did; they would have no need of it. Truly able girls might attempt it, but only those "who would not be tempted by vain curiosity, would conceal what they had learned, and would study it only for their own edification."[153] The sixteenth-century saint and scholar Thomas More had educated his daughters, but, as

Fénelon would later advise, only for their own edification. He instructed his daughter Margaret Roper, learned in both Latin and Greek, not to "seek for the praise of the public, nor value it . . . but because of the great love you bear us, you regard us—your husband and myself—as a sufficiently large circle of readers for all that you write."[154] In the seventeenth, Sir Ralph Verney advised his goddaughter, who wished to study Hebrew, Greek, and Latin, to be content with the Bible and the catechism, more appropriate to her sex.[155] At the same time, the English Marquess of Halifax discouraged his daughter's ambitions: advising her to accept the disposition of law and custom, he explained that "there is inequality in the sexes, and that for the better economy of the world the men, who were to be the lawgivers, had the larger share of reason bestowed upon them."[156]

Fathers of daughters were the lawgivers of men, and though some were supportive of their female children's ambitions, most were eager to sustain the order that placed men in charge and left women subordinate. Male hostility to female learning (like the broader tendencies of misogyny and misogamy) was widespread: because men feared to lose their dominion over women, explained the angry scholar Lucrezia Marinelli.[157] Such could well have been the aim of the sixteenth-century pedagogue Silvio Antoniano, who recommended the minimal instruction of women: "As to those of humble status, it is not necessary that they even know how to read; as to those of middle condition, do not teach them to read; as to noblewomen who must be mothers to the children of grand families, I would certainly approve their learning to read a little [*mediocremente*] and do some arithmetic."[158] Those who ventured further endangered themselves and others. In seventeenth-century New England, the governor of Massachusetts charged that the wife of the governor of Connecticut had gone mad from delving into problems of theology: "For if she had attended her household affairs, and such things as belong to women, and not gone out of her way and calling to meddle in such things as are proper for men, whose minds are stronger, etc., she had kept her wits, and might have improved them usefully and honorably in the place God had set her."[159] Two centuries earlier, the guardian of orthodoxy Jean Gerson wrote against the written works of women: they are to be "held suspect," unless "diligently examined" by male spiritual superiors, "much more than the teaching of men. . . . Why? Because women are too easily seduced, because they are too obstinately seducers, because it is not fitting that they should be knowers of divine wisdom."[160]

The problem of women's capacity for learning was an element in the notorious *querelle des femmes* sparked by Jean de Meung's hostile addition to the thirteenth-century *Roman de la Rose*, which was enthusiastically affirmed in the commentary of Jean de Montreuil (1401). The responses it elicited from such luminaries as Christine de Pizan and Jean Gerson launched a debate fought out in several languages, over at least three centuries, and in a plenitude of books—one scholar lists 251 of them.[161] The *querelle* raged in Latin and in the vernacular, in Italy, in France, in England, in the German states, among Catholics, Protestants, and Jews. The period 1595 to 1655 saw at least twenty-one works for and against women published in France. The "problem of women" was discussed in England in a series of works beginning with the misogynistic *The Schole House of Women* (1541), culminating in the famous *Hic mulier*, or the "Man—Woman" (1620), and fading only after 1639. On the one side, proponents of female dignity argued the essential worthiness of femininity; on the other, its essential deficiency. In the end such an astonishing effusion of proud and angry words accumulated on the single issue that it is difficult to name a twentieth-century debate that has dominated the culture of the learned to such an extent or enlisted, at one time or another, so many of its soldiers.

A cameo of the debate is contained in the pages of Castiglione's *Book of the Courtier*, where one of the principal interlocutors, Giuliano de' Medici champions the female cause against the traditional misogynist, Gasparo Pallavicino. Giuliano, the "Magnifico," denies that men are more perfect than women, for both men and women are of the same human essence: "For just as no stone can be more perfectly a stone than another, as regards the essence stone, nor one piece of wood more perfectly wood than another piece—so one man cannot be more perfectly man than another; and consequently the male will not be more perfect than the female as regards their formal substance, because the one and the other are included under the species man, and that in which the one differs from the other is an accident and is not of the essence. Thus, if you tell me that man is more perfect than woman, if not in essence, at least in accidental qualities, I will answer that these accidental qualities necessarily belong either to the body or to the mind; if to the body, man being more robust, more quick and agile, and more able to endure toil, I say that this little argues perfection, because among men themselves those who have these qualities more than others are not more esteemed for that; and in wars, where the operations are, for the most part, laborious and call for strength, the sturdiest are not more esteemed; if to the mind, I say that women can understand all the things men can understand and that the intellect of a woman can penetrate wherever a man's can."[162] Since women are the equals of men in fundamental qualities, "you will find that worth has constantly prevailed among women as among men; and that there have always been women who have undertaken wars and won glorious victories, governed kingdoms with the greatest prudence and justice, and done all that men have done. As for the sciences, do you not remember reading of many women who were learned in philosophy? Others who excelled in poetry? Others who prosecuted, accused and defended before judges with great eloquence? As for manual works, it would be too long to tell of them."[163]

Signor Gasparo opposed the Magnifico's concession to the female sex of capacity for both virtue and knowledge. "For it should have been enough for you to make this Court Lady beautiful, discreet, chaste, affable, and able to entertain . . . in dancing, music, games, laughter, witticisms . . . ; but to wish to give her knowledge of everything in the world, and allow her those virtues that have so rarely been seen in men during the past centuries, is something one cannot endure or listen to at all."[164] Woman's very existence is flawed, he argued, repeating the generally accepted Aristotelian view: "when a woman is born, it is a defect or mistake of nature."[165] To elevate them to the ranks of men is to subvert the order of nature itself. "I am quite surprised," he objected, "that you do not wish them to govern cities, make laws, lead armies, and let the men stay at home to cook or spin."[166] The mention of spinning alerts us to the obdurate substratum of Renaissance thinking about women: their role is to reproduce, their home is their fortress and their prison, their destiny is endless work with needle and spindle. If they step beyond these limits they have become what women must not be: they become men, and turn men into women.

Amazons and Armed Maidens

The possibility of the reversal of sexual roles threatened the Renaissance men who wrote books, governed cities, and guided social behavior. The man ridden by a woman—as Phyllis humiliated the philosopher Aristotle—was the butt of jokes and the subject of the popular village carnivals called *charivari*, so characteristic especially of the sixteenth century.[167] In Renaissance Florence, the same humorous but fearful emblem appeared on the decorated chests and dishes that accompanied a bride, along with her dowry, to a new husband.[168] The English *Hic mulier*, or *The Man-Woman*, crystallizes the hatred felt by men for women who aspired to literary or public roles: the unsexed "Masculine-Feminine," it charged, should throw off her "deformities" and clothe herself properly in the purposes intended for her: chastity, silence, piety, obedience towards her husband, nurture for her children.[169] Masculine women represented a "refusal of obedience" to the prevailing culture, and like the ancient Amazons, a repudiation of the very domesticity defined as woman's natural and proper condition: they were "monstruous women," said John Knox, "that could not abide the regiment of men, and therefore killed their husbands."[170] Hostile representations of such disordered nature cautioned matrons and brides to respect their natural limits. Women whose ambitions or destinies pushed them to adopt an Amazonian role, to stride boldly into the male realms of culture and society, took on the burden of confused or illegitimate sexuality.

The pages of Renaissance books bristle and thunder with armed and dangerous women, the personifications, both fearful and admirable, of inverted sexual order.[171] From Ariosto and Tasso to Spenser and Milton, Bradamantes and Britomarts stalk the pages of the first two centuries of print, the only type of women in imaginative literature possessing "liberty and authority on a par with man."[172] Some are malevolent and perverse, quickly slain, fated to destruction like the armed protagonists of Boccaccio's catalogue. Some are righteous and pure, and uphold the male values that their very existence would seem to threaten. Ariosto's Bradamante battles to win her lover Ruggiero, by whom she will herself be mastered, while his Marfisa, who looked like a man but was a woman, "in battle wonderfully fierce,"[173] pledges to remain everchaste. Edmund Spenser's *Faerie Queene* features the armed confrontation of two warrior-maidens, icons respectively of evil and good: Radigund, destructive and disobedient, and Britomart, equally fierce, but submissive to male order and the taming institution of marriage.[174] By the seventeenth century, fascination with the "manly woman" would peak in the odd exaltation of the *femme forte*, especially in France and Italy: the armed and powerful woman who strutted in images both verbal and visual.

If it is surprising that such a crowd of men-women existed in literature, it is more surprising still that they existed in fact: for in these centuries two sworn virgins—Joan of Arc, who donned armor, and Elizabeth Tudor, who ruled a nation—were living Amazons who aroused the same combination of fear and admiration as the warrior ladies of epic literature did. The bold refusal of the latter "sublime androgyne"[175] to secure the biological continuity of her dynasty, choosing the man's direct exercise of power instead of a traditional role, has already been considered. The transvestism of the former is of deeper concern here. Her male habit was a major concern at her trial, for it represented a disturbance of divine order as fundamental as the claim of visions and voices. She had "given up and rejected female dress," her accusers charged, and wore "a shirt, breeches, a doublet with hose attached by twenty laces, leggings laced on the outside, a short robe, to the knees, a cap, tight boots, long spurs, a sword, a dagger, a coat of mail, a lance, and other arms," all of which was "in violation of canon law, abominable to God and men, and prohibited by the sanctions of the Church."[176] Condemned once and persuaded to abjure, she shed masculine attire, but within a few days repented of her abjuration and donned her tunic and cap once again. A virgin and a soldier, she refused to be contained by the barriers of sex, and went to her death neither male nor female.

The proliferation of the Amazon is striking enough, but still more curious is the extension of that symbolism to the figure who most concerns us here: the learned woman. She was identified with the female ruler and the female soldier because she, like they, had invaded the masculine—that is, the public—realm: war, politics, learning; they all inhabited the same country, in clear contradistinction to the nation of those who spin. One laid down her distaff for a spear, another for a scepter, another for a pen; all alike had transgressed the adamantine limits of female activity. By that act, represented in both literature and the arts by the assumption of arms, the exceptional woman is distanced (not by herself, but by male observers) from the female norm. The refiguration of such a woman as masculine accounts for the appearance of extraordinary qualities in a creature otherwise known to be inferior: it exalts "masculinity and reasserts the inferiority of women."[177]

Female trespassers of the boundaries of sexual definition were hated and feared, as the large corpus of misogynist literature bears witness. But extraordinary women, depicted in fearful Amazonian array, aroused admiration as well: precisely because their achievements were manly! Boccaccio admired Andrea Acciaiuoli, to whom he addressed his catalogue of famous women, precisely because she had become, in a sense, a man: "and when I saw that what Nature has taken from the weaker sex God in His liberality has granted to you, instilling marvelous virtues within your breast, and that He willed you to be known by the name you bear (since in Greek *andres* means "man"), I [judged] that you should be set equal to the worthiest men, even among the ancients."[178] Christine de Pizan was likewise acclaimed by the theologian Gerson as a "distinguished woman, manly female."[179] Christine herself, in her auto-biographical poem bewailing the turns of Fortune's wheel, *Le livre de la Mutacion de Fortune*, said that circumstances had made a man of her: the mutation of fortune had caused her own transmutation from female to male, as she picked up her pen to support her family.[180] Lauro Quirini would praise Isotta Nogarola by declaring she had "overcome your own nature. For that true virtue, which is essentially male, you have sought with singular zeal, such as befits the whole and perfect virtue that men attain."[181] The same sexual transformation was recognized in Olimpia Morata, carved in her epitaph years after her death: her body was female, her mind male, her spirit, God's.[182]

When women were merely women, on the other hand, they were despised. Disordered, unstable, cold and wet, "hysterical," they were all womb, the Greek *hysteros*. Rabelais's memorable passage epitomizes the Renaissance view of the womanly woman: within her body, "in a secret and intestinal place," Nature had placed "a certain animal or member which is not in man, in which are engendered, frequently, certain humours, brackish, nitrous, boracious [*sic*], acrid, mordant, shooting and bitterly tickling, by the painful prickling and wriggling of which . . . the entire feminine body is shaken, all the senses ravished, all the passions carried to a point of repletion, and all thought thrown into confusion."[183] A "manly" woman was altogether more sympathetic—except that she could not bear children and fulfill familial roles. Physicians confronting the problem of amenorrhea admired the patient whom they needed nevertheless to recall to her state of defective nature. Women who were naturally hot and manly were actually healthier than "moister" women, and not sick at all, though they were sterile. For that reason, as John Pechy wrote in his 1696 *General Treastise of the Diseases of Maids, Big-bellied Women, Child-bed Women, and Widows*, "Such as are robust and of a manly Constitution must by all means be reduced to a womanly state; that they

may become fit for generation, they must forbear strong meats and Labour, and the Courses must be forced, and by Bleeding and Purging and
the like, the habit of the Body must be rendred cold and moist."[184] The
manly woman, the aberration from the natural, who could perform great
works, was both liked and feared more than the womanly woman, the
defect of nature, who, despised, bore the world's children, male and
female alike.

Could the manly woman be tamed? Could the achieving woman
present herself in such a way that she might win respect for her attainments but not upset her culture's axial balance of sexual roles? There
was a road open to her, and male advisers pointed her to the gate
where she might pay her toll and gain the right of entry. That road had
been prepared by the female saints and martyrs, who like the *femme
forte* of the Renaissance centuries performed heroic deeds and declined
to accept a domestic role. Since such a woman had defied her own
sexuality, she could deny it too and be both virgin and Amazon, a
maiden armed.

In antiquity and the Middle Ages, women of surpassing spiritual
achievement had been masculinized, as the female rulers and scholars
and fictitious heroines of the Renaissance would be later. The Fathers of
the Church had hailed the manliness of virginal women, adopting the
classical ideal of the *virago*: "the female military hero who achieves
equivalence, or indeed eminence, in the world by becoming not a great
woman but, as it were, a man (*vir*)."[185] Jerome had made the sexual aspects of sanctity pellucid: "as long as woman is for birth and children,
she is different from man as body is from soul. But when she wishes to
serve Christ more than the world, then she ceases to be a woman and will
be called a man."[186] Many of the female saints, like the bellicose Amazons, were pictured wearing or indeed wore men's clothing.[187] Learned
women could assume the inheritance of the transvestite virgin of
Christian antiquity, abjure a domestic role, avoid the convent, and win
the praise of a small circle of male observers. Grudgingly these cen-
sorious judges gave their blessing to the women who created a new
model of female existence, an alternative to those of Eve (woman in the
family) and of Mary (woman in the cloister): the sexless virago, a hybrid
of virgin and crone; the female-man, dangerously competent; the frigid
Amazon, the armed maiden. Late in the trecento, the Veronese Antonio
Loschi introduced into humanist discourse the images that would shape

the persona of the learned woman in a poetic eulogy, with prose commentary, of the earliest known female humanist, Maddalena Scrovegni.[188]

Loschi was the scion of a noble Vicentine family that had turned on its native lords to support the Visconti of Milan; Scrovegni was the daughter of a noble Paduan family that had made the same choice. The two young humanists were caught up in the exchange of services, letters, and eulogies that such political choices entailed in the cultivated northern Italian arena. Thus made aware of Scrovegni's learning, Loschi stepped aside from his official role to offer his eulogy in 1389. He would build for Scrovegni a Temple of Chastity on foundations of poetry, Loschi explained in his letter, which provides an indispensable gloss. She had so earnestly cultivated the virtue of chastity that she had become its embodiment. The Temple itself, which he would build with the mortar of poetic imagery, would be modeled on the little study—*sacellum*—in her father's house where the widowed Scrovegni sat with her books, a sight that had so moved Loschi "that it first gave birth to this meditation within me."[189]

The learned Scrovegni seated in her study is thus transformed by Loschi's poetic imagination into the analogous figure of Chastity seated in her Temple. This temple is located in Scythia, the inaccessible homeland of the pure and warlike Amazons, where a lofty and wooded mountain rises from the center of an immense plain encircled by the sea. At its summit, white marble walls enclose a courtyard planted with laurel and resonant with the cries of turtle doves. Within that courtyard stands the Temple of Chastity; within it burns the sacred flame of Vesta, and on its walls are incised images of men and women famed for the virtue it memorializes in stone: Hippolytus, Penelope, Arethusa, Dido, Lucretia, and others. Inside, Chastity presides as queen, enthroned on glass, surrounded by the attendant figures of Continence, Penitence, and Virginity, while her gatekeeper, Frugality, successfully repulses the attacks of the warlike Cupid. This poetic representation blends images of power and chastity, intelligence and frigidity, virile Amazons and the womblike recess of the mind itself, the Temple set at the deep center of a system of concentric circles. Rigid on her throne, surrounded by her virtuous keepers, within a temple within a courtyard within tall walls on a mountaintop ringed by an icy plain enclosed by the sea, Chastity-Scrovegni is as much prisoner as sovereign.

Learned Women

Both captive and goddess in the frozen wasteland of the Amazons, Scrovegni was the first of the women humanists who would flower and die over the next two centuries, first in Italy, then elsewhere in western Europe, prodigies of Renaissance culture. Within a generation after Loschi had written in Latin prose and verse to Scrovegni, Leonardo Bruni had outlined a serious classical curriculum for Battista Montefeltro. She should read Latin works of history, moral philosophy, and poetry, the whole spectrum of the *studia humanitatis* that men of this generation had formed for themselves, with the striking exception of rhetoric: "For why should the subtleties of . . . rhetorical conundrums consume the powers of a woman, who never sees the forum? The art of delivery . . . [is] so far . . . from being the concern of a woman that if she should gesture energetically with her arms as she spoke and shout with violent emphasis, she would probably be thought mad and put under restraint. The contests of the forum, like those of warfare and battle, are the sphere of men."[190] Since a woman had no role outside of household or convent, the art of oratory would be for her useless.

Scrovegni and Montefeltro were the forerunners of a group of women humanists who possessed a genuine Latin erudition (sometimes Greek as well) and were productive in a number of genres. Others would follow; a dozen can easily be named and perhaps another twenty could be found, while others continue to elude us. They came from ruling or patrician families, often from families that specialized in learning, and even families that specialized in learning for women. For some—such as Cecilia Gonzaga, Costanza Varano, Isabella Sforza, Alessandra Scala— we have the testimony of contemporaries and a few slight works to bear witness to humanist training and achievement. But of four notable women whose careers span the early fifteenth to the early sixteenth century, rich records survive to memorialize their considerable learning and intellectual courage: the Veronese noblewoman Isotta Nogarola; the Brescian Laura Cereta, daughter of a physician; the Venetian Cassandra Fedele, of a cultivated citizen dynasty active in that city's secretariat; and Olimpia Morata, daughter of the Ferrarese court humanist, later émigré spouse of a young German Lutheran. These women turned to the finest curriculum available to men of the day: that forged by the quattrocento humanists. Unlike their contemporaries, who, if they read at all, consumed the diet of advice books, prayer books, and romances that circulated in the vernacular, these women mastered the authors whose works were the foundation of the grand edifice of European thought. These women's letters, poems, orations, and treatises place them alongside the humanists of the day. They set a standard for female academic achievement that was scarcely equaled before the modern era.

Isotta Nogarola was born to a noble Veronese family that had already honored learning in at least one woman: her aunt, Angela.[191] Nogarola's widowed mother, exceptional among the mothers of the learned women encountered in these pages, chose to have both her young daughters educated in the finest curriculum available. She hired for their instruction the tutor Martino Rizzoni, himself an alumnus of the famed Guarinian school that was shaped in the Veneto and later migrated to the court city of Ferrara. Under this tutelage flourished the two sisters Isotta (Isolde, or Iseult) and Ginevra (Guinevere), whose names aped the heroines of romance, not Latinity. As adolescents, they were already famous, and admiring letters from several humanists of the northern Italian region were directed to them both. But by 1438, when Isotta was twenty and Ginevra twenty-one, the latter married the Brescian nobleman Brunoro Gambara. Thereafter her studies ceased. Isotta was determined to continue her scholarly pursuits, and did so for the rest of her life. But not the classical studies of her youth: too much disdain and plain opposition greeted her attempts to enter the male circles of the learned. At the sere age of twenty-three, she renounced secular studies for sacred ones, and forsook her gay life amid the highly born and cultivated for the isolation of a room in her mother's house. In this she replicated the pattern of the saints, nuns, and holy women who, avoiding marriage, sought the seclusion of the convent or hermitage. But Isotta was no holy woman; a scholar she remained, and she is known not for her miracles or her ascetic feats, but for her letters, orations, and treatises.

Why did Nogarola turn from the exciting world of the learned and the powerful to seek seclusion in her "book-lined cell"?[192] Her decision must have been influenced by the reception accorded so bold a woman by the men she encountered. Beginning at age eighteen, Nogarola had initiated correspondence with statesmen, churchmen, and professional humanists, ranking among the great men of her age. Those who responded to her letters praised her; but their words of praise were sometimes faint and concealed disdain. The male humanists who admired Isotta compared her not to learned men but to other women—whom she clearly excelled—making her a strange prodigy who, though exalted, could only be a stranger to the very society of learned men she begged to enter. Not all the reactions to her learning were subtle. One pseudonymous writer accused her, in an obscene letter to his friend, of acts that would crumble a woman's reputation: promiscuity and incest. The slanderer assumed a link between Nogarola's unnatural erudition and the unnatural sexuality he alleged. She "who has won such praise for her eloquence, does things which little befit her erudition and reputation. . . . Before she made her body generally available for promiscuous intercourse, she had first permitted, and indeed even earnestly desired, that the seal of her virginity be broken by none other than her brother, so that by this tie she might be more tightly bound to him. Alas for God in whom men trust . . . when she, who sets herself no limit in this filthy lust, dares to engage so deeply in the finest literary studies."[193] This charge of lewdness was apparently provoked by the offense to masculine propriety perceived in her attempt to enter the male preserve of humanist studies.

While Nogarola could not have been encouraged in her scholarly ambition by this attack, the events that more immediately propelled her decision to retreat from the world occurred early in 1437. It was known that Nogarola had written to Guarino Veronese, her compatriot, at the summit of his fame. When Guarino did not reply, the women of Verona ridiculed Nogarola, and rejoiced in her humiliation at his silence. Nogarola wrote Veronese a second time, reproaching him for having exposed her to the mockery of her sex. The letter is a fine portrait of the emotions experienced by a woman caught between female resentment and male disdain: "There are already so many women in the world! Why then was I born a woman, to be scorned by men in words and deeds? I ask myself this question in solitude. I do not dare to ask it of you, who have made me the butt of everyone's jokes. Your unfairness in not writing to me has caused me such suffering, that there could be no greater suffering. . . . You might have cared for me more if I had never been born. For they jeer at me throughout the city, the women mock me. I cannot find a quiet stable to hide in, and the donkeys [the women] tear me with their teeth, the oxen [the men] stab me with their horns."[194] When Guarino received this plaintive letter, he replied immediately both to reassure and to reprove the young woman. She was wondrously learned, he acknowledged. "But now you seem so humbled, so abject, and so truly a woman, that you demonstrate none of the estimable qualities that I thought you possessed."[195] She must set her sex aside and create "a man within the woman."

She had done so by 1441: pledging herself to virginity, she retreated to a solitary room where she combined religious devotions with the study of sacred letters. In this hermetic existence, she won the praise that had never been unqualifiedly hers when, young and nubile, she had circulated in the world. The Venetian nobleman Lauro Quirini outlined for her a program of study that did not neglect rhetoric or philosophy, pursuits considered by Bruni earlier and Vives later to be beyond a woman's range.[196] He congratulated her at the outset for her already great and unusual achievements: "dissatisfied with the lesser studies, you have applied your noble mind also to the higher disciplines, in which there is need for keenness of intelligence and mind."[197] She was engaged, he noted approvingly, in the study of dialectic, after which the next step was philosophy. Read, above all, Aristotle (the central authority of the community of scholars at Padua, where Quirini studied and taught), along with the commentaries of Boethius and the Arab philosophers Avicenna, Averroes, and Al Ghazali, all available in Latin. As she had no Greek, the commentators who wrote in that language were closed to her until translations had been made. Of scholastic authors, he advises only Thomas Aquinas. By this difficult curriculum, she would ascend to knowledge of philosophy, than which "there is nothing among human things more divine." She should give her whole heart to these demanding studies, "for I want you to be not semi-learned, but to have knowledge of all the good arts, that is, to know the art of good speaking and the discipline of correct disputation, as well as the science of human and divine things."[198] And he promised his love.

More powerful and more personal was the admiration of another nobleman of Venice, Ludovico Foscarini, which clearly exceeded friendship. His acquaintance with her had begun when he was the Venetian *podestà*, or governor, of Verona. Their rich correspondence documents their mature relationship, which, though intimate and enduring, respected the limits on their relationship set by her vows of sanctity and his political and marital responsibilities. He praised her for her poverty, her simple dress contrasting with "the golden robes," "the bursting wardrobes" of her family.[199] Recalling a recent visit, he surveyed in his memory "your little cell, which from every corner breathes forth sanctity. I think of the sacred relics touched by my hands. . . . I put before my eyes those pictures portraying the saints, the robes embroidered with designs of crosses and the images of the blessed . . . and all the other things . . . which brought me a kind of foretaste of paradise."[200]

A chorus of voices reminded Nogarola to guard her virginity intact: it was the prime credential for a woman in all her pursuits, including that of studious solitude. One urged upon her the model of the Virgin Mary. Another declined to visit her, unwilling to expose himself—and her—to temptation. A third discouraged the dangerous visits of the enamored Foscarini. Foscarini himself rebuked Nogarola when she, at age thirty-five, gave serious thought to a proposal of marriage. It was not proper, he wrote, "that a virgin should consider marriage, nor even think about that liberty of lascivious morals, that libidinous cohabitation."[201] When Nogarola suggested to him, however, that he should join her in holy solitude, he declined to play Abelard to her Héloise: he could not abandon his career of state service and the responsibilities of his social position. It was her job to pursue a holy life, and his to do the Senate's bidding.

It was in a discussion with Foscarini, first worked out in letters and then recorded by Nogarola in dialogue form in one of the most interesting of female humanist works, that this beleaguered figure fully confronted the predicament of her sexual identity.[202] The subject of the debate was an old one—it had been argued by Augustine, and would reappear in the works of Castiglione and Agrippa von Nettesheim and others: the relative gravity of the sins of Adam and Eve in the garden of Eden. Upon that judgment rested the world's opinion of masculinity and femininity. In the dialogue, Nogarola defended Eve, and Foscarini Adam. But even while championing Eve, Isotta deprecated the female sex. Her defense, paradoxically, was based on the weakness of female nature. Created imperfect, Eve could not be held responsible for universal sin. God had made Eve ignorant; but Adam He had created perfect: "When God created man, from the beginning he created him perfect, and gave him a greater understanding and knowledge of truth, and also a greater profundity of wisdom."[203] At the summit of her literary career, Nogarola here declares her conviction that woman was essentially inferior to man, and that all women were to bear the burden of the first acts of creation. She lived with that construction of relations between the genders for the quarter-century of her voluntary solitude, and for the rest of her life.

Cassandra Fedele, born in the decade of Nogarola's death, followed a different trajectory: her studious activities were begun in childhood, interrupted by marriage, and pursued into extreme old age.[204] Of the citizenry rather than the aristocracy, Fedele's male relatives tended to respected employment in the bureaucracies of the Venetian state and church. Her father, grandfather, and great-grandfather, moreover, had all been renowned for their learning. She was thereby well placed to win the attention of the governors of Venice and of Italy, and such attention was the objective of her father. For Angelo Fedele, his intelligent daughter Cassandra represented a powerful instrument in his own quest for reputation. His son, who attained a standard of intellectual achievement appropriate and traditional for Fedele males, could serve no such function. But a learned daughter would be a prodigy truly remarkable in an age that admired genius especially in its rarer forms.

Accordingly, Angelo had his daughter tutored in Latin and Greek by the Servite theologian and humanist Gasparino Borro, even permitting these studies priority over the domestic activities which typically constituted the education of young Venetian women. Fedele mastered Latin—by age twelve—as well as Greek, rhetoric, history, some philosophy, and the inevitable sacred studies. Her precocious career was crowned by her successful public appearances as a reciter of orations at the University of Padua, to the people of Venice, and before the Venetian Doge Agostino Barbarigo. She won great favor with the Doge, who invited her and the proud Angelo to banquets where she shone among a circle of Venetian citizens, writers, and poets. When Queen Isabella of Aragon invited Fedele to join her court, the young woman's decision to leave her fatherland was countermanded by the Venetian Senate, which issued a decree forbidding so great an asset to leave Venice. In 1491, when Fedele was twenty-six and already an object of international fame, the Florentine poet and humanist Angelo Poliziano testified to her achievements. Using the words with which Virgil had honored the warrior maiden Camilla, he hailed Fedele as the "ornament" of Italy and, still more powerfully, as companion in his affections with the heroic genius Pico: "Indeed, I used to admire Giovanni Pico della Mirandola, than whom there never was a mortal more brilliant, nor, I judge, more excellent in all branches of knowledge. Now behold, I began to revere also you, Cassandra, immediately after him, and even perhaps alongside of him."[205] Fedele's grand success served as a model for other women as well: the French poet Catherine des Roches held her up as an example, and she was celebrated by the young German jurist Christoph Scheurl alongside his compatriot Caritas Pirckheimer.[206]

The meteoric success of Cassandra Fedele, acclaimed by both the monarchs and the intellectuals of her day, is a little disturbing: for her literary achievements were rather slight. Her ample letters and orations lack originality, and other works mentioned in her correspondence were begun but never completed. Though she was remarkable in having achieved as much as she did in an environment unreceptive to female genius, Fedele also appears to have been a victim of her father's quest for prestige and her city's for yet another symbol of civic excellence—a woman of intelligence. Once she reached the age—about thirty-three—when she could no longer garner admiration for the precocity that had graced her beauty, she was married to a Vicentine physician—despite her original intention not to do so. The productive period of her studies came to an end. She was not heard from again for sixteen years, after which there was silence for seven years more, and then silence again for twenty-six.

Fedele's life after her marriage would have been unremarkable were it not for three facts: she had no children; her husband died young; and she herself survived to the astonishing age of ninety-three. After her husband's death, having no further domestic responsibilities, she returned to her studies. But that pursuit has left no traces. Two letters survive from this period, testifying not to her literary activity but to her anxious poverty. Her husband had died poor, his patrimony lost in an accident at sea, and her family was unwilling or unable to alleviate her poverty. Thus the "ornament of Italy" and the glory of the female sex was in her old age inadequately succored by her family and shamefully ignored by her city and even, at first, by the Church. For it was to Pope Leo X that Fedele addressed her first importunate letter of 1521, soon after her husband's death. She aimed (unsuccessfully, it appears) for a pension to support the impoverished old woman who had once been renowned for her knowledge. Twenty-six years later, at the age of eighty-two, she wrote in greater distress to Pope Paul III: "Age and necessity, most blessed Father, afflict me with deep anguish, misfortunes press me on every side, I lead my life in the face of all extremities."[207] She felt that death was imminent and implored his immediate assistance. He responded to her plea, interceding with the Venetian Senate to appoint her prioress of the orphanage attached to the church of San Domenico di Castello, where she worked until her death and where she was buried. The Senate, which had for nearly thirty years neglected the learned woman it had once jealously forbidden to emigrate, allowed her one final honor. In 1556, at the age of ninety-one, she delivered a Latin oration to welcome the visiting Queen of Poland: a prodigy again, of senectitude as she had been of youth. Two years later she died. Her will left a small sum to the friars of San Domenico, her residual property to her maid and her nephew's wife, and her books to his sons. Could the thought have occurred to her, as she bequeathed to them those valuable objects, that they who looked forward to careers as lawyers, doctors, and civil servants might discover in them a utility that she had never found?

Laura Cereta, the daughter of a learned physician of the troubled city of late quattrocento Brescia, was gifted with a temperament more defiant than either Nogarola or Fedele.[208] The opinion of the community of learned men had cowed one into a book-lined cell and the pressures of domesticity had reduced the other to a nearly interminable silence. But Cereta as a girl and as a widow—her marriage at age fifteen to a Brescian merchant ended with his death eighteen months later—would not pull in her horns. She was proud of her knowledge, and recorded it in some detail: as her mind acquired small particles of knowledge, she learned to supply words to adorn them; her mind yearned for studies even more challenging, and as her understanding expanded, so did her diligence; she loved philosophy above all; she burned with desire for mathematics; she delved deeply into theology, and she found there knowledge not "shadowy and vaporous" but "perpetually secure and perfect."[209] The main targets of her prose, supercharged with elaborate locutions, obscure allusions, and anachronisms, were the falsely learned men of her acquaintance and the idle, useless women who abused her for her ambitions. Such women search out others who have risen above them by their genius and destroy them with poisonous envy, she wrote. "I cannot bear the babbling and chattering women, glowing with drunkenness and wine, whose impudent words harm not only our sex but even more themselves. . . . Inflamed with hatred, they would noisily chew up others, [except that] mute, they are themselves chewed up within." Virtue and learning are not acquired through destiny but through effort; women who are unable to ascend to knowledge fall into sloth and sink into the filth of pleasures.[210] Look at the women in the piazza! she mocked. "Among them . . . is one who ties a towering knot—made of someone else's hair—at the very peak of her head; another's forehead is submerged in waves of crimped curls; and another, in order to bare her neck, binds with a golden ribbon her golden hair. One suspends a necklace from her shoulder, another from her arm, another from neck to breast. Others choke themselves with pearl necklaces; born free, they boast to be held captive. . . . O the weakness of our sex, stooping to voluptuousness!"[211]

Outspoken as she was, Cereta aroused enmities, foremost among them spokesmen of the traditional church who wished to channel her intellectual fire in the usual direction: cold and wet, consistent with the humoral composition, as it was thought, of the female. Cereta's mind is excellent, the Dominican Tommaso of Milan wrote the young woman's father Silvestro, but "she gives herself to things unworthy of her"— that is, to classical learning, when she would more fittingly lead a holy life in the shadow of a holy man, as did Magdalene in Christ's, Paula and Eustochium in Jerome's, or Scholastica in Benedict's.[212] "Blunt your pen and temper it with the file of modesty," he advised Cereta.[213] A few months later she did: she published the letters she had written in three busy years, and, eighteen years old, retired into silence.

It was astonishing that Laura Cereta was bold enough to defy custom and opinion and to continue in the labored language of the scholar to clear a space in the world she knew for female achievement; but bolder still was Olimpia Morata, daughter of the erudite and heterodox Fulvio Pellegrino Morata, who lived during his daughter's adolescence at the Ferrarese court.[214] In that glittering center of Renaissance culture, Morata's friends were the ladies-in-waiting of the duchess Renée, and her close companion was the latter's daughter Anne, who later married into the French Guise family of Catholic zealots. The two girls studied together under the young German humanist Chilian Senf (Latin Sinapius), and Olimpia, at least, mastered both ancient tongues, read widely in the secular classics, and began to compose the poems, letters, and dialogues that are the not inconsiderable relics of her brief twenty-nine years of life. Unlike so many of her predecessors, female humanists and holy women alike, the young Olimpia had little interest in sacred studies. But she was moved in their direction by an event beyond her control: the establishment of the Roman Inquisition of 1542. In the climate of accusation and persecution that followed, Morata was pressed to declare herself. Among her circle of erudite male friends and advisers were adherents of the Reform—including her own father, his friend Celio Secundo Curione, her tutor Sinapius and his brother, and their friend and her future husband, the physician Andreas Grunthler. Soon after her father's death in 1548, she was dismissed from court, stripped even of the clothes she had worn while in its company. She was in disgrace, perhaps, for the dangerous habit it seems she had acquired: reading the Old and New Testaments. She married Grunthler in 1550, and with him returned to his native town of Schweinfurt in German Franconia.

Now a Lutheran physician's wife in the zestful days of early Protestantism, Morata poured forth letters in Latin and Italian to the friends of her youth: to the Catholic noblewomen Lavinia della Rovere, Cherubina Orsini, and Anne of Guise, urging upon the first the works of Luther and upon the third the need for tolerance and mercy, two traits not much cultivated among the Guises; and to the Italian exiles and converts to the reform, Curione in Basel and Pier Paolo Vergerio in Tübingen. Soon she was caught up in the wars caused by the questions of conscience that tormented her generation. Schweinfurt was besieged, and she and her husband fled, sick, naked, penniless, and at the limits of fatigue. The Grunthlers survived their ordeal and were reestablished at Heidelberg in 1554, though Olimpia never recovered from the malarial illness she contracted during the siege.

From Heidelberg, Olimpia wrote Curione of her experiences, lamenting amid her other hardships that her books and her own manuscript writings had been lost. Curione attempted to fill the void made by the burning of those previous volumes in Latin and Greek: "I have given directions to our booksellers that on my account you may receive whatever you require. Homer and several other books have been sent for you to Frankfurt as presents. If to be found in that city, I have taken care that you shall have the commentaries on the Lamentations of Jeremiah that with him you may lament your husband's country. Remember that we have sent you whatever remains of Sophocles."[215] On her deathbed in 1555, she dictated in Latin to her husband her last letter, addressed to Curione. "I must inform you that there are no hopes of my surviving long. No medicine gives me any relief; every day, indeed every hour, my friends look for my dissolution. It is probable that this may be the last letter you receive from me. My body and strength are wasted; my appetite is gone; night and day the cough threatens to suffocate me. The fever is strong and unremitting; and the pains which I feel over the whole of my body, deprive me of sleep. . . . Farewell! excellent Celio, and do not distress yourself when you hear of my death. . . . I send you such of the poems as I have been able to write out from memory since the destruction at Schweinfurt—all my other writings have perished. I request that you will be my Aristarchus and polish them. Again, farewell."[216] Her husband dispatched this letter to Curione with his own describing

her death. Three years later, Curione published her surviving works—
those she had sent to friends over the years—which include a variety of
works in the humanist genres of oration, dialogue, and poem, some in
Greek; two Latin versions of stories from Boccaccio's *Decameron*; and a
Greek paraphrase of the psalms. Curione's elegant volume may be the
finest memorial to a Renaissance woman humanist: *The Orations, Dialogues, Letters and Poems, both Latin and Greek, of Olimpia Fulvia Morata, a
Learned and almost Divine Woman (Olympiae Fulviae Moratae foeminae doctissimae ac plane divinae orationes, dialogi, epistolae, carmina, tam Latina quam
Graeca).*[217] The works are slim but interesting: among them are an oration on Cicero's *Paradoxes* delivered in her sixteenth year; eight poems, of
which five are in Greek; and two dialogues in which two women interlocutors discuss learning and destiny. The first edition was dedicated to
another female exile of the reform—Isabella Bresegna; the second and
all later editions to Queen Elizabeth, an exile of a different sort.

Morata's achievement carried the tradition of the Italian female humanist to the other side of the Alps, where there had been few of that
stamp. The patrician nun and abbess Caritas Pirckheimer of Nuremberg
had, a generation before Morata, pursued the study of sacred letters in
the humanist vein.[218] From one of the leading families of that flourishing
city long reputed for its tradition of learning, she was the most famous of
the Pirckheimer circle of seven sisters and five daughters, all of whom
received a serious education. A testimony to the endurance of the tradition that women of learning belonged in the convent, nine of these
twelve women became nuns. Caritas Pirckheimer entered the Franciscan
convent of St. Clare in 1479 at the age of twelve, and there continued the
studies that would make her famous before the end of the century. In the
years following 1498, she exchanged refined Latin letters, subsequently
republished and circulated, with her brother Willibald, a patron of the
new learning who was later recruited to the reform; Sixtus Tucher;
Christoph Scheurl; and most notably Conrad Celtis, the poet and first
bright light of German humanism. These learned men spread her reputation to a widening circle of pre-reform humanists. These included
those in her brother's circle, most notably Celtis, Dürer, Reuchlin,
Melanchthon, and above all, Erasmus, in whose colloquy on the
"Learned Woman and the Abbot" the Pirckheimer sisters are mentioned
next to the More sisters (of whom more below) as paragons of female
erudition. Willibald, a ceaseless promoter of his sister's (and his family's) glory, had sent the prince of northern humanists samples of their

letters, "which will wondrously reveal to you women who are more learned than many men who think themselves to be so."[219] In the convent, the Pirckheimer sisters Caritas and Clara studied and admired Erasmus's works, which worked subversion elsewhere, but not for them.

Like Isotta Nogarola, whose intellectual efforts were rebuffed while she remained in the world but extolled once she had retreated into the solitude of her self-designed cell, Pirckheimer's learning won an admiration for which her sacred reclusion was the precondition. Representing the fused radiance of the learned and the holy woman, *virgo docta* and *virgo sacra*, she became for the men of her generation not just a scholar who happened to be female, but a symbol of a complex series of cultural ideals. Celtis uncovered in 1494 the Latin works of the tenth-century abbess Hrotswitha in the cloister of Emmeram in Regensburg, and proceeded to publish them in 1501. The dedication was to Caritas Pirckheimer, whom he envisioned as the reincarnation of Hrotswitha herself, of an ancient German-Latin tradition concretized in a holy virgin: *monialem nostram, mulierem doctissimam et Germanam* ("our nun, a woman both learned and German").[220] The following year he hailed her in an ode, the "Norimberga," in which these symbols also melded: she was the virgin "learned in the language of the Romans," "the ornament of Germany": *virgo Romana benedocta lingua, virgo Germanae decus omne terrae.*[221] The object of the humanist's praise responded gratefully but reproved him for his excessive enthusiasm for the secular classics: she begged him "to give up celebrating the unseemly tales of Jupiter, Venus, Diana and other heathen beings whose souls are burning in Gehenna and who are condemned by right-minded men as detestable and deserving of oblivion; make the saints of God your friends by honouring their names and their memory, that they may guide you to the eternal home when you leave this earth."[222]

While Caritas Pirckheimer aroused the admiration and filled the imagination of the circle of male humanists of Germany's proto-reform, she provoked the censure of the church. She was selected abbess of her convent in 1503, which position she filled amply and heroically until her death in 1532; she died in the convent consigned to die with its last residents under the hostile eye of Protestant Nuremberg. Soon after her election—greeted again with humanist celebration—she received an instruction from the Franciscan superiors of St. Clare: she was forbidden to write any more in Latin. Her brother complained of the "roguery" of these "hypocrites" to Celtis, but there was nothing to be done.[223]

Pirckheimer's vocation had defined her role for her, apart from the symbolization of the humanists, and her destiny was as sacred, not learned, virgin. Obedient to her superiors, she wrote no more in the language of the advanced intellectual culture of her day—though she continued to read the holy books in that language sent to her by Willibald and his friends. The memoirs recording her struggle with the Nuremberg reformers, looked at in the previous chapter, were written in German. The brother who had shown the sparkling examples of her Latin prose to the smart humanist set devoted himself to securing her safety in the violent climate of the Reformation.

Unlike Pirckheimer, Morata, Cereta, and Fedele, Marguerite d'Angoulême, sister to the king of France and patroness of proto-reform, belonged to the world of the court and was safe from the jealous rivalries of the learned, if not isolated from more profound historical currents.[224] She was not a humanist, but she was richly educated in the new tradition and deeply involved in the vital humanism of her generation as patron, reader, and transmitter of its ideas. A writer whose interests included but transcended classical scholarship, she authored the *Heptaméron*, a collection of stories on the model of Boccaccio's *Decameron* that has much to say about women's roles; and such devotional works as *The Mirror of a Sinful Soul (Le Miroir de l'âme pécheresse)*, an Erasmian work condemned by the orthodox censors at the Sorbonne two years after its publication, but later translated into English by the young Elizabeth Tudor.[225] She also composed a book of letters defending the female sex. In this work, now lost but known from a seventeenth-century summary, she asserted the superior nature of women as God's last and finest work and their original status as rulers in an age of matriarchy.[226] Fertile in ideas and fierce in commitments, Marguerite d'Angoulême influenced other court women who, as rulers and mothers of rulers, would use their intellects, if not for humanist studies, then to further the success of their religious faiths, the central issue of their generation.

Marguerite d'Angoulême's position at the center of French cultural life was typical of the ultramontane female humanist—if one may call typical a phenomenon that was so very rare. In the French and English monarchies, the learned woman more commonly came from the highest nobility, and even royalty. As Agrippa d'Aubigné wrote to his daughters a generation after Marguerite had reigned at court, education for them was unnecessary, but suited the needs of one born to rule: "And so I conclude that I would be most reluctant to encourage girls to pursue book learning unless they were princesses, obliged by their rank to assume the responsibilities, knowledge, competence, administration, and authority of men. Then doubtless, as in the case of Queen Elizabeth, an education can stand girls in good stead."[227] Before the history of female humanism disappears entirely, the phenomenon of the female monarch and the female scholar will very nearly coalesce.

Sir Thomas More, gentleman and saint, friend of Erasmus and John Colet and the other great minds of England's early sixteenth century, was perhaps the single greatest inspiration to the emergence of female humanism in England.[228] He himself trained his three daughters (alongside their brother) in classical studies at the highest level—including the rarer elements of Greek, rhetoric, philosophy, and mathematics. As he explained in a letter to the tutor of his daughters, learning was useful for girls as well as boys: "They both have the name of human being whose nature reason differentiates from that of beasts; both, I say, are equally suited for the knowledge of learning by which reason is cultivated, and, like plowed land, germinates a crop when the seeds of good precepts have been sown."[229] His aim was not to create professional scholars of his daughters, but effective mothers and companionate wives for the governors of England. Of the three, his daughter Margaret was the star product of More's domestic school. Married to William Roper, she seemed to achieve her father's ideal as an intellectual companion for her learned husband and the generator of further generations of female talent. From her own hand comes an English translation of Erasmus's commentary on the Lord's Prayer, completed at age nineteen, which demonstrates her easy command of Latin, her fluent and imaginative English, and her considerable theological sensitivity. Her main surviving work, this translation was published in her lifetime by Richard Hyrde (also the translator of Vives' *Instruction of a Christian Woman*), whose introduction to the volume contains a valuable argument for the classical education of women. Roper in turn taught her own daughters and the daughter of her nurse. The descendants of these learned women carried on the tradition into the next century, when members of both lines retreated childless to the continental convents sought by Catholic exiles.

The girls of the More line constitute a significant fraction of all the women scholars that England was to produce in the Tudor century that alone knew their existence. The same period that saw the takeoff of secondary humanist education for boys, as guided by Thomas Elyot's *The Governor*, failed to respond to Vives' *Instruction of a Christian Woman* and

provide in the safety of the home a classical education for daughters. Including the women whose learning is known only by shadowy reputation, the female humanists of Tudor England may have totaled 60: "a
number that can be put into perspective by comparing it to the 153 boys
admitted to St. Paul's in its opening year early in the reign of Henry
VIII."[230] Many fewer are well known. Fewer still have left documentary
traces of their erudition, and fewer yet wrote in Latin or Greek—the
hallmark of serious humanist achievement. Most of the works of English
women humanists—in the vernacular or in classical languages—were
of a devotional or pious nature. There were exceptions: Jane Fitzalan,
daughter of the Earl of Arundel whose books form the core of one of the
most valuable manuscript collections in today's British Library, translated Euripides' *Iphigenia in Aulis* from the Greek! On the whole, though,
the literary production of England's female humanists was concentrated
in devotional genres, and in translation rather than original composition.
More striking still is the pattern of their social origin. With the exception
of the descendants of the More circle, the classically trained women of
England nearly all derived from families who moved in the circuit of royalty. Theirs was a court humanism: its object was never primarily to
make new contributions to the world of learning, but rather to enhance
with the gloss of learning the families that held or struggled for power.

Daughter of the formidable Isabella, herself well read in the
Christian tradition, Catherine of Aragon, the first wife of Henry VIII,
was a scholar of considerable dimension. Skilled herself in Latin, she encouraged the work, as has been seen, of the leading humanists of the day.
Her daughter, Mary Tudor, received the education of a Christian prince
(for the possibility of her accession did not escape her father). Her firm
mastery of Latin allowed her to read More's *Utopia* and the works of
Erasmus in the original. She translated a prayer of Thomas Aquinas's
and one of the paraphrases of Erasmus. Her interests did not range beyond the pious, however, so her advanced ability in Latin escaped the
notice of the intellectuals of the age. Catherine Parr, the sixth wife and
surviving queen of Henry VIII, the first Protestant king of England, was
a patron in the same pious mode as his first wife.[231] The center of what
might be seen as a "Protestant salon" that predated the full impact of
reform in England, she promoted the publication of holy works and the
advancement of serious people. Her most ambitious project was the supervision of the translation of Erasmus's *Paraphrases of the New Testament*,
which would become upon its much later publication (1548) a vehicle of

the newly aggressive reform in the reign of her stepson, King Edward VI. Parr studied Latin as an adult, encouraged by the young Edward, ten of whose thirteen letters to her in the years 1546–47 are in that language. The author of a series of *Prayers or Meditations* extracted from Thomas à Kempis and a treatise entitled *The Lamentation of a Sinner* (published in 1545 and 1547 respectively), Parr was one of only eight English women writers published between 1486 and 1548, "and one of only three . . . to have a statement of her faith appear in print."[232] The *Lamentation* included an explanation of the doctrine of justification by faith and marks the beginning of female learning in the Protestant mode.[233] For her predecessors, like all the More girls, were Catholic.

Two figures of the following generation—both queens, like all three of their predecessors—exceeded these women in learning to emerge as truly lustrous representatives of the humanist tradition: Lady Jane Grey, the great-granddaughter of Henry VII and the vehicle of her family's ambitions for the throne of England, and Elizabeth Tudor, Henry VIII's daughter and successor to that throne. Jane Grey—curiously one of four classically trained daughters of English noble families all named Jane—pursued under John Aylmer a serious humanist curriculum similar to that provided for the royal children whose future she was programmed to share.[234] From a family linked with reformers in England and on the continent, she studied Hebrew as well as Latin and Greek and modern languages, and corresponded in Latin with Heinrich Bullinger and Martin Bucer. Maneuvered by her family to the throne of England, which she held for nine days in 1553, she was executed in 1554 by her cousin, the Latinist Mary Tudor, alongside the father whose ambitions had nurtured her learning and her death. An Italian visitor lauded her with the now-familiar words of praise accorded the exceptional woman: she "faced death with far greater gallantry than it might be expected from her sex," and "submitted to the axe with more than manly courage."[235] Her extant works, including letters and poems written during the last six months of her life, were published later in part by the Protestant martyrologist John Foxe. They are statements of faith and preparations for death, powerfully mixed in the thoughts of a sixteen-year-old facing execution. Touching is the succinct counsel to her sister Katherine, written in the blank pages at the end of a New Testament in recommendation of that volume: it "shall teach you to live, and learn you to die."[236]

For Lady Jane Grey, as for some of the Italian *erudite*, learning represented the possibility of liberation from a confined existence.

Roger Ascham reports a conversation with the young woman, whom he found at her home studying Plato's *Phaedo* (in the Greek), "with as much delight as some gentleman would read a merry tale in Boccaccio," while her kin were out hunting. Asked why she passed up such sport, she replied that Plato afforded her greater pleasure. "Alas, good folk, they never felt what true pleasure meant." When Ascham asked how she had come to such an understanding of true pleasure achieved by "not many women," and "very few men," Grey explained that in all else she did, she was subject to others' control; when she studied, she was free. "One of the greatest benefits that ever God gave me is that he sent me so sharp and severe parents and so gentle a schoolmaster. For when I am in presence either of father or mother, whether I speak, keep silence, sit, stand, or go, eat, drink, be merry or sad, be sewing, playing, dancing, or doing anything else, I must do it, as it were, in such weight, measure, and number, even so perfectly as God made the world, or else I am so sharply taunted, so cruelly threatened, yea, presently sometimes, with pinches, nips, and bobs, and other ways which I will not name for the honor I bear them, so without measure misordered, that I think myself in hell till time come that I must go to Master Aylmer, who teacheth me so gently, so pleasantly, with such fair allurements to learning, that I think all the time nothing whilst I am with him."[237] Limited by her social position and her brief life span, she was never able to pursue studies into maturity, but Grey's discovery of liberation in speculative work is reminiscent of the experience of the great Italian humanists.

Elizabeth Tudor flourished under the guidance of her stepmother Catherine Parr and the tutelage of Roger Ascham, the leading English-born scholar of the reform generation. Encouraged by the former, she translated Marguerite d'Angoulême's *The Mirror of a Sinful Soul* from French to English, and Parr's English prayers from English into Latin, French, and Italian. Taught by Ascham for about two years, she acquired the elements of a serious classical education. Fluent in Latin, competent in Greek, she read Isocrates and Sophocles in the morning and Cicero and Livy, the Fathers, and the New Testament in the afternoon. In addition, she studied history, theology, philosophy, and the other sciences that comprised the advanced curriculum of the day. Ascham wrote his friend Jacob Strum in 1550 of her achievements: "She has just passed her sixteenth birthday and shows such dignity and gentleness as are wonderful at her age and in her rank. Her study of true religion and learning is most eager. Her mind has no womanly weakness, her perseverance is equal to that of a man, and her memory long keeps what it quickly picks up."[238] A leading scholar of the age, Ascham provided Elizabeth with a man's education: that which he had outlined for the gentlemen of England in his *Scholemaster*, the third of the great pedagogical works of the age (preceded by Vives' and Elyot's), published posthumously in 1570. Unlike her kinswoman Grey, Elizabeth survived to exercise the formidable talents that a man's education had honed.

After Elizabeth was graduated from student to queen, the phenomenon of female humanism in the country she ruled dwindled to near extinction. The fault was not Elizabeth's, but the brand of Protestantism that flourished on the island. Latin learning of any sort was considered to be very nearly popish, and to be on the safe side, elite families had both their sons and daughters read vernacular translations of works sound in reformed doctrine. At the same time, the Protestant vision of the family displaced the female as the carrier of charismatic piety, and fathers became "bishops" in their own households. Intelligent women were herded into submissive roles, and recommended these to their daughters. But Catholic women were free of these limitations, and the possibilities of the convent were still available to them. Among the only truly erudite women of the first Jacobean generation were two Catholics who had to leave England: Mary Ward, already encountered as the founder of the teaching Institute of the Blessed Virgin Mary; and Elizabeth Jane Weston, a Latin poet, who took refuge in Prague and added to the usual accomplishments of Latin, Greek, and Italian a command of Czech.

The tradition of female humanism that began in the generation after Petrarch with the Paduan widow Maddalena Scrovegni had died everywhere in Europe by the seventeenth century. Its place was taken by the study of dancing, drawing, and needlework, and perhaps French and Italian. A few women were known for their remarkable learning in the difficult subjects that made up the humanist and more advanced curricula of science, philosophy, and theology: Anne Marie van Schurmann in the Netherlands, Sor Juana Inés de la Cruz in Mexico in New Spain. One of the last representatives of such learning among women was the Venetian noblewoman Elena Lucrezia Cornaro Piscopia. She was also the first in another line of achievement that was to have no successor for two centuries more. Trained in Latin and Greek, as well as Hebrew, Arabic, and Chaldaic, and, like the most skilled of her predecessors, in philosophy and the other advanced disciplines of the age, she was in 1678 the first

woman—unmarried, aged thirty-two, a *consecrata* to God—to receive
the university degree of "doctor of philosophy."[239] By that time, she had
achieved an enormous reputation for her learning, and had written orations, letters, and poems, some in Greek. But the awarding of the doc-
toral degree was to be the peak of her career. Thereafter she suffered a
painful and wasting illness that lasted until her death six years later.

Urged by her father, Cornaro had sought the rare honor of the doc-
torate from the University of Padua as official recognition of her mastery
of the most advanced disciplines. It was awarded according to proper
procedure, the candidate having been examined on two *puncta* from, respectively, the logical and physical works of Aristotle. But the success
was a little sour for a number of reasons. She had intended, in fact, to be
credentialed in theology. Her preferred studies were in that revered
branch of knowledge, and she was herself committed to a pious life. Refusing to marry, she had become at age nineteen a Benedictine oblate in
the pattern of the holy women who were the predecessors of the female
learned in the Renaissance. As a secular oblate, she assumed vows and
duties towards a Benedictine convent as suited her condition, but residence and the stricter obligations were not required. She took the name
"Scolastica," the spiritual friend of the founder Benedict, and under the
robes of a noblewoman wore the habit of a nun of that order; in these she
would also be buried. Despite her legitimate vocation, the degree in theology was not to be. The opposition of the Cardinal Gregorio Barbarigo,
bishop of Padua and chancellor of that university, had forestalled the astonishing prospect of the award of a theological degree to a woman—a
defect of nature who could in no way hope to teach or preach or adminis-
ter the sacraments. Cornaro herself faltered a little, too, on the brink of
her success. When it was time to rise and speak, she stumbled: "This I
cannot do, because after all I am only a woman."[240]

The lack of self-confidence betrayed by this thirty-two-year-old descendant of an ancient lineage as she reached the pinnacle of success recalls the reaction of the earlier humanists who had dared to challenge
men in the sphere of advanced learning, but had paled in doing so. In the
same way the adolescent orator Constanza Varano had hesitated to begin
her oration to Bianca Maria Visconti: for at this challenge "the spirits of
even the wisest and most learned men would tremble"; so certainly "my
girlish style without cultivation or polish does not suffice"; "what then
can I do, an ignorant, rustic and inexperienced girl?"[241] With such self-
deprecation Isotta Nogarola had written the Cardinal Giuliano Cesarini:

"It should be little wondered at, venerable Father, if I be in awe and a fearful tremor run through my bones, and for this reason the more, when I realize that I was born a woman, who breaks words rather than pronounces them, and since I write to you, whose eloquence and force of sweetness of style are so great. . . ."[242] Caritas Pirckheimer abased herself in much the same way before her admirer Celtis, who had just dedicated to her his edition of the works of Hrotswitha. She had received the work with its dedicatory letter and read it with admiration and astonishment, contrasting its brilliance with "the rusticity, slowness, and weakness of my small intellect, nor can I wonder enough that so great a learned man, so expert a philosopher, has deigned to salute me, an ignorant and simple girl, in whom there dwells neither knowledge, nor eloquence, nor anything worthy of praise, in a letter of such sweetness."[243]

Such self-deprecation was in part customary, for men as well as for women. But the women humanists are especially abject, adopting the passive posture that their unequal role in the realm of humanist culture required. Moreover, to the extent that there is no such thing as "mere" rhetoric, these reductions of the self at the moment of achievement cannot be seen as mere gestures, but expressions of a profound discontent or anxiety with the role of learned woman. And why not? Such women had been educated to do nothing and go nowhere.[244] By the seventeenth century, the possibility of their participation in the rhetorical culture of the humanists or the academic culture of the professionals had contracted to a zero. Marie de Gournay complained in defiant words that avoided the self-abnegation of her fellows, but made clear the low perception that women possessed of themselves: "Happy are you, Reader," she opened one of her works, "if you do not belong to this sex to which all good is forbidden, since to us liberty is proscribed . . . so that the sole joy and sovereign virtue allowed us is to be ignorant, to play the dullard, and to serve."[245] Not even the possibility of sanctity could beckon the learned women in their book-lined, not holy, cells. Warriors without weapons, speakers without an audience, holy women without vocation, they could not know that the seed of their achievement would bear fruit in the words of their spiritual descendants.

Those descendants did not speak Latin but their own vernacular languages in works which blossom during the Renaissance from the traditional genres into new ones. In them, before the end of that era, the seeking and questioning female voice will be heard in a new key. The increase in the tempo of women's writing (and at the same time of writing about women) is striking. In England, for instance, where between 1486 and 1548 only eight works by women had been printed, ninety-five more had appeared by 1640. By 1690, works by women made up nearly 2 percent of all published material: a small fraction still, but visible and growing.[246] Women's works that were not devotional revolved around the families in which women led their lives: advice books written by mothers and wives for their daughters and other women who faced motherhood and widowhood, as noted in the first chapter; and letters, diaries, and histories centered on their own experiences.[247]

Such works were private and personal, and did not claim to enter upon the masculine territory of literary production. They drew on personal experience and were addressed to an intimate circle. As the English Countess of Lincoln Elizabeth Knevet Clinton explained, amid pages of exhortations to her daughter-in-law about the proper care and nurture of her children: "I leave the larger and learneder discourse here-of unto men of art, and learning: only I speake of so much as I reade, and know in my owne experience, which if any of my sexe, and condition do receave good by, I am glad."[248] With equal humility, Dorothy Kemp Leigh addressed her children in her *Mother's Blessing*: "But lest you should marvell, my children, why I doe not according to the usual custome of women, exhort you by words and admonitions, rather than by writing: . . . know therefore that it was the motherly affection I bare unto you all, which made mee now . . . forget my self in regard of you."[249] Such endeavors resulted, before the end of our period, in biographies of people and even histories of public events. Unlike the male historian, whose viewpoint was universal, women generally wrote of significant events from the small corner of the world in which they dwelled: as the English Duchess of Newcastle said of her biography of her husband late in our era, she wrote "a particular history" which is "the more secure, because it goes not out of its own circle, but turns on its own axis, and for the most part keeps within the circumference of the truth."[250]

There are exceptions: Christine de Pizan's biography of Charles V and Lucrezia Marinelli's history of the Fourth Crusade broke through the circumference of the domestic circle. Other kinds of works were devoted to a circle beyond the family, as well. Businesswomen who had long kept account books for their fathers and husbands also wrote diaries, letters, and petitions. The widows of the pioneers of the first century of print carried on their husbands' labors, industrial and intellectual at once. Twenty-five of them labored in sixteenth-century Paris, like Charlotte Guillard who for twenty-two years in between marriages and after the death of her husbands herself directed the publication of (and sometimes wrote the prefaces to) works of theology, philosophy, and history.[251] Nuns and holy women continued to write of the spiritual turmoil within: the saints Caterina Vegri, Camilla da Varano (sister Battista), Catherine of Genoa, Teresa of Avila, among others, no longer spoke through amanuenses but wielded their pens independently to produce rich documents of female authorship. Camilla da Varano, for instance, produced some twenty-two works between 1479 and her death in 1524: letters, prayers, and treatises in a fine Latin style, crowned by the autobiographical reflections of her *Spiritual Life* (*Vita spirituale*).[252] Quite a different endeavor was that of the poets, who wrote of love and of themselves.

The great female poets of the sixteenth century—in France, that patron of reform and mainstay of royal power, Marguerite d'Angoulême, and Louise Labé, and the des Roches mother and daughter, Madeleine and Catherine; in Italy, Vittoria Colonna, Veronica Gambara, Isabella di Morra, Veronica Franco, and Gaspara Stampa; in England, the two Mary Sidneys, Lady Wroth and the Countess of Pembroke; in Mexico the nun Juana de la Cruz—achieved in some cases the very highest level of literary composition in that great epoch of poetry that they shared with Shakespeare and Spenser, Du Bellay, Scève, and Tasso. Above all, they were concerned with love: sometimes the love of God, but most remarkably the love of men—the very sex that did not always value women at their worth—love that was inflaming, deceitful, and tormenting. Labé, daughter and wife of twiners of rope, writes of nothing else. She wants to be kissed and to kiss:

> Kiss me again, again, kiss me again!
> Give me one of the luscious ones you have,
> Give me one of the loving ones I crave:
> Four hotter than burning coals I shall return.[253]

—and lose her self in her lover, as she expects him to do, too:

> A double life for each of us ensues.
> Each in the self and in the lover lives.[254]

—for without him, she has nothing, and with him, everything:

> You alone my good and evil are:
> With you I'm rich, without you I am poor.[255]

Now that he has gone, she feels she must die, but she will not stop loving even then; her epitaph will read:

> For you, my love, I lived in such desire
> That, languishing, I've been consumed by fire,
> Which still will smoulder underneath my clay
> Unless your tears will its distress allay.[256]

In love with the passion which she imagines is the main good of life and the only afterlife she appears to consider, Labé gave up all her other pursuits, at which she was proficient: needlework, studies, and martial exercises. Cupid had called her away:

> . . . The God of Love was irritated
> To see my heart to books and Mars devoted;
> Determining to give me other cares,
> Smiling he said, "Do you think that, with these
> You'll flee my flames, O lady of Lyon?
> You won't succeed.[257]

The Venetian courtesans Veronica Franco and Gaspara Stampa are equally entranced with love. Stampa suffers from the Frenchwoman's sickness of the annihilation of self in the quest of another. When her lover leaves, exercising the tyranny over her that is his prerogative as a male with better things to do, she is helpless, left behind without a heart:

> Send back my heart to me, relentless one,
> Who, tyrantlike, do hold and tear it so,
> And do to it, and me, just what is done
> By tigers and lions to the hapless doe.
>
> . . . .
>
> Am I Hercules or Samson, do you suppose,
> To bear such sorrow now that we're apart?
> I'm young, a woman, half out of my mind,
> And, most of all, I'm here without my heart.[258]

Franco seems less vulnerable, and boldly invites love and admiration at the same time, offering prizes of poetic and sexual performance. Attacked as a whore (*puttana*) by one of her clever acquaintances in a verse whose title punned her name (*Veronica, Ver unica puttana*), Franco fought back, with words that conjured up the Amazons, in whose martial but unnatural form her age described the extraordinary woman.[259] The coterie that was the source of her reputation could also cause its destruction, lovers and predators impossibly confounded. Her trade exposed her to such attacks, and even more her boldness in taking up a pen in a world where women's mental efforts were seen as laughable, yet dangerous.

Like Labé and Stampa, Franco openly defied the triune convention of female chastity, silence, and obedience. These women owed the possibility of freedom in their work to the urban context in which they existed—complex, fluid, pulsating—and to the fact that their own social identities lay between the usual interstices of class.[260] So much for opportunity. These women were also limited by their unique social position: seeking to pursue their ambitions, they were dependent on male admiration, male attention, male audiences. Rebels against sexual propriety, they were dependent in the end on men of high social position as much, ironically, as if they had never left the drawing room. Those men could turn against them, too, as Franco's interlocutor did so sharply. Labé's unknown lover abandoned her, and so did Stampa's known one— the Collaltino who alone of her partners serves to inspire her poetry. Indeed, it is not so much of love that they write as of its loss.

The Mexican nun Juana de la Cruz may have had through personal experience some acquaintance of the world familiar to Stampa and Franco but had certainly left such matters behind her before she entered the convent where she crafted her poems. Yet in one deceptively simple *redondillas* she turned viciously on the men who first prostitute women, and then condemn them:

> Stupid men, fond of abusing
> All women, without any shame,
> Not seeing you're the ones to blame
> For the very faults that you're accusing.
>
> . . . .
> You strive to conquer her resistance,
> Then with a solemn treachery
> Attribute to her lechery
> What was only done through your persistence.
>
> . . . .
> No female reputation's sure:
> The most cautious woman in the town
> Is an ingrate if she turns you down;
> If she gives in to you she's a whore.[261]

The grandes dames among the women poets, like Colonna or Gambara or Marguerite d'Angoulême, while still immersed in the thematics of love, are better able to distance themselves from male aggression. Nor did such concerns trouble the Roches women, who from the safe perch of a wealthy home without a male superior explored the possibility of an independent life for women, enriched by learning but free of harsh austerities. Madeleine, the mother, urged her daughter, Catherine, to undertake such a life (which she subsequently did), in the name of the great love she bore her. Her daughter, precious to her not only because she resembles her mother in every way, not only because of the great labors she expended in raising her, but also because of her own great spirit, she advises thus:

> I cannot grant you a greater gift
> Than to urge you to do your duty
> Toward the Muse and divine learning.
>
> . . . .
>
> You may become immortal some day through your virtue,
> It is thus that I have always wished you to be.[262]

Among the themes that Catherine explored when she accepted her mother's challenge was that of female learning and, more broadly, the female predicament. It is not wholly surprising to find that Amazons, more than once, make their appearance in her verse: powerful, chaste, free, and triumphant. Here they sing:

> We make war
> On the Kings of the earth. . . .
> We flee like the plague
> The grievous flame
> Which burns the heart:
> For the purity
> Of our chastity
> Forever protects us.
>
> We hold men prisoners
> In the places where we rule
> And force them to spin.[263]

The Female Voice

Amid this wealth of words bearing women's insight that circulated more richly in the Renaissance centuries than ever before, a few writers began for the first time to probe in a critical and comprehensive mode the predicament of female existence in male society. Of these, space can be made to consider three: the Frenchwoman Christine de Pizan, the first woman of the Western tradition to live by the product of her pen; the Venetian citizen Modesta da Pozzo; and the English lady Mary Astell. Writing in turn in the fifteenth, the sixteenth, and the seventeenth centuries, they sum up a tradition of the perception of women that stretches from Boccaccio in the fourteenth century to Mary Wollstonecraft in the eighteenth. With these pioneers of female consciousness, this exploration of the life of Renaissance women may proceed to its close.

Born in Italy but raised from early childhood in France, Christine took her name, through her father Tommaso di Benvenuto da Pizzano, not from Pisa but a from small town near Bologna.[264] She had followed her physician father to France, where he was invited to join the court of Charles V as resident astrologer and sage. In that privileged circle, guided by her learned father, Christine acquired an excellent education, to be perfected later by extensive reading in her widowhood. Her culture was that of the elegant late-Gothic French court in an age of political turbulence. For the century-long war with England continued throughout her lifetime, and she would see the throne of the prudent Charles V pass to the mad Charles VI and the impotent Charles VII, crowned years later only through the strength of the maiden soldier Joan of Arc. At the center of such events, she experienced those of her own life: her youthful marriage to the notary Etienne de Castel, learned and loving like her father, who encouraged her "long estude" of the books she loved as her father had taught her to do; the birth of her children and the deaths of both father and spouse; and the prospect of poverty, so often the fate of a woman bereft of male protectors. In 1389, at age twenty-five, this widow, endowed only with the knowledge of letters and the experience of court life, established herself in an unprecedented career for women. She wrote verse and prose on commission or in hope of reward, producing works of such excellence for the forty years until her death that her clients forbore to notice that their author was female. With the profits of this handiwork she maintained herself, her three children, a niece, and an aging mother: she was "six times one person."[265] The story in itself is remarkable, but scarcely prepares us for the enormous achievement (only recognized in recent years) of her most important work, composed in 1404–5, *The Book of the City of Ladies (Le Livre de la cité des dames)*.[266]

The City of Ladies breathes the same active and positive spirit that must have inspired its author to become master and not victim of circumstance. Its central goal is to refute the charges, heretofore unchallenged, that men had made against women. This task of refutation Christine had already begun in works written from 1399 to 1402 against the *Roman de la Rose*, constituting a first volley in the *querelle des femmes* already described. In these verse polemics, women drawn from all social classes complain to Cupid about their detractors, including Ovid and Jean de Meung, the misogynist author of the notorious addendum to the *Rose*; while for the "knights" who defended female honor, she founded a new chivalric "Order of the Rose." Why did men write such books, Christine asked herself, and answered the question in a way that opened new doors to the future: "If women had been the authors of these books, they would have written otherwise, for they know well that they have been falsely accused."[267] In *The City of Ladies*, Christine exposes the falsity of the representation of women by the male authorities of the past whom she had been raised to reverence.

The work opens in Christine's study, the setting of her "long estude," with a reconsideration of those authorities: "One day as I was sitting alone in my study surrounded by books on all kinds of subjects, devoting myself to literary studies, my usual habit, my mind dwelt at length on the weighty opinions of various authors whom I had studied for a long time."[268] She picked up a volume disparaging to women, and wondered "how it happened that so many different men—and learned men among them—have been and are so inclined to express both in speaking and in their treatises and writings so many wicked insults about women and their behavior" (3–4; 1.1.1). So many books, and so much agreement: "it seems they all speak from one and the same mouth" (4; 1.1.1). Were they right? Christine reflected on all the women she knew, of many different stations, and could not be convinced: for most were worthy of praise. Yet how could so many excellent authors be wrong? They must be right, and she must be wrong, she decided, as she sank into self-detestation: "Like a gushing fountain, a series of authorities, whom I recalled one after another, came to mind, along with their opinions on this topic. And I finally decided that God formed a vile creature when He made woman, and I wondered how such a worthy artisan could have deigned to make such an abominable work which, from what they say, is the vessel as well as the refuge and abode of every evil and vice. As I was thinking this, a great unhappiness and sadness welled up in my heart, for I detested myself and the entire feminine sex, as though we were monstrosities in nature" (5; 1.1.1).

Solitary in her despair in her book-lined cell that was the best destiny of the learned woman, Christine was like Boethius in prison, a man without hope; and like him, as described in his *Consolation of Philosophy*—one of the books that everyone in that age who could read in Latin would have read—she would receive comfort. Boethius was visited by the lady Philosophy, Christine by three extra-terrestrial ladies: Reason, Rectitude, and Justice. These ladies explained to her the misogyny of male authors. The philosophers could be wrong; the poets dream up fictions; the misogamists attack a holy institution (6–7; 1.2.2). Some writers, seeking to correct the faults of a few, have attacked all women in general. Others acted out of resentment and jealousy: old and repenting their misspent youth, they blame women for their sins; crazed by impotence, they lash out at women they cannot possess (17–20; 1.8.3–8). It is the viciousness of men, not the fault of women, that causes these latter to be attacked.

In the same way, men grieve when their wives bear them daughters, fearing the cost of a dowry and the risk of dishonor; yet daughters are more loyal than sons, and care to the end for their aging parents (110–13; 2.7.1). Men attack wives for inconstancy, infidelity, self-indulgence, and selfishness (118–19; 2.13.1), but (although a few women are perverse) most women are loyal and long suffering, and many "because of their husband's harshness spend their weary lives in the bond of marriage in greater suffering than if they were slaves among the Saracens" (119; 2.13.1). God who created all things good created woman good, as well. He molded Eve out of Adam's rib, not the gross dirt, "signifying that she should stand at his side as a companion and never lie at his feet like a slave, and also that he should love her as his own flesh" (23; 2.9.2). Not woman as a sex, but those women or those men who commit sin are evil: "The man or the woman in whom resides greater virtue is the higher; neither the loftiness nor the lowliness of a person lies in the body according to the sex, but in the perfection of conduct and virtues" (24; 1.9.3). No writer of the next three centuries would exceed Christine's statement here of the equality of the sexes.

What of the charge, Christine asked, that women's minds can learn only very little? Again untrue, replied Lady Reason. "If it were customary to send daughters to school like sons, and if they were then taught the natural sciences, they would learn as thoroughly and understand the subtleties of all the arts and sciences as well as sons. . . . for . . . just as women have more delicate bodies than men, weaker and less able to perform many tasks, so do they have minds that are freer and sharper whenever they apply themselves" (63; 1.27.1). It seems that men know more than women because men are out in the world, while women must stay at home and tend the household, "and there is nothing which so instructs a reasonable creature as the exercise and experience of many things" (63; 1.27.1). While men charge that women are good "only for bearing children and sewing" (77; 1.37.1), in fact they have been inventors, leaders, scholars. Why have all these gifted women not responded in all these spans of years to the slanders found in the books of men? That, Lady Rectitude replied, is the task designated for Christine: "The composition of this work has been reserved for you and not for them" (185; 2.53.2). Indeed, it is not only a book that she is destined to create.

Christine is commanded by the three ethereal ladies to build a city, a city that will protect the good women of past, present, and future, and house them forever. "Thus, fair daughter," explains Lady Reason, "the prerogative among women has been bestowed on you to establish and build the City of Ladies. For the foundation and completion of this City you will draw fresh waters from us as from clear fountains, and we will bring you sufficient building stone, stronger and more durable than any marble with cement could be. Thus your City will be extremely beautiful, without equal, and of perpetual duration in the world" (11; 1.4.1). From now on, those good women "who have been abandoned for so long, exposed like a field without a surrounding hedge, without finding a champion to afford them an adequate defense," will have a refuge from their assailants (10; 1.3.3). The controversy, then, ends here. No more will Christine engage in the fruitless thrust and counterattack of the *querelle* against the armies of learned men, but she will construct a new base of operation, an armed fortress, indomitable. Christine will build it herself, wielding the "pick of her understanding" (16; 1.8.1), engaging in the physical labor that was considered to be the task of men although women often performed it. And she will be aided by the tools her guiding spirits will supply: mortar, a ruler, a balance, the instruments of builders, mathematicians, and judges—men's tools. She will bring them to the

Field of Letters, a plain "flat and fertile," and dig a great ditch where Lady Rectitude has marked it out; and she will help Christine bear off the disinterred earth on her strong shoulders (16; 1.8.1). The City of Ladies is a woman's proud response to the negative message of world literature, crafted by male minds in annihilation of her worth. Heretofore, men had had their cities and God His. Now women will have theirs.

The construction of the city is the story of the book. In the first part, the foundations are laid. In the second, the houses are built and peopled. In the third, the towers and rooftops are completed. In the first, Christine is aided by Reason; in the second, by Rectitude; and in the third, by Justice. In the first, we are told about the active women of the past who led armies and ruled states; for these are the foundations of the city, and they employed their reason as independent spirits unbounded by the conventions of men. In the second, we are told about obedient women who guarded their chastity, honored their parents, loved their husbands, persevered in their duties; for they are most women, those who inhabit and enliven the houses and inns and mansions, and they served righteousness. In the third, we are told about the women who martyred themselves for their faith and are the closest handmaidens of the Virgin; for they are the towers and roofs that reach up to God, and the incarnate principle of His justice. The clear logic of Christine's scheme is breathtaking, not unlike Dante's. The parts of the book and the parts of the city are one, an integral system comprehending the whole of the past, a perfect congruence of book, city and the universal story of womankind.

The brilliance of Christine's scheme is all the more striking when compared to the work of her predecessor Boccaccio, upon which source more than any other she depends.[269] Of the 106 portraits of Boccaccio's *Concerning Famous Women*, Christine draws more or less directly on 75. (In addition, she uses three female characters from the same author's *Decameron*, and draws as well on other sources, especially the Old Testament and Christian hagiography.) From one point of view, Christine has simply milked the scholar's Latin text for a vernacular French portrayal of famous women. From another, she has done much more: for her reorganization of Boccaccio's structure is fundamental, and at once serves her very different purpose and comments on his. Boccaccio's work is an erudite catalogue of exceptional women, curious in their striking nonconformity, a curiousness heightened by their exoticism: except for Eve and six modern figures, they were all pagan. Christine's work is systematic, as has been seen, but more, it claims the universality rather than the exceptionalism of female virtue. Nowhere is Christine's tilting of Boccaccio's delineation of character more conspicuous than in her treatment of the armed maidens who dominate the whole of the Italian's book and the first part of the Frenchwoman's.

Where Boccaccio's fierce pagan warriors are condemned for their boldness or subjected to humiliation and death, Christine's are displayed as uncomplicated models of achievement: "what Boccaccio presents as notorious is reformulated so that fame replaces notoriety."[270] Boccaccio's Semiramis is a monster. Christine recites her achievement, and concludes with a defense. Some people, it is true, might reproach that queen for having taken her own son as a husband; but this lady who lived before the time of written law must not have known the act was sinful, "for there can be no doubt that if she thought this was evil or that she would incur the slightest reproach, she would never have done this, since she had such a great and noble heart and so deeply loved honor" (40; 1.15.2). Boccaccio admired the queen Zenobia of Palmyra, but takes pains to describe her capture and humiliation: "There Aurelian's triumph was celebrated and it was marvelous because of Zenobia's presence. Among other great things worthy of remembrance, he brought the precious chariot of gold and gems which Zenobia had had built hoping to come to Rome, not as a prisoner, but as a triumphant conqueror arriving to take possession of the Roman empire. With gold chain around her neck and fettered hand and foot with shackles of gold, Zenobia went before the chariot with her children. She wore her crown and royal robes and was loaded with pearls and precious stones, so that in spite of her great strength she often stopped, exhausted by the weight."[271] Christine's halcyon portrait of Zenobia's successes concludes with a tribute to her learning. Master of her own language and the Egyptian, Latin, and Greek, she taught her children and applied her own leisure to study, receiving instruction from the philosopher Longinus; so that it must be confessed that there has never been "any prince or knight more complete in every virtue" (54–55; 1.20.2).

Christine fondly recounts the deeds of the Amazon queens and warriors, breastless and husbandless, who through the course of hundreds of years sent their sons to be raised by their fathers and left the legacy of their power to their daughters: Lampheto and Marpasia, Synoppe, Thamiris, Orithyia and Penthesilea, all queens; Menalippe and Hippolyta, prized bride of Theseus (40–51; 1.16.1–19.3). Armed, they marched in battalions, irresistible, conquering much of Europe and Asia, founding rich cities and towns. They battled successfully with the greatest men and heroes of antiquity: Thamiris defeated Cyrus, the Persian king of kings, while Menalippe and Hippolyta withstood Hercules and Theseus nearly to the end; Penthesilea avenged Hector's death on the son of Achilles. Among the strongest were those pledged to virginity—no Christian scruple here, merely a statement of their independence from men. Synoppe "had such a great and lofty heart that not for a day in her life did she deign to couple with a man, but remained a virgin her entire lifetime. Her only love and care was the exercise of arms" (42; 1.16.1). Penthesilea was "so high-minded that she never condescended to couple with a man, remaining a virgin her whole life" (48; 1.19.1). Other warrior maidens not of the Amazon community had the same disdain for a sexual link with men: Camilla, raised on the milk of beasts, Aeneas's opponent celebrated by Virgil (61; 1.24.1), and Minerva, here a heroine, but more familiar as the goddess Athena, who scorned male contact as she had scorned to be born from woman, but burst forth from the head of her divine father (74; 1.34.4).

In much the same way, Christine would praise the Amazonian virgin, her younger contemporary Joan of Arc, shortly before her own death and two years before the maid of Orléans had been downgraded by dangerous enemies from hero to witch.[272]

> Oh! What honour for the female sex! It is perfectly obvious that God has special regard for it when all these wretched people who destroyed a whole kingdom—now recovered and made safe by a woman, something 5000 men could not have done—and the traitors [have been] exterminated. Before the event they would scarcely have believed this possible.
>
> A little girl of 16 (is not this something quite supernatural?) who does not even notice the weight of the arms she bears—indeed her whole upbringing seems to have prepared her for this, so strong and resolute is she! And her enemies go fleeing before her, not one of them can stand up to her. She does this in full view of everyone.[273]

To this female poet, the Amazon Joan does not appear monstrous, but bold, competent, triumphant. The Ditié de Jehanne d'Arc is de Pizan's last work and perhaps her final statement about the condition of women. It was the only work written in praise of its solitary subject during her lifetime.

The Amazons, as an autonomous woman's community, have particular importance for Christine, beyond the same fascination that they
seemed to exercise on many other Renaissance authors. They are a secular model for her City of Ladies, for which otherwise only the model of
the convent was available. While the inhabitants of the convent could
surely claim the title of righteousness, the power and success of the
Amazons were useful values to attach to the notion of an independent
refuge for womankind, safe from the viciousness of male opinion. Not
surprisingly, the Amazons appear in contexts outside of the series of profiles of worthy women of the past. When Lady Reason assured Christine
that her city would never fall, she compared it to the kingdom of the
Amazons: "this City which you must construct will be far stronger" (12;
1.4.3). And when the houses of the city were ready, empty and waiting to
be supplied with residents, Lady Rectitude explained how their condition would exceed that even of the Amazons: "It is therefore right that we
start to people this noble City now, so that it does not remain vacant or
empty, but instead is wholly populated with ladies of great excellence,
for we do not want any others here. How happy will be the citizens of our
edifice, for they will not need to fear or worry about being evicted by
foreign armies, for this work has the special property that its owners cannot be expelled. Now a New Kingdom of Femininity is begun, and it is
far better than the earlier kingdom of the Amazons, for the ladies resid-
ing here will not need to leave their land in order to conceive or give birth
to new heirs to maintain their possessions throughout the different ages,
from one generation to another, for those whom we now place here will
suffice quite adequately forever more" (116–17; 2.12.1). Every burden
of sexuality is lifted for the residents of the City of Ladies, even the requirement to reproduce, as Genesis had decreed, in sorrow.

Although the society of the Amazons is a pattern for Christine's city,
not all its residents will be Amazonian. Those armed maidens formed, as
has been said, its foundation. In the second part of the *Book* are encountered women of considerable valor, but neither armed nor virginal.
These are the patient wives and daughters of men, loyal to fathers and
husbands, both chaste and beautiful: among them Dido, Thisbe, and
Hero (2.55, 57, 58), who died for love; Lucretia, who died for honor
(2.44); Judith, who killed Holofernes for the sake of her people (2.31);
Griselda, who suffered her husband's testing without complaint—who
came, naked, when summoned, and departed naked and robbed of her
children when dismissed (2.50); Artemisia, who mixed with her wine the

ashes of her husband and drank, so that the remains of the man she loved might have no "other sepulcher than the heart and body where the root of this great love resided" (2.16.1); Penelope, who for twenty years awaited the return of her husband, weaving (2.41). Christine's deep sympathy for these and the other women who people the houses of her city does not disguise her pity for those who, thus tied up in the toils of life, were often its victims. For the Christian martyrs of part three, on the other hand, tortured, torn, and burned, she speaks with plain admiration, but without the enthusiasm expressed for the maidens in arms whose pagan world did not require their martyrdom.

Her city complete, Christine called upon all its residents, the sum total of virtuous womankind, to rejoice: for the city could be "not only the refuge for you all, . . . but also the defense and guard against your enemies and assailants, if you guard it well" (254; 3.19.1). For the defense of women against the assaults of men—verbal, psychological, and sexual—was the first and only aim of her grand structure. She urges no realignment of social roles. Indeed, in the concluding section of *The Book of the City of Ladies* that follows this last invitation to rejoice, she urges upon her listeners of all social categories forbearance with their husbands and the careful observance of chastity. For all her admiration of the Amazon, she did not plan that women should rule in the world of men—only in her City of Ladies. Earlier she had asked Lady Reason why women do not govern states or plead cases in the courts of justice. That lady had responded that men and women were forever assigned to different roles: "One could just as well ask why God did not ordain that men fulfill the offices of women, and women the offices of men. . . . God has . . . ordained man and woman to serve Him in different offices and also to aid and comfort one another, each in their ordained task, and to each sex has given a fitting and appropriate nature and inclination to fulfill their offices" (31; 1.11.1). Women are capable of understanding, but are not suited, according to Christine, to action.

The same author's *Book of Three Virtues* (*Le livre des trois vertues*), also called *The Treasure of the City of Ladies* (*Le Trésor de la cité des dames*), continues where *The Book of the City of Ladies* ended. Far more popular with its audience than *The Book of the City of Ladies*, it affirmed a social order in which women were subordinate, rather than creating one in which women achieved both safety and autonomy. It outlines the duties appropriate to women in different social categories: royalty, the high nobility, and all the lower social orders (including women of the bourgeoisie, artisanry, and peasantry). Of these, considerably more attention is given to women of the highest social orders, whose social functions Christine sees as genuinely important, indeed indispensable. In each category, women are called on to work productively and behave well. Leaving intact the hierarchical structures of her society, she called on women to perform the duties attached to their positions in the same way that men had always been required to do. The clear message throughout is that "each woman ought to keep to her own station in life."[274] It poses a striking contrast to the message of *The City of Ladies*, which posed so deep a challenge to the traditional concepts of women. That two such diverse messages could have been generated by the same guiding ideas and produced in the same span of time by the same pen reveals much about the differences between that age and our own. The categories of social life were adamantine in their inflexibility. Yet it is notable that Christine, unlike nearly all other Renaissance commentators on women as a social group, classes women by social and not sexual criteria: as aristocrat, bourgeoise, peasant, not as virgin, matron, crone.

The vision of female secession, of the creation of a space for womankind apart from the world of men, would reappear in the work of the Venetian Modesta da Pozzo (writing under the name of Moderata Fonte) entitled *Women's Worth* (*Il merito delle donne*).[275] Lacking the bold verticals and martial tone of Christine's community, Fonte's is a fluid and spontaneous gathering over two days of seven friends—virgins, matrons, and crones—in a garden decorated with statues of Chastity, Solitude, and Liberty. All progeny of illustrious families of high repute, the women have come at the invitation of Leonora, a young and wealthy widow: they are "noble and spirited, . . . equal by blood and breeding, genteel, virtuous, and high-minded, . . . and impeded in no way by the presence of men, they conversed among themselves about those things that most intrigued them" (Fonte 1600, 10–11). This drama comments not on the cities of men, as Christine's roofed and towered edifices did, but on the dialogues of the philosophers and humanists. How many times, in the history of Western literature, had two or three or a handful of men gathered in gardens, under porticos, at banquets, to discuss the soul, or knowledge, or the virtues! Now their place is taken by women, suave and insouciant.

The key figure is the maiden Corinna, whose name echoes that of the woman who was said to have exceeded Pindar in eloquence.[276] Unarmed and furnished with both breasts, Corinna is no Amazon, but her spiritual stance is nonetheless Amazonian. She is and intends to remain free, and free of men: "I would rather die," she states unequivocably, "than subordinate myself to any man; that life for me is perfectly blessed that I live with you, not fearing the beard of a man who could command me" (Fonte 1979, 160). She would express the same sentiment in impromptu verse applauded by all present:

> Free is the heart beating inside my breast,
> I serve no one, nor do I belong to any other but myself;
> Modesty and gentility fill me,
> Virtue exalts me and chastity adorns me.
>
> . . . .
>
> So in my youth and my maturity,
> Since I am undisturbed by the fallacy of man,
> I await fame and glory in life, and then in death."
>
> (Fonte 1600, 14)

Corinna's decision for autonomy was inspired by her view of the structure of power, shared by some of her friends: men rule and make slaves of the women they secretly envy for their great beauty and worth. Naturally aggressive, they trick, rob, destroy, and ruin each other; they commit assassination, usurpation, perjury, bestiality, murder, assault, and theft (Fonte 1979, 162). Thus they treat each other; they deal still more roughly with the other sex. "Fathers, brothers, sons, husbands, lovers" alike abuse, debase, and negate women (Fonte 1979, 162–63). We're crazy, added Cornelia, "to suffer their cruelty, and not to flee as from flames their undeclared, continuous persecution, and the particular hatred that they show to us" (Fonte 1979, 162).

Corinna's counterfoil is Virginia, the other maiden participant in the dialogue, whose being is fully encompassed by the virginity that names her. Her quiet passivity contrasts with the angry claims of her friends, as her small intelligence does with Corinna's sparkling mind. Unlike that proud virago, she will marry, though with some reluctance; does Fonte suggest that then, her virginity lost, she will be, nameless, nothing at all? She would rather preserve her liberty, but must obey her elders: as she is rich, her inheritance must not be allowed to be alienated to strangers. She hopes for a husband better than the others (Fonte 1979, 159). Aware like her friends of the difficulties women have suffered, she believes they are due to men's ignorance, not malice (Fonte 1979, 162). Or if men do not love women, perhaps it is because women do not deserve their love—a

possibility vividly refuted by Corinna, Cornelia, and Leonora, who argue, on the contrary, women's superior virtue and indispensable services
to men (Fonte 1979, 168). Not the least of these is the dowry, brought by
a bride to her husband—with which, if she could live on it alone, she
could "live like a queen" (Fonte 1979, 170). Consider, Corinna warned
the docile Virginia, what is the fate of the woman who marries: "she
loses her property, loses herself, and does this for no gain but to have
children, who are a nuisance, and be subject to a man, who does with her
as he pleases" (Fonte 1979, 170). Rather, men who wish to marry should
give dowries to women, and what a bargain it would be: "giving little
they would acquire much, gaining so great a treasure as the sweet conversation and sincere love of a dear wife" (Fonte 1979, 171).

In the course of the second day's diffuse conversation, the merits of
women and defects of men are discussed in various contexts, culminating
in the restatement of the diverse fates of the two leading figures, who
close by singing a song in praise of their sex. One purpose of the clever
but meandering discussion is the demonstration of the ample learning
the participants possess. Wherever the words lead, knowledge of disciplines is displayed: "cosmology, ornithology, ichthyology, zoology, bot-
any, . . . the medicinal use of herbs, the relative merits of painting and
sculpture, the application of cosmetics, and the cities and rivers of the
Veneto." The interlocutors list "the best lawyers, the best doctors, the
best writers, the best painters of the city, every one of them male."[277] But
punctuating the presentation of masculine knowledge assimilated by
women, and male authorities admired by them, are assaults on the male
sex. Whether they discuss marine or terrestrial life, countries near or far,
the discourse eventually intersects the principal issue: women's victimiz-
ation by men. The symbiosis between one type of conch shell and one
type of shrimp which allows them both to dine on a captured fish elicits
from Leonora the complaint, "would that we might have a similar support from men, but they would take all the catch for themselves and then
eat us as well if they could" (Fonte 1600, 82; quoted by Labalme 1981,
89). A consideration of the risks faced by sailors on the sea concludes
with a comparison in favor of navigation: women run more risk in the
hands of men than "sailors at the mercy of sea and wind"; more ships
than women get home safely (Fonte 1600, 83).

Amid this random efflorescence of learning, there appears in the
mouth of Lucrezia the eulogy to Venice well-nigh obligatory in literary
works produced in that proud city. Nowhere are there laws and princi-

ples better than "in this our glorious city, where there are most holy laws, worthy of being embraced and executed in any realm, not otherwise than in ancient times were the laws of prudent Athens" (Fonte 1979, 185). The senate, the people, the doge, all excel in this city ruled by "courage, counsel, wisdom, knowledge, intellect, piety and the fear of God" (Fonte 1979, 186). The praise of Venice does not pass by without analysis, though, from the female perspective. The magistracies listed and admired, Leonora points out, are the tools of the oppression of women: "What do we have to do with magistracies, lawcourts, and such twists and turns of the government? For don't men use all this official machinery against us, don't they command us if we do not willingly obey, don't they win things to our loss, don't they treat us like aliens, don't they make our property their own?" (Fonte 1979, 187). The political apparatus of serene and beautiful Venice fascinated the statesmen of Europe with its order, justice, and endurance; but for women it was a tyranny like any other.

As the ladies of Christine's city gathered together to find an asylum forever safe, the ladies in Fonte's garden enjoy solidarity and mutual respect not otherwise available in the society of Venice. It is the prospective loss of the company of female friends that persuades Virginia to accept marriage, as it was the loss of freedom consequent upon marriage that causes Corinna to forswear it. Her mother had described her choices: "If you do not marry, you will need to stay always inside your house, and you will dress drably, without lovely clothes, nor lovely conversations, as we are having now, because it is not proper that a maiden who does not wish to marry to do otherwise; and you will be deprived of that [female] companionship which otherwise would be all your delight" (Fonte 1600, 146). Elsewhere that choice is shown to be flawed. Women seek marriage so as not to lead the life of beasts, "trapped within walls," but find they have gained only "a hateful warder."[278] It would be better, Leonora suggested, to be among the Amazons, when armed women combatted and defeated their oppressors.[279] The fearful prospect of war between the genders raised, the participants retreat to milder themes, their courtly diction and graceful movements in constant tension with their virulent anger.

The garden retreat of the seven grand ladies of Fonte's vision form, if only for a moment, a perfect female society. Here they speak freely of their predicament and gain strength from each other, and above all, from the fiercely independent Corinna. The primary interlocutor, Corinna speaks with Fonte's own voice. Yet Fonte's situation was, ironically, not Corinna's: she was married (with what success we do not know but may presume that some experience of her own marriage informs her construction of it in *Woman's Worth*), and she was a mother. Pregnant as she wrote that defense of her sex, she died giving birth to a fourth child, at the age of thirty-seven, one day after its completion. It was published with prefatory material by two of her surviving children in 1600, eight years after her premature death and nearly two hundred after that of the indefatigable widow Christine de Pizan.

In 1694, not quite a century later, a third writer would describe the architecture of a female community secluded from men for refuge and strength: the Englishwoman Mary Astell, never mother, wife, nor widow, but one of those spinsters who formed so large a fraction of her class.[280] Educated by her uncle Ralph, an Anglican clergyman suspended from his post for "bad behaviour" when Astell was eleven, she acquired a serious education that included philosophy, mathematics, and at least some modern languages. Her works testify to some knowledge of classical literature, which she probably read in translation, and wide reading in theology, history, and politics. These were considerable attainments, although her education may be judged not quite to equal that of either Fonte or Christine. Soon after her uncle's death she also lost both parents, and, left with few prospects or plans, proceeded at about the age of twenty to forge a literary career in London. Established in Chelsea, in a circle of well-educated aristocratic women and earnest high-church theologians, she wrote prolifically over a period of ten years, producing a number of works that included *Reflections upon Marriage*, which cast more than a few aspersions on that institution, and, the work that will concern us here, *A Serious Proposal to the Ladies, for the Advancement of Their True and Greatest Interest, by a Lover of her Sex*.[281] It circulated widely, running to five editions by 1701, and, having gained inspiration from such older contemporaries as Bathsua Makin and Hannah Wolley, it sparked fresh thinking by men and women alike, including Defoe, Elizabeth Elstob, and Lady Mary Wortley Montagu. Recommending the secession of women from the society of men (at least for a while), for their own benefit and for the sake of the productive work that they could thereby be prepared to perform, the book proposes an institution a little like the convents that had been suppressed 150 years earlier during England's Reformation, and a little like the female colleges not yet born that would in many ways resemble the lost nunneries.

Astell's proposed place of retreat was to be, like a Roman Catholic convent, a place of religious contemplation: she calls it, straightforwardly, a "monastery" (150). Her intention was perfectly earnest. In this place of "Religious Retirement," women would live in a community, gathering daily to pray, weekly to worship, and—as nearly outworn tradition required—on occasions to fast (150–51, 156–57). They would reap from this communal life of dedication to God the same joy and peace that the dedicated nuns of another age had known. Protestantism provided no such mechanism, and Astell would restore what had been lost. "Happy Retreat! which will be the introducing you into such a *Paradise* as your Mother *Eve* forfeited, where you shall feast on Pleasures, that do not like those of the World, disappoint your expectations . . . ; but such as will make you *truly* happy *now*, and prepare you to be *perfectly* so hereafter. Here are no Serpents to deceive you, whilst you entertain your selves in these delicious Gardens. . . . In fine, the place to which you are invited is a Type and Antepast of Heav'n" (151). Astell's Protestant nunnery lacked the authoritarian structure of the traditional one: no abbesses, or confessors, or inquisitors, would intervene to direct the mental life of the ladies who willingly gathered there and who were quite competent independently to design the course of their lives of contemplation. In their religious retreat, persuasion would take the place of authority: "piety shall not be roughly impos'd, but wisely insinuated," and there were to be no "Vows or irrevocable Obligations, not so much as the fear of Reproach to keep our Ladies here any longer than they desire" (158). The discipline of the holy life would coexist with the highest personal freedom.

For the main purpose of this holy retreat is apparently not so much "Monastic" as "Academical" (179), not so much salvation as self-development, and Astell's vision of a female community differs from several others offered contemporaneously in this: it centered on the need for the higher education of women. "One great end of this Institution shall be, to expel that cloud of Ignorance which Custom has involv'd us in, to furnish our minds with a stock of solid and useful Knowledge, that the Souls of Women may no longer be the only unadorn'd and neglected things" (152). She offers in realization of this end, rather than a formal curriculum, an invitation to conversation—like that of the ladies, perhaps, in Leonora's Venetian garden, encircled by the principles of chastity, solitude, and freedom? The usual injunction was given to avoid idle romances and frivolous stories, heard from pedagogues of virtually every ideological, confessional, and sexual vantage point. Better would be the works of the contemporary philosophers Descartes and Malebranche, accessible in French, and the female authors Anne d'Acier and Madeleine de Scudéry (called "Sappho") (155). Astell seems to find French sufficient, and does not recommend the humanist program of sustained study of the ancient languages. She envisions a course of study that "will neither be too troublesome nor out of the reach of a Female Virtuoso," who need not be bothered with "turning over a great number of Books," when it is sufficient to "understand and digest a few well-chosen and good ones" (152, 153). Following Bacon, in an orientation adopted also by Makin, she believed that women's efforts should be expended not "in learning words but things" (152). These things, perhaps, had to do with the service that educated women could perform when they left their "nunnery" behind and reentered the world.

Astell's "monastery" would be a "Seminary to stock the Kingdom with pious and prudent Ladies," who might in turn guide and inspire the rest of their sex so that women might no longer be taken for "useless and impertinent animals" (152). Those who marry would be fit to perform well the task which for this author stands out as the main point of matrimony: the education of children. Merely to bring children into the world "is no matter of choice and therefore the less obliging"; but through kindness to guide others "to live wisely and happily in it, and be capable of endless Joys hereafter" is a truly grand achievement (144). (Here follows an injunction to mothers to nurse their own children, in which Astell adds her voice to a centuries-old male tradition.) The mother who can richly educate her children fits her son to transmit to posterity the honor borne by his family name, and does no less for her daughter, through whom subsequent unnamed generations will be molded. Yet though the education of women implies the education of mothers and through them the whole of the future, the childless woman is also educated to a purpose. Indeed, the responsibility to be shouldered by unmarried women is far more challenging: reaching outward beyond the limits of the family, they can further the education of many. Knowledge will not "lie dead upon their hands," because "the whole World is a single Lady's Family, her opportunities of doing good are not lessen'd but encreas'd by her being unconfin'd. Particular Obligations do not contract her Mind, but her Beneficence moves in the largest Sphere" (178). Such women will be suited to give the best possible tuition to the children "of persons of quality." While the routine tasks of child rearing can be left to "meaner Persons deputed to that Office, . . . the forming of their minds shall be the particular care of those of their own Rank" (165). They can also profitably serve as tutors to the daughters of distressed gentlemen unable to provide for their own offspring: by their doing so "many Souls will be preserv'd from great Dishonours and put in a comfortable way of subsisting" (166).

The fruit of education for women, then, according to Astell, is educative and, to a lesser extent, the more traditional caritative work. She does not suggest that women take over the social positions for which a man's education suited him: in politics, in business, in the church. Women will not, she assures her audience, "usurp authority," as has been heard in the passage already quoted, or dare to "teach in the Church" (154). While women can learn as much as men can (155), they do not intend to learn so much as to challenge men in their own sphere, but only enough so as to develop their own sense of self-worth. "The Men therefore may still enjoy their prerogatives for us. . . . They may busy their Heads with Affairs of State, and spend their Time and Strength in recommending themselves to an uncertain Master, or a more giddy Multitude, our only endeavour shall be to be absolute Monarchs in our own Bosoms. . . . and whilst they have unrival'd the glory of speaking as *many* Languages as *Babel* afforded, we only desire to express ourselves pertinently and Judiciously in *One*. We will not vie with them in thumbing over Authors, nor pretend to be walking Libraries, provided they'll but allow us a competent Knowledge of the Books of God, nature I mean and the Holy Scriptures: And whilst they accomplish themselves with the Knowledge of the World, . . . we'll aspire no further than to be intimately acquainted with our own Hearts" (179). In spite of the modesty of her goals, Astell's "serious proposal" met with hostility from some readers. The male satirists of *The Tatler* trotted out the deadly metaphors that those who have read to this point will recognize as the regular currency of masculine disdain: the abandonment of the tools of textile for those of literary production; the revivification of the Amazons. Astell, wrote one, had recommended a "College for Young Damsels; where instead of Scissors, Needles, and Samplers; pens, Compasses, Quadrants, Books, Manuscripts, Greek, Latin, and Hebrew are to take up the whole Time." Another charged that the inmates would have "at least a superficial tincture of the Ancient and Modern Amazonian Tacticks!"[282]

Astell's critics were right: it was her aim in a certain sense to woo women away from scissors, needles, and samplers and to turn them into

Amazons—that is, into emotionally and intellectually self-sufficient human beings. As Louise Labé had wished the women of her bourgeois circle to lift their minds a little above their distaffs, Astell wished those of her elegant set to think of more than their milliners and tailors (cf. 146). She calls her contemporaries to a higher vision of themselves, aiming, she tells them, "to improve your Charms and heighten your Value, by suffering you no longer to be cheap and contemptible." The women of her class and age thought only of their beauty, and each would sadly learn that their admirers would disappear *pari passu* with their loveliness. They must find in themselves their real beauty, "to make it lasting and permanent, . . . and to place it out of the reach of Sickness and Old Age." They must learn not to debase themselves with trinkets that have no real value, available to anyone at all who has money to purchase them, but to procure "such Ornaments as all the Treasures of the Indies are not able to purchase" (139). In Astell's world, which packaged women like sugar plums to be sold in marriage, an untutored girl was "taught to think Marriage her only Preferment, the Sum-total of her Endeavours, the completion of all her hopes."[283] For that end their insufficient education prepared them, but Astell would have them extend their wills to a better one. Let us not, she implores, "entertain such a degrading thought of our own *worth*, as to imagine that our Souls were given us only for the service of our Bodies, and that the best improvement we can make of these, is to attract the Eyes of Men" (141). If women received an adequate education, "had they obtain'd a well inform'd and discerning Mind, they would be proof against all those Batteries, see through and scorn those little silly Artifices which are us'd to ensnare and deceive them. Such an one would value her self only on her Vertue. . . . She would know, that not what others *say*, but what she her self *does*, is the true Commendation and the only thing that exalts her" (146). The spiritual requirements of Astell's "monastery" were none too stiff, and the curriculum she prescribed for the residents was somewhat meager, but the summons to a higher vocation for women is stated as boldly as the sounding of a trumpet.

By the year 1700, the Renaissance was well over; Astell lived in greater proximity to Robespierre than to Boccaccio. Yet her concept of a Protestant nunnery where women without families might enrich themselves with knowledge and in freedom develop their personalities for productive expression within society is linked with the experience of women who had lived in centuries past. The holy women and saints of that age had done what Astell now proposed as a goal for her sorority of upper-

upper-class Anglicans: they had sought God, mastering what they could of the learned male tradition, and verdant with spiritual growth had tended the sick and the old and the young and the abandoned, men as well as women, from their overflowing love. The women humanists of the past—the handful who had succeeded in finding time and resources for the "long estude," the years of disciplined study that groomed a learned man—had attained an education equal to (in terms of the knowledge available in that time, not yet scientific), or perhaps surpassing that which Astell envisioned. Astell may have earned with her striking "Serious Proposal" the title of the "first modern feminist." But she may also be claimed as the last of the learned women of the Renaissance.

Further, Astell's "Protestant nunnery" is a "city of ladies," like Fonte's and Christine de Pizan's: a place of refuge from the violence and tyranny of the male, and a place of nurture for the virtue and dignity of the female. When Renaissance women confronted the predicament in which women found themselves, their solution was not to change society, irreparably dominated by male concerns, but to escape it. All three of the feminists considered in these last pages were social conservatives. They challenged the tyranny of men but not the tyranny of class or potentate. Within the structures their critique left undisturbed there was no place for women: no role for women in cities where only men could be citizens or kings. Until those ancient structures fell to a male assault in the name of civil rights and natural law in the revolutions of the late eighteenth century, no truly modern feminist claim could be made. Following the American declaration of the equality of all men and the French declaration of the rights of man, such a feminist claim was finally taken in 1792 by Mary Wollstonecraft, who claimed for women the same human rights won by American and French revolutionaries. And it was succinctly expressed by the American women who gathered at the small town of Seneca Falls, New York, in 1848, to declare these truths to be self-evident: "that all men and women are born equal, and are endowed by their creator with certain inalienable rights."[284] Years, then, would pass before women would demand not liberty from men but the same liberty enjoyed by men. Such a victory could not be gained until acceptance grew universal of the principle stated by Marie de Gournay: "the human animal is neither male nor female."[285]

A final question remains—the one implied in the title of a work aiming to describe "Women of the Renaissance." Was there a Renaissance for women? Joan Kelly wrote boldly in 1977 that there was not: "at least, not during the Renaissance."[286] At the time, her insight was powerful. For she was the first historian to point unremittingly to the dismal realities of women's lives in the Renaissance centuries. Within the family, they were subject to fathers and husbands and their surrogates in modes that did not relent before the end of Renaissance centuries. They bore special burdens of economic hardship, which limited their dowries and determined their destinies if they were of the elite, or which condemned them (much as it condemned their brothers) to lives of servitude if they were not. Within the church, they were powerless as well. In Roman Catholic countries, those women who chose or were consigned to the religious life were increasingly enclosed, scrutinized, and constrained. In Protestant countries, they were denied the option of convent or anchorage and placed under the spiritual supervision of the same men who decided their social destiny. In both settings, they could seize, at their peril, the option of nonconformity: they could be heretics, prophets, sectaries, or witches. In the world of learning, women remained suspect throughout the period. They snatched an education, in a few cases, from affectionate fathers, brothers, uncles, and grandfathers. But if they wrote, they were declared to be unwomanly; and if they wrote very well, they were labeled Amazons, fearsome and unnatural beings. This does not look like a Renaissance, a rebirth into a new life, but a continuation and in some ways an intensification of the disabilities and prejudices inherited from the Middle Ages and from antiquity.

Yet an argument can be made to the contrary, and has been, for instance, by the splendid historian of Italian society, David Herlihy.[287] Women's charismatic role, her astonishing success as intermediary with the divine, rooted in her female role as mother projected on a cosmic scale, gave her special prominence precisely in the Renaissance centuries. As it did, in the case of a few exceptional women. One might wonder if the far greater numbers of those who burned and suffered the torments of the torture chamber might overshadow the figures of spiritual prominence; or if the ordinary suffering of the great mass of women overshadows them, for though these women were subject to the same harsh austerities as men of the age, they were deprived, unlike men, of all autonomy. Nevertheless, Herlihy's suggestion is persuasive. Something changed during the Renaissance in women's sense of themselves, even if very little changed or changed for the better in their social condition. That change did have its roots in the spiritual experience of women, and it culminates in the consciousness put into words by the first feminists of the Renaissance. Not monsters, not defects in nature, but the intelligent seekers of a new way, these women wielded the picks of their understanding to build a better city for ladies.

NOTES

Chapter One

1. See inter alia Bugge 1975, esp. 141–54; Bynum 1982; Gold 1985; Warner 1976, esp. part 4.

2. Ariès 1962, 35–37; Goldthwaite 1972, 1009–11; Lasareff 1938; see also previous note. For the antithesis and identification of Mary and Eve, see also Guldan 1966.

3. See for instance N. Z. Davis 1979, "City Women" 69; Flandrin 1979, 58–59; McLaren 1985, esp. 27.

4. Flandrin 1979, 202, 204; McLaren 1985, 22.

5. J. C. Davis 1975, 73; also McLaren 1985, 27–28; Slater 1984, 65.

6. Slater 1984, 65.

7. J. C. Davis 1962; Dante, *Paradiso* 15.106–8; for the oblique reference to birth control in this passage of Dante's, see Biller 1982, 21–22.

8. Alberti 1969, 25.

9. Kristeller 1956, "Un codice padovano," 348.

10. Alberti 1969, 115; F. Barbaro 1916, book 1, passim.

11. Quoted by Ozment 1983a, 161.

12. N. Z. Davis 1979, "City Women" 69.

13. E. A. R. Brown 1987, 316–19.

14. Fraser 1984, 59.

15. Slater 1984, 7–8.

16. Martines 1974, 19; from Guasti's introduction to Strozzi 1877.

17. J. C. Davis 1975, 63.

18. Klapisch-Zuber 1985, "Blood Parents and Milk Parents" 135 n. 11.

19. Perleone, *Laudatio*, 190–91.

20. Schutte 1980b, 487; also Rodocanachi 1922, 3–5.

21. Schutte 1980b, esp. 486ff.

22. Correr 1983, 99.

23. Origo 1957, 165–67.

24. M. L. King 1978, 818–20.

25. Erasmus 1979, 19.

26. Quoted in Shepherd 1985, 19.

27. Quoted by Martines 1974, 25.

28. Quoted by Power 1926, 409.

29. See below, chap. 2, pp. 133–34.

30. Macfarlane 1970, 84–85.

31. Flandrin 1979, 217.

32. Eccles 1982, 125.

33. Eccles 1982, 126.

34. Stone 1977, fig. 7 following p. 192.

35. Hill 1984, 102.

36. Flandrin 1979, 217. Of his first wife, nothing is known, and the fifth still lived, but had not given birth, when the diary came to an end.

37. D'Aubigné 1969, 385.

38. Dati 1967, 112, 117, 132.

39. Carmichael 1986, 41–53, 90–92; Flandrin 1979, 53.

40. Kieckhefer 1984, 22.

41. Chrisman 1972, 155.

42. Slater 1984, 117.

43. Flandrin 1979, 59.

44. Herlihy 1967, 86.

45. Klapisch-Zuber 1987, 340.

46. Albini 1983, 152, table 2, based on first seven months of year.

47. Dati 1967, 134–36.

48. Perleone, *Laudatio*, 190–91.

49. Quoted by Mendelson 1985, 195.

50. Brucker 1971, 48, from Strozzi 1987, no. 17, 123.

51. Christian 1981, 182.

52. Cited in Mendelson 1985, 197.

53. Stone 1977, 215; see also Ariès 1962.

54. Shahar 1983, 104.

55. Shahar 1983, 105.

56. J. C. Davis 1975, 63; Klapisch-Zuber 1985, "Childhood in Tuscany," 96–97.

57. Klapisch-Zuber 1985, "Childhood in Tuscany," 99.

58. Hanawalt 1986a, 179.

59. Hanawalt 1986a, 175–78.

60. Cited by Kellum 1973–74, 367.

61. Langer 1973–74 and 1974–75; also, among many other sources, Boswell 1989; Brissaud 1972; Helmholz 1975; Herlihy 1985b, 25–27; Kellum 1973–74; Trexler 1973–74b.

62. Hanawalt 1986a, 194–97; Stone 1977, 610, graph 15.

63. Kellum 1973–74, 372.

64. Kellum 1973–74, 381–82.

65. Cecchetti 1886, 339.

66. Shahar 1983, 118.

67. Quoted by Wiesner 1986c, 61.

68. Wiesner 1986c, 71.

69. Trexler 1973–74b, esp. 103–4.

70. Cherubino da Siena 1888, 100.

71. Quoted by Origo 1962, 198.

72. Monter 1976, 197–98; Monter 1980, 196–98; Trexler 1973–74b, 103–5.

73. Larner 1981, 51–52; Monter 1976, 197–98; Monter 1980, 196–98; Quaife 1987, 132; for witch prosecutions, see below, chap. 2, pp. 144–56.

74. Trexler 1973–74b, 105.

75. Larner 1981, 52; Quaife 1987, 132.

76. Shahar 1983, 20; Monter 1980, 196.

77. Shahar 1983, 119.

78. O'Faolain and Martines 1973, 227.

79. The above two examples: Monter 1976, 198 n. 14.

80. Monter 1980, 197.

81. This discussion of abandonment depends on Boswell 1989.

82. Quoted by Trexler 1973–74b, 98, in his trans.; also quoted in different trans. by Boswell 1989, 414.

83. Boswell 1989, 409–12.

84. Langer 1973–74, 356; Trexler 1973–74b, 99; Boswell 1989, 416–17.

85. Otis 1986, 84.

86. Trexler 1973–74a, 263.

87. Klapisch-Zuber 1985, "Childhood in Tuscany," 104.

88. Quoted by Trexler 1973–74a, 261.

89. Herlihy 1985b, 150–51, table 6.5.

90. Klapisch-Zuber 1985, "Kin, Friends, and Neighbors," 73 n. 24.

91. Flandrin 1979, 180–88; Mitterauer and Sieder 1982, chap. 2, esp. 43–44.

92. Quoted by Still 1931, 64.

93. Macfarlane 1970, 87.

94. Shahar 1982–83, 284.

95. R. Bell 1985, 29–34; Shahar 1982–83, 295.

96. Still 1931, 49. Among many other discussions of this literature see: E. A. R. Brown 1987, 318 n. 123; Klapisch-Zuber 1985, "Blood Parents and Milk Parents," esp. 161–62; Rodocanachi 1922, 12ff.; Ross 1974, 185–86; and a general survey in Fildes 1988, 32–111.

97. F. Barbaro 1978, 223.

98. Ross 1974, 186.

99. Vives 1783, 4:70 (1.1).

100. Davies 1982, 73.

101. Cherubino da Siena 1888, 63–64.

102. Flandrin 1979, 198–207; Klapisch-Zuber 1985, "Blood Parents and Milk Parents," 158–62; McLaren 1985, "Marital Fertility and Lactation," 27–28; Shahar 1982–83, 295–98.

103. McLaren 1985, 45.

104. Klapisch-Zuber 1985, "Blood Parents and Milk Parents," 135; Klapisch-Zuber 1986, 57; also table 4 and fig. 2 at 65 and 67 respectively.

105. E. A. R. Brown 1987, 318.

106. M. L. King 1988, 211; Perleone, *Laudatio*, 212–15.

107. Still 1931, 71, citing Bartholomaeus Metlinger's *Ein Regiment der Jungen Kinder* (1473), who repeats the advice offered by experts for more than 1,000 years. See also Ross 1974, 185–86; Shahar 1982–83, 285–86, 296.

108. Klapisch-Zuber 1985, "Blood Parents and Milk Parents," 139–53.

109. Alberti 1969, 51.

110. Klapisch-Zuber 1985, "Blood Parents and Milk Parents," 142–44.

111. Klapisch-Zuber 1985, "Blood Parents and Milk Parents," 153–58.

112. Klapisch-Zuber 1985, "Blood Parents and Milk Parents," 136.

113. Shahar 1982–83, 296.

114. Klapisch-Zuber 1985, "Blood Parents and Milk Parents," 138.

115. Klapisch-Zuber 1985, "Blood Parents and Milk Parents," 140.

116. Trexler 1973–74b, 100, from Origo 1957, 216.

117. Quoted by Trexler 1973–74a, 274 and 275.

118. Owen 1978, 338–39.

119. Montaigne 1958, 2.8.290–91; also Ross 1974, 187, for the artist Vasari's report of an infant suckled by a goat.

120. Shahar 1982–83, 287.

121. Klapisch-Zuber 1985, "Blood Parents and Milk Parents," 146, table 7.4.

122. McLaren 1985, 30.

123. Hill 1984, 107.

124. Quoted by Origo 1957, 231.

125. Cellini 1985, 400.

126. Klapisch-Zuber 1985, "Blood Parents and Milk Parents," 133.

127. Cardan 1930, 9; quoted by Ross 1974, 192.

128. Stone 1977, 106.

129. Trexler 1975, 229.

130. Quoted by Marcus 1978, 60, 143.

131. Ross 1974, 199; see also Klapisch-Zuber 1985, "Childhood in Tuscany," 114–16.

132. Quoted by Hanawalt 1986a, 186.

133. Cohn 1988, 224.

134. Flandrin 1979, 194–235, for this thesis.

135. Biller 1982, 20ff. For Florence, Herlihy 1985b, 146–49.

136. Biller 1982, 19 n. 67, from Del Lungo 1926, 107.

137. Ruggiero 1985, 42.

138. Cherubino da Siena 1888, 100.

139. Alberti 1969, 50.

140. Flandrin 1979, 138–39; Herlihy 1985b, 122–24.

141. Vives 1783, 2.11, 258.

142. Cohn 1988, 206.

143. Reyerson 1986, 122, 130.

144. Chojnacki 1985.

145. Zeno, *Consolatio*.

146. Chrisman 1972, 158.

147. Blaisdell 1972, 216ff.

148. Roelker 1972b, esp. 170; 1972a; and 1968, esp. 395–401.

149. Ignatius of Loyola 1956, 461–66.

150. Ignatius of Loyola 1956, 463.

151. Strozzi 1877.

152. Martines 1974, 27–28, from Strozzi 1987, no. 65, 290.

153. Quoted by Bainton 1971, 93–94.

154. Quoted by Bainton 1971, 142.

155. Emerson 1984, 12ff.; Hogrefe 1977, 136–53.

156. Quoted by Hogrefe 1977, 142.

157. Quoted by Hogrefe 1977, 142.

158. For excerpts, Dronke 1984, chap. 2; Wilson 1984, 12–29.

159. Lucas 1983, 163–64; Willard 1984, 173–74.

160. Bainton 1971, 125–44.

161. Travitsky 1980, 38.

162. Travitsky 1980, 39 and n. 21.

163. Casagrande 1978, introduction, reprint of Consiglia de' Matteis 1986, 259–73; Le Goff 1977, 114.

164. Cherubino da Siena 1888, 3.

165. M. L. King 1975, 554–56.

166. Vives 1783, 4:66 (Praefatio).

167. Wiesner 1986c, 152.

168. Mendelson 1985, 199.

169. *Paradiso* 15:103–4, quoted by several scholars; Datini letter quoted in Ross 1974, 206 and n. 155; for the negligent treatment of females generally, Herlihy and Klapisch-Zuber 1978, 326–49.

170. Excerpt in Trexler 1975, 247, from Morelli 1956, 504–5.

171. Trexler 1975, 234, from Morelli 1956, 212–13.

172. Quoted by Wiesner 1986a, 101.

173. Quoted by Eccles 1982, 44, from Ambroise Paré.

174. Eccles 1982, 44; Klapisch-Zuber 1985, "Childhood in Tuscany," 101–2; Tamassia 1971, 266ff.; Horowitz 1979.

175. Trexler 1975, 229, from Morelli 1956, 143.

176. Klapisch-Zuber 1985, "Childhood in Tuscany," 102 n. 17.

177. Klapisch-Zuber 1985, "Childhood in Tuscany," 101–6; Trexler 1973–74b, 100–102.

178. Trexler 1973–74b, 100–102; Kellum 1973–74, 368–69; see also the titles cited above n. 61.

179. Herlihy and Klapisch-Zuber 1978, 361–62; Klapisch-Zuber 1985, "Childhood in Tuscany," 98–104.

180. J. C. Davis 1975, 63.

181. Klapish-Zuber 1985, "Blood Parents and Milk Parents," 138–39, 155; "Childhood in Tuscany," 105–6.

182. Klapish-Zuber 1985, "Childhood in Tuscany," 106–7; see also Hufton 1982.

183. For this analysis of shifting family functions, Mitterauer and Sieder 1982, esp. chap. 4.

184. Herlihy 1976b, 7, 19; Herlihy 1985b, 98–103; D. Hughes 1978.

185. Klapisch-Zuber 1985, "The Griselda Complex," 213–17.

186. Chojnacki 1974, 194; Chojnacki 1976, 173.

187. Chojnacki 1976, 175.

188. Sanuto 1879–1903, 30:29.

189. Chojnacki 1976, 173–74.

190. Cohn 1988, 126.

191. Martines 1974, 27 n.

192. Herlihy 1976b.

193. Nearly 74 percent of investors were fathers, and an additional 11 percent were other male relatives: Kirshner and Molho 1978, 412, table 2, and passim; Kirshner 1978; Kirshner and Molho 1980; Molho 1986.

194. Kirshner and Molho 1978, 413.

195. Molho 1986, 169, table 2.

196. Kirshner and Molho 1978, 414.

197. Chojnacki 1976.

198. Le Roy Ladurie 1978, 36.

199. Stone 1977, 51, stating the conclusion of many studies on the European family; see also Mitterauer and Sieder 1982, 35–37.

200. Hufton 1982.

201. Klapisch-Zuber 1985, "Childhood in Tuscany," 106–7.

202. Ciammitti 1983.

203. L. Ferrante 1983; see esp. 511, table 2.

204. Cohn 1988, 28.

205. Quoted in Molho 1969, 202, from Strozzi 1987, no. 1, 61.

206. Hanawalt 1986b, ix.

207. Le Roy Ladurie 1978, 179.

208. Stone 1977, 44.

209. Slater 1984, 84–89, at 85.

210. Wiesner 1986c, 4–5.

211. Thrupp 1962, 170.

212. Klapisch-Zuber 1985, "Female Celibacy and Service"; Chabot 1986.

213. Klapisch-Zuber 1985, "Female Celibacy and Service," 172.

214. Klapisch-Zuber 1985, "The 'Cruel Mother,'" 119 n. 7; Chabot 1986, 12.

215. Ruggiero 1987, 756. See also Cohen 1988, 172-73.

216. Le Roy Ladurie 1978, 199-200.

217. Quoted by Brucker 1986, 78.

218. Quoted by Origo 1962, 67.

219. Ruggiero 1985, 17.

220. Ruggiero 1987, 761.

221. Robin in press, chap. 2.

222. See, for a Bolognese case, L. Ferrante 1983.

223. Hanawalt 1986a, 194-96; Stone 1977, 610, graph 15.

224. Hufton 1982, 201.

225. Cohen 1988; Ruggiero 1985, chap. 2.

226. Ruggiero 1985, 44.

227. Brucker 1986.

228. For example, the cases in Cohen 1988.

229. Hill 1984, 33.

230. Klapisch-Zuber 1985, "Childhood in Tuscany," 111.

231. Hallett 1984, chap. 3.

232. Duby 1983, 267; see also D. Hughes 1975a, 1975b; Herlihy 1985a, 9-11, 13.

233. Gregory 1987, 217-18.

234. F. Barbaro 1916, 32.20-22. See also M. L. King 1976a, 33-35.

235. F. Barbaro 1916, 41.19-20.

236. F. Barbaro 1916, 51.18-20.

237. Quoted in Kolsky 1987, 81.

238. Macfarlane 1970, 93-94.

239. Quoted in Slater 1984, 76.

240. Emmanuel Downing to John Winthrop, 1643, quoted by Morgan 1966, 57.

241. Martines 1974, 25, from Strozzi 1987, no. 1, 63. Trans. of the entire letter, Molho 1969, 202-5.

242. J. C. Davis 1975, 107-8.

243. Among others see Brucker 1986, 82–84; Brundage 1987, chaps. 9–11; Duby 1978, 1–24; Klapisch-Zuber 1985, "Zacharias, or the Ousted Father"; and Ozment 1983b, 25–49.

244. Quoted by Noonan 1973, 434.

245. Rossiaud 1985, 93.

246. Quoted by Ozment 1983b, 28.

247. Nicholas 1985, 53; Dillard 1984, 41.

248. O'Faolain and Martines 1973, 172–74; Haskell 1973, 466–68.

249. Fraser 1984, 12–20; Stone 1977, 182.

250. Quoted by Stone 1977, 182.

251. Hogrefe 1977, xxii; the testator is William Shaftoe of Northumberland.

252. Houlbrooke 1984, 72–73; Stone 1977, 191–93.

253. Hanawalt 1986a, 198; discussion at 198–99 for what follows.

254. Quoted by Stone 1977, 192.

255. Davies 1982.

256. Barbaro 1978, 197.

257. Alberti 1969, 98.

258. Quoted by Origo 1962, 57.

259. Quoted by Ozment 1983b, 7.

260. Quoted by Herlihy 1985b, 117.

261. Vives 1783, 4:172 (1.15).

262. Quoted by Warnicke 1983, 178.

263. Quoted by Morgan 1966, 47 and 48.

264. Quoted by Morgan 1966, 61–62.

265. Gies and Gies 1987, 246.

266. Chojnacki 1988, 134.

267. Quoted by Chojnacki 1988, 135.

268. Chojnacki 1988, 138.

269. Cohn 1988, 202–3.

270. Ozment 1986.

271. Ozment 1986, 41, 43.

272. Quoted by Slater 1984, 67.

273. Mendelson 1985, 193.

274. D. Hughes 1986.

275. Stone 1977, 202.

276. Stone 1977, 3.5, "The Reinforcement of Patriarchy" for England, 1540–1640.

277. Quoted by Stone 1977, 197.

278. Goodman of Paris 1928; *Menagier de Paris* 1981.

279. Goodman of Paris 1928, 112 (1.6); *Menagier de Paris* 1981, 1.6.7.

280. Cherubino da Siena 1888, 7, 18.

281. Stone 1977, 196.

282. Ozment 1983b, 69.

283. Quoted by Kelso 1956, 96.

284. Quoted by Gentile 1986, 93 n. 1.

285. Quoted by Stone 1977, 151.

286. *The Second Treatise of Civil Government* 7:82, in Locke 1988, 321.

287. Casagrande 1978, xxi; reprint of Consiglia de' Matteis 1986, 270–71.

288. Casagrande 1978, xxiii; reprint of Consiglia de' Matteis 1986, 272.

289. Quoted by Origo 1962, 270 n. 39.

290. F. Barbaro 1978, 202.

291. F. Barbaro 1978, 204.

292. Tentler 1977, 165 and chap. 4; also Braswell 1986, 83–85; Flandrin 1979, 162–63; Flandrin 1985; Kamen 1985, 205ff.

293. Cherubino da Siena 1888, 47.

294. Quoted by Cadden 1986, 165; text in n. 66.

295. Flandrin 1979, 163–64; Tentler 1977, 170ff.

296. Quoted by Origo 1962, 54–55 n. 34.

297. Cherubino da Siena 1888, 55–71, at 66, 61.

298. Cherubino da Siena 1888, 80–99, at 99.

299. Cherubino da Siena 1888, 73, 75.

300. N. Z. Davis 1979, "Women on Top." See also below, chap. 3, 188–93.

301. Quoted by Camden 1952, 126, from Joseph Swetnam, *The Arraignment of Lewd, Idle, Froward and Unconstant Women* (London 1622).

302. *Les Quinze joies de mariage* 1963, 4, lines 120–23.

303. Dillard 1976, 81.

304. O'Faolain and Martines, 1973, from François Serpillon, *Code criminel.*

305. Cecchetti 1886, 55.

306. Douglass 1974, 302–3; Ozment 1983b, 84, 93; and 80–98 for the Protestant position; R. Phillips 1988, chap. 2.

307. Nicholas 1985, chap. 2.

308. Chojnacki 1974, 188.

309. Camden 1952, 117.

310. Stone 1977, 38.

311. Chabot 1986, 16.

312. L. Ferrante 1983, 507.

313. Shahar 1983, 89–90; Stone 1977, 197–98.

314. Le Roy Ladurie 1978, 192.

315. Quoted in Flandrin 1979, 123.

316. Nicholas 1985, 45.

317. Demos 1970 93–94; N. Z. Davis 1979, "City Women," 90–91.

318. Quoted by Ozment 1983b, 54–55 from Irwin 1979, 104.

319. Cherubino da Siena 1888, 10–13, at 13.

320. Quoted by Origo 1962, 49.

321. Quoted by Flandrin 1979, 149.

322. Excerpt in O'Faolain and Martines 1973, 165.

323. Kristeller 1956, "The School of Salerno," 505; Kristeller 1980, 102–3 and nn. 50–51; a more positive view in Herlihy 1990, 104–7.

324. Modern translations in Mason-Hohl 1940 and Rowland 1981; *editio princeps* Strasbourg 1544.

325. Shahar 1983, 201; J. Ferrante 1980, 18.

326. J. Ferrante 1980, 18.

327. Quoted, among other places, by Kristeller 1980, 115 n. 52.

328. Wiesner 1986c, 49–50.

329. Anderson and Zinsser 1988, 1:421–22.

330. Wiesner 1986c, 50.

331. Wiesner 1986a.

332. Quoted by N. Z. Davis 1986, 187.

333. Quoted by Wiesner 1986c, 54.

334. Quoted by Wiesner 1986c, 52.

335. Quoted by Wiesner 1986c, 52.

336. Excerpt in Ross and McLaughlin 1966, 635–40, from H. Denifle, *Cartularium Universitatis parisiensis* (Paris 1891) 257–67.

337. M. Hughes 1943, 85–86 n. 21.

338. O'Faolain and Martines 1973, 165.

339. Anderson and Zinsser 1988, 1:420.

340. Filippini 1985.

341. Savonarola 1952; see Demaitre 1976–77, 162–63 and passim; O'Neill 1975.

342. Lemay 1985.

343. Lemay 1985, 326.

344. Ozment 1983b, chap. 3; Still 1931, 94ff.; Wiesner 1986c, 66.

345. Anderson and Zinsser 1988, 1:423, citing Carolyn Merchant, *The Death of Nature: Women, Ecology and the Scientific Revolution* (New York: Harper & Row, 1980) 153.

346. Duby 1983, xx.

347. Among other titles: Bullough 1973a, 1973b; d'Alverny 1977; Mac-Lean 1980; Okin 1979, chaps. 1 and 2.

348. Lemay 1978.

349. Quoted by Demaitre 1976–77, 482.

350. The conclusion (not undisputed) of many authorities: see, among others, Stone 1977, 202 and passim, for the period from the sixteenth century forward, and Flandrin 1979, 124–26, for that from the late Middle Ages. Also N. Z. Davis 1979, "Women on Top," 126.

351. For the following discussion, Goody 1983, esp. chap. 2; Herlihy 1985a, 11–14; 1985b, 61, 135–36.

352. Bellomo 1968, chap. 1.

353. Herlihy 1976a, 24–40; Dillard 1984; 1976.

354. Chojnacki 1974, 190.

355. Nicholas 1985, 26, 73–76, and table 6.

356. Stone 1977, 195, alluding to the well-known statement of the English jurist William Blackstone.

357. F. Barbaro 1916, 51.6–11.

358. Kuehn 1982.

359. Kirshner 1985, 299.

360. Nicholas 1985, 42.

361. Klapisch-Zuber 1985, "Kin, Friends, and Neighbors," 78.

362. Quoted by Kuehn 1982, 318, with text.

363. Nicholas 1985, part 1, passim.

364. Quoted by Wiesner 1986c, 25.

365. Kuehn 1982, esp. 329–33.

366. Hanawalt 1986b, "Peasant Women's Contribution"; Stone 1977, 199–200; Wiesner 1986c, chap. 1.

367. D. Hughes 1975a, 124ff.; 1975b, 22ff.

368. Quoted by Origo 1962, 270 n. 39.

369. Stone 1977, 200.

370. Wiesner 1986c, 31.

371. Quoted by Braswell 1986, 92, with text.

372. Strocchia 1990.

373. Klapisch-Zuber 1985, "Female Celibacy and Service," "The Griselda Complex"; Klapisch-Zuber 1986.

374. Klapisch-Zuber 1985, "The Griselda Complex," 220, 227.

375. Caldiera, *De oeconomia veneta*, fol. 82v.

376. Martines 1974, 26, from Strozzi 1987, no. 49, 234.

377. Harris 1982, 375, 377.

378. Quoted by Muzzarelli 1986, 374.

379. Muzzarelli 1986, 374.

380. Muzzarelli 1986, 388.

381. Muzzarelli 1986, 390.

382. D. Hughes 1975a, 1975b.

383. Chojnacki 1974, 177.

384. Betto 1981, 53.

385. Chojnacki 1974, 203.

386. Klapisch-Zuber 1985, "Kin, Friends, and Neighbors," 81.

387. Betto 1981, 45.

388. Chojnacki 1974, 196.

389. Chojnacki 1974, esp. 185 for bequests to females.

390. Betto 1981, 56–57.

391. Chojnacki 1974, 190; also 195.

392. Chojnacki 1974, 201–2.

393. Cohn 1988, 207.

394. The following depends on Cohn 1988, esp. 198–210.

395. Cohn 1988, 201–2.

396. Cohn 1988, 202.

397. Vann 1977, 195.

398. Wiesner 1986c, 76.

399. Wiesner 1986c, 157, 162.

400. D. Hughes 1975a, 124ff.; 1975b, 22–25.

401. Mitterauer and Sieder 1982, esp. 54–62; Shahar 1983, 94–98; Stone 1977, 50–60.

402. Quoted by Demos 1970, 85.

403. Quoted by Murray 1988, 379.

404. Quoted by Macfarlane 1986, 112.

405. Reyerson 1986, 137.

406. Quoted by Roelker 1972b, 171.

407. Migne, *Patrologia latina*, Epistola 123.11; quoted by Herlihy 1985b, 22.

408. Quoted by Mendelson 1985, 199.

409. For the following esp.: Chabot 1986; Klapisch-Zuber 1985, "The 'Cruel Mother,'" Herlihy 1985b, 154–55; Tamassia 1971, 327ff.

410. Herlihy and Klapisch-Zuber 1978, 406.

411. Betto 1981, 58.

412. Tamassia 1971, 348.

413. For the following, Klapisch-Zuber 1985, "The 'Cruel Mother.'"

414. Klapisch-Zuber 1985, "The 'Cruel Mother,'" 123.

415. Klapisch-Zuber 1985, "The 'Cruel Mother,'" 124.

416. Quoted by Ross 1974, 201.

417. D. Hughes 1975a.

418. Quoted by Klapisch-Zuber 1985, "The 'Cruel Mother,'" 125.

419. Cecchetti 1886, 55.

420. Klapisch-Zuber 1985, "The Griselda Complex," 226 n. 45.

421. Quoted by Origo 1962, 68.

422. Tamassia 1971, 327.

423. Klapisch-Zuber 1985, "Female Celibacy and Service," 167ff. and figs. 8.1–8.3; Herlihy 1985b, 154–55.

424. Chabot 1986, 23.

425. Lombardi 1986, 27.

426. Quoted by Lombardi 1986, 26.

427. Quoted by Klapisch-Zuber 1985, "Kin, Friends, and Neighbors," 78 and 74.

428. Klapisch-Zuber 1985, "The 'Cruel Mother,'" 118.

429. Quoted in Hanawalt 1986a, 162.

430. Quoted in Lewenhak 1980, 108.

431. A. Clark 1968, 293.

432. Wiesner 1986c, 92–93.

433. Mendelson 1985, 190; Braunstein 1987, 747.

434. Herlihy 1985a, 12; 1990.

435. Alberti 1969, 208–9.

436. Quoted by Origo 1962, 57.

437. Cherubino da Siena 1888, 30–31.

438. Power 1975, 60.

439. McDonnell 1954, 85.

440. Howell 1986a, 70ff.

441. Howell 1986a, 124ff.

442. Wiesner 1986b, 193.

443. O'Faolain and Martines 1973, 154.

444. Wiesner 1986b, 193.

445. Nicholas 1985, chap. 5, esp. 85–86, table 7.

446. Monter 1980, 200, 201.

447. Shahar 1983, 190–91; also Herlihy 1990, 145, fig. 6.4 for distribution of occupations.

448. O'Faolain and Martines, 1973, 155–56.

449. Reyerson 1986, 120–21.

450. N. Z. Davis 1986.

451. N. Z. Davis 1986, 172.

452. N. Z. Davis 1979, "City Women and Religious Change," 70.

453. N. Z. Davis 1986, 181ff.

454. Shahar 1983, 198.

455. O'Faolain and Martines 1973, 157.

456. This section is much indebted to Howell 1986a, which in turn confirms the central thesis of A. Clark 1968 (orig. 1919) and Wiesner 1986b and 1986c.

457. Herlihy 1985a, 13; in general, Herlihy 1990, chaps. 2, 4.

458. Quoted by Wiesner 1986b, 191.

459. Prior 1985, "Women and the Urban Economy," 95.

460. Wiesner 1986b, 202.

461. Quoted in Hill 1984, 134–35.

462. The following depends on Wiesner 1986b, 1986c; see also N. Z. Davis 1986, 185ff.; Herlihy 1990, chap. 7 and conclusion; and Monter 1980, 200, 203–4.

463. Wiesner 1986b, 201.

464. For the following, Howell 1986a; also Howell 1986b and A. Clark 1968.

465. Bennett 1986.

466. Bennett 1986, 23.

467. Reyerson 1986, 122–38.

468. N. Z. Davis 1986.

469. Ozment 1986, 72–73.

470. Nicholas 1985, chap. 5.

471. Chojnacki 1974, 198–99.

472. O'Faolain and Martines 1973, 154–55.

473. Favalier 1985, 192–93, 196.

474. Tarabotti 1979, 213–14.

475. The following depends especially on J. C. Brown 1986a.

476. For the following, J. C. Brown 1986a, 220ff.

477. A. Clark 1968, 146.

478. Alberti 1969, 207.

479. Lombardi 1986; also Stone 1977, 201; Wiesner 1986c, 5.

480. Cohn 1988, 201; also Ciammitti 1983; L. Ferrante 1983; Trexler 1982.

481. N. Z. Davis 1986, 169.

482. Herlihy 1990, 145–46, fig. 6.4, table 6.5.

483. Herlihy 1990, 159, table 7.1; I have combined "servants" with "servants of state officials" and "servant of church" to achieve 126 of 270 known employments.

484. N. Z. Davis 1986, 177; Klapisch-Zuber 1985, "Childhood in Tuscany," 106–7; "Women Servants in Florence," 68; Wiesner 1986c, 46, 91–92. Herlihy and Klapisch-Zuber 1978, 331, show that between 40 and 50 percent of persons registered as "servants" in Tuscany were under seventeen years old, and that 23.1 percent of all female servants were under twelve. See also Martines 1974, 15 n. 2.

485. N. Z. Davis 1986, 178; Lewenhak 1980, 113; Stone 1977, 196; Wiesner 1986c, 91–92.

486. Mitterauer and Sieder 1982, esp. chap. 1; Flandrin 1979, chap. 2.

487. J. C. Brown 1986a, 211.

488. Wiesner 1986c, 92.

489. Shahar 1983, 203.

490. Goodman of Paris 1928, 220; *Menagier de Paris* 1981, 2.3.18.

491. F. Barbaro 1978, 216–20.

492. Barbaro 1978, 219.

493. Klapisch-Zuber 1986, 61–68.

494. Klapisch-Zuber 1985, "Female Celibacy and Service," 176–77.

495. Hanawalt 1986a, 164, 163.

496. Hufton 1982.

497. Klapisch-Zuber 1985, "Female Celibacy and Service," 177.

498. Ariès 1962, 26–27; Boswell 1989, 27.

499. Quoted by Hanawalt 1986a, 157, from an anonymous Venetian *relazione*.

500. Herlihy 1985b, table 6.5, pp. 150–51; discussion at pp. 149–54.

501. Klapisch-Zuber 1986, esp. 68–70; Origo 1955; Stuard 1986.

502. Quoted by Slater 1984, 72.

503. Origo 1955, 347; Trexler 1973–74a, 266–68.

504. Kirshner and Molho 1978, 428–29.

505. Nicholas 1985, 106.

506. Rossiaud 1988, 12.

507. Flandrin 1980, 31.

508. Quoted by Flandrin 1980, 43.

509. Ruggiero 1985, chap. 5.

510. Ruggiero 1985, 108; also table 5, 94.

511. Otis 1985a, 1985b; M. Perry 1978; Rossiaud 1988.

512. Pavan 1980; Rossiaud 1988, 59; Trexler 1981.

513. Wiesner 1986c, 97.

514. Rossiaud 1988, 59.

515. Otis 1985b, 137.

516. Rossiaud 1988, 10.

517. M. L. King 1975, 556.

518. Rossiaud 1988, 50.

519. Otis 1985a, 42.

520. Ascham 1967, 60–75.

521. Erasmus 1968, 48, lines 73, 80–83.

522. Rossiaud 1988, 131–32.

523. Santore 1988, 46–47, and passim.

524. Rosenthal 1989, 236.

525. Thirsk 1985, 10.

526. Da Barberino 1957, 17.

527. Stone 1977, 350–51.

Chapter Two

1. Herlihy 1975, 4–5; also J. C. Davis 1975, 106ff.; Ruggiero 1985, 76ff.

2. For the following, see , among others: Bolton 1976; Eckenstein 1963; Grundmann 1974; Paschini 1960; Southern 1970, 309–18; Vauchez 1981.

3. Boswell 1984.

4. Vanja 1984, 139–52; 255–336 for lists.

5. Kirshner and Molho 1978, 423, 428.

6. Trexler 1972, 1338; J. C. Davis 1975, 108.

7. J. C. Davis 1975, 109.

8. Pia Pedani 1985, 70 n. 148, 67, 37.

9. Trexler 1972, 1333, 1334, 1337, 1345; Kirshner and Molho 1978, 424, report figures similar to Trexler's: of 1,814 registrants in the *monte di dote* in the early fifteenth century, 2.59 percent became nuns.

10. D. Hughes 1986, 28–29 and passim.

11. Eckenstein 1963, chap. 11.

12. Power 1964, 215, 602; Power 1975, 89–96; Ozment 1983b, 14; Shahar 1983, 49–50.

13. Trexler 1972, 1347 n. 99.

14. Southern 1970, 317 n. 19.

15. Vanja 1984, 119–25.

16. Shahar 1983, 49–50.

17. Chrisman 1972, 163, 165; Pia Pedani 1985, 70.

18. Chrisman 1972, 164.

19. Shahar 1983, 48; Willard 1984, 43.

20. Quoted by Paschini 1960, 32.

21. Quoted by Paschini 1960, 35–36, from the *Consilium delectorum cardinalium de emendanda ecclesia* of 9 March 1537.

22. Quoted by Paschini 1960, 38.

23. Quoted by Paschini 1960, 43, from the *Diaries* of Marino Sanuto.

24. Paschini 1960, 46; cited by Trexler 1972, 1345 n. 88.

25. Ruggiero 1985, 77–84, for the following.

26. Southern 1970, 311 and n. 7; Lawrence 1989, 220.

27. Ruggiero 1985, 182 n. 23.

28. Caldiera, *De oeconomia veneta*, fol. 94v, quoted by M. L. King 1975, 556.

29. Erasmus 1965, 99–111 and 111–14 respectively.

30. Erasmus 1965, 109, 114.

31. Quoted by Lazard 1985, 156.

32. Quoted by Ruggiero 1985, 77.

33. Bainton 1973, 89.

34. Kohl and Witt 1978, 115 n. 1; the following based on Salutati's letter to Caterina di Vieri at 115–18.

35. Kohl and Witt 1978, 116–17.

36. Kohl and Witt 1978, 117.

37. Kohl and Witt 1978, 93–114.

38. From Witt's introduction to the Salutati letters, 81–90, at 90.

39. For the following, Weaver 1986.

40. Weaver 1986, 192.

41. For the following, Tarabotti 1979; also Labalme 1981, at 98–102.

42. Quoted by Conti Oderisio 1979, 81.

43. Tarabotti 1979, 202.

44. Tarabotti 1979, 200.

45. Tarabotti 1979, 200.

46. Tarabotti 1979, 203.

47. Tarabotti 1979, 207.

48. Tarabotti 1979, 201.

49. Tarabotti 1979, 205, quoting Dante, *Inferno* 3:9, and Psalm 17 (18):5–7.

50. Tarabotti 1979, 208.

51. Tarabotti 1979, 213.

52. Tarabotti 1979, 214.

53. Tarabotti 1979, 210.

54. Tarabotti 1979, 211.

55. Chojnacki 1988, 133.

56. J. C. Davis 1975, 110–11.

57. Quoted by Flandrin 1979, 140.

58. Quoted by J. C. Davis 1975, 137, from Goldoni's *Memoirs*.

59. J. C. Davis 1975, 142.

60. Stone 1977, 112–13.

61. Höhler 1984, 180.

62. Bellonci 1965, 152.

63. Kirshner and Molho 1978, 409 n. 16.

64. For the following, esp. Bugge 1975; Liebowitz 1979; Lucas 1983, chap. 2; and McNamara 1976.

65. Quoted by D. C. Brown 1987, 226–27, from *Poenitemini, de la chasteté*, G.7, 845–47.

66. Vives 1783, 1:6, 90–91.

67. Ledochowska 1969, 1:266; quoted by Liebowitz 1979, 133–34.

68. Quoted by M. Perry 1987, 151.

69. N. Z. Davis 1979, "City Women and Religious Change"; Eckenstein 1963, esp. 477–84; Magli 1972; E. C. McLaughlin 1979.

70. For the following, M. L. King 1976b, 291–92, 302–3; Correr 1983 for letter to Cecilia Gonzaga.

71. Correr 1983, 100.

72. Musto 1985.

73. Ignatius of Loyola 1956, 336; the letter at 336–37, 5 February 1550.

74. For the following, M. L. King 1976b, 289–90 and 302.

75. A. M. Quirini 1743, 95.

76. F. Barbaro 1983.

77. F. Barbaro 1983, 111.

78. Quoted by Di Mattia Spirito 1988, 305.

79. Excerpt in Petroff 1986, 245–46.

80. Bainton 1971, 23–44.

81. Quoted by Ozment 1983b, 17.

82. Quoted by Ozment 1983b, 18.

83. Ozment 1983b, 19–20.

84. Chrisman 1972, 165–66.

85. Eckenstein 1963, 432–57, for the dissolution of the English nunneries.

86. For the following, Douglass 1974, 309–313.

87. Quoted by Douglass 1974, 312.

88. For the following, introduction, by Gwendolyn Bryant, 287–94, and translation of a section of Pirckheimer's *Denkwurdigkeiten*, 296–302, in Wilson 1987; also Eckenstein 1963, 467–76.

89. Pirckheimer in Wilson 1987, 298.

90. Pirckheimer in Wilson 1987, 297.

91. Pirckheimer in Wilson 1987, 298–99.

92. For the following, esp. Southern 1970, 310–18; also Bolton 1976,

141-44; Grundmann 1974, 147-372; Lawrence 1989, chap. 11 and 264-65; E. C. McLaughlin 1974, 241-45; Pásztor 1984; and McDonnell 1954, 81-119 and passim.

93. E. C. McLaughlin 1979, 100-130, at 105, 106.

94. Quoted by Southern 1970, 314, from the *Annales Praemonstratenses*; see also McDonnell 1954, 103.

95. Quoted by McDonnell 1954, 105, from Jacques de Vitry, *Historia occidentalis*; also Lawrence 1989, 228.

96. Thompson 1978, 227.

97. Thompson 1978, 238-42; also McDonnell 1954, 119 for the coexistence of formal Cistercian nunneries and informal related communities.

98. Brooke and Brooke 1978, 275; also Bolton 1976, 148-50; Sensi 1984, 93-94.

99. McDonnell 1954, 187-204.

100. Bolton 1976, 149, 151-52; Brooke and Brooke 1978, 287.

101. Bolton 1976, 150.

102. Bynum 1982, 185, 247-62; E. C. McLaughlin 1974, 243-44; an example of male scrutiny of a female community in J. C. Brown 1986b.

103. Casagrande 1984, 157.

104. For the following McDonnell 1954; also Bolton 1976, 144-54; Grundmann 1974, 273-302; Koorn 1986; Lawrence 1989, 231-35; D. Phillips 1941; Schmitt 1978; Southern 1970, 319-31.

105. Southern 1970, 420; Lawrence 1989, 233.

106. Quoted by Southern 1970, 319, from *Chronica majora*.

107. Quoted by Southern 1970, 320, from *Chronica majora*.

108. D. Phillips 1941, 226, table 9, and 213-29, for the following.

109. D. Phillips 1941, 226.

110. Schmitt 1978, 141, table 2, for the pattern of the decline of the beguinages in Cologne, Mainz, Strasbourg and Basel.

111. Koorn 1986; Southern 1970, 337ff.; Wyntjes 1977, 168-69.

112. Excerpt in O'Faolain and Martines 1973, 157.

113. M. Perry 1987.

114. Sensi 1984, 108, and 105-6.

115. Bolton 1976, 146-48; Brooke and Brooke 1978; Bynum 1982, 182-83; Bynum 1987, 21; Liebowitz 1979, 145-46; McDonnell 1954, 81-100; 97-98 for examples of leading Beguines from affluent backgrounds. According to Bynum 1987, 21, females were more likely to be upper class than men.

116. Bolton 1976, 147.

117. Benvenuti Papi 1986, 277 n. 5.

118. Brentano 1984, 78–79.

119. Craveri 1981, 110–27.

120. For the following, M. M. McLaughlin 1989. Höhler 1984 traces the history of a similar community, which was to enjoy a "libero stato," being neither linked to an order nor subjected to a bishop. Within two centuries, it had become wealthy, and had lost its original liberty.

121. M. M. McLaughlin 1989, 298.

122. For the following, Ledochowska 1969; also Latz 1986; Liebowitz 1979.

123. Merici's *Regola*, in Ledochowska 1969, 1:272.

124. A free translation by Latz 1986, 122, from Cozzano's *Risposta contro quelli persuadono la clausura alle vergini di Sant'Orsola*, published in Ledochowska 1969, 2:308–335, at 325–26.

125. A free translation by Latz 1986, 130, from Cozzano, *Risposta*, in Ledochowska 1969, 2:325.

126. Liebowitz 1979, 143.

127. Ledochowska 1969, vol. 2, esp. parts 3–5; for the Ursulines of Paris, Jégou 1981.

128. Liebowitz 1979, 136–46; D. Phillips 1941, 217ff. for the impact of the publication of the Vienne decree in 1318.

129. Teresa of Avila 1957, 51 (chap. 7).

130. Liebowitz 1979; Oliver 1959; Rowlands 1985, 168–74; Warnicke 1983, 174–81.

131. Quoted by Rowlands 1985, 169.

132. Quoted by Warnicke 1983, 180.

133. Rowlands 1985, 168.

134. R. Bell and Weinstein 1982, 86.

135. In general: Beard 1973, 266ff.; Grundmann 1974, esp. 303–72; Herlihy 1971 and 1973; Koch 1962; E. C. McLaughlin 1973. See also references to individual movements in the following notes.

136. Bolton 1976, 150; Herlihy 1973, 137–38; here and for the following, also Herlihy 1971, 6, 11–12.

137. Herlihy 1971, 11.

138. Herlihy 1971, 12.

139. Cross 1978; Wyntjes 1977, 169.

140. Cross 1978, 360.

141. Cross 1978, 366.

142. Cross 1978, 369.

143. Cross 1978, 375.

144. Martin 1987, 122.

145. M. Perry 1987, 157, 160, and passim.

146. Lerner 1972; E. C. McLaughlin 1973.

147. Wessley 1978.

148. Wessley 1978, 289–303.

149. Wessley 1978, 303.

150. Excerpt in Petroff 1986, 289.

151. Lerner 1972, 175–76.

152. Lerner 1972, 200–208.

153. Excerpt in Petroff 1986, 297, 298.

154. McDonnell 1954, 367–68.

155. E. C. McLaughlin 1979, 124.

156. Quoted by Bynum 1982, 153.

157. Bynum 1982, 110–69; Børresen 1978.

158. Bynum 1982, 136, 167.

159. Julian of Norwich 1978, 582–83, Long Text, chap. 58; spelling modernized here and in following notes.

160. Julian of Norwich 1978, 588, Long Text, chap. 58.

161. Julian of Norwich 1978, 586, Long Text, chap. 58.

162. Julian of Norwich 1978, 589, Long Text, chap. 59.

163. Excerpt from the biography of Jacques de Vitry in Petroff 1986, 9.

164. Quoted by Joseph R. Berrigan in his "introduction" to excerpts from Saint Catherine of Bologna, in Wilson 1987, 82.

165. Di Agresti 1966, 22–23.

166. Kempe 1936, 25.

167. Kempe 1936, 354–55.

168. Craveri 1981, 20.

169. Birgitta of Sweden 1977, 245–46 (1:2:3–4, 8).

170. R. Bell 1985, xi.

171. Excerpt in Craveri 1981, 70.

172. Quoted by Craveri 1981, 83.

173. Catherine of Siena 1975, 216, quoted by Craveri 1981, 71.

174. Quoted by Craveri 1981, 123.

175. Quoted by Craveri 1981, 159.

176. Kieckhefer 1984, 28–29.

177. Petroff 1986, 347.

178. Excerpt in Petroff 1986, 352–53.

179. Teresa of Avila 1957, 208 (chap. 29).

180. Teresa of Avila 1957, 209, 210 (chap. 29).

181. Teresa of Avila 1957, 210 (chap. 29).

182. For illness, esp. R. Bell 1985, 175–77; Petroff 1986, 42.

183. R. Bell 1985, 154.

184. R. Bell and Weinstein 1982, 93.

185. R. Bell 1985, 98; Craveri 1981, 114.

186. R. Bell 1985, 99; see also Schulenburg 1986.

187. R. Bell 1985, 91; Kieckhefer 1984, 188; Petroff 1986, 36, 38–40.

188. Kieckhefer 1984, 26, 117.

189. R. Bell 1985, 89, 142, 152, 42; Benvenuti Papi 1986, 281–82. Elsewhere Catherine of Siena (1970, 4:34) consoles a mother for the loss of her son, inviting her to find peace "nella cella del cognoscimento di voi medesima."

190. R. Bell 1985, 22–53; other notable cases of self-starvation in Bell: for instance, Colomba da Rieti's, 158.

191. Craveri 1981, 73–74.

192. R. Bell 1985, 108.

193. Excerpt in Craveri 1981,148.

194. Excerpt in Craveri 1981, 146.

195. Excerpt in Wilson 1987, 74, trans. Donald C. Nugent.

196. Bynum 1987, 193. For the following, R. Bell 1985 and Bynum 1987. The two authors are in some tension with each other, Bell proposing a modern (perhaps anachronistic) and areligious diagnosis of "anorexia" for Italian holy women from 1200 to the present, Bynum a subtle argument hinging on the importance of food to medieval people and the central role of food preparation in women's lives. But both argue that avoidance of food correlates with a kind of psychological autonomy. See also Kieckhefer 1984, 140–42 and passim.

197. R. Bell 1985, 134–35, 146–47 for tables 1 and 2.

198. Bynum 1987, esp. 117.

199. Excerpt in Craveri 1981, 114.

200. R. Bell 1985, 160–61.

201. Excerpt in Petroff 1986, 275; 273–75 for Catherine's letter describing the incident to Raymond of Capua.

202. Quoted by D. C. Brown 1987, 223, from *De examinatione doctrinarum.*

203. M. Perry 1987, 157.

204. E. C. McLaughlin 1979, 115.

205. Birgitta of Sweden 1929, Cumming introduction, xxv; Jelsma 1986.

206. Jorgensen 1954, 1:171–82; also Birgitta of Sweden 1929, Cumming introduction, xxvi; Atkinson 1983, 170–75; Eckenstein 1963, 385ff.; Jelsma 1986.

207. Catherine of Siena 1988, 106.

208. Catherine of Siena 1970, 2:249.

209. Catherine of Siena 1905, 234; Catherine of Siena 1970, 4:84.

210. E. C. McLaughlin 1979, 124.

211. The thesis of Herlihy 1985a and 1985b, chap. 5.

212. Erba 1986; Prosperi 1986.

213. Scapparone 1987, 153, for Giorgi; Barozzi's *Vita B. Eustochii virginis paduanae.*

214. R. Bell 1985, 161, 169.

215. Bolton 1976; also Petroff 1986, 173–74.

216. Quoted by Joseph R. Berrigan, in his "introduction" to excerpts from Saint Catherine of Bologna in Wilson 1987, 85.

217. Petroff 1986, 18–19; see also Bynum 1982, 162; Bynum 1987, esp. 251–59.

218. Passage cited above, n. 202.

219. Christian 1981, 188–203, esp. 192, 197.

220. J. C. Brown 1986b, 60.

221. J. C. Brown 1986b, 112–13.

222. J. C. Brown 1986b, 73; Christian 1981, 185; Craveri 1981, 17.

223. Teresa of Avila 1957, 207, 206 (chap. 29).

224. R. Bell 1985, 57–58.

225. M. Perry 1987, 149.

226. Monter 1986.

227. E. C. McLaughlin 1979, 125.

228. E. C. McLaughlin 1979, 127.

229. Petroff 1986, 235.

230. Schulenburg 1978, 122, 127, 131 n. 11, cited by Bynum 1982, 137; Bynum 1987, 20 and 314 n. 31, with additional figures from other sources.

231. Herlihy 1985a, 3; 1985b, 113.

232. Vauchez 1981, 315–17.

233. Benvenuti Papi 1986, 278; Bynum 1987, 21.

234. Bolton 1976, 147; see also Bynum 1987, 222–26.

235. Bolton 1978, 258–60, two of five holy women (including Marie d'Oignies) discussed as typifying the early thirteenth-century Flemish milieu. Two others became spiritual adepts from a young age without prior marital experience.

236. Bolton 1978, 256; McDonnell 1954, 144–45.

237. Benvenuti Papi 1986, 282; R. Bell 1985, 87–91.

238. Brooke and Brooke 1978, 284.

239. R. Bell 1985, 126 narrates the story with gusto.

240. Kieckhefer 1984, 44–45.

241. Sorelli 1984.

242. R. Bell 1985, 57.

243. Quoted in Warnke 1987, 82.

244. Atkinson 1983, 169–70; Birgitta of Sweden 1929, Cumming introduction, xxiv.

245. See Goodman 1978, 352–53.

246. Kempe 1936, 23. See also Atkinson 1983, 15.

247. Kempe 1936, 24.

248. Kempe 1936, 27.

249. Kempe 1936, 23–25, 47ff.

250. Excerpt from Craveri 1981, 116, 117.

251. Kieckhefer 1984, 22–33.

252. Bell and Weinstein 1982, 95.

253. Excerpt in Petroff 1986, 256.

254. Bolton 1976, 147; Bynum 1987, 18–19; Herlihy 1971, 6; Herlihy 1985b, 102; McDonnell 1954, 81–100.

255. R. Bell and Weinstein 1982, 97, give these figures for the medieval through early modern period: 64 of 151 (or 42 percent) female saints; 137 of 713 (slightly more than 19 percent) male saints.

256. Benvenuti Papi 1986, 282.

257. Herlihy 1973, 135–39.
258. R. Bell and Weinstein 1982, 97.
259. Bynum 1987, 225.
260. Chrisman 1972, 147–54.
261. Quoted by Douglass 1974, 297, from Luther, *Enarrationes in 1 librum Mose.*
262. Douglass 1974, 298; from Luther, as above.
263. Quoted by Wyntjes 1977, 174.
264. Quoted by Douglass 1974, 299.
265. Chrisman 1972, 147ff.
266. Bainton 1971, 79–96; Chrisman 1972, 155–56.
267. Bainton 1971, 88.
268. Bainton 1971, 55–76; Chrisman 1972, 151ff.
269. Chrisman 1972, 152.
270. Quoted by Chrisman 1972, 157, from Zell, n. 49.
271. N. Z. Davis 1979, "City Women and Religious Change," 79–80.
272. N. Z. Davis 1979, "City Women and Religious Change," 81.
273. N. Z. Davis 1979, "City Women and Religious Change," 86–87.
274. Warnicke 1983, 174; 174–179 for the following discussion.
275. Stone 1977, 680–86.
276. Warnicke 1983, 74.
277. Chrisman 1972, 159–60.
278. Chrisman 1972, 160–61.
279. Quoted by Wyntjes 1977, 176.
280. Quoted by Demos 1982, 64.
281. Warnicke 1983, 72.
282. Testimony quoted by Bainton 1971, 147–49.
283. Huber 1979; Mack 1986, esp. 462–64; Mullett 1980, 119–29.
284. Mack 1982, 24.
285. Quoted by Huber 1979, 164.
286. Huber 1979, 173.
287. Roelker 1972b, 169, and for the following discussion; Roelker 1968.
288. Bainton 1973, 43.
289. Bainton 1973, chaps. 4 and 5; Wyntjes 1977, 179.

290. Blaisdell 1972, 198; for the following, Blaisdell and Bainton 1973, 235–51.

291. Bainton 1971, 201–18; Jung 1951.

292. Jung 1951, 150.

293. Bainton 1971, 212; Fragnito 1972, 785–86.

294. Jung 1951, 153–54, 157.

295. Bainton 1971, 219–33.

296. Bainton 1971, 253–68; Bonnet 1856.

297. Bainton 1971, 171–85; Oliva 1985.

298. De Valdés 1985, 14–16, 75.

299. De Valdés 1938; De Valdés 1985, 15–16 and n. 11.

300. De Valdés 1985, 14.

301. Bainton 1971, 183.

302. Russell 1980, 79. For the following also, among many others, Bonomo 1971; Bonomo 1986; Cardini 1979; Demos 1982; Karlsen 1987; Kieckhefer 1976; Larner 1981; Levack 1987; Midelfort 1972; Monter 1971; Monter 1976; Quaife 1987; Romanello 1975.

303. Levack 1987, 21; see also Monter 1977, 130. This is a low figure; other authorities give figures from 100,000 to 1,500,000.

304. Based on the figure for Italy, 1300–1700, of 151 used by R. Bell 1985.

305. Midelfort 1972, 98, table 6; O'Faolain and Martines 1973, 215; Russell 1980, 86.

306. Quoted by O'Faolain and Martines 1973, 215.

307. Larner 1981, 8.

308. Levack 1987, 104–110.

309. Midelfort 1972, 32–33.

310. Larner 1981, 89, 63.

311. Larner 1981, 74–75.

312. Monter 1976, 105–9.

313. Monter 1976, 52, 60–61, 49. Monter excludes the 1571–72 panic in which many accused *engraisseurs* perished.

314. Levack 1987, 123–39; Monter 1976, 115–141; Quaife 1987, 79–95; 162–74; but Quaife places age as the most important factor (162).

315. Demos 1982, 57–94: "A Collective Portrait" of New England witches; also Karlsen 1987.

316. Demos 1982, 65, table 4: 55 of 68, 50 of them between 40 and 60. These figures are for communities outside of nontypical Salem.

317. Demos 1982, 85, table 11. I have added the five downwardly mobile to the sixty-three of middle-low to low rank to arrive at 79 percent of the sample.

318. Larner 1981, 89, 2–3, 97–98, 103.

319. Monter 1976, 119, table 7.

320. Midelfort 1972, 180–81, table 14.

321. Larner 1981, 94.

322. Monter 1977, 133.

323. Levack 1987, 8–9; Kieckhefer 1976, chap. 5.

324. Bonomo 1971, part 2; Cuccu and Rossi, 1986; Russell 1980, 66; Midelfort 1972, 16–18.

325. Burke 1977.

326. Excerpt in Abbiati, Agnoletto, and Lazzati 1984, 244–45.

327. Quoted by Midelfort 1972, 19.

328. Montaigne 1958, 784–92, 791, 792.

329. Levack 1987, 56; Midelfort 1972, 24–26; Monter 1976, 32–34; Russell 1980, 84, 96.

330. Excerpt from O'Faolain and Martines 1973, 214, from Weyer (Wier), *De praestigiis daemonum*.

331. West 1984.

332. West 1984, 50.

333. Levack 1987, 36–39; Russell 1980, 60–72.

334. Monter 1976, 22.

335. Russell 1980, 61.

336. Midelfort 1972, 18–19.

337. Levack 1987, 9; Russell 1980, 69–70.

338. Larner 1981, 88.

339. Levack 1987, 63–70; Quaife 1987, 120ff.

340. Midelfort 1972, 20–21; West 1984, 16.

341. Midelfort 1972, 22, 27.

342. Larner 1981, 58.

343. Larner 1981, 107–10; Monter 1976, 157–66.

344. Levack 1987, 70–77.

345. Russell 1980, 82.

346. Midelfort 1972, 107, 111, 164.

347. Levack 1987, 13; also 48.

348. Midelfort 1972, 108.

349. Francia, Verde, and Zanella 1984, 115–40.

350. Francia, Verde, and Zanella 1984, 125.

351. Francia, Verde, and Zanella 1984, 140.

352. Levack 1987, 201.

353. Kamen 1985, 210–14.

354. Kamen 1985, 212, 213; also Henningsen 1980; Lea 1922, 4:233–34.

355. Monter 1986 for the following figures; see also M. O'Neil 1987.

356. Ginzburg 1983.

357. For the resemblance between saints and witches, esp. Craveri 1981; also R. Bell 1985, passim; Larner 1981, 94. For the resemblance between witch activity and healing, Forbes 1966; Herlihy 1985a, 12.

358. Larner 1981, 94.

359. R. Bell 1985, 27.

360. R. Bell 1985, 158, 160.

361. Forbes 1966, chap. 8; Herlihy 1985a, 12; Larner 1981, 138–44.

362. Krämer and Sprenger 1928, 66.

363. Testimony in Mammoli 1972, 29.

364. Mammoli 1972, 32.

365. Mammoli 1972, the formula used repeatedly for each charge in the indictment.

366. Mammoli 1972, 32–38, some examples among many charges.

367. The testimony is published by Craveri 1981, 168–93.

368. Excerpt in Craveri 1981, 177.

369. Excerpt in Craveri 1981, 184.

370. Excerpt in Craveri 1981, 193.

371. Russell 1980, 59.

372. Larner 1981, 10.

373. Russell 1980, 116.

374. Karlsen 1987, 173; Krämer and Sprenger 1928, 47 (part 1, question 6).

375. Quoted by Larner 1981, 93.

376. Monter 1976, 17.

377. Levack 1987, 191.

378. Quoted in Huber 1979, 177. The jury had already presented a verdict of not guilty.

Chapter Three

1. Gies 1981, 222 for text in English; also Craveri 1981, 109; for the following Gies 1981; Pernoud 1964; Warner 1981; also Barstow 1986.

2. Breisach 1967; Clough 1963–65.

3. ffolliott 1986; in general, Cloulas 1981; Héritier 1963.

4. The standard biography is Neale 1957; for the monarchial imagery Marcus 1986, 137–45; Montrose 1986; Yates 1975.

5. Neale 1954, 2:391.

6. Quoted by Haigh 1988, 24.

7. Marcus 1986, among many studies.

8. Montrose 1986.

9. Jordan 1987b, discussion at 432–36 for the following; for the problem of a woman ruling, also Haigh 1988, chap. 1.

10. Knox 1985, 38, 42; quoted by Jordan 1987b, 432, from an older edition.

11. Knox 1985, 42–43; quoted by Bullough 1973b, 201, from an older edition.

12. Knox 1985, 74–75; quoted by Jordan 1987b, 434, from an older edition.

13. Quoted by Bullough 1973b, 202.

14. Jordan 1987b, 426–27 n. 7, from 1606 English ed., pp. 746–54.

15. Quoted by Ambrosini 1984, 36.

16. Ambrosini 1984, 60, quoting Pietro Contarini in 1618 and Pietro Mocenigo in 1671.

17. Stock 1978, 45.

18. Bainton 1973, 13–41; Blaisdell 1980; Stock 1978, 45–47; the major biography is Jourda 1930.

19. For these figures, see chap. 2 at nn. 288 and 290; for Morata, see below.

20. Hogrefe 1977, 155–78; Stock 1978, 50–55.

21. Emerson 1984, 12; Hogrefe 1977, 136–53.

22. Felisatti 1982; also Ady 1903; Bellonci 1965.

23. Brion 1945; H. Brown 1907; Robbert 1980.

24. Castiglione 1959, 204–5 (3.3).

25. Castiglione 1959, 257–58 (3.52).

26. Castiglione 1959, 206 (3.4).

27. Castiglione 1959, 207 (3.5).

28. Castiglione 1959, 206 (3.4).

29. Castiglione 1959, 207 (3.5).

30. Castiglione 1959, 206 (3.4).

31. Kelso 1956; Grendler 1989, 87–89.

32. Vives 1783. Among many discussions: Wayne 1985; Kaufman 1978; Kelso 1956, 72–74; Stock 1978, 50–54; Bullough 1973b, 211–12. Vives' *Instruction* is the basis of Ludovico Dolce's *Dialogo della institutione delle donne* (1545), among other works: Grendler 1989, 87–88; Kelso 1956, 336 no. 90 and 359 no. 302.

33. Vives 1783, vol. 1, Praefatio, 65.

34. Vives 1783, 1:5, 89.

35. Rousseau 1964, 220 (book 5).

36. Vives 1783, 1:5, 87.

37. Vives 1783, 1:3, 74.

38. Vives 1783, vol. 1, Praefatio.

39. Vives 1783, 1:4, 83, 84.

40. Vives 1783, 1.4, 79.

41. Vives 1783, vol. 1, Praefatio, 66.

42. A. Smith 1952, 341b.

43. Frequently encountered terms, their tedious incessancy pointed out in Hull 1982.

44. See above, chap. 1, pp. 64–72; Herlihy 1985a, 12–13.

45. Da Barberino 1957, esp. 17–19.

46. Paolo da Certaldo 1945, 126–28, no. 155.

47. Origo 1962, 65.

48. Wiesner 1986c, 81.

49. Excerpt in O'Faolain and Martines 1973, 250–51.

50. Rousseau 1964, 222 (book 5).

51. Gies and Gies 1987, 255; Lucas 1983, 141–42.

52. Martines 1974, 24–25.

53. N. Z. Davis 1979, "City Women," 72.

54. Goodman of Paris 1928, 1:4, 105–6.

55. Grendler 1989, 71, quoting Giovanni Villani, *Chronica*.

56. Grendler 1989, 72.

57. Grendler 1989, 90; 90–93 for the following; see also Klapisch-Zuber 1984.

58. J. Ferrante 1980, 11 and 36 n. 17; Power 1975, 83–84; Shahar 1983, 215.

59. N. Z. Davis 1979, "City Women," 73.

60. Thrupp 1962, 171.

61. Bullough 1973b, 214.

62. Stock 1978, 69–70.

63. Stock 1978, 70–72.

64. J. Ferrante 1980, 11 and n. 18; Shahar 1983, 215.

65. Stock 1978, 70.

66. Power 1975, 84.

67. For the following, Wiesner 1986c, 79ff.

68. Wiesner 1986c, 79.

69. Wiesner 1986c, 80.

70. Douglass 1974, 304; Stock 1978, 62.

71. Stock 1978, 62–63.

72. Ozment 1983a, 174; see also Stock 1978, 63.

73. Douglass 1974, 304; Monter 1980, 204–6.

74. Stock 1978, 63–64.

75. M. Clarke 1978.

76. Stock 1978, 67, 70.

77. Quoted Eby 1931, 204–5, from Bugenhagen's *School Ordinance* for the town of Brunswick.

78. Wiesner 1986c, 81.

79. Wiesner 1986c, 81–82.

80. J. Ferrante 1980, 11–12; Grendler 1989, 96–100; Power 1975, 78ff.; Shahar 1983, 216.

81. Ledochowska 1969, vol. 2; Stock 1978, 74–77.

82. Jégou 1981, 153 and chap. 9, passim.

83. Stock 1978, 77–78.

84. Wiesner 1986c, 83; also Stock 1978, 64.

85. Stock 1978, 68.

86. N. Z. Davis 1979, "City Women," 72.

87. Stock 1978, 80.

88. Grendler 1989, 46.

89. Thrupp 1962, 171.

90. Stock 1978, 73–74.

91. S. Bell 1982 for the following.
92. Grundmann 1974, 373ff.
93. S. Bell 1982, 745.
94. Power 1975, 85.
95. S. Bell 1982, 749–50 n. 24.
96. S. Bell 1982, 749–50 n. 24.
97. S. Bell 1982, 750.
98. S. Bell 1982, 748.
99. Ady 1903, 2:27; from S. Bell 1982, 751 n. 31.
100. Hull 1982, 21, and for the following.
101. Hull 1982, 7.
102. J. Ferrante 1980, 12.
103. Jorgensen 1954, 1:180.
104. Hess 1983, 182.
105. McDonnell 1954, 376.
106. Quoted by Eckenstein 1963, 359.
107. McDonnell 1954, 385.
108. Correr 1983, 103.
109. E. Barbaro (vecchio), *Vita S. Athanasii*; E. Barbaro (vecchio) 1972.
110. Tarabotti 1979, 213; Weaver 1986.
111. McDonnell 1954, 377–81.
112. Bolton 1978, 269; also Mack 1982.
113. Petroff 1986, 20–29.
114. Atkinson 1983, 171; Birgitta of Sweden 1977, Undhagen introduction, 7; 5–7 for the following.
115. Birgitta of Sweden 1977, quoted by Undhagen, introduction, 5.
116. De Pizan 1982, 63 (1.27.1).
117. Published in Conti Oderisio 1979, 197–98.
118. Conti Oderisio 1979, 57.
119. Aynard, 1924, 157.
120. Ilsley 1963; Stock 1978, 83.
121. Irwin 1980; Stock 1978, 83–84.
122. Quoted by Irwin 1980, 74.
123. Houlbrooke 1984, 99; also H. Smith 1982, chap. 3.
124. Stock 1978, 84.
125. Quoted by Brink 1980, "Bathsua Makin," 93.

126. Astell 1986, 179, 154.

127. Excerpt in O'Faolain and Martines 1973, 204.

128. Quoted by Bainton 1971, 98.

129. Aynard 1924, 158.

130. As quoted in Wiesner 1986d, 13, 14.

131. Trans. in Bainton 1971, 254.

132. Fedele 1636, 156.

133. Excerpt in O'Faolain and Martines 1973, 192, from Erasmus *Christiani matrimonii institutio.*

134. Sowards 1982, 84; and for the following discussion.

135. Quoted in Sowards 1982, 83.

136. "The Abbot and the Learned Lady" (*Abbatis et eruditae*), in Erasmus 1965, 217–23.

137. Excerpt in O'Faolain and Martines 1973, 184.

138. Agrippa 1529; for Bercher (Barker) and Domenichi, see Kelso 1956, 336, no. 90, and 359, no. 302.

139. Conti Oderisio 1979, 47–69.

140. Boccaccio 1963, 1970; Jordan 1987a, Tomalin 1982, chap. 1 for the following.

141. Analysis of sources in Boccaccio 1963, 253–57.

142. These and many others are frequently cited. An eighteenth-century listing of works in praise of women containing many of these titles is quoted at length in Beard 1973, 256–57. Kelso 1956, 463 and 465 indexes vernacular works of women's lives and in defense of women from her bibliography of 891 items.

143. Gundersheimer 1980 for the following; also Fahy 1956.

144. Quoted by Gundersheimer 1980, 183.

145. For the following, Jordan 1986.

146. Quoted by Jordan 1986, 255.

147. For the Italian women humanists, M. L. King esp. 1976b and 1980a, 67–68.

148. Conti Oderisio 1979, 50–51; Schutte, "Irene da Spilimbergo."

149. De Pizan 1982, 2.36.4; the English translation quoted by O'Faolain and Martines 1973, 182, preferred here.

150. Travitsky 1980, 33–34.

151. Travitsky 1980, 38–40.

152. O'Faolain and Martines 1973, 186.

153. Excerpt in O'Faolain and Martines 1973, 250; see Lougee 1976, chap. 11.

154. More 1967, 155.

155. Brink 1980, "Bathsua Makin," 87.

156. Houlbrooke 1984, 99–100.

157. Conti Oderisio 1979, 55.

158. Quoted in Maschietto 1978, 78; cf. Labalme 1981, 83.

159. Quoted by Morgan 1966, 44.

160. Passage cited above, chap. 2, n. 202.

161. Kelso 1956, bibliography at 326–424, followed by index at 465, showing 90 titles against women, 161 in favor; Hicks 1977 and Willard 1984, chap. 4 for the *Roman de la Rose* controversy; for the *querelle* in general, among many titles, Camden 1952, 241–71; Conti Oderisio 1979, chap. 2; Henderson and McManus, 1985; Kelly 1984, "Early Feminist Theory"; Lougee 1976, parts 1 and 2; MacLean 1977; Rogers 1966, chaps. 3 and 4; Shepherd 1985; Utley 1944. For the Jewish phase of the *querelle*, Zinberg 1974, 4:97–98 (with thanks to Rosalie Bachana).

162. Castiglione 1959, 214 (3.12).

163. Castiglione 1959, 215 (3.13).

164. Castiglione 1959, 213 (3.11).

165. Castiglione 1959, 213 (3.11).

166. Castiglione 1959, 212 (3.10).

167. N. Z. Davis 1979, "Women on Top."

168. Schutte 1980b.

169. Camden 1952, 263–64.

170. Quoted by Shepherd 1981, 14, from Knox's works, 1878 ed., 13.

171. For Amazon imagery and confusion of gender, see among many others Conti Oderisio 1979, 69–79; Freccero 1986; Jordan 1986, 256–57; Kelly 1984, "Early Feminist Theory," 83–93; Kleinbaum 1983; MacLean 1977, chap. 3; Montrose 1986; Shepherd 1981; Stallybrass 1986; Tomalin 1982.

172. Tomalin 1982, 14.

173. *Inammorato* 18, 98; quoted by Tomalin 1982, 109.

174. See the discussion in Shepherd 1981, 14ff.

175. Ambrosini 1984, 74.

176. Quoted by Gies 1981, 192; for Joan's transvestism, Warner 1981, chap. 7.

177. Wayne 1987, 52.

178. Boccaccio 1963, xxxiii–xxxiv.

179. Quoted by N. Z. Davis 1980, 158.

180. Altman 1980, 11.

181. Nogarola 1886, 2:12.

182. Bainton 1971, 264.

183. Rabelais 1946, 477; see also Freccero 1986.

184. Quoted in Eccles 1982, 27.

185. E. C. McLaughlin 1974, 233; also McNamara 1976; Schulenburg 1986, 32–33.

186. Quoted by J. C. Brown 1986b, 169 n. 29, from Jerome, *Commentarius in Epistolam ad Ephesios* 3, 5 (658); in PL 26:567.

187. Bynum 1987, 263; Delcourt 1961.

188. For the following, M. L. King 1980b, which publishes the prose *Domus pudicicie* at 119–27; the verse in Zaccaria 1957–58.

189. M. L. King 1980b, *Domus pudicicie*, lines 36–37.

190. Bruni 1987, 244.

191. For the following M. L. King 1976b, 283–89, 293, and M. L. King 1980a, which provides further bibliography; see also Jardine 1983. Isotta, Ginevra, and Angela's works are in Nogarola 1886; also Nogarola 1983.

192. For this phrase and its wider implications, esp. M. L. King 1980a, 71–75.

193. Segarizzi 1904, 53; whole passage at 50–54.

194. Guarino 1915–19, 11:305–6; for text and the reading of donkey and oxen as the two sexes, see M. L. King 1980a, 86–87 n. 31.

195. Guarino 1915–19, 11:306.

196. L. Quirini 1983.

197. L. Quirini 1983, 113.

198. L. Quirini 1983, 116.

199. Nogarola 1886, 2:40.

200. Nogarola 1886, 2:123–24.

201. Nogarola 1886, 2:98.

202. Nogarola 1886, 2:187–216; English trans. in Nogarola 1983.

203. Nogarola 1886, 2:199.

204. For the following, M. L. King 1976b, 295–99; Jardine 1985.

205. Fedele 1636, 157.

206. Wilson 1987, 255, trans. Anne R. Larsen; Eckenstein 1963, 464.

207. Quoted by Cavazzano 1906, 365.

208. For the following, M. L. King 1980a, 71–73; see also King and Rabil 1983, 77–86 and 122–25. The principal study is Rabil 1981.

209. Cereta 1640, 3.

210. Cereta, no. 15, in King and Rabil 1983, 85–86.

211. Cereta, no. 13, 79 in King and Rabil 1983.

212. Cereta, no. 21, 123 in King and Rabil 1983.

213. Cereta no. 22, 125, in King and Rabil 1983, 125.

214. The following is based on Bainton 1971, 253–67, and Caretti, "La vita" in Morata 1954, 1:37–53; see also Bonnet 1856; Southey 1834.

215. Southey 1834, 296 (Basel, September 1554).

216. Southey 1834, 240–41 (Heidelberg, October 1555).

217. Morata 1570.

218. For the following, Hess 1983 and Eckenstein 1963, 458–76.

219. Quoted in Hess 1983, 180; see also Sowards 1982, 82.

220. Hess 1983, 183.

221. Quoted in Hess 1983, 184.

222. Quoted by Eckenstein 1963, 463.

223. Hess 1983, 202.

224. See above at n. 18.

225. Prescott 1985 for the relations between Marguerite and Elizabeth.

226. Bullough 1973b, 218.

227. Excerpt in O'Faolain and Martines 1973, 186.

228. For the following, Verbrugge 1985, Warnicke 1983, passim, Warnicke 1988, Wilson 1987, Elizabeth McCutcheon's introduction to Margaret Roper's works, 449–65.

229. More 1967, 105.

230. Warnicke 1988, 39.

231. For the following, Hoffman 1960, J. N. King 1985, in addition to earlier titles cited.

232. Warnicke 1983, 95.

232. Wyntjes 1977, 171; Warnicke 1983, 93–96.

234. For the following Levin 1985, in addition to titles earlier cited.

235. Quoted by Levin 1985, 97.

236. Quoted by Levin 1985, 103.

237. Ascham 1967, 36.

238. Neale 1957, 26.

239. Maschietto 1978; also Kristeller 1980, 97–104; Labalme 1980, "Women's Roles."

240. Quoted by Labalme 1980, "Women's Roles," 142.

241. Feliciangeli 1894, 51–52. A translation of Varano's oration is in King and Rabil 1983, 39–41.

242. Nogarola 1886, 1:147.

243. Quoted by Hess 1983, 197.

244. For this point, see also Jardine 1983; Grafton and Jardine 1986, chap. 2.

245. Quoted by Ilsley 1963, 216.

246. Crawford 1985, 266; Travitsky 1981, 3.

247. See above, chap. 1, 22–23 for mothers' advice books; for these, and diaries and histories also N. Z. Davis 1980; Mendelson 1985; Rose 1986, "Gender, Genre and History"; Travitsky 1981; for letters, Swain 1987.

248. Quoted by Travitsky 1980, 36.

249. Excerpt in Travitsky 1981, 56.

250. Quoted by N. Z. Davis 1980, 157.

251. Beech 1983.

252. Boccanera 1957.

253. Excerpt in Warnke 1987, 37–39.

254. Warnke 1987, 39.

255. Warnke 1987, 45.

256. Warnke 1987, 45.

257. Warnke 1987, 49.

258. Excerpt in Warnke 1987, 70–71.

259. Jones 1986, 312–13; Rosenthal 1989, 249–57.

260. Jones 1986, for this insight in the cases of Labé and Franco.

261. Warnke 1987, 108–11.

262. Wilson 1987, 244–45, trans. Anne R. Larsen.

263. Wilson 1987, 249, trans. Anne R. Larsen.

264. For the following, esp. Willard 1984; also S. Bell 1976; De Pizan 1982, Richards's introduction, xix–li.

265. Quoted by Willard 1984, 39.

266. De Pizan 1982.

267. Quoted by Richards in De Pizan 1982, xxxii.

268. De Pizan 1982, 3; 1.1.1. Further references in the next several pages will be given in the text in parentheses.

269. De Pizan 1982, Richards' introduction, xxxviii–xl; S. Bell 1976, 176–77.

270. De Pizan 1982, Richards's introduction, xxxviii.

271. Boccaccio 1963, 229 (no. 98).

272. Altman 1980, 19–20; Barstow 1986, 75–78; Willard 1984, 204–7.

273. De Pizan 1977, 46.34–35, with text in French and English.

274. De Pizan 1985, 153 (3.3).

275. Fonte 1979, a partial edition; Fonte 1600; references to these texts supplied henceforth within parentheses in the text. The following discussion indebted to Conti Oderisio's introduction to the former, 57–63, and Labalme 1981, 84–91.

276. Labalme 1981, 88.

277. Labalme 1981, 89.

278. Conti Oderisio 1979, 62.

279. Conti Oderisio 1979, 62.

280. For the following Astell 1986, introduction by Bridget Hill, pp. 1–64; Kinnaird 1983; R. Perry 1986; H. Smith 1982, 117–39.

281. Astell 1986, 135–72 for part 1, 173–79 for part 2, from 1697 ed. Subsequent references appear in parentheses in the text.

282. Quoted by Hill in Astell 1986, 17.

283. Astell 1986, *Reflections upon Marriage*, 114.

284. *Declaration of Sentiments* 1969, 70.

285. Quoted by Ilsley 1963, 207.

286. Kelly 1977, 139.

287. Herlihy 1985a.

WORKS CITED

Full information is provided here for all works cited in the notes. The notes give the author's last name (and initials and/or brief title as required) and date of publication. The date of publication given here for contemporary works is that of the edition used in this volume. Works are divided into primary sources and secondary sources. The following abbreviations are used:

AHR	(*American Historical Review*)
Annales: ESC	(*Annales: Economies-Sociétés-Civilisations*)
ASI	(*Archivio storico italiano*)
AV	(*Archivio veneto*)
GSLI	(*Giornale Storico della Letteratura Italiana*)
JMH	(*Journal of Modern History*)
JMRS	(*Journal of Medieval and Renaissance Studies*)
NRS	(*Nuova rivista storica*)
QS	(*Quaderni Storici*)
RQ	(*Renaissance Quarterly*)
RSCI	(*Rivista di Storia della Chiesa in Italia*)
RSI	(*Rivista storica italiana*)
SLA	(Scienze, Lettere ed Arti)
SV	(*Studi veneziani*)

Primary Sources

Agrippa, Heinrich Cornelius. 1529. *De nobilitate et praecellentia foeminei sexus.* Antwerp: apud Michaelem Hillenium.

Alberti, Leon Battista. 1969. *The Family in Renaissance Florence.* Trans. Renée Neu Watkins. Columbia, S.C.: University of South Carolina Press.

Ascham, Roger. 1967. *The Schoolmaster (1570).* Ed. Lawrence V. Ryan. Ithaca: Cornell University Press, for The Folger Shakespeare Library.

Astell, Mary. 1986. *The First English Feminist: Reflections on Marriage and Other Writings.* Ed. Bridget Hill. Aldershot, Hants, England: Gower, 1986.

Aynard, Joseph, ed. 1924. *Les poètes lyonnais précurseurs de la Pléiade: Maurice Scève—Louise Labé—Pernette du Guillet*. Paris: Editions Bossard.

Barbaro, Ermolao, vecchio. N.d. *Vita S. Athanasii Alexandrini episcopi, cum translatione eius corporis*. Cod. Marc. Lat. 2, 123 (10383), fols. 23–48.

―――. 1972. "Proemium in beatissimi Athanasii, Alexandrini Episcopi, vitam ac eius corporis ad inclitam Venetiarum civitatem translationem," to the nuns of Santa Croce di Giudecca. In *Orationes contra poetas; Epistolae*, ed. Giorgio Ronconi. Facoltà di Magistero dell'Università di Padova, 14, 157–59. Florence: G. C. Sansoni.

Barbaro, Francesco. 1916. *De re uxoria liber*. Ed. Attilio Gnesotto. In *Atti e memorie della R. Accademia di SLA in Padova*, n.s. 32:6–105.

―――. 1978. "On Wifely Duties." Trans. from *De re uxoria* by Benjamin G. Kohl, 177–228. In *The Earthly Republic: Italian Humanists on Government and Society*, ed. Kohl and Ronald G. Witt. Philadelphia: University of Pennsylvania Press.

―――. 1983. *Consolatory Letter to Costanza Barbaro (1447)*, 106–11. In *Her Immaculate Hand*, trans. King and Rabil. Binghamton, N.Y.

Barozzi, Pietro. N.d. *Vita B. Eustochii virginis paduanae*. Padua, Museo Civico, cod. BP 1273.

Birgitta of Sweden, Saint. 1929. *The Revelations of Saint Birgitta*. Ed. by William Patterson Cumming from the fifteenth-century manuscript in the Garrett Collection in the Library of Princeton University. Early English Text Society, by Humphrey Milford. London: Oxford University Press.

―――. 1977. *Sancta Birgitta, Revelaciones, Book I*. Ed. Carl-Gustaf Undhagen. The Royal Academy of Letters, History and Antiquities. Stockholm: Almquist & Wiksell, 1977.

Boccaccio, Giovanni. 1963. *Concerning Famous Women*. Trans. Guido A. Guarino. New Brunswick, N.J.: Rutgers University Press.

―――. 1970. *De mulieribus claris*. In *Tutte le opere di Giovanni Boccaccio*, 2d ed., vol. 10, ed. Vittore Branca. Verona: Arnoldo Mondadori.

Brucker, Gene, ed. 1967. *Two Memoirs of Renaissance Florence: The Diaries of Buonaccorso Pitti and Gregorio Dati*. Trans. Julia Martines. New York: Harper & Row.

―――, ed. 1971. *The Society of Renaissance Florence: A Documentary Study*. New York: Harper & Row (Harper Torchbooks).

Bruni, Leonardo. 1987. *On the Study of Literature [De studiis et litteris]*. In *The Humanism of Leonardo Bruni: Selected Texts*, ed. Gordon Griffiths, James Hankins, and David Thompson, 240–50. Binghamton, N.Y.: Medieval and Renaissance Texts and Studies/Renaissance Society of America.

Caldiera, Giovanni. *De oeconomia veneta libri duo*, to Tommaso Gradenigo. Oxford, Bodleian Library, cod. laud. misc. 717, fols. 79–99v.

Cardan, Jerome. 1930. *The Book of My Life*. Trans. Jean Stoner. New York: E. P. Dutton.

Castiglione, Baldesar. 1959. *The Book of the Courtier*. Trans. Charles S. Singleton, ed. Edgar de N. Mayhew. Garden City: Doubleday (Anchor).

Catherine of Siena. 1905. *Catherine of Siena as Seen in Her Letters*. Trans. and ed. Vida Scudder. New York: E. P. Dutton; London: J. M. Dent.

————. 1970. *Le lettere di Santa Caterina da Siena*. Ed. Piero Misciatelli. 6 vols. Florence: Bemporad Marzocco. Reprint Florence: Giunti-G. Barbèra, 1940.

————. 1975. *Il libro della divina provvidenza*. Ed. D. Umberto Meattini. Collana Patristica e del pensiero cristiano. Siena: Edizioni Paoline.

————. 1988. *The Letters of Catherine of Siena, Vol. I: Letters 1–88*. Ed. by Suzanne Noffke. Medieval and Renaissance Texts and Studies, Binghamton, N.Y.

Cellini, Benvenuto. 1985. *The Autobiography of Benvenuto Cellini*. Trans. John Addington Symonds. New York: Modern Library (Random House).

Cereta, Laura. 1640. *Laurae Ceretae brixiensis feminae clarissimae epistolae jam primum e manuscriptis in lucem productae*. Ed. Giacomo Filippo Tomasini. Padua: Sebastiano Sardi.

Cherubino da Siena, Frate. 1888. *Regola della vita matrimoniale*. Ed. Francesco Zambrini and Carlo Negroni. Bologna: Presso G. Romagnoli dall'Aqua.

Correr, Gregorio. 1983. *Letter to the Virgin Cecilia Gonzaga, On fleeing this worldly life*. In *Her Immaculate Hand*, trans. King and Rabil, 91–105. Binghamton, N.Y.

D'Aubigné, Agrippa. 1969. *Sa vie à ses enfants*. In *Oeuvres*, 383–463. Paris: Gallimard.

Da Barberino, Francesco. 1957. *Del reggimento e costume di donne*. Ed. G. C. Sansone. Turin: Loescher-Chiantore.

Dati, Gregorio. 1967. *Diary*. In *Two Memoirs of Renaissance Florence: The Diaries of Buonaccorso Pitti and Gregorio Dato*, ed. Gene Brucker, trans. Julia Martines, 107–41. New York: Harper & Row.

De Pizan, Christine. 1977. *Ditié de Jehanne d'Arc*. Ed. Angus J. Kennedy and Kenneth Varty. Medium Aevum Monographs, n.s. 9. Oxford: Society for the Study of Medieval Languages and Literature.

————. 1982. *The Book of the City of Ladies*. Trans. Earl Jeffrey Richards. New York: Persea.

————. 1985. *The Treasure of the City of Ladies, Or the Book of the Three Virtues.* Trans. Sarah Lawson. Harmondsworth: Penguin.

De Valdés, Juan. 1938. *Alfabeto Cristiano: Dialogo con Giulia Gonzaga.* Ed. B. Croce. Bari: Gius. Laterza e Figli.

————. 1985. *Lo evangelio di S. Matteo.* Ed. Carlo Ossola and Anna Maria Cavalloni. Rome: Bulzoni.

Declaration of Sentiments and Resolutions, Seneca Falls, 1848. 1969. In *History of Women Suffrage,* ed. Elizabeth Cady Stanton, Susan B. Anthony, and Matilda J. Gage, 1:70–73. New York: Arno and the New York Times.

Di Agresti, Guglielmo, ed. 1966. *Santa Caterina de' Ricci: documenti storici, biografici, spirituali.* Collana ricciana, Fonti, 4. Florence: L. S. Olschki.

Dronke, Peter. 1984. *Women Writers of the Middle Ages: A Critical Study of Texts from Perpetua (+203) to Marguerite Porete (+1310).* Cambridge: Cambridge University Press.

Erasmus, Desiderius. 1965. *The Colloquies of Erasmus.* Trans. Craig R. Thompson. Chicago and London: University of Chicago Press.

————. 1968. *Julius Excluded from Heaven.* Trans. Paul Pascal, ed. J. Kelley Sowards. Bloomington: Indiana University Press.

————. 1979. *The Praise of Folly.* Trans. Clarence H. Miller. New Haven and London: Yale University Press.

Fedele, Cassandra. 1636. *Clarissimae feminae Cassandrae Fidelis venetae epistolae et orationes.* Ed. Giacomo Filippo Tomasini. Padua: apud Franciscum Bolzettam.

Fonte, Moderata (Modesta da Pozzo). 1979. *Il merito delle donne.* In *Donne e società nel Seicento: Lucrezia Marinelli e Arcangela Tarabotti,* ed. Ginevra Conti Oderisio, 159–96. Biblioteca di cultura, 167. Rome: Bulzoni. Orig. Venice: Dom. Imberti, 1600.

Francia, Adolfo, A. Verde and H. Zanella. 1984. *Caterina e le altre: i processi per stregoneria nel savonese nel XVI e XVII secolo: una lettura criminologica.* Savona: Editrice Liguria.

The Goodman of Paris. 1928. *A Treatise on Moral and Domestic Economy by A Citizen of Paris (c. 1393).* Trans. and ed. Eileen Power. London: George Routledge & Sons.

Guarino Veronese. 1915–19. *Epistolario di Guarino Veronese.* Ed. Remigio Sabbadini. R. Deputazione Veneta di Storia Patria. Ser. 3: Miscellanea di Storia Veneta. Vols. 8, 11, 14. Venice: la Società. Photostatic reproduction Turin: Bottega d'Erasmo, 1967.

Henderson, Katherine U., and Barbara F. McManus. 1985. *Half Humankind: Contexts and Texts of the Controversy About Women in England, 1540–1650.* Urbana and Chicago: University of Illinois Press.

Hicks, Eric, ed. and trans. 1977. *Le Débat sur le Roman de la Rose*. Bibliothèque du XVᵉ siècle, 43. Paris: Honoré Champion.

Hill, Bridget, ed. 1984. *Eighteenth-Century Women: An Anthology*. London: George Allen & Unwin.

Ignatius of Loyola. 1956. *Ignatius von Loyola: Briefwechsel mit Frauen*. Ed. and trans. Hugo Rahner, S.J. Freiburg: Verlag Herder.

Julian of Norwich. 1978. *A Book of Showings to the Anchoress Julian of Norwich*. Ed. Edmund Colledge and James Walsh. Toronto: Pontifical Institute of Medieval Studies.

Kempe, Margery. 1936. *The Book of Margery Kempe, 1436*. Trans. W. Butler-Bowden. London: Jonathan Cape.

————. 1940. *The Book of Margery Kempe*, Vol. 1. Ed. Sanford Brown Meech and Hope Emily Allen. Early English Text Society, by Humphrey Milford. London: Oxford University Press.

King, Margaret L., and Albert Rabil, Jr., ed. and trans. 1983. *Her Immaculate Hand: Selected Works By and About the Women Humanists of Quattrocento Italy*. Medieval and Renaissance Texts and Studies, 20. Binghamton, N.Y.

Knox, John. 1985. *The Political Writings of John Knox: The First Blast of the Trumpet against the Monstrous Regiment of Women and Other Selected Works*. Ed. Marvin A. Breslow. Washington: Folger Shakespeare Library; London and Toronto: Associated University Presses.

Kohl, Benjamin G., and Ronald G. Witt. 1978. *The Earthly Republic: Italian Humanists on Government and Society*. Philadelphia: University of Pennsylvania Press.

Kors, Alan C., and Edward Peters, ed. 1972. *Witchcraft in Europe, 1100–1700: A Documentary History*. Philadelphia: University of Pennsylvania Press.

Krämer (Institoris), Heinrich, and Jacob Sprenger. 1928. *Malleus Maleficarum*. Ed. and trans. Montague Summers. London. Reprint. New York: Benjamin Blom, 1971.

Lenzi, Maria Ludovica. 1982. *Donne e madonne: l'educazione femminile nel primo Rinascimento italiano*. Turin: Loescher.

Locke, John. 1988. *Two Treatises of Government*. Ed. Peter Laslett. Cambridge: Cambridge University Press.

Mammoli, Domenico. 1972. *The Record of the Trial and Condemnation of a Witch, Matteuccia di Francesco, at Todi, 20 March 1428*. Res tudertinae 14. Todi. Trans. of 1969: *Processo alla strega Matteuccia di Francesco, 20 marzo 1428. Res tudertinae 8*. Todi.

Marinelli, Lucrezia. 1979. *La nobiltà e l'eccellenza delle donne co' diffetti et mancamente degli uomini*. In *Donne e società nel Seicento: Lucrezia Marinelli e Ar-*

cangela Tarabotti, ed. Ginevra Conti Oderisio, 114–57. Biblioteca di cultura, 167. Rome: Bulzoni. Orig. Venice: Ciotti. 1601.

Mason-Hohl, Elizabeth, ed. and trans. 1940. *The Diseases of Women by Trotula of Salerno: A Translation of "Passionibus Mulierum Curandorum."* New York: Ward Richie.

Le Menagier de Paris. 1981. Ed. Georgine E. Brereton and Janet M. Ferrier. Oxford: Clarendon Press.

Montaigne, Michel de. 1958. *The Complete Essays of Montaigne.* Trans. Donald M. Frame. Stanford, Calif.: Stanford University Press.

Morata, Olimpia. 1570. *Olympiae Fulviae Moratae foeminae doctissimae ac plane divinae orationes, dialogi, epistolae, carmina, tam Latina quam Graeca.* Ed. Celio Secundo Curione. 3d ed. Basel: apud Petrum Pernam.

———. 1954. *Opere.* Ed. L. Caretti. Deputazione provinciale ferrarese di storia patria, Atti e memorie, n.s. 11: parts 1 (*Epistolae*) and 2 (*Orationes, dialogi et carmina*).

More, Thomas. 1967. *Selected Letters.* Ed. Elizabeth Frances Rogers. Vol. 1 of *Selected Works of St. Thomas More.* 2d ed. New Haven: Yale University Press.

Morelli, Giovanni di Pagolo. 1956. *Ricordi.* Ed. Vittore Branca. Florence: Felice Le Monnier.

Nogarola, Isotta. 1886. *Isotae Nogarolae opera quae supersunt omnia,* with works of Angela and Ginevra Nogarola. Ed. Eugenius Abel. 2 vols. Vienna and Budapest: apud Gerold et socios.

———. 1983. *On the Equal or Unequal Sin of Adam and Eve.* In *Her Immaculate Hand,* trans. King and Rabil, 57–68. Binghamton, N.Y.

O'Faolain, Julia, and Lauro Martines, eds. 1973. *Not in God's Image: Women in History from the Greeks to the Victorians.* New York: Harper & Row (Harper Torchbooks).

Ozment, Steven. 1986. *Magdalena and Balthasar: An Intimate Portrait of Life in Sixteenth-Century Europe Revealed in the Letters of a Nuremberg Husband and Wife.* New York: Simon & Schuster.

Paolo da Certaldo. 1945. *Il libro di buoni costumi, documento di vita trecentesca.* Ed. Alfredo Schiaffini. Florence: Felice Le Monnier.

Perleone, Pietro. *Laudatio in Valerium eius filium puerum eximium,* to Jacopo Antonio Marcello. In MS 201 (U.1.5.) of the Hunterian Museum Library, University of Glasgow, pp. 189–248.

Petroff, Elizabeth A. 1986. *Medieval Women's Visionary Literature.* Oxford and New York: Oxford University Press.

Les Quinze joies de mariage. 1963. Ed. Jean Rychner. Textes Littéraires Français. Geneva: Librairie Droz; Paris: Librairie Minard.

Quirini, Angelo Maria, ed. 1743. *Francisci Barbari et aliorum ad ipsum epistolae.* Brescia: Joannes-Maria Rizzardi.

Quirini, Lauro. 1983. *Letter to Isotta Nogarola.* In *Her Immaculate Hand,* trans. King and Rabil, 112–16. Binghamton, N.Y.

Rabelais, François. 1946. *The Portable Rabelais.* Ed. Samuel Putnam. New York: Viking Press. Reprint 1968; orig. 1929.

Ross, J. B., and Mary McLaughlin, eds. 1953. *The Portable Renaissance Reader.* New York: Viking.

————. 1966. *The Portable Medieval Reader.* New York: Viking.

Rousseau, Jean Jacques. 1964. *Emile, Julie and Other Writings.* Trans. R. L. Archer. Woodbury, N.Y.: Barron's Educational Series.

Savonarola, Michele. 1952. *Il trattato ginecologico-pediatrico in volgare.* Ed. Luigi Belloni. Milan: Società italiana di medicina interna.

Shepherd, Simon, ed. 1985. *The Woman's Sharp Revenge: Five Women's Pamphlets from the Renaissance.* London: Fourth Estate; New York: St. Martin's Press.

Smith, Adam. 1952. *An Inquiry into the Nature and Causes of the Wealth of Nations.* Great Books of the Western World, 39. Chicago and London: Encyclopedia Brittanica.

Strozzi, Alessandra de' Macinghi. 1877. *Lettere di una gentildonna fiorentina del secolo XV.* Ed. Cesare Guasti. Florence: G. C. Sansoni.

————. 1987. *Tempo di affetti e di mercanti: Lettere ai figli esuli.* Ed. Angela Bianchini. Milan: Garzanti.

Tarabotti, Arcangela. 1979. *La semplicità ingannata: Tirannia paterna,* and *Inferno monacale.* In *Donne e società nel Seicento: Lucrezia Marinelli e Arcangela Tarabotti,* ed. Ginevra Conti Oderisio, 199–214 and 231–38 respectively. Biblioteca di cultura, 167. Rome: Bulzoni.

Teresa of Avila, Saint. 1957. *The Life of Saint Teresa of Avila by Herself.* Trans. J. M. Cohen. Harmondsworth: Penguin.

Travitsky, Betty S., ed. 1981. *The Paradise of Women: Writings by Englishwomen of the Renaissance.* Contributions in Women's Studies, 22. Westport, Conn., and London: Greenwood Press.

Vives, Juan Luis. 1783. *De institutione feminae christianae.* In *Joannis Ludovici Vivis Valentini Opera omnia,* ed. Gregorius Majansius, 4:70–304. 8 vols. Valentiae: Benedictus Montfort, 1782–1790. Facs. reprint. London: Gregg Press, 1964.

Warnke, Frank J. 1987. *Three Women Poets, Renaissance and Baroque: Louise Labé, Gaspara Stampa, and Sor Juana Inés de la Cruz.* Lewisburg: Bucknell University Press; London and Toronto: Associated University Presses.

Wilson, Katharina M., ed. 1984. *Medieval Women Writers*. Athens, Georgia, and London: University of Georgia Press.

————, ed. 1987. *Women Writers of the Renaissance and Reformation*. Athens, Georgia, and London: University of Georgia Press.

Zeno, Jacopo. *Consolatio pro obitu matris*. To his brother Marino (Padua: 1 August 1434). London, British Museum, cod. Arundel 70, fols. 169–74.

Secondary Studies

Abbiati, Sergio, Attilio Agnoletto, and Maria Rosario Lazzati, eds. 1984. *La stregoneria: diavoli, streghe, inquisitori dal Trecento al Settecento*. Milan: Arnoldo Mondadori.

Ady, Julia Cartwright. 1903. *Isabella d'Este, Marchioness of Mantua, 1474–1539: A Study of the Renaissance*. 2 vols. London: John Murray.

Albini, Giuliana. 1983. "L'infanzia a Milano del Quattrocento: note sulle registrazioni delle nascite e sugli esposti all'Ospedale Maggiore." *NRS* 67:144–9.

Altman, Leslie. 1980. "Christine de Pisan: First Professional Woman of Letters (1364–1430?)." In *Female Scholars: A Tradition of Learned Women before 1800*, ed. Jeanie R. Brink, 7–23. Montreal: Eden Press Women's Publications.

Ambrosini, Federica. 1984. "'Mestier da donne?' Opinioni su Elisabetta d'Inghilterra e sul governo femminile nella Venezia della Controriforma." *AV*, ser. 5, 123:27–76.

Anderson, Bonnie S., and Judith P. Zinsser. 1988. *A History of Their Own: Women in Europe from Prehistory to the Present*. 2 vols. New York: Harper & Row.

Ariès, Philippe. 1962. *Centuries of Childhood: A Social History of Family Life*. Trans. Robert Baldick. New York: Random House (Vintage).

Ariès, Philippe, and André Béjin. 1985. *Western Sexuality: Practice and Precept in Past and Present Times*. Trans. Anthony Forster. Oxford and New York: Basil Blackwell. Orig. *Sexualité occidentale*. Paris: Editions du Seuil/Communications, 1982.

Atkinson, Clarissa W. 1983. *Mystic and Pilgrim: The Book and the World of Margery Kempe*. Ithaca and London: Cornell University Press.

Bainton, Roland H. 1971. *Women of the Reformation in Germany and Italy*. Minneapolis: Augsburg Publishing House.

————. 1973. *Women of the Reformation in France and England*. Minneapolis: Augsburg Publishing House.

————. 1977. *Women of the Reformation from Spain to Scandinavia.* Minneapolis: Augsburg Publishing House.

Baker, Derek. 1978. *Medieval Women: Dedicated and Presented to Professor Rosalind M. T. Hill.* Oxford: Basil Blackwell for the Ecclesiastical History Society.

Barstow, Anne. 1986. *Joan of Arc: Heretic, Mystic, Shaman.* Studies in Women and Religion, 17. Lewiston, New York, and Toronto: Edwin Mellen.

Beard, Mary (Ritter). 1973. *Woman as Force in History: A Study in Traditions and Realities.* 3d ed. New York: Collier. Orig. New York: Macmillan, 1946.

Beech, Beatrice. 1983. "Charlotte Guillard: A Sixteenth-Century Business Woman." *RQ,* 36:345–67.

Bell, Rudolph M. 1985. *Holy Anorexia.* Chicago and London: University of Chicago Press.

Bell, Rudolph M., and Donald Weinstein. 1982. *Saints and Society: The Two Worlds of Western Christendom, 1000–1700.* Chicago: University of Chicago Press.

Bell, Susan Groag. 1976. "Christine de Pizan (1364–1430): Humanism and the Problem of a Studious Woman." *Feminist Studies* 3:172–84.

————. 1982. "Medieval Women Book Owners: Arbiters of Lay Piety and Ambassadors of Culture." *Signs* 7:742–68. Reprint *Women and Power in the Middle Ages,* ed. Mary Erler and Maryanne Kowaleski, 149–87. Athens, Georgia, and London: University of Georgia Press, 1988.

Bellomo, Manlio. 1968. *Problemi di diritto familiare nell'età dei comuni.* Pubblicazioni dell'Istituto di Scienze Giuridiche, Economiche, Politiche e Sociali della Università di Messina, 69. Milan: Dott. A. Giuffrè.

Bellonci, Maria. 1965. "Beatrice and Isabella d'Este." In *Renaissance Profiles,* ed. J. H. Plumb, 139–56. New York: Harper & Row (Harper Torchbook).

Bennett, Judith M. 1986. "The Village Ale-Wife: Women and Brewing in Fourteenth-Century England." In *Women and Work in Pre-Industrial Europe,* ed. Barbara A. Hanawalt, 20–36. Bloomington: Indiana University Press.

Benvenuti Papi, Anna. 1986. "Frati mendicanti e pinzochere in Toscana: dalla marginalità sociale a modello di santità." In *Donna nel Medioevo: aspetti culturali e di vita quotidiana,* ed. Maria Consiglia de Matteis, 275–95. Il mondo medievale, 10. Bologna: Patron Editore. Orig. in *Temi e problemi della mistica femminile trecentesca,* Atti del XX Convegno del Centro di Studi sulla spiritualità medievale, 109–35. Todi: L'accademia tudertina, 1983.

Betto, Bianca. 1981. "Linee di politica matrimoniale nella nobiltà veneziana fino al XV secolo: Alcune note genealogiche e l'esempio della famiglia Mocenigo." *ASI* 139:3–64.

Biller, P. A. 1982. "Birth Control in the Medieval West." *Past and Present* 94:3–26.

Blaisdell, Charmarie Jenkins. 1972. "Renée de France between Reform and Counter-Reform." *Archiv für Reformationsgeschichte* 63:196–225.

———. 1980. "Marguerite d'Angoulême." In *Female Scholars: A Tradition of Learned Women before 1800*, ed. Jeanie R. Brink, 36–53. Montreal: Eden Press Women's Publications.

Boccanera, Giacomo. 1957. *Biografia e scritti della B. Camilla Battista da Varano, clarissa di Camerino (1458–1524)*. Rome: Editrice "Miscellanea Francescana."

Boesch Gaiano, Sofia. 1988. "Lavoro, povertà, santità fra nuove realtà sociali e luoghi comuni agiografici." In *Cultura a società nell'Italia medievale: studi per Paolo Brezzi*, 117–30. 2 vols. Rome: Istituto storico italiano per il medioevo.

Bolton, Brenda M. 1976. "*Mulieres sanctae.*" In *Women in Medieval Society*, ed. Susan Mosher Stuard, 141–58. Philadelphia: University of Pennsylvania Press. Orig. in *Studies in Church History, 10: Sanctity and Secularity: The Church and the World*, ed. Derek Baker, 77–85. 1973.

———. 1978. "*Vitae matrum*: A Further Aspect of the Frauenfrage." In *Medieval Women: Dedicated and Presented to Professor Rosalind M. T. Hill on the Occasion of her Seventieth Birthday*, ed. Derek Baker, 253–74. Oxford: Basil Blackwell for the Ecclesiastical History Society.

Bonnet, Jules. 1856. *Vie d'Olympia Morata, épisode de la Renaissance et de la Réforme en Italie*. 3d ed. Paris: Libraire de Charles Meyrners.

Bonomo, Giuseppe. 1971. *Caccia alle streghe: la credenza nelle streghe dal secolo XIII al XIX con particolare riferimento all'Italia*. Palermo: Palumbo.

———. 1986. "Nuove ricerche sulla stregoneria." In *La strega, il teologo, lo scienziato: Atti del Convegno "Magia, stregoneria e superstizione in Europe e nella zona alpina," Borgosesia, 1983*, ed. M. Cucco and P. A. Rossi, 21–73. Genoa: Edizioni culturali internazionali.

Børresen, Kari Elisabeth. 1978. "Christ notre mère, la théologie de Julienne de Norwich." *Mitteilungen und Forschungsbeiträge der Cusanus-Gesellschaft* 13:320–29.

Boswell, John E. 1984. "*Expositio* and *oblatio*: The Abandonment of Children and the Ancient and Medieval Family." *AHR* 89:10–33.

———. 1989. *The Kindness of Strangers: The Abandonment of Children in Western Europe from Late Antiquity to the Renaissance*. New York: Pantheon.

Braswell, Mary Flowers. 1986. "Sin, the Lady, and the Law: The English Noblewoman in the Late Middle Ages." *Medievalia et Humanistica*, n.s. 14:81–101.

Braunstein, Philippe. 1987. "Les forges champenoises de la comtesse de Flandres (1372–1404)." *Annales: ESC* 42:747–77.

Breisach, Ernst. 1967. *Caterina Sforza: A Renaissance Virago*. Chicago and London: University of Chicago Press.

Brentano, Robert. 1984. "Il movimento religioso femminile a Rieti nei secoli XIII–XIV." In *Il movimento religioso femminile in Umbria nei secoli XIII–XIV*, Quaderni del Centro per il collegamento degli studi medievali e umanistici nell'Università di Perugia, 12, ed. Roberto Rusconi, 67–83. Florence: La Nuova Italia.

Bridenthal, Renate, and Claudia Koonz, eds. 1977. *Becoming Visible: Women in European History*. Boston: Houghton-Mifflin. 2d ed. rev. 1987: ed. Renate Bridenthal, Claudia Koonz, and Susan M. Stuard.

Brink, Jeanie R., ed. 1980. "Bathsua Makin, Educator and Linguist (1608?–1675?)." In *Female Scholars: A Tradition of Learned Women before 1800*, ed. Jeanie R. Brink, 86–100. Montreal: Eden Press Women's Publications.

Brion, Marcel. 1945. *Catherine Cornaro, reine de Chypre*. Paris: A. Michel.

Brissaud, Yves. 1972. "L'infanticide à la fin du moyen âge, ses motivations psychologiques et sa repression." *Revue historique de droit français et étranger* 50:229–56.

Brooke, Rosalind B., and Christopher N. L. Brooke. 1978. "St Clare." In *Medieval Women: Dedicated and Presented to Professor Rosalind M. T. Hill on the Occasion of her Seventieth Birthday*, ed. Derek Baker, 275–87. Oxford: Basil Blackwell for the Ecclesiastical History Society.

Brown, D. Catherine. 1987. *Pastor and Laity in the Theology of Jean Gerson*. Cambridge: Cambridge University Press.

Brown, Elizabeth A. R. 1987. "The Prince is Father of the King: The Character and Childhood of Philip the Fair of France." *Mediaeval Studies* 49:282–334.

Brown, H. Rawdon. 1907. "Caterina Cornaro, Queen of Cyprus." In *Studies in the History of Venice*, 2 vols., 1:255–92. London: John Murray; New York: E. P. Dutton.

Brown, Judith C. 1986a. "A Woman's Place Was in the Home: Women's Work in Renaissance Tuscany." In *Rewriting the Renaissance: The Discourses of Sexual Difference in Early Modern Europe*, ed. Margaret W. Ferguson, Maureen Quilligan, and Nancy J. Vickers, 206–224. Chicago: University of Chicago Press.

―――――. 1986b. *Immodest Acts: The Life of a Lesbian Nun in Renaissance Italy*.

Studies in the History of Sexuality. Oxford and New York: Oxford University Press.

Brucker, Gene. 1986. *Giovanni and Lusanna: Love and Marriage in Renaissance Florence*. Berkeley: University of California Press.

Brundage, James A. 1987. *Law, Sex, and Christian Society in Medieval Europe*. Chicago and London: University of Chicago Press.

Bugge, John. 1975. *Virginitas: An Essay in the History of a Medieval Ideal*. The Hague: Martinus Nijhoff.

Bullough, Vern L. 1973a. "Medieval Medical and Scientific Views of Women." In "Marriage in the Middle Ages," ed. John Leyerle, 485–500. *Viator* 4:413–501.

————. 1973b. *The Subordinate Sex: A History of Attitudes towards Women*. Urbana: University of Illinois Press.

Burke, Peter. 1977. "Witchcraft and Magic in Renaissance Italy: Gianfrancesco Pico and his Strix." In *The Damned Art: Essays in the Literature of Witchcraft*, ed. Sidney Anglo, 32–52. London, Henley, and Boston: Routledge & Kegan Paul.

Bynum, Caroline Walker. 1982. *Jesus as Mother: Studies in the Spirituality of the High Middle Ages*. Berkeley and Los Angeles: University of California Press.

————. 1987. *Holy Feast and Holy Fast: The Religious Significance of Food to Medieval Women*. Berkeley and Los Angeles: University of California Press.

Cadden, Joan. 1986. "Medieval Scientific and Medical Views of Sexuality: Questions of Propriety." *Medievalia et Humanistica*, n.s. 14:157–71.

Camden, Charles Carroll. 1952. *The Elizabethan Woman: A Panorama of English Womanhood, 1540–1640*. Houston: Elsevier Press.

Cardini, Franco. 1979. *Magia, stregoneria, superstizioni nell'occidente medievale*. Florence: La Nuova Italia.

————. 1983. "La predicazione popolare alle origini della caccia alle streghe." In *La strega, il teologo, lo scienziato: Atti del Convengo "Magia, stregoneria e superstizione in Europe e nella zona alpina," Borgosesia, 1983*, ed. M. Cucco and P. A. Rossi, 247–93. Genoa: Edizioni culturali internazionali.

Carmichael, Ann G. 1986. *Plague and the Poor in Renaissance Florence*. Cambridge History of Medicine. Cambridge and New York: Cambridge University Press.

Casagrande, Carla. 1978. Introduction to *Prediche alle donne del secolo XIII: Testi di Umberto da Romans, Gilberto da Tournai, Stefano di Borbone*, v–xxv. Milan: Bompiani.

Casagrande, Giovanna. 1984. "Forme di vita religiosa femminile nell'area di Città di Castello nel secolo XIII." In *Il movimento religioso femminile in Umbria nei secoli XIII–XIV,* Quaderni del Centro per il collegamento degli studi medievali e umanistici nell'Università di Perugia, 12, ed. Roberto Rusconi, 123–57. Florence: La Nuova Italia.

Cavazzano, Cesira. 1906. "Cassandra Fedele erudita veneziana del Rinascimento." *Ateneo veneto* 29.2:73–91, 249–75, 361–97.

Cecchetti, Bartolomeo. 1886. "La donna nel medioevo a Venezia." *AV,* n.s. 31:33–69, 305–45.

Chabot, Isabelle. 1986. "'Sola, donna, non gir mai': Le solitudini femminili nel Tre-Quattrocento." *Memoria* 18:3:7–24.

Chojnacki, Stanley. 1974. "Patrician Women in Early Renaissance Venice." *Studies in the Renaissance* 21:176–203.

————. 1976. "Dowries and Kinsmen in Early Renaissance Venice." In *Women in Medieval Society,* ed. Susan Mosher Stuard, 173–98. Philadelphia: University of Pennsylvania Press. Orig. *Journal of Interdisciplinary History* 1975, 4:571–600.

————. 1985. "Kinship Ties and Young Patricians in Fifteenth-Century Venice." *RQ* 38:240–70.

————. 1988. "The Power of Love: Wives and Husbands in Late Medieval Venice." In *Women and Power in the Middle Ages,* ed. Mary Erler and Maryanne Kowaleski, 126–48. Athens, Georgia, and London: University of Georgia Press.

Chrisman, Miriam U. 1972. "Women and the Reformation in Strasbourg, 1490–1530." *Archiv für Reformationsgeschichte,* 63:143–68.

Christian, William A., Jr. 1981. *Apparitions in Late Medieval and Renaissance Spain.* Princeton, N.J.: Princeton University Press.

Ciammitti, Luisa. 1983. "Quanto costa essere normali: La dote nel Conservatorio femminile di Santa Maria del Baraccano (1630–1680)." *QS* 53:469–98.

Clark, Alice. 1968. *Working Life of Women in the Seventeenth Century.* New York: A. M. Kelley; London: Frank Cass. Orig. London: Routledge, 1919.

Clarke, M. L. 1978. "The Making of a Queen: The Education of Christina of Sweden." *History Today* 28.4:228–35.

Clough, Cecil H. 1963–65. "The Sources of the Biography of Caterina Sforza and for the History of Her State during Her Rule with some Hitherto Unpublished Letters." Atti e Memorie della Deputazione di Storia Patria per le Provincie di Romagna 15–16:57–143.

Cloulas, Ivan. 1981. *Catherine de Médicis.* Paris: Fayard.

Cohen, Elizabeth Storr. 1988. "La verginità perduta: autorappresentazione di giovani donne nella Roma barocca." *QS*, n.s. 67:1:169–91.

Cohn, Samuel K., Jr. 1988. *Death and Property in Siena, 1205–1800: Strategies for the Afterlife*. Johns Hopkins University Studies in Historical and Political Science, 106th Series, 2. Baltimore and London: Johns Hopkins University Press.

Consiglia de Matteis, Maria, ed. 1981. *Idee sulla donna nel Medioevo: fonti e aspetti giuridici, antropologici, religiosi, sociali e letterari della condizione femminile*. Il mondo medievale, Sezione di storia delle istituzioni, della spiritualità e delle idee, 10. Bologna: Patron Editore.

———. 1986. *Donna nel Medioevo: aspetti culturali e di vita quotidiana*. Il mondo medievale, Sezione di storia delle istituzioni, 10. Bologna: Patron Editore.

Conti Oderisio, Ginevra. 1978. "Matriarcato e patriarcalismo nel pensiero politico di Hobbes e Locke." In *Matriarcato e potere delle donne*, ed. Ida Magli, 37–56. Milan: Feltrinelli.

———. 1979. *Donne e società nel Seicento: Lucrezia Marinelli e Arcangela Tarabotti*. Biblioteca di cultura, 167. Rome: Bulzoni.

Craveri, Marcello. 1981. *Sante e streghe: biografie e documenti dal XIV al XVII secolo*. Milan: Feltrinelli, 1980; 2d. ed., 1981.

Crawford, Patricia. 1985. "Women's Published Writings 1600–1700." In *Women in English Society, 1500–1800*, ed. Mary Prior, 211–82. London and New York: Methuen.

Cross, Claire. 1978. "'Great Reasoners in Scripture': The Activities of Women Lollards 1380–1530." In *Medieval Women: Dedicated and Presented to Professor Rosalind M. T. Hill on the Occasion of her Seventieth Birthday*, ed. Derek Baker, 359–80. Ecclesiastical History Society, by Oxford: Basil Blackwell.

Cuccu, M., and P. A. Rossi, eds. 1986. *La strega, il teologo, lo scienziato: atti del Covegno "Magia, stregoneria e superstizione in Europa e nella zona alpina," Borgosesia, 1983*. Genoa: Edizioni culturali internazionali.

D'Alverny, M. T. 1977. "Comment les théologiens et les philosophes voient la femme." *Cahiers de civilisation médiévale* 20:105–29; also trans. Ital. in *Idee sulla donna nel Medioevo: fonti e aspetti giuridici, antropologici, religiosi, sociali e letterari della condizione femminile*, ed. Maria Consiglia de Matteis, 259–303. Il mondo medievale. Bologna: Patron Editore, 1981.

Davidson, Jane P. 1987. *The Witch in Northern European Art, 1470–1750*. Freren: Luca Verlag.

Davies, Kathleen. 1982. "Continuity and Change in Literary Advice on Marriage." In *Marriage and Society: Studies in the Social History of Mar-*

riage, ed. R. B. Outhwaite. London: Europa Publications (1981); New York: St. Martin's Press.

Davis, James Cushman. 1962. *The Decline of the Venetian Nobility as a Ruling Class.* Johns Hopkins University Studies in Historical and Political Science, Series 80, 2. Baltimore: Johns Hopkins University Press.

————. 1975. *A Venetian Family and its Fortune, 1500–1900: the Donà and the Conservation of Their Wealth.* Philadelphia: University of Pennsylvania Press.

Davis, Natalie Zemon. 1979. *Society and Culture in Early Modern France.* Stanford, Calif.: Stanford University Press. "City Women and Religious Change," 65–95. "Women on Top," 124–51.

————. 1980. "Gender and Genre: Women as Historical Writers, 1400–1820." In *Beyond their Sex: Learned Women of the European Past,* ed. Patricia H. Labalme, 153–82. New York: New York University Press.

————. 1986. "Women in the Crafts in Sixteenth-Century Lyon." In *Women and Work in Pre-Industrial Europe,* ed. Barbara A. Hanawalt, 167–97. Bloomington: Indiana University Press; orig. *Feminist Studies* 1982, 8:47–80.

De la Serna Gonzalez, Clemente, ed. 1986. *Mujeres del absoluto: el monacato femenino, historia, instituciones, actualidad: XX Semana de Estudios Monasticos.* Burgos, Spain: Abadia de Silos.

Del Lungo, Isidoro. 1926. *La donna fiorentina del buon tempo antico.* 2d ed. Florence: R. Bemporad & Figli.

Delcourt, Marie. 1961. "Appendix: Female Saints in Masculine Clothing." In *Hermaphrodite: Myths and Rites of the Bisexual Figure in Classical Antiquity,* trans. Jennifer Nicholson, 84–102. London: Studio Books.

Demaitre, Luke. 1976–77. "The Idea of Childhood and Child Care in Medical Writings of the Middle Ages." *Journal of Psychohistory* 4:461–90.

Demos, John. 1970. *A Little Commonwealth: Family Life in Plymouth Colony.* New York: Oxford University Press.

————. 1982. *Entertaining Satan: Witchcraft and the Culture of Early New England.* New York: Oxford University Press.

Di Mattia Spirito, Silvana. 1988. "Una figura del francescanesimo femminile tra Quattrocento e Cinquecento: Camilla Battista da Varano (problemi e ricerche)." In *Cultura a società nell'Italia medievale: studi per Paolo Brezzi,* 2 vols., 295–314. Rome: Istituto storico italiano per il medioevo.

Dillard, Heath. 1976. "Women in Reconquest Castile: the Fueros of Sepùlveda and Cuenca." In *Women in Medieval Society,* ed. Susan M. Stuard, 71–94. Philadelphia: University of Pennsylvania Press.

_____. 1984. *Daughters of the Reconquest: Women in Castilian Town Society, 1100–1300.* Cambridge and New York: Cambridge University Press.

Douglass, Jane Dempsey. 1974. "Women and the Continental Reformation." In *Religion and Sexism: Images of Women in the Jewish and Christian Traditions,* ed. Rosemary Radford Ruether, 291–318. New York: Simon & Schuster.

Duby, Georges. 1978. *Medieval Marriage: Two Models from Twelfth-Century France.* Trans. Elborg Forster. Baltimore: Johns Hopkins University Press.

_____. 1983. *The Knight, the Lady and the Priest: The Making of Modern Marriage in Medieval France.* Trans. Barbara Brays. New York: Pantheon Books. Orig. *Le Chevalier, la femme et le prêtre: le mariage dans la France féodale.* Paris: Hachette, 1981.

Eby, Friedrich. 1931. *Early Protestant Educators.* New York and London: McGraw Hill.

Eccles, Audrey. 1982. *Obstetrics and Gynaecology in Tudor and Stuart England.* Kent, Ohio: Kent State University Press.

Eckenstein, Lina. 1963. *Woman under Monasticism: Chapters on Saint-Lore and Convent Life between A.D. 500 and A.D. 1500.* New York: Russell & Russell. Orig. Cambridge: Cambridge University Press, 1896.

Emerson, Kathy Lynn. 1984. *Wives and Daughters: The Women of Sixteenth Century England.* Troy, New York: Whitson.

Erba, Andrea. 1986. "Il 'caso' di Paola Antonia Negri nel Cinquecento italiano." In *Women and Men in Spiritual Culture, XIV–XVII Centuries: A Meeting of South and North,* ed. Elisja Schulte Van Kessel, 193–212. Studien Nederlands Instituut te Rom, 8. The Hague: Netherlands Government Publishing Office.

Erler, Mary, and Maryanne Kowaleski, eds. 1988. *Women and Power in the Middle Ages.* Athens, Georgia, and London: University of Georgia Press.

Fahy, Conor. 1956. "Three Early Renaissance Treatises on Women." *Italian Studies* 11:30–55.

Favalier, Sylvie. 1985. "Le attività lavorative in una parrocchia del centro di Venezia (San Polo—secolo XVI)." *SV,* n.s. 9:187–94.

Feliciangeli, B. 1894. "Notizie sulla vita e sugli scritti Costanza Varano-Sforza (1426–1447)." *GSLI* 23:1–75.

Felisatti, Massimo. 1982. *Isabella d'Este, la primadonna del Rinascimento.* Milan: Bompiani.

Ferguson, Margaret W., Maureen Quilligan, and Nancy J. Vickers, eds.

1986. *Rewriting the Renaissance: The Discourses of Sexual Difference in Early Modern Europe*. Chicago: University of Chicago Press.

Ferrante, Joan. 1980. "The Education of Women in the Middle Ages in Theory, Fact, and Fantasy." In *Beyond Their Sex: Learned Women of the European Past*, ed. Patricia H. Labalme, 9–42. New York: New York University Press.

Ferrante, Lucia. 1983. "L'onore ritrovato: donne nella Casa del Soccorso di S. Paolo a Bologna (sec. XVI–XVII)." *QS*, 53:499–527.

ffolliott, Sheila. 1986. "Catherine de' Medici as Artemisia: Figuring the Powerful Widow." In *Rewriting the Renaissance: The Discourses of Sexual Difference in Early Modern Europe*, ed. Margaret W. Ferguson, Maureen Quilligan and Nancy J. Vickers, 227–41. Chicago: University of Chicago Press.

Fildes, Valerie. 1988. *Wet Nursing: A History from Antiquity to the Present*. Oxford: Basil Blackwell.

Filippini, Nadia Maria. 1985. "Levatrici e ostetricanti a Venezia tra Sette e Ottocento." *QS* 20:1:149–80.

Flandrin, Jean-Louis. 1979. *Families in Former Times: Kinship, Household and Sexuality in Early Modern France*. Trans. Richard Southern. Cambridge: Cambridge University Press.

————. 1980. "Repression and Change in the Sexual Life of Young People in Medieval and Early Modern Times." In *Family and Sexuality in French History*, ed. Robert Wheaton and Tamara K. Hareven, 27–48. Philadelphia: University of Pennsylvania Press.

————. 1985. "Sex in Married Life in the Early Middle Ages: The Church's Teaching and Behavioral Reality." In *Western Sexuality: Practice and Precept in Past and Present Times*, ed. Philippe Ariès and André Béjin, trans. Anthony Forster, 114–29. Oxford and New York: Basil Blackwell.

Forbes, Thomas Rogers. 1966. *The Midwife and the Witch*. New Haven and London: Yale University Press.

Fragnito, Gigliola. 1972. "Gli 'spirituali' e la fuga di Bernardino Ochino." *RSI* 84:777–813.

Fraser, Antonia. 1984. *The Weaker Vessel*. New York: Alfred A. Knopf.

Freccero, Carla. 1986. "The Other and the Same: The Image of the Hermaphrodite in Rabelais." In *Rewriting the Renaissance: The Discourses of Sexual Difference in Early Modern Europe*, ed. Margaret W. Ferguson, Maureen Quilligan, and Nancy J. Vickers, 145–58. Chicago: University of Chicago Press.

Garrard, Mary D. 1989. *Artemisia Gentileschi: The Image of the Female Hero in Italian Baroque Art*. Princeton: Princeton University Press.

Gentile, Cecilia. 1986. "La società coniugale nella trattatistica italiana del Settecento: appunti per una ricerca." *RSCI* 40:92–102.

George, Margaret. 1988. *Women in the First Capitalist Society: Experiences in Seventeenth-Century England.* Urbana and Chicago: University of Illinois Press.

Gies, Frances. 1981. *Joan of Arc: The Legend and the Reality.* New York: Harper & Row.

Gies, Frances, and Joseph Gies. 1978. *Women in the Middle Ages.* New York: Thomas Y. Crowell.

—————. 1987. *Marriage and the Family in the Middle Ages.* New York: Harper & Row.

Ginzburg, Carlo. 1983. *The Night Battles: Witchcraft and Agrarian Cults in the Sixteenth and Seventeenth Centuries.* Trans. John and Anne Tedeschi. Baltimore: Johns Hopkins University Press. Orig. *I benandanti.*

Gold, Penny Schine. 1985. *The Lady and the Virgin: Image, Attitude and Experience in Twelfth-Century France.* Chicago: University of Chicago Press.

Goldthwaite, Richard. 1972. "The Florentine Palace as Domestic Architecture." *AHR,* 77:977–1012.

Goodman, Anthony. 1978. "The Piety of John Brunham's Daughter, of Lynn." In *Medieval Women: Dedicated and Presented to Professor Rosalind M. T. Hill on the Occasion of her Seventieth Birthday,* ed. Derek Baker, 347–58. Oxford: Basil Blackwell, for the Ecclesiastical History Society.

Goody, Jack. 1983. *The Development of the Family and Marriage in Europe.* Cambridge and New York: Cambridge University Press.

Grafton, Anthony, and Lisa Jardine. 1986. *From Humanism to the Humanities: Education and the Liberal Arts in Fifteenth- and Sixteenth-Century Europe.* Cambridge, Mass.: Harvard University Press.

Gregory, Heather. 1987. "Daughters, Dowries and the Family in Fifteenth-Century Florence." *Rinascimento,* ser. 2, 27:215–37.

Grendler, Paul F. 1989. *Schooling in Renaissance Italy: Literacy and Learning, 1300–1600.* Baltimore and London: Johns Hopkins University Press.

Grundmann, Herbert. 1974. *Movimenti religiosi del Medioevo: ricerche sui nessi storici tra l'eresia, gli Ordini mendicanti e il movimento religioso femminile nel XII e XIII secolo e sulle origini storiche della mistica tedesca.* Trans. Maria Ausserhofer and Lea Nicolet Santini. Bologna: il Mulino. Orig. *Religiöse Bewegungen im Mittelalter.* Berlin: Eberings historische Studien, Band 267, 1935; 2d ed., Darmstadt: Wissenschaftliche Buchgesellschaft, 1961.

Guldan, Ernst. 1966. *Eva und Maria: Eine Antithese als Bildmotiv.* Graz-Cologne: Verlag Hermann Böhlaus Nachfolge.

Gundersheimer, Werner. 1980. "Bartolommeo Goggio: A Feminist in Renaissance Ferrara." *RQ* 23:175–200.

Haigh, Christopher. 1988. *Elizabeth I.* London and New York: Longman.

Haliczer, Stephen, ed. and trans. 1987. *Inquisition and Society in Early Modern Europe.* London: Rowman & Littlefield; Sydney: Croom Helm.

Hallett, Judith P. 1984. *Fathers and Daughters in Roman Society: Women and the Elite Family.* Princeton: Princeton University Press.

Hanawalt, Barbara A. 1974. "The Female Felon in Fourteenth-Century England." *Viator* 5:253–68. Reprint *Women in Medieval Society,* ed. Susan Mosher Stuard, 125–40. Philadelphia: University of Pennsylvania Press, 1976.

—————. 1986a. *The Ties that Bound: Peasant Families in Medieval England.* New York: Oxford University Press.

—————, ed. 1986b. *Women and Work in Pre-Industrial Europe.* Bloomington: Indiana University Press. "Peasant Women's Contribution to the Home Economy in Late Medieval England," 2–19.

Hannay, Margaret P., ed. 1985. *Silent but for the Word: Tudor Women as Patrons, Translators, and Writers of Religious Works.* Kent, Ohio: Kent State University Press.

Hanning, Robert W. 1977. "From Eva and Ave to Eglentyne and Alisoun: Chaucer's Insight into the Roles Women Play." *Signs* 2:580–599.

Harris, Barbara J. 1982. "Marriage Sixteenth Century Style: Elisabeth Stafford and the Third Duke of Norfolk." *The Journal of Social History,* 371–82.

Haskell, Ann S. 1973. "The Paston Women on Marriage in Fifteenth-Century England." In "Marriage in the Middle Ages," ed. John Leyerle, 459–72. *Viator* 4:413–501.

Helmholz, Richard H. 1975. "Infanticide in the Province of Canterbury During the Fifteenth Century." *History of Childhood Quarterly* 2:379–90.

Henningsen, Gustav. 1980. *The Witches' Advocate: Basque Witchcraft and the Spanish Inquisition, 1609–1614.* Reno: University of Nevada Press.

Héritier, Jean. 1963. *Catherine de Medici.* Trans. Charlotte Haldane. London: George Allen & Unwin. Orig. *Catherine de Médicis.* Paris: Libraire Arthème Fayard, 1959.

Herlihy, David. 1967. *Medieval and Renaissance Pistoia: The Social History of an Italian Town, 1200–1430.* New Haven and London: Yale University Press.

—————. 1969. "Viellir à Florence au Quattrocento." *Annales: ESC,* 24:1338–52. Trans. in Peter N. Stearns, *Old Age in Preindustrial Society,*

"Growing Old in the Quattrocento," 104–18. New York: Holmes & Meier, 1982.

————. 1971. "Women in Medieval Society." The Smith History Lecture: University of St. Thomas, Houston, Texas, 1971. Reprint in Herlihy, *The Social History of Italy and Western Europe 700–1500: Collected Studies.* London: Variorum, 1978.

————. 1973. "Alienation in Medieval Culture and Society." In *Alienation: Concept, Terms and Meanings*, ed. Frank Johnson, 125–40. New York. Reprint in Herlihy, *The Social History of Italy and Western Europe 700–1500: Collected Studies.* London: Variorum, 1978.

————. 1975. "Life Expectancies for Women in Medieval Society." In *The Role of Women in the Middle Ages*, ed. Rosemarie T. Morewedge, 4–22. Albany: State University of New York Press. Reprint in Herlihy, *The Social History of Italy and Western Europe, 700–1500: Collected Studies.* London: Variorum, 1978.

————. 1976a. "Land, Family and Women in Continental Europe, 701–1200." In *Women in Medieval Society*, ed. Susan Mosher Stuard, 13–46. Philadelphia: University of Pennsylvania Press. Reprint in Herlihy, *The Social History of Italy and Western Europe 700–1500: Collected Studies.* London: Variorum, 1978. Orig. *Traditio* 1962, 18:89–120.

————. 1976b. "The Medieval Marriage Market." *Medieval and Renaissance Studies* 6:3–27. Reprint in Herlihy, *The Social History of Italy and Western Europe 700–1500: Collected Studies.* London: Variorum, 1978.

————. 1978. *The Social History of Italy and Western Europe, 700–1500: Collected Studies.* London: Variorum.

————. 1985a. "Did Women Have a Renaissance? A Reconsideration." *Medievalia et Humanistica*, n.s. 13:1–22.

————. 1985b. *Medieval Households.* Cambridge, Mass.: Harvard University Press.

————. 1990. *Opera muliebria: Women and Work in Medieval Europe.* New York: McGraw-Hill.

Herlihy, David, and Christiane Klapisch-Zuber. 1978. *Les Toscans et leurs familles: une étude du catasto florentin de 1427.* Paris: Fondation nationale des sciences politiques: Ecole des hautes études en sciences sociales. Trans. *Tuscans and Their Families: A Study of the Florentine Catasto of 1427.* Yale Series in Economic History. New Haven: Yale University Press, 1985.

Hess, Ursula. 1983. "Oratrix humilis: Die Frau als Briefpartnerin von Humanisten, am Beispiel der Caritas Pirckheimer." In *Der Brief im Zeitalter der Renaissance*, ed. Franz Josef Worstbrock, 173–203. Deutsche Forschungsgemeinschaft: Kommission für Humanismusforschung, 9. Weinheim: Acta humaniora.

Hill, Bridget. 1987. "A Refuge from Men: The Idea of a Protestant Nunnery." *Past and Present* 117:107–30.

Hoffman, C. Fenno, Jr. 1960. "Catherine Parr as a Woman of Letters." *Huntington Library Quarterly* 23:349–67.

Hogrefe, Pearl. 1977. *Women of Action in Tudor England: Nine Biographical Sketches.* Ames, Iowa: Iowa State University Press.

Höhler, Peter. 1984. "Il monastero delle Clarisse di Monteluce in Perugia (1218–1400)." In *Il movimento religioso femminile in Umbria nei secoli XIII–XIV,* Quaderni del Centro per il collegamento degli studi medievali e umanistici nell'Università di Perugia, 12, ed. Roberto Rusconi, 159–81 Florence: La Nuova Italia.

Horowitz, Maryanne C. 1979. "Aristotle and Women." *Journal of the History of Biology* 9:182–213.

Houlbrooke, Ralph A. 1984. *The English Family, 1450–1700.* Themes in British Social History. White Plains, New York: Longman.

Howell, Martha C. 1986a. *Women, Production, and Patriarchy in Late Medieval Cities.* Women in Culture and Society. Chicago and London: University of Chicago Press.

————. 1986b. "Women, the Family Economy, and the Structures of Market Production in Cities of Northern Europe during the Late Middle Ages." In *Women and Work in Pre-Industrial Europe,* ed. Barbara A. Hanawalt, 198–222. Bloomington: Indiana University Press.

Huber, Elaine C. 1979. "'A Woman Must Not Speak': Quaker Women in the English Left Wing." In *Women of Spirit: Female Leadership in the Jewish and Christian Traditions,* ed. Rosemary Ruether and Eleanor McLaughlin, 153–81. New York: Simon & Schuster.

Hufton, Olwen H. 1982. "Women, Work and Marriage in Eighteenth-Century France." In *Marriage and Society: Studies in the Social History of Marriage,* ed. R. B. Outhwaite, 186–203. London: Europa Publications, 1981; New York: St. Martin's Press.

Hughes, Diane Owen. 1975a. "Domestic Ideals and Social Behavior: Evidence from Medieval Genoa." In *The Family in History,* ed. Charles E. Rosenberg, 115–44. Philadelphia: University of Pennsylvania Press.

————. 1975b. "Urban Growth and Family Structure in Medieval Genoa." *Past and Present* 66:3–28.

————. 1978. "From Brideprice to Dowry in Mediterranean Europe." *Journal of Family History* 3:262–96.

————. 1986. "Representing the Family: Portraits and Purposes in Early Modern Italy." *Journal of Interdisciplinary History* 17:7–38.

Hughes, Muriel J. 1943. *Women Healers in Medieval Life and Literature.* New York: King's Crown Press.

Hull, Suzanne W. 1982. *Chaste, Silent and Obedient: English Books for Women, 1475–1640.* San Marino, California: The Huntington Library.

Ilsley, M. 1963. *A Daughter of the Renaissance: Marie le Jars de Gournay, Her Life and Works.* The Hague: Mouton & Co.

Irwin, Joyce L., ed. 1979. *Womanhood in Radical Protestantism, 1525–1675.* Lewiston, N.Y.: The Edwin Mellen Press.

————. 1980. "Anna Maria van Schurman: The Star of Utrecht (1607–1678)." In *Female Scholars: A Tradition of Learned Women before 1800,* ed. Jeanie R. Brink, 68–85. Montreal: Eden Press Women's Publications.

Jardine, Lisa. 1983. "Isotta Nogarola: Women Humanists—Education for What?" *History of Education* 12:231–44.

————. 1985. "'O decus Italiae virgo,' or the Myth of the Learned Lady in the Renaissance." *Historical Journal* 28:799–819.

Jégou, Marie-Andrée. 1981. *Les Ursulines du Faubourg St. Jacques à Paris, 1607–1662: Origine d'un monastère apostolique.* Bibliothèque de l'Ecole des Hautes Etudes, Section des Sciences Réligieuses, 82. Paris: Presses universitaires de France.

Jelsma, Auke. 1986. "The Appreciation of Bridget of Sweden (1303–1373) in the Fifteenth Century." In *Women and Men in Spiritual Culture, XIV–XVII Centuries: A Meeting of South and North,* ed. Elisja Schulte Van Kessel, 163–76. Studien Nederlands Instituut te Rom, 8. The Hague: Netherlands Government Publishing Office.

Jones, Anne R. 1986. "City Women and Their Audiences: Louise Labé and Veronica Franco." In *Rewriting the Renaissance: The Discourses of Sexual Difference in Early Modern Europe,* ed. Margaret W. Ferguson, Maureen Quilligan and Nancy J. Vickers, 299–316. Chicago: University of Chicago Press.

Jordan, Constance. 1986. "Feminism and the Humanists: The Case of Sir Thomas Elyot's Defence of Good Women." In *Rewriting the Renaissance: The Discourses of Sexual Difference in Early Modern Europe,* ed. Margaret W. Ferguson, Maureen Quilligan and Nancy J. Vickers, 242–58. Chicago: University of Chicago Press. Orig. *RQ* 1983, 36:181–201.

————. 1987a. "Boccaccio's In-Famous Women." In *Ambiguous Realities: Women in the Middle Ages and Renaissance,* ed. Carole Levin and Jeanie Watson, 25–48. Detroit: Wayne State University Press.

————. 1987b. "Woman's Rule in Sixteenth-Century British Political Thought." *RQ* 40:421–51.

Jorgensen, Johannes. 1954. *Saint Bridget of Sweden.* 2 vols. Trans. Ingeborg Lund. London and New York: Longmans, Green.

Joshel, Sandra R. 1986. "Nurturing the Master's Child: Slavery and the Roman Child-Nurse." *Signs* 12:3–22.

Jourda, Pierre. 1930. *Marguerite d'Angoulême, duchesse d'Alençon, Reine de Navarre (1492–1549), Etude biographique et littéraire.* 2 vols. Bibliothèque littéraire de la Renaissance. Paris: Honoré Champion.

Jung, Eva-Maria. 1951. "Vittoria Colonna between Reformation and Counter-Reformation." *The Review of Religion* 15:144–59.

Kamen, Henry Arthur Francis. 1985. *Inquisition and Society in Spain in the Sixteenth and Seventeenth Centuries.* London: Weidenfeld and Nicolson.

Karlsen, Carol F. 1987. *The Devil in the Shape of a Woman: Witchcraft in Colonial New England.* New York and London: W. W. Norton.

Kaufman, G. 1978. "Juan Luis Vives on the Education of Women." *Signs* 3:891–96.

Kellum, Barbara A. 1973–74. "Infanticide in England in the Later Middle Ages." *History of Childhood Quarterly* 1:367–88.

Kelly, Joan. 1977. "Did Women Have a Renaissance?" In *Becoming Visible: Women in European History*, ed. Renate Bridenthal and Claudia Koonz, 137–64. Boston: Houghton Mifflin. Reprint *Women, History and Theory*, ed. Kelly, 19–50 (Chicago: University of Chicago Press, 1984); and *Becoming Visible: Women in European History*, 2d ed., ed. Bridenthal, Koonz, and Susan Mosher Stuard, 175–201 (Boston: Houghton Mifflin, 1987).

————. 1984. *Women, History, and Theory: The Essays of Joan Kelly.* Women in Culture and Society. Chicago: University of Chicago Press. "Early Feminist Theory and the *Querelle des Femmes*, 1400–1789," 65–109.

Kelso, Ruth. 1956. *Doctrine for the Lady of the Renaissance.* Urbana: University of Illinois Press.

Kieckhefer, Richard. 1976. *European Witch Trials: Their Foundations in Popular and Learned Culture, 1300–1500.* London and Henly: Routledge & Kegan Paul.

————. 1984. *Unquiet Souls: Fourteenth-Century Saints and Their Religious Milieu.* Chicago: University of Chicago Press.

King, John N. 1985. "Patronage and Piety: The Influence of Catherine Parr." In *Silent but for the Word: Tudor Women as Patrons, Translators, and Writers of Religious Works*, ed. Margaret P. Hannay, 43–60. Kent, Ohio: Kent State University Press.

King, Margaret L. 1975. "Personal, Domestic, and Republican Virtues in the Moral Philosophy of Giovanni Caldiera." *RQ* 28:535–74.

———. 1976a. "Caldiera and the Barbaros on Marriage and the Family: Humanist Reflections of Venetian Realities." *JMRS* 6:19–50.

———. 1976b. "Thwarted Ambitions: Six Learned Women of the Renaissance." *Soundings* 59:280–304.

———. 1978. "The Religious Retreat of Isotta Nogarola (1418–1466)." *Signs* 3:807–22.

———. 1980a. "Book-Lined Cells: Women and Humanism in the Early Italian Renaissance." In *Beyond Their Sex: Learned Women of the European Past*, ed. Patricia H. Labalme, 66–90. New York: New York University Press.

———. 1980b. "Goddess and Captive: Antonio Loschi's Epistolary Tribute to Maddalena Scrovegni (1389)." *Medievalia et humanistica*, 103–27.

———. 1988. "The Death of the Child Valerio Marcello." In *Renaissance Studies: Intertext and Context*, ed. Maryanne C. Horowitz, Anne J. Cruz, and Wendy A. Furman, 205–25. Urbana and Chicago: University of Illinois Press.

Kinnaird, Joan K. 1983. "Mary Astell: Inspired by Ideas." In *Feminist Theorists: Three Centuries of Key Women Thinkers*, ed. Dale Spender, 28–30. New York: Pantheon.

Kirshner, Julius. 1978. "Pursuing Honor while Avoiding Sin: The Montedelle Doti of Florence." *Quaderni di "Studi Senesi"* 41:177–258.

———. 1985. "Wives' Claims against Insolvent Husbands in Late Medieval Italy." In *Women of the Medieval World*, ed. Kirshner and Suzanne F. Wemple, 256–93. Oxford: Oxford University Press.

Kirshner, Julius, and Anthony Molho. 1978. "The Dowry Fund and the Marriage Market in Early Quattrocento Florence." *JMH* 50:403–38.

———. 1980. "Il monte delle doti a Firenze dalla sua fondazione nel 1425 alla metà del sedicesimo secolo: abbozzo di una ricerca." *Ricerche storiche* 10:2:21–47.

Kirshner, Julius, and Suzanne Wemple, eds. 1985. *Women of the Medieval World: Essays in Honor of John H. Mundy*. Oxford: Basil Blackwell.

Klapisch-Zuber, Christiane. 1984. "Le chiavi fiorentine di Barbablù: l'apprendimento della lettura a Firenze nel XV secolo." *QS* 19:3:765–92.

———. 1985. *Women, Family, and Ritual in Renaissance Italy*. Trans. Lydia G. Cochrane. Chicago: University of Chicago Press.

    "'A uno pane e uno vino': The Rural Tuscan Family at the Beginning of the Fifteenth Century," 36–67. With Michel Demonet. Orig.

"'A uno pane e uno vino': la famille rurale toscane au début du XVe siècle." *Annales: ESC* 1972, 27:873–901.

"Kin, Friends, and Neighbors: The Urban Territory of a Merchant Family in 1400," 68–93. Orig. "'Parenti, amici, e vicini': Il territorio urbano d'una famiglia mercantile nel XV secolo." *QS* 1976, 33:953–82.

"Childhood in Tuscany at the Beginning of the Fifteenth Century," 94–116. Orig. "L'enfance en Toscane au début du XVe siècle." *Annales de démographie historique* 1973, 99–122.

"The 'Cruel Mother': Maternity, Widowhood, and Dowry in Florence in the Fourteenth and Fifteenth Centuries," 117–31. Orig. "Maternité, veuvage et dot à Florence." *Annales: ESC* 1983, 38:1097–1109.

"Blood Parents and Milk Parents: Wet Nursing in Florence, 1300–1530," 132–64. Orig. "Parents de sang, parents de lait: La mise en nourrice à Florence (1300–1530)." *Annales de démographie historique* 1983, 33–64.

"Female Celibacy and Service in Florence in the Fifteenth Century," 165–77. Orig. "Célibat et service féminins dans la Florence du XVe siècle." *Annales de démographie historique* 1981, 289–302.

"Zacharias, or the Ousted Father: Nuptial Rites in Tuscany between Giotto and the Council of Trent," 178–212. Orig. "Zacharie ou le père évincé: les rituels nuptiaux toscans entre Giotto et le Concile de Trente." *Annales: ESC* 1979, 34:1216–43.

"The Griselda Complex: Dowry and Marriage Gifts in the Quattrocento," 213–6. Orig. "Le complexe de Griselda." *Mélanges de l'Ecole Française de Rome* 1982, 94:1:7–43.

"The 'Mattinata' in Medieval Italy," 261–82. Orig. *Journal of Family History* 1980, 5:2–27.

———. 1986. "Women Servants in Florence." In *Women and Work in Pre-Industrial Europe*, ed. Barbara Hanawalt, 56–80. Bloomington, Indiana: Indiana University Press.

———. 1987. "La donna e la famiglia." In *L'uomo medievale*, ed. Jacques Le Goff, 321–49. Rome: Editori Laterza.

Kleinbaum, Abby W. 1983. *The War Against the Amazons.* New York: McGraw Hill.

Koch, Gottfried. 1962. *Frauenfrage und Ketzertum im Mittelalter: die Frauenbewegung im Rahmen des Katharismus und der Waldensertums und ihre sozialen Wurzeln, 12.–14. Jahrhundert.* Berlin: Akademie Verlag.

Kolsky, Stephen. 1987. "Culture and Politics in Renaissance Rome: Marco Antonio Altieri's Roman Weddings." *RQ* 40:49–90.

Koorn, Florence. 1986. "Women Without Vows: The Case of the Beguines and the Sisters of the Common Life in the Northern Netherlands." In

Women and Men in Spiritual Culture, XIV–XVII Centuries: A Meeting of South and North, ed. Elisja Schulte Van Kessel, 138–48. Studien Nederlands Instituut te Rom, 8. The Hague: Netherlands Government Publishing Office.

Kowaleski-Wallace, Beth. 1986. "Milton's Daughters: The Education of Eighteenth-Century Women Writers." *Feminist Studies* 12:275–94.

Kristeller, Paul Oskar. 1956. *Studies in Renaissance Thought and Letters*. Rome: Edizioni di Storia e Letteratura.

———. "Un codice padovano di Aristotile postillato da Francesco ed Ermolao Barbaro: Il manoscritto Plimpton 17 della Columbia University Library," 337–53.

———. "The School of Salerno," 495–551.

———. 1980. "Learned Women of Early Modern Italy: Humanists and University Scholars." In *Beyond Their Sex: Learned Women of the European Past*, ed. Patricia H. Labalme, 91–116. New York: New York University Press.

Kuehn, Thomas. 1982. "'Cum consensu mundualdi': Legal Guardianship of Women in Quattrocento Florence." *Viator* 13:309–33.

Labalme, Patricia H., ed. 1980. *Beyond Their Sex: Learned Women of the European Past*. New York: New York University Press. "Women's Roles in Early Modern Venice: An Exceptional Case," 129–52.

———. 1981. "Venetian Women on Women: Three Early Modern Feminists." *AV*, Ser. 5, 197:81–109.

Langer, William L. 1973–74. "Infanticide: A Historical Survey." *History of Childhood Quarterly* 1:353–65.

———. 1974–75. "Further Notes on the History of Infanticide." *History of Childhood Quarterly* 2:129–33.

Larner, Christina. 1981. *Enemies of God: The Witch-Hunt in Scotland*. Baltimore and London: Johns Hopkins University Press.

Lasareff, Victor. 1938. "Studies in the Iconography of the Virgin." *Art Bulletin* 20:26–65.

Latz, Dorothy. 1986. *Saint Angela Merici and the Spiritual Currents of the Italian Renaissance*. Lille: Université de Lille III.

Lawrence, C. H. 1989. *Medieval Monasticism: Forms of Religious Life in Western Europe in the Middle Ages*. 2d ed. London and New York: Longman.

Lazard, Madeleine. 1985. *Images littéraires de la femme à la Renaissance*. Paris: Presses Universitaires de France.

Lea, Henry Charles. 1922. *A History of the Inquisition of Spain*. 4 vols. New York and London: Macmillan.

Le Goff, Jacques. 1977. *Time, Work, and Culture in the Middle Ages.* Trans. Arthur Goldhammer. Chicago: University of Chicago Press.

Le Roy Ladurie, Emmanuel. 1978. *Montaillou: The Promised Land of Error.* Trans. Barbara Bray. New York: George Braziller. Orig. *Montaillou, village occitan de 1294 a 1324.* Paris: Editions Gallimard, 1975.

Ledochowska, Teresa. 1969. *Angela Merici and the Company of St. Ursula.* Trans. Mary Teresa Neylan. Rev. ed. 2 vols. Rome, Ancona, and Milan: Typis Pontificiae Universitatis Gregoriana.

Lemay, Helen Rodnite. 1978. "Some Thirteenth- and Fourteenth-Century Lectures on Female Sexuality." *International Journal of Women's Studies* 1:391–400.

———. 1985. "Anthonius Guarinerius and Medieval Gynecology." In *Women of the Medieval World: Essays in Honor of John H. Mundy*, ed. Julius Kirshner and Suzanne Wemple, 317–36. Oxford: Basil Blackwell.

Lerner, Robert E. 1972. *The Heresy of the Free Spirit in the Later Middle Ages.* Berkeley and Los Angeles: University of California Press.

Levack, Brian P. 1987. *The Witch Hunt in Early Modern Europe.* London and New York: Longman.

Levin, Carole. 1983. "Advice on Women's Behavior in Three Tudor Homilies." *International Journal of Women's Studies* 6:176–85.

———. 1985. "Lady Jane Grey: Protestant Queen and Martyr." In *Silent but for the Word: Tudor Women as Patrons, Translators, and Writers of Religious Works*, ed. Margaret P. Hannay, 92–106. Kent, Ohio: Kent State University Press.

Levin, Carole, and Jeanie Watson, eds. 1987. *Ambiguous Realities: Women in the Middle Ages and Renaissance.* Detroit: Wayne State University Press.

Lewenhak, Sheila. 1980. *Women and Work.* New York: St. Martin's Press.

Liebowitz, Ruth P. 1979. "Virgins in the Service of Christ: The Dispute Over an Active Apostolate for Women During the Counter-Reformation." In *Women of Spirit: Female Leadership in the Jewish and Christian Traditions*, ed. Rosemary Ruether and Eleanor McLaughlin, 132–52. New York: Simon & Schuster.

Lombardi, Daniela. 1986. "Le altre famiglie: assistite e serve nella Firenze dei Medici." *Memoria* 18:3:25–36.

Lougee, Carolyn C. 1976. *Le Paradis des femmes: Women, Salons and Social Stratification in Seventeenth-Century France.* Princeton: Princeton University Press.

Lucas, Angela M. 1983. *Women in the Middle Ages: Religion, Marriage and Letters.* New York: St. Martin's Press; Brighton: Harvester Press.

McDonnell, Ernest W. 1954. *The Beguines and Beghards in Medieval Culture with Special Emphasis on the Belgian Scene.* New Brunswick, N.J.: Rutgers University Press. Reprint New York, 1969.

Macfarlane, Alan. 1970. *The Family Life of Ralph Josselin, A Seventeenth-Century Clergyman: An Essay in Historical Anthropology.* Cambridge and New York: Cambridge University Press.

————. 1986. *Marriage and Love in England: Modes of Reproduction, 1300–1840.* New York: Basil Blackwell.

Mack, Phyllis. 1982. "Women as Prophets During the English Civil War." *Feminist Studies* 8:19–46.

————. 1986. "Feminine Behavior and Radical Action: Franciscans, Quakers, and the Followers of Gandhi." *Signs* 11:457–77.

McLaren, Dorothy. 1985. "Marital Fertility and Lactation, 1570–1720." In *Women in English Society, 1500–1800*, ed. Mary Prior, 22–53. London and New York: Methuen.

McLaughlin, Eleanor Commo. 1973. "The Heresy of the Free Spirit and Late Medieval Mysticism." *Medievalia et Humanistica* 4:37–54.

————. 1974. "Equality of Souls, Inequality of Sexes: Woman in Medieval Theology." In *Religion and Sexism: Images of Women in the Jewish and Christian Traditions*, ed. Rosemary Radford Ruether, 213–66. New York: Simon & Schuster.

————. 1979. "Women, Power and the Pursuit of Holiness in Medieval Christianity." In *Religion and Sexism: Images of Women in the Jewish and Christian Traditions*, ed. Rosemary Radford Ruether, 100–139. New York: Simon & Schuster.

McLaughlin, Mary Martin. 1989. "Creating and Recreating Communities of Women: The Case of Corpus Domini, Ferrara, 1406-1452." *Signs* 14:2:293–320.

MacLean, Ian. 1977. *Women Triumphant: Feminism in French Literature, 1610–1652.* Oxford: Clarendon Press.

————. 1980. *The Renaissance Notion of Women: A Study in the Fortunes of Scholasticism and Medical Science in European Intellectual Life.* Cambridge Monographs on the History of Medicine. Cambridge and New York: Cambridge University Press.

McNamara, Jo Ann. 1976. "Sexual Equality and the Cult of Virginity in Early Christian Thought." *Feminist Studies* 3:145–58.

McNamara, Jo Ann, and Suzanne Wemple. 1977. "Sanctity and Power: The Dual Pursuit of Medieval Women." In *Becoming Visible*, ed. Renate Bridenthal and Claudia Koonz, 90–118. Boston: Houghton Mifflin. Rev. in *Becoming Visible*, 2d ed., ed. Bridenthal, Koonz, and

Susan Mosher Stuard. Wemple, 131–51. Boston: Houghton Mifflin, 1987.

Magli, Ida. 1972. "Il problema antropologico-culturale del monachesimo femminile." In *Encliclopedia delle religioni* 4, 627–41. Florence.

Marcus, Leah S. 1978. *Childhood and Cultural Despair: A Theme and Variations in Seventeenth-Century Literature.* Pittsburgh: University of Pittsburgh Press.

—————. 1986. "Shakespeare's Comic Heroines, Elizabeth I, and the Political Uses of Androgyny." In *Women in the Middle Ages and the Renaissance: Literary and Historical Perspectives*, ed. Mary Beth Rose, 135–54. Syracuse: Syracuse University Press.

Martin, John. 1987. "Popular Culture and the Shaping of Popular Heresy." In *Inquisition and Society in Early Modern Europe*, ed. Stephen Haliczer, 115–28. London: Rowman & Littlefield; Sydney: Croom Helm.

Martines, Lauro. 1974. "A Way of Looking at Women in Renaissance Florence." *JMRS* 4:15–28.

Maschietto, Francesco Ludovico. 1978. *Elena Lucrezia Cornaro Piscopia (1646–1684), prima donna laureata nel mondo.* Contributi alla storia dell'Università di Padova, 10. Padua: Editrice Antenore.

Mendelson, Sara Heller. 1985. "Stuart Women's Diaries and Occasional Memoirs." In *Women in English Society, 1500–1800*, ed. Mary Prior, 181–210. London and New York: Methuen.

Midelfort, Erik H. C. 1972. *Witchhunting in Southwestern Germany, 1562–1684: the Social and Intellectual Foundations.* Stanford, Calif.: Stanford University Press.

Mitterauer, Michael, and Reinhard Sieder. 1982. *The European Family: Patriarchy to Partnership from the Middle Ages to the Present.* Trans. Karla Oosterveen and Manfred Hörzinger. Chicago: University of Chicago Press.

Molho, Anthony. 1969. *Social and Economic Foundations of the Italian Renaissance.* New York: John Wiley.

—————. 1986. "Investimenti nel Monte delle Doti di Firenze: un'analisi sociale e geografica." *QS*, n.s. 61:147–70.

Monter, E. William. 1971. "Witchcraft in Geneva (1537–1662)." *JMH*, 43:179–204.

—————. 1976. *Witchcraft in France and Switzerland: the Borderlands during the Reformation.* Ithaca: Cornell University Press.

—————. 1977. "Courtly Love and Witchcraft." In *Becoming Visible: Women in European History*, ed. Renate Bridenthal and Claudia Koonz, 119–36. Boston: Houghton Mifflin.

————. 1980. "Women in Calvinist Geneva (1550–1800)." *Signs* 6:189–209.

————. 1986. "Women and the Italian Inquisitions." In *Women in the Middle Ages and the Renaissance: Literary and Historical Perspectives*, ed. Mary Beth Rose, 73–88. Syracuse: Syracuse University Press.

Montrose, Louis A. 1986. "*A Midsummer Night's Dream* and the Shaping Fantasies of Elizabethan Culture: Gender, Power, Form." In *Rewriting the Renaissance: The Discourses of Sexual Difference in Early Modern Europe*, ed. Margaret W. Ferguson, Maureen Quilligan, and Nancy J. Vickers, 65–87. Chicago: University of Chicago Press.

Morgan, Edmund S. 1966. *The Puritan Family: Religion and Domestic Relations in Seventeenth-Century New England*. Rev. ed. New York: Harper & Row.

Mueller, Janel M. 1986. "Autobiography of a New 'Creatur': Female Spirituality, Selfhood and Authority in *The Book of Margery Kempe*." In *Women in the Middle Ages and the Renaissance: Literary and Historical Perspectives*, ed. Mary Beth Rose, 155–172. Syracuse: Syracuse University Press.

Mullett, Michael A. 1980. *Radical Religious Movements in Early Modern Europe*. London: George Allen & Unwin.

Murray, Jacqueline. 1988. "The Perception of Family by Clergy and Laity." *Albion* 20:369–85.

Musto, Ronald G. 1985. "Queen Sancia of Naples (1286–1345) and the Spiritual Franciscans." In *Women of the Medieval World: Essays in Honor of John H. Mundy*, ed. Julius Kirshner and Suzanne Wemple, 179–214. Oxford: Basil Blackwell.

Muzzarelli, Maria Giuseppina. 1986. "'Contra mundanas vanitates et pompas': Aspetti della lotta contro i lussi nell'Italia del XV secolo." *RSCI* 40:371–90.

Neale, John E. 1954. *Elizabeth I and her Parliaments*. 2 vols. London: Jonathan Cape.

————. 1957. *Queen Elizabeth I*. London: Jonathan Cape. Orig. 1934.

Nicholas, David. 1985. *The Domestic Life of a Medieval City: Women, Children, and the Family in Fourteenth-Century Ghent*. Lincoln, Nebraska, and London: University of Nebraska Press.

Noonan, John T., Jr. 1973. "Power to Choose." In "Marriage in the Middle Ages," ed. John Leyerle, 419–34. *Viator* 4:413–501.

Okin, Susan Moller. 1979. *Women in Western Political Thought*. Princeton: Princeton University Press.

Oliva, Mario. 1985. *Giulia Gonzaga Colonna: tra Rinascimento e Controriforma*. Milan: Mursia.

Oliver, Mary. 1959. *Mary Ward, 1585–1645.* New York: Sheed & Ward.

O'Neil, Mary. 1987. "Magical Healing, Love Magic and the Inquisition in Late Sixteenth-Century Modena." In *Inquisition and Society in Early Modern Europe*, ed. Stephen Haliczer, 88–114. London: Rowman & Littlefield; Sydney: Croom Helm.

O'Neill, Ynez Violé. 1975. "Giovanni Michele Savonarola: An Atypical Renaissance Practitioner." *Clio Medica* 10:77–93.

Origo, Iris. 1955. "The Domestic Enemy: Eastern Slaves in Tuscany in the Fourteenth and Fifteenth Centuries." *Speculum* 30:321–66.

————. 1957. *The Merchant of Prato: Francesco di Marco Datini.* New York: Knopf.

————. 1962. *The World of San Bernardino.* New York: Harcourt, Brace & World.

Otis, Leah Lydia. 1985a. *Prostitution in Medieval Society: The History of an Urban Institution in Languedoc.* Women in Culture and Society. Chicago: University of Chicago Press.

————. 1985b. "Prostitution and Repentence in Late Medieval Perpignan." In *Women of the Medieval World: Essays in Honor of John H. Mundy*, ed. Julius Kirshner and Suzanne Wemple, 137–60. Oxford: Basil Blackwell.

————. 1986. "Municipal Wet Nurses in Fifteenth-Century Montpellier." In *Women and Work in Pre-Industrial Europe*, ed. Barbara Hanawalt, 83–93. Bloomington, Indiana: Indiana University Press.

Outhwaite, R. B., ed. 1982. *Marriage and Society: Studies in the Social History of Marriage.* New York: St. Martin's Press; London: Europa Publications, 1981.

Owen, Dorothy M. 1978. "White Annays and Others." In *Medieval Women: Dedicated and Presented to Professor Rosalind M. T. Hill on the Occasion of her Seventieth Birthday*, ed. Derek Baker, 331–46. Oxford: Basil Blackwell for the Ecclesiastical History Society.

Ozment, Steven. 1983a. "The Family in Reformation Germany: The Bearing and Rearing of Children." *Journal of Family History* 8:159–76.

————. 1983b. *When Fathers Ruled: Family Life in Reformation Europe.* Studies in Cultural History. Cambridge, Mass., and London: Harvard University Press.

Paschini, Pio. 1960. "I monasteri femminili in Italia nel Cinquecento." In *Problemi di vita religiosa in Italia nel Cinquecento: Atti del Convegno di Storia della Chiesa in Italia (Bologna, 2–6 settembre 1958)*, = *Italia sacra*, 2, 31–60. Padua: Editrice Antenore.

Pásztor, Edith. 1984. "I papi del Duecento e Trecento di fronte alla vita religiosa femminile." In *Il movimento religioso femminile in Umbria nei secoli XIII–XIV: Atti del Convegno internazionale di studio nell'ambito delle celebrazioni per l'VIII centenario della nascita di S. Francesco d'Assisi, Città di Castello, 27–29 ottobre 1982.* Quaderni del "Centro per il collegamento degli studi medievali e umanistici nell'Università di Perugia," 12, ed. Roberto Rusconi, 29–65. Perugia: Regione dell'Umbria; Scandicci (Firenze); La Nuova Italia.

Pavan, Elisabeth. 1980. "Police des moeurs, société et politique à Venise à la fin du Moyen Age." *Revue historique* 536:241–88.

Pernoud, Régine. 1964. *Joan of Arc, By Herself and Her Witnesses.* Trans. Edward Hyams. New York: Stein & Day. Orig. *Jeanne d'Arc par elle-même et par ses témoins.* Paris: Editions du Seuil, 1962.

Perry, Mary Elizabeth. 1978. "'Lost Women' in Early Modern Seville: The Politics of Prostitution." *Feminist Studies* 4:195–214.

—————. 1987. "Beatas and the Inquisition in Early Modern Seville." In *Inquisition and Society in Early Modern Europe,* ed. Stephen Haliczer, 147–68. London: Rowman & Littlefield; Sydney: Croom Helm.

Perry, Ruth. 1986. *The Celebrated Mary Astell: An Early English Feminist.* Chicago: University of Chicago Press.

Phillips, Dayton. 1941. *The Beguines in Medieval Strasburg: A Study of the Social Aspect of Beguine Life.* Stanford, Calif.: Stanford University Press.

Phillips, Roderick. 1988. *Putting Asunder: A History of Divorce in Western Society.* Cambridge and New York: Cambridge University Press.

Pia Pedani, Maria. 1985. "Monasteri di Agostiniane a Venezia." *AV,* ser. 5, 125:35–78.

Power, Eileen. 1926. "The Position of Women." In *The Legacy of the Middle Ages,* ed. C. G. Crump and E. F. Jacob, 401–34. New York: Oxford University Press.

—————. 1964. *Medieval English Nunneries.* New York: Biblio & Tannen.

—————. 1975. *Medieval Women.* Ed. M. M. Postan. Cambridge and New York: Cambridge University Press, 1975.

Prescott, Anne Lake. 1985. "The Pearl of the Valois and Elizabeth I: Marguerite de Navarre's *Miroir* and Tudor England." In *Silent but for the Word: Tudor Women as Patrons, Translators, and Writers of Religious Works,* ed. Margaret P. Hannay, 61–76. Kent, Ohio: Kent State University Press.

Prior, Mary, ed. 1985. *Women in English Society, 1500–1800.* London and New York: Methuen. "Women and the Urban Economy: Oxford, 1500–1800," 93–117.

Prosperi, Adriano. 1986. "Dalle 'divine madri' ai 'padri spirituali.'" In *Women and Men in Spiritual Culture, XIV–XVII Centuries: A Meeting of South and North*, ed. Elisja Schulte Van Kessel, 71–92. Studien Nederlands Instituut te Rom, 8. The Hague: Netherlands Government Publishing Office.

Quaife, G. R. 1987. *Godly Zeal and Furious Rage: The Witch in Early Modern Europe*. London and Sydney: Croom Helm.

Rabil, Albert, Jr. 1981. *Laura Cereta: Quattrocento Humanist*. Medieval and Renaissance Texts and Studies, 3. Binghamton, N.Y.

Reyerson, Kathryn L. 1986. "Women in Business in Medieval Montpellier." In *Women and Work in Pre-Industrial Europe*, ed. Barbara A. Hanawalt, 127–44. Bloomington: Indiana University Press.

Rigolot, François. 1986. "Gender vs. Sex Difference in Louise Labé's Grammar of Love." In *Rewriting the Renaissance: The Discourses of Sexual Difference in Early Modern Europe*, ed. Margaret W. Ferguson, Maureen Quilligan, and Nancy J. Vickers, 287–98. Chicago: University of Chicago Press.

Robbert, Louise Buenger. 1980. "Caterina Corner, Queen of Cyprus." In *Female Scholars: A Tradition of Learned Women before 1800*, ed. Jeanie R. Brink, 24–35. Montreal: Eden Press Women's Publications.

Robin, Diana. In press. *Forms of Resistance: The Writings of Francesco Filelfo*. Princeton: Princeton University Press.

Rodocanachi, Emmanuel Pierre. 1922. *La Femme italienne: avant, pendant et après la Renaissance, sa vie privée et mondaine, son influence sociale*. Paris: Hachette.

Roelker, Nancy L. 1968. *Queen of Navarre, Jeanne d'Albret, 1528–1572*. Cambridge, Mass.: Harvard University Press.

———. 1972a. "The Appeal of Calvinism to French Noblewomen in the Sixteenth Century." *Journal of Interdisciplinary History* 2:391–418.

———. 1972b. "The Role of Noblewomen in the French Reformation." *Archiv für Reformationsgeschichte* 63:168–95.

Rogers, Katherine. 1966. *The Troublesome Helpmate: A History of Misogyny in Literature*. Seattle: University of Washington Press.

Romanello, Marina, ed. 1975. *La stregoneria in Europa (1450–1650)*. Bologna: Il Mulino.

Rose, Mary Beth, ed. 1986. *Women in the Middle Ages and the Renaissance: Literary and Historical Perspectives*. Syracuse: Syracuse University Press. "Gender, Genre and History: Seventeenth-Century English Women and the Art of Autobiography," 245–78.

Rosenthal, Margaret F. 1989. "Veronica Franco's *Terᶎe Rime*: the Venetian Courtesan's Defense." *RQ* 42:227–57.

Ross, J. B. 1974. "The Middle-Class Child in Urban Italy, Fourteenth to Early Sixteenth Century." In *The History of Childhood*, ed. Lloyd de Mause, 183–228. New York: Psychohistory Press.

Rossiaud, Jacques. 1985. "Prostitution, Sex and Society in French Towns in the Fifteenth Century." In *Western Sexuality: Practice and Precept in Past and Present Times*, ed. Philippe Ariès and André Béjin, trans. Anthony Forster, 76–94. Oxford and New York: Basil Blackwell.

———. 1988. *Medieval Prostitution*. Trans. Lydia G. Cochrane. London: Blackwell.

Rowland, Beryl. 1981. *Medieval Woman's Guide to Health: The First English Gynecological Handbook*. Kent, Ohio: Kent State University Press.

Rowlands, Marie B. 1985. "Recusant Women, 1560–1640." In *Women in English Society, 1500–1800*, ed. Mary Prior, 149–80. London and New York: Methuen.

Ruether, Rosemary Redford, ed. 1974. *Religion and Sexism: Images of Women in the Jewish and Christian Traditions*. New York: Simon & Schuster.

Ruether, Rosemary, and Eleanor McLaughlin, eds. 1979. *Women of Spirit: Female Leadership in the Jewish and Christian Traditions*. New York: Simon & Schuster.

Ruggiero, Guido. 1985. *The Boundaries of Eros: Sex Crime and Sexuality in Renaissance Venice*. New York and London: Oxford University Press.

———. 1987. "'Più che la vita caro': onore, matrimonio e reputazione femminile nel tardo Rinascimento." *QS*, n.s. 66:3:753–55.

Rusconi, Roberto, ed. 1984. *Il movimento religioso femminile in Umbria nei secoli XIII–XIV: Atti del Convegno internaᶎionale di studio nell'ambito delle celebraᶎioni per l'VIII centenario della nascita di S. Francesco d'Assisi, Città di Castello, 27–28–29 ottobre 1982*. Quaderni del "Centro per il collegamento degli studi medievali e umanistici nell'Università di Perugia," 12. Perugia: Regione dell'Umbria; Scandicci (Firenze); La Nuova Italia.

Russell, Jeffrey Burton. 1980. *A History of Witchcraft, Sorcerers, Heretics and Pagans*. London: Thames and Hudson.

Santore, Cathy. 1988. "Julia Lombardo, 'Somtuosa Meretrize': A Portrait by Property." *RQ* 41:44–83.

Scapparone, Elisabetta. 1987. "'Sapienza Riposta' e lingua volgare: Note sull'*Elegante poema* di Francesco Giorgio Veneto." *SV* 13:147–92.

Schleiner, Winfried. 1978. "*Divina virago*: Queen Elizabeth as an Amazon." *Studies in Philology* 75:163–80.

Schmitt, Jean-Claude. 1978. *Mort d'une hérésie, l'église et les clercs face aux béguines et aux bégards du Rhin supérieur du XIVe au XVe siècle.* Ecole des hautes études en sciences sociales, centre de recherches historiques. Civilisations et sociétés, 56. Paris: Mouton.

Schulenburg, Jane T. 1978. "Sexism and the Celestial Gynecaeum from 500 to 1200." *Journal of Medieval History* 4:117–33.

————. 1986. "The Heroics of Virginity." In *Women in the Middle Ages and the Renaissance: Literary and Historical Perspectives*, ed. Mary Beth Rose, 29–72. Syracuse: Syracuse University Press.

Schutte, Anne Jacobson. 1980a. "Printing, Piety and the People in Italy: The First Thirty Years." *Archiv für Reformationsgeschichte* 71:5–10.

————. 1980b. "'Trionfo delle donne': tematiche di rovesciamento dei ruoli nella Firenze rinascimentale." *QS* 44:474–96.

————. 1991. "Irene di Spilimbergo: The Image of a Creative Woman in Late Renaissance Italy." *RQ*, 44:42–61.

Segarizzi, Arnaldo. 1904. "Niccolò Barbo, patrizio veneziano del secolo XV e le accuse contro Isotta Nogarola." *GSLI* 43:47–54.

Sensi, Mario. 1984. "Incarcerate e recluse in Umbria nei secoli XIII e XIV: un bizzocaggio centro-italiano." In *Il movimento religioso femminile in Umbria nei secoli XIII–XIV*, Quaderni del Centro per il collegamento degli studi medievali e umanistici nell'Università di Perugia, 12, ed. Roberto Rusconi, 85–121. Florence: La Nuova Italia.

Shahar, Shulamith. 1982–83. "Infants, Infant Care, and Attitudes Toward Infancy in the Medieval Lives of Saints." *Journal of Psychohistory* 10:281–309.

————. 1983. *The Fourth Estate: A History of Women in the Middle Ages.* Trans. Chaya Galvi. London and New York: Methuen.

Shank, Michael H. 1987. "A Female University Student in late Medieval Kraków." *Feminist Studies* 12:373–80.

Sheehan, Michael M. 1985. "The Wife of Bath and her Four Sisters: Reflections on a Woman's Life in the Age of Chaucer." *Medievalia et Humanistica*, n.s. 13:23–42.

Shepherd, Simon. 1981. *Amazons and Warrior Women: Varieties of Feminism in Seventeenth-Century Drama.* New York: St. Martin's Press.

Slater, Miriam. 1984. *Family Life in the Seventeenth Century: The Verneys of Claydon House.* London and Boston: Routledge & Kegan Paul.

Smith, Hilda L. 1982. *Reason's Disciples: Seventeenth-Century English Feminists.* Urbana: University of Illinois Press.

Sorelli, Fernanda. 1984. *La santità imitabile: 'Leggenda di Maria da Venezia' di*

Tommaso da Siena. Deputazione di storia patria per le Venezie; Miscellanea di studi e memoria, 23. Venice: Deputazione editrice, 1984.

Southern, R. W. 1970. *Western Society and the Church in the Middle Ages.* The Pelican History of the Church, 2. Harmondsworth: Penguin.

Southey, E. A. B. 1834. *Olympia Morata, Her Times, Life and Writings.* London: Smith Elder & Co.

Sowards, J. Kelley. 1982. "Erasmus and the Education of Women." *Sixteenth Century Journal* 13:77–90

Stallybrass, Peter. 1986. "Patriarchal Territories: The Body Enclosed." In *Rewriting the Renaissance: The Discourses of Sexual Difference in Early Modern Europe,* ed. Margaret W. Ferguson, Maureen Quilligan, and Nancy J. Vickers, 123–42. Chicago: University of Chicago Press.

Still, George F. 1931. *The History of Pediatrics: The Progress of the Study of Diseases of Children up to the End of the XVIIIth Century.* London: H. Milford, Oxford University Press. Reprint not seen, London: Dawson of Pall Mall, 1953.

Stock, Phyllis. 1978. *Better than Rubies: A History of Women's Education.* New York: G. P. Putnam's Sons (Capricorn Books).

Stone, Lawrence. 1977. *Family, Sex, and Marriage in England, 1500–1800.* London and New York: Weidenfeld & Nicolson, 1977. Abr. ed. 1979: New York: Harper & Row.

Strocchia, Sharon. 1990. "Remembering the Family: Women, Kin, and Commemorative Masses in Renaissance Florence." *RQ* 43:635–55.

Stuard, Susan Mosher, ed. 1976. *Women in Medieval Society.* Philadelphia: University of Pennsylvania Press. "Women in Charter and Statute Law: Medieval Ragusa/Dubrovnik," 199–208.

———. 1986. "To Town to Serve: Urban Domestic Slavery in Medieval Ragusa." In *Women and Work in Pre-Industrial Europe,* ed. Barbara A. Hanawalt, 39–55 Bloomington: Indiana University Press.

———. 1987. "The Dominion of Gender: Women's Fortunes in the High Middle Ages." In *Becoming Visible: Women in European History,* 2d ed., ed. Renate Bridenthal, Claudia Koonz, and Susan M. Stuard. Boston: Houghton Mifflin.

Swain, Elisabeth Ward. 1987. "Il potere di un'amicizia." *Memoria* 21:3:7–23.

Tamassia, Nino. 1971. *La famiglia italiana nei secoli decimoquinto e decimosesto.* Rome: Multigrafica. Orig. Milan, 1914.

Tentler, Thomas N. 1977. *Sin and Confession on the Eve of the Reformation.* Princeton: Princeton University Press.

Thirsk, Joan. 1985. Foreward to *Women in English Society, 1500–1800*, ed. Mary Prior, 7–21. London and New York: Methuen.

Thompson, Sally. 1978. "The Problem of the Cistercian Nuns in the Twelfth and Early Thirteenth Centuries." In *Medieval Women: Dedicated and Presented to Professor Rosalind M. T. Hill on the Occasion of her Seventieth Birthday*, ed. Derek Baker, 227–52. Oxford: Basil Blackwell for the Ecclesiastical History Society.

Thrupp, Sylvia L. 1962. *The Merchant Class of Medieval London (1300–1500)*. Ann Arbor: University of Michigan Press. Orig. Michigan, 1948.

Todd, Barbara J. 1985. "The Remarrying Widow: A Stereotype Reconsidered." In *Women in English Society, 1500–1800*, ed. Mary Prior, 54–92. London and New York: Methuen.

Tomalin, Margaret. 1982. *The Fortunes of the Warrior Heroine in Italian Literature: An Index of Emancipation*. Ravenna: Longo Editore.

Travitsky, Betty S. 1980. "The New Mother of the English Renaissance: Her Writings on Motherhood." In *The Lost Tradition: Mothers and Daughters in Literature*, ed. Cathy N. Davidson and E. M. Broner, 33–43. New York: Frederick Ungar.

Trexler, Richard C. 1972. "Le Célibat à la fin du Moyen Age: les réligieuses de Florence." *Annales: ESC* 27:1329–50.

―――. 1973–74a. "The Foundlings of Florence, 1395–1455." *History of Childhood Quarterly* 1:259–84.

―――. 1973–74b. "Infanticide in Florence: New Sources and First Results." *History of Childhood Quarterly* 1:98–116.

―――. 1975. "In Search of Father: The Experience of Abandonment in the Recollections of Giovanni di Pagolo Morelli." *History of Childhood Quarterly* 3:225–52.

―――. 1981. "La Prostitution florentine au XVe siècle: patronages et clienteles." *Annales: ESC* 36:983–1015.

―――. 1982. "A Widows' Asylum of the Renaissance: the Orbatello of Florence." In *Old Age in Preindustrial Society*, ed. Peter N. Stearns, 119–49. New York: Holmes & Meier.

Utley, Francis L. 1944. *The Crooked Rib*. Columbus: Ohio State University Press.

Van Kessel, Elisja Schulte, ed. 1986. *Women and Men in Spiritual Culture, XIV–XVII Centuries: A Meeting of South and North*. Studien Nederlands Instituut te Rom, 8. The Hague: Netherlands Government Publishing Office.

Vanja, Christina. 1984. *Besitz- und Sozialgeschichte der Zisterzienserinnenkloster*

Caldern und Georgenberg und des Prämonstratenserinnenstiftes Hachborn in Hessen im späten Mittelalter. Darmstadt: Hessische Historische Kommission Darmstadt und Historische Kommission für Hessen.

Vann, R. T. 1977. "Women in Preindustrial Capitalism." In *Becoming Visible: Women in European History,* ed. Renate Bridenthal and Claudia Koonz, 192–216. Boston: Houghton Mifflin.

Vauchez, André. 1981. *La sainteté en Occident aux derniers siècles du Moyen Age après les procès de canonisation et les documents hagiographiques.* Bibliothèque des Ecoles françaises d'Athènes et de Rome, fasc. 241. Rome.

Verbrugge, Rita. 1985. "Margart More Roper's Personal Expression in the *Devout Treatise Upon the Pater Noster.*" In *Silent but for the Word: Tudor Women as Patrons, Translators, and Writers of Religious Works,* ed. Margaret P. Hannay, 30–42. Kent, Ohio: Kent State University Press.

Warner, Marina. 1976. *Alone of All Her Sex: The Myth and the Cult of the Virgin Mary.* New York: Random House (Vintage).

———. 1981. *Joan of Arc: The Image of Female Heroism.* New York: Alfred A. Knopf.

Warnicke, Retha M. 1983. *Women of the English Renaissance and Reformation.* Contributions in Women's Studies, 38. Westport, Conn., and London: Greenwood Press.

———. 1988. "Women and Humanism in England." In *Renaissance Humanism: Foundations, Forms, and Legacy,* ed. Albert Rabil, Jr., 3 vols., 2:39–54. Philadelphia: University of Pennsylvania Press.

Wayne, Valerie. 1985. "Some Sad Sentences: Vives' Instruction of a Christian Woman." In *Silent but for the Word: Tudor Women as Patrons, Translators, and Writers of Religious Works,* ed. Margaret P. Hannay, 15–29. Kent, Ohio: Kent State University Press.

———. 1987. "Zenobia in Medieval and Renaissance Literature." In *Ambiguous Realities: Women in the Middle Ages and Renaissance,* ed. Carole Levin and Jeanie Watson, 48–65. Detroit: Wayne State University Press.

Weaver, Elissa. 1986. "Spiritual Fun: A Study of Sixteenth-Century Tuscan Convent Theater." In *Women in the Middle Ages and the Renaissance: Literary and Historical Perspectives,* ed. Mary Beth Rose, 173–206. Syracuse: Syracuse University Press.

Wessley, Stephen E. 1978. "The Thirteenth-Century Guglielmites." In *Medieval Women: Dedicated and Presented to Professor Rosalind M. T. Hill on the Occasion of her Seventieth Birthday,* ed. Derek Baker, 289–303. Oxford: Basil Blackwell for the Ecclesiastical History Society.

West, Robert Hunter. 1984. *Reginald Scot and Renaissance Writings on Witch-craft.* Twayne's English Author Series. Boston: Twayne.

Wiesner, Merry E. 1986a. "Early Modern Midwifery: A Case Study." In *Women and Work in Pre-Industrial Europe,* ed. Barbara A. Hanawalt, 94–113. Bloomington: Indiana University Press.

————. 1986b. "Spinsters and Seamstresses, Women in Cloth and Clothing Production." In *Rewriting the Renaissance: The Discourses of Sexual Difference in Early Modern Europe,* ed. Margaret W. Ferguson, Maureen Quilligan, and Nancy J. Vickers, 191–205. Chicago: University of Chicago Press.

————. 1986c. *Working Women in Renaissance Germany.* Douglass Series on Women's Lives and the Meaning of Gender. New Brunswick, N.J.: Rutgers University Press.

————. 1986d. "Women's Defense of Their Public Role." In *Women in the Middle Ages and the Renaissance: Literary and Historical Perspectives,* ed. Mary Beth Rose, 1–28. Syracuse: Syracuse University Press.

Willard, Charity Cannon. 1984. *Christine de Pizan: Her Life and Works.* New York: Persea Books.

Wyntjes, Sherrin M. 1977. "Women in the Reformation Era." In *Becoming Visible: Women in European History,* ed. Renate Bridenthal and Claudia Koonz, 165–91. Boston: Houghton Mifflin.

Yates, Frances A. 1975. *Astraea: The Imperial Theme in the Sixteenth Century.* London: Routledge & Kegan Paul.

Zaccaria, Vittorio. 1957–58. "Una epistola metrica di Antonio Loschi a Maddalena Scrovegni." *Bollettino del Museo Civico di Padova.* 46:153–68.

Zinberg, Israel. 1974. *A History of Jewish Literature.* Trans. and ed. Bernard Martin. Vol. 4: *Italian Jewry in the Renaissance Era.* Cincinnati, Ohio: Hebrew Union College Press; New York: KTAV Publishing House.

INDEX